for

Nigl

Meter in Poetry

Many of the great works of world literature are composed in metrical verse, that is, in lines which are measured and patterned. *Meter in Poetry: A New Theory* is the first book to present a single simple account of all known types of metrical verse, which is illustrated with detailed analyses of poems in many languages, including English, Spanish, Italian, French, classical Greek and Latin, Sanskrit, classical Arabic, Chinese, Vietnamese, and Latvian. This outstanding contribution to the study of meter is aimed both at students and scholars of literature and languages, as well as anyone interested in knowing how metrical verse is made.

NIGEL FABB is Professor of Literary Linguistics at the University of Strathclyde. His publications include *Linguistics and Literature* (1997) and *Language and Literary Structure* (Cambridge, 2002).

MORRIS HALLE is Institute Professor Emeritus in the Department of Linguistics and Philosophy at Massachusetts Institute of Technology. His publications include *The Sound Pattern of English* (with Noam Chomsky, 1968/1991) and *From Memory to Speech and Back* (2002).

Meter in Poetry

A New Theory

NIGEL FABB AND MORRIS HALLE

with a chapter on Southern Romance meters by
CARLOS PIERA

CAMBRIDGE
UNIVERSITY PRESS

CAMBRIDGE UNIVERSITY PRESS
Cambridge, New York, Melbourne, Madrid, Cape Town, Singapore, São Paulo, Delhi

Cambridge University Press
The Edinburgh Building, Cambridge CB2 8RU, UK

Published in the United States of America by Cambridge University Press, New York

www.cambridge.org
Information on this title: www.cambridge.org/9780521713252

First published 2008

Printed in the United Kingdom at the University Press, Cambridge

A catalogue record for this publication is available from the British Library

ISBN 978-0-521-88564-5 hardback
ISBN 978-0-521-71325-2 paperback

For Janet and Rosamond

Contents

Acknowledgments

We are grateful for help and advice of many people, most especially to those who have provided us with information about the poetry in the languages that neither of us has command of. Foremost among these is Carlos Piera, whose advice about metrical poetry in Spanish, Portuguese and Italian was so complete and extensive that, with his permission, we have included it as Chapter 4 in the book. Other consultants include Elitzur Bar Asher, Tim Barnes, Andrea Calabrese, Benoît de Cornulier, Ashwini Deo, François Dell, San Duanmu, Mohamed Elmedlaoui, Juan Jose Garcia Gonzalez, John Huehnergard, Samuel Jay Keyser, Kristīne Konrāde, Clint M. Lohse, Angelo Mercado, Andrea Moro, Martin Orwin, Mits Ota, Aziz Qutbuddin, Renate Sohnen, and Richard Widdess. We have been greatly helped in preparing this book by Janet Fabb, Margaret Fabb, John Halle, Caroline Heycock, Cassie Mayo, Steven Paton, Craig Thiersch, Gary Thoms and Stefano Versace. Very special thanks are due to Ewa Jaworska, who helped us in the final stages of preparation of the book. We thank Andrew Winnard, Sarah Green, and Rosina Di Marzo at Cambridge University Press. We thank Curt Rice for his invitation to us to teach a course on metrics at Tromsø, from which this book developed. Nigel Fabb thanks his colleagues in the Department of English Studies, University of Strathclyde for giving him research leave to complete this book.

Our book has been greatly improved by the detailed and persistent criticisms of Sylvain Bromberger.

1

A theory of poetic meter

1.1 On different kinds of verse

Poetry is a form of verbal art that has been found in all languages and in all times. Most, perhaps all human societies put their language to the special use of composing poetry. What distinguishes all poetry from prose is that poetry is made up of lines (verses). Syllables, words, phrases, clauses and sentences are found in both prose and poetry, but only poetry has lines. It is the organization of the text into lines that defines poetry in all languages and literary traditions.[1]

Poetry is, of course, not produced simply by segmenting a prose passage into arbitrary sequences of words or syllables and calling these lines. For a sequence of syllables or words to count as poetry it must satisfy a set of conditions which differ for different kinds of poetry. In metrical poetry, which is the subject of this book, lines must satisfy requirements on length and on the location in the line of marked syllables, and different conditions are met by different kinds of non-metrical poetry.

One type of non-metrical poetry is based not on line length, but on syntactic parallelism, where corresponding lines must be composed of syntactic constituents of the same kind. An example of such poetry is that of the Old Testament, of which an example in quoted in (1), where syntactic units of the same kind are labeled with the same capital letter.

---

[1] Dissenting from a colleague's remark that there is nothing in poetry that is not also in language, Boris Tomaševskij, the Russian literary scholar, wrote that the statement needed one correction: 'in language [outside of poetry – NF&MH] the phenomenon of verse itself does not exist' (Tomaševskij 1959: 60n). Note that this is not a matter of the usage of the word 'poetry' (or 'verse'), which can be applied to any kind of text (or even to non-textual material); instead it is a claim that there is a well-founded distinction between texts divided into lines and texts not divided into lines. Like Tomaševskij we reserve the term 'poetry' to name the former type.

(1)   A voice^A calls:^{B}

In the wilderness^C open^D a road for Yahweh;^{E}
Make straight^D in the desert^C a highway for our God!^{E}

Every valley ^{A} shall be exalted,^{B}
And every mountain and hill^A ⟨shall be⟩ made low,^{B}

And the crooked^A shall become straight,^{B}
And the mountain crags^A ⟨shall become⟩ a ravine.^{B}

And Yahweh's glory^A shall be revealed^B
And all flesh^A shall see ⟨it⟩ together^B

For Yahweh's mouth^A has spoken.^{B}

Isaiah 40, 3–5

In translating the biblical text in (1), we attempted to preserve the syntactic parallelism of the original, and we succeeded in this except in lines 8–9, where in the original Hebrew the verb precedes the subject. It is fortunate that English syntax is sufficiently similar to Old Testament Hebrew to make this possible.[2]

The ten lines of (1) consist of five pairs, where the lines of each pair are composed of the same syntactic constituents. The first and last line of (1) make up one of the five pairs, the remaining four pairs are constituted by adjacent lines in the text: 2–3, 4–5, 6–7, 8–9. Line 1 and its complement, line 10, are composed of a subject phrase labeled A and a predicate phrase, labeled B. This also true of three of the remaining pairs (lines 4–5, 6–7, and 8–9). Unlike these, the line pair 2–3 has a tripartite syntactic structure: prepositional phrase labeled C, verb labeled D, and its object labeled E. The three constituents appear in the order CDE in line 2, but in the order DCE in line 3.

Another kind of non-metrical verse, in wide use since the end of the 19th century, is Free Verse. As Ezra Pound, one of the foremost proponents of Free Verse, famously remarked, his purpose was 'to break the

---

[2] In the 1611 King James translation of the Bible, which is still in wide use today, the first two lines in (1) are translated as 'The voice of him that crieth in the wilderness, Prepare ye the way of the Lord...'. This mistranslation, which fails to preserve the syntactic parallelism of the original, is found already in the Septuagint, the earliest, pre-Christian translation of the Old Testament (into Greek), and is quoted in that form in Matthew 3:3, and John 1:23. The incorrect translation has become a standard locution in many languages.

pentameter, that was the first heave' (Canto LXXXI), and he and the many poets who have adopted Free Verse have composed poems with lines that violate the principles and rules not only of the pentameter, but of all other meters as well. Free Verse does not rest on a generally agreed upon set of principles and units; rather each poem – and often also each line in the poem – is based on principles and units of its own, and the poem achieves its esthetic impact by asking the reader or listener to discover the units and principles that give shape to the line. The one aspect that Free Verse shares with other kinds of poetry is lineation: even the most experimental kind of Free Verse is composed of lines. (For additional discussion of Free Verse, see Steele 1990.)

This brings us to metrical verse, which is the most widely used kind of poetry and is also the subject of this book. It is used in the *Odyssey*, the Vedic hymns, Classical Arabic poetry, the regulated verse of Chinese, *Beowulf*, the *Chanson de Roland*, *The Divine Comedy*, *The Canterbury Tales*, and much more. Metrical verse, illustrated in (2) is obviously different from the non-metrical verse in (1), as well as from Free Verse.

(2)   a.   Ever let the Fancy roam,
                    Pleasure never is at home;
                    At a touch sweet pleasure melteth,
                    Like to bubbles when rain pelteth;

John Keats, 'Fancy'

        b.   For the Angel of Death spread his wings on the blast,
                    And breathed in the face of the foe as he passed;
                    And the eyes of the sleepers waxed deadly and chill,
                    And their hearts but once heaved, and forever grew still.

George Gordon, Lord Byron, 'The Destruction of Sennacherib'

An essential characteristic of (2a) and(2b) is that the lines in each poem are of (approximately) the same length. If we count the syllables, there are seven or eight syllables in each of the lines of (2a) and eleven or twelve syllables in each of the lines of (2b). The lines, moreover, have a definite rhythm, and on our view the rhythm is a by-product of the way line length is restricted. In this respect our approach departs radically from most other approaches to meter, as these have been focused almost exclusively on rhythm. As already noted, lines are the defining aspect of poetry. In language outside of poetry, there are no lines, nor is there any equivalent of the mechanism for restricting line length that is described below. It is this mechanism that accounts also for the rhythm of metrical poems.

Line length in (2) is not measured by counting the syllables directly, for example, by counting them off on the fingers, or assigning numbers to the syllables. Instead, line length is measured indirectly by a special procedure for grouping the syllables. In the formal theory developed in this book the syllables are not directly subject to grouping. Grouping rather is imposed on *projections* of syllables. The projections – represented by asterisks – are shown in (3), with a single asterisk projecting from each syllable. We call the asterisk sequence a *Gridline*. As we will see, a line projects a set of Gridlines, forming a grid.

(3)   Ever let the Fancy roam,
       * * *   * * * *   Gridline

In addition to asterisks a Gridline may also include parentheses, which segment the asterisk sequence into groups. A left parenthesis groups the asterisks on its right, and a right parenthesis groups the asterisks on its left. In (4) we illustrate grouping with left parentheses; grouping with right parentheses is shown in (5b).

(4)   Ever let the Fancy roam,
       (* * (*   * (* * (*   Gridline

The parentheses are inserted into the asterisk sequence by a rule of a special kind: an iterative rule. This rule starts at one edge of the asterisk sequence, inserts a parenthesis, skips either two or three asterisks and inserts a parenthesis. The rule repeats this operation until the opposite edge of the asterisk sequence is reached, and no further asterisks remain to be grouped. We look at the iterative rules in detail in section 1.4. In (5), we show the effects of iterative rules for each of the lines in (2).

(5)   a. Ever let the Fancy roam,
           (* * (*   * (* * (*
           Pleasure never is at home;
           (* *   (* *(* * (*
           At a touch sweet pleasure melteth,
           (* * (*   * (* *   (* *(
           Like to bubbles when rain pelteth;
           (*   * (* *   (* * (* *(
       b. For the Angel of Death spread his wings on the blast,
)*   * *)* * *)   * * *) *   * *)
           And breathed in the face of the foe as he passed:
           *   *)   *   * *) * * *)* * *)
           And the eyes of the sleepers waxed deadly and chill,
)*   * *) *   * *)* *   *) * *   *)

And their hearts but once heaved, and forever grew still.
)*   *   *)   * *   *)   *   * *) *   *   *)

In (5a) the syllables are grouped into pairs, and there are four such pairs, of which the rightmost may be incomplete, i.e., contain only one syllable. Traditionally the groups are called *feet*, but we use this term only intermittently below. The same picture emerges in (5b), but here each group has three syllables, except in the second line of (5b), where the first group is incomplete and has only two syllables. The lines in both (5a) and (5b) are composed of four groups, but the groups in (5a) consists of (at most) two syllables, while those in (5b) include as many as three syllables. This illustrates that the meter controls primarily the number of groups in the line, and only secondarily the number of syllables.

The groups formed by parenthesis insertion are not just sub-sequences of asterisks, but have a special property of their own: each group includes a *head* element, which in a given Gridline is either the left- or rightmost element in the group, and which is subject to rule (6).

(6)   Project the head of a group to the next Gridline.

In Keats's lines quoted in (5a), the Gridline 0 groups are left-headed; in the lines by Browning quoted in (5b), Gridline 0 groups are right-headed. The heads of Gridline 0 groups are in both cases projected as asterisks on the next Gridline, which is Gridline 1; this is shown in (7).

(7)   a.   Pleasure never is at home;

         (*   *   (* *(* *   (*   0
           *   *   *   *   1

        At a touch sweet pleasure melteth,

         (* * (*   *   (*   *   (* *(0
         *   *   *   *   1

     b.   For the Angel of Death spread his wings on the blast,

)*   * *) * *   *)   *   * *) *   * *) 0
            *   *   *   *   1

        And breathed in the face of the foe as he passed:

         *   *)   *   * *) *   * *)*   * *)   0
            *   *   *   *   1

The mechanism of projecting the heads of groups and generating a new line of asterisks (a new Gridline) is also the way of using grouping in order to restrict the length of lines. To see this, recall that there is one head in each group and that groups normally include more than one syllable. The number of heads in a line is therefore smaller than the number of syllables, and as a consequence there are fewer asterisks on Gridline 1 than on Gridline 0.

The number of asterisks is further reduced by forming groups on Gridline 1, and projecting their heads onto Gridline 2, as shown in (8).

(8)   a.   Pleasure never is at home;

```
( *    *    ( * *( *   *    ( *                    0
( *         *   ( *        * (                     1
    *               *                              2
```

At a touch sweet pleasure melteth,

```
(*    * ( *        *      ( *   *      ( *  *(      0
(*        *             ( *          * (           1
    *                       *                      2
```

b.   For the Angel of Death spread his wings on the blast,

```
) *      * * )  *   *    * )      *    *   * )   *    *   * )   0
         ) *            * )                    *        * )    1
                         *                                *    2
```

And breathed in the face of the foe as he passed:

```
*       * )     *     * * )  *    * * ) *    *   * )           0
        ) *           * )            *         * )            1
                       *                        *            2
```

We repeat the same procedure in (9), forming Gridline 3.

(9)   a.   Pleasure never is at home;

```
( *    *    ( * *( *   *    ( *                    0
( *         *   ( *        * (                     1
( *              *  (                              2
    *                                              3
```

At a touch sweet pleasure melteth,

```
(*    * ( *        *      ( *   *      ( *  *(      0
(*        *             ( *          * (           1
(*                       *  (                      2
    *                                              3
```

b.   For the Angel of Death spread his wings on the blast,

```
) *      * * )  *   *    * )      *    *   * )   *    *   * )   0
         ) *            * )                    *        * )    1
                        ) *                              * )   2
                         *                                *    3
```

And breathed in the face of the foe as he passed:

```
*       * )     *     * * )  *    * * ) *    *   * )           0
        ) *           * )            *         * )            1
                       ) *                       * )          2
                        *                          *          3
```

Since there is only a single asterisk on Gridline 3, additional groupings are vacuous, for they do not reduce the number of asterisks on the next Gridline. The grouping operation therefore comes to an end at this point, with the formation of a complete grid.

The grids in both (9a) and (9b) have asterisk groupings on three Gridlines. This reflects the fact that in generating the metrical grids above, there have been rules for grouping asterisks only on three Gridlines. Since in (9a) the groups on all three Gridlines are binary (i.e., are composed of two asterisks), the maximum length of line in this meter (trochaic tetrameter) is two times two times two, equalling eight syllables. The same reasoning applies to the anapaestic tetrameter lines in (9b), but since there the Gridline 0 groups consist of three asterisks, whereas the groups on Gridlines 1 and 2 both consist of two asterisks, the maximum length of the line in this meter is three times two times two, equalling twelve syllables. We show in (10) how the grouping rules used for (8a) deal with a sequence of ten syllables.

(10)   (*   * (*   * (*   * (*   * (*   * (0
        (*   *   (*   *   (*   1
        (*   *   (*   2
          *   *   3

The obvious difference between (10) and the grids in (9a) is that in (10) there are two asterisks on the bottom-most Gridline, but there is only a single one in (9a). This shows that if line length is limited by restricting the number of Gridlines for which iterative grouping rules are stipulated, it will be necessary to allow only a single asterisk on the bottom-most line of the grid. We express this formally by means of condition (11).

(11)   The bottom-most Gridline in a well-formed grid must contain exactly one asterisk.

The length of the line is determined on the one hand by the size of groups on each Gridline, and on the other hand by the number of Gridlines for which rules of syllable grouping are specified. The majority of metrical poetry that we have studied has metrical grids with three Gridlines on which groups are formed, as in the examples above. The fact that poems with longer lines, requiring four or more Gridlines, are rare, may reflect restrictions on the perception of the lines.

1.2 Other functions of the metrical grid

Restricting the length of lines of verse is not the only function performed by the grid. While for grouping purposes all syllables that make up the line of poetry are treated alike, the effect of the grouping in the grid is to supply columns with different numbers of asterisks to different syllables in the line. Thus, in the grids in (9a) the first syllable has a column with four asterisks, the second syllable only a single asterisk, the third two asterisks, etc. These differences between syllables are the basis for patterns in the metrical line. For example, we shall see in section 1.8 below that the syllable with the most asterisks – which we call *the head of the verse* – plays a special role in the meter of many poetic traditions.

It is well known that most English words include a syllable that is more prominent than the rest, and this syllable is said to bear the word stress. Some examples can be seen in (12).[3]

(12)   África enígma contradíct emancipátion individualístic

In English syllabo-tonic verse, of which the lines in (2) are particular examples, syllables bearing word stress are preferentially placed in positions that are heads of Gridline 0 groups. In (13) below we have reproduced the lines and grids from (9), and added accents to indicate word stresses. It can be seen that stressed syllables tend to project to Gridline 1.

(13)   a. Pléasure néver is at hóme;

```
( *   *   ( *  *( *   *   ( *              0 ⇒
( *         *  ( *        * (              1 ⇒
( *            *  (                        2 ⇒
  *                                        3
```

At a tóuch swéet pléasure mélteth,

```
(*   * ( *        *   ( *   *   ( *  * (    0 ⇒
(*     *          ( *        * (           1 ⇒
(*               *  (                       2 ⇒
  *                                        3
```

b. For the Ángel of Déath spréad his wíngs on the blást,

```
) *     * *) *  *   *)       *    *   *)  *    *   *)   0 ⇐
    ) *          *)                    *          *)   1 ⇐
        ) *                                       *)   2 ⇐
          *                                        3
```

And bréathed in the fáce of the fóe as he pássed:

```
*       *)   *    * *) *   * *)*   *  *)       0 ⇐
    ) *          *)          *         *)      1 ⇐
        ) *                            *)      2 ⇐
          *                             3
```

---

[3] As discussed in section 1.11 the placement of stresses on different syllables of the word requires metrical grids of the same kind as those employed for the representation of meters here, and the columns of asterisks in the metrical grids representing word stress reflect differences in degrees of stress (prominence). Thus, the fact that stress is multi-valued in many languages is a consequence of it being represented with a metrical grid. (For some details of the multi-valued stress feature in English, see Chomsky and Halle 1968/1991.)

It is important to recognize that though stressed syllables tend to project to Gridline 1, there are stressed syllables which do not project to Gridline 1, and there are Gridline 1 asterisks which do not project from stressed syllables. The meter (represented by the grid below the line) does not necessarily follow the same pattern as the rhythm (represented by the accent marks on the syllables).

Different metrical traditions impose restrictions on aspects other than the word stress. For example, restrictions are imposed on syllable quantity (see Chapters 6, 7, and 8), word boundary placement (Chapter 5), tone or alliteration (Chapter 10). As documented below, all of these restrictions are directly related to aspects of the metrical grid.The fact that the grid controls these aspects of lines in addition to their length is important evidence for the centrality of the grid in metrical poetry.

In composing metrical verse, the poet selects metrically well-formed syllable sequences and rejects sequences that are not well-formed, and readers are, of course, aware of the fact that they are reading metrical verse, rather than prose. To the extent that the grids and the conditions allow us to distinguish metrically well-formed lines from other syllable sequences, the grids (and the conditions they must meet) reflect a function that must also be performed by poets and by readers of metrical verse. In saying this, however, we are not asserting that poets and their readers project asterisks and insert parentheses in the manner sketched just above. The metrical grids present one way in which the well-formedness of lines might be determined. We have not shown that this is the way that poets and readers do it, nor have we shown that this is the only logically possible way in which this can be done.

The modern study of syntax and semantics is based on groupings of morphemes and words, and considerable advances have been made in this domain during the last half-century (see, for example, Chomsky 2002). But at this time next to nothing is known about the neurophysiology of syntax and semantics, and about how actual speakers compute the well-formedness of the sentences they produce. This problem might be solved in the future, as we get a better understanding of how the human brain and mind work. The discoveries by Chomsky and others about syntax and semantics will then be explained in terms of aspects of a theory that is yet to be developed. In much the same way, the metrical grids in (9) and elsewhere in this book constitute the data to be accounted for by a future theory of human cognition. We return to these issues in section 1.4.

1.3 Phrase and word boundaries may be disregarded in metrical verse

As already noted, metrical verse is distinguished from ordinary language in having properties that are not present in ordinary language.[4] In particular, lines, which are the defining property of poetry, have no counterpart in ordinary language. Support for this assertion is provided by enjambment, the fact that lines of verse end in the middle of a syntactic phrase. A few examples of syntactic enjambment are given in (14).

(14)   ... time will run
        On smoother, till Favonius re-inspire
        The frozen earth; ...

> John Milton, 'Lawrence of Virtuous Father'

        Death be not proud, though some have called thee
        Mighty and dreadful, ...

> John Donne, Holy Sonnet 10

                ... and it brought
        Into his mind the turbid ebb and flow
        Of human misery; we
        Find also in the sound a thought,

> Matthew Arnold, 'Dover Beach'

It is much less widely known that there is also morphological enjambment: lines of metrical verse may end in the middle of words, or put differently, that enjambment occurs not only in the middle of a syntactic phrase, but also in the middle of the word, as illustrated with the English examples in (15).

(15)   To separate these twi-
        Lights, the Discouri;

> Ben Jonson, 'To the immortal memory ... Sir H. Morison'

        I caught this morning morning's minion, king-
        dom of daylight's dauphin, dapple-dáwn-drawn Falcon, in
              his riding

> Gerard Manley Hopkins, 'The Windhover'

---

[4] Here we differ from approaches which assume that literary language is a development of ordinary language, using the resources already available to it; for a proposal along these lines see Hanson and Kiparsky (1996).

in simple, shining lines, in pages stretched
plain as a bleaching bedsheet under a gutter-
ing rainspout; glad for the sputter

Derek Walcott, 'Nearing Forty'

Though rare in the corpus of English poetry, such lines with word-internal enjambment are not uncommon in other poetic traditions. They are found in classical Greek poetry (see Chapter 6), in Sanskrit poetry (Chapter 8), in the medieval Hebrew poetry of Spain (7.8), in the poetry of the Tashlhiyt dialect of Berber studied by Dell and Elmedlaoui (2007, 2008), and elsewhere. Lines ending in the middle of a word are thus not a minor anomaly to be set aside, but exemplify a fundamental property of metrical poetry: the fact that lines are sequences of syllables, rather than of words or phrases.

1.4 The metrical grid

The central claim of this study is that every well-formed line of metrical verse consists not only of the phonemes and syllables that determine its pronunciation, but also of what we have called a metrical grid, i.e., a pattern, which though not pronounced, determines the perception of a sequence of syllables as a line of metrical verse, rather than as an ordinary bit of prose. Our further claim is that each grid is the output of a computation whose input is the string of syllables that make up the verse line: the grid is not preconstructed and then attached to the line, but is generated separately from each individual line. Our third claim is that the computation consists in the ordered application of a licensed set of rules selected from a finite set of rules that we describe in detail below. (A set of rules is 'licensed' when it is observed by a poetic school or tradition.) Our fourth and final claim is that a verse line is well formed metrically if and only if its grid is well formed (i.e., the grid is the output of a licensed set of ordered rules) and if the syllables composing the line satisfy certain further conditions.

Words and syllables are not overtly present in the acoustic speech signal of the utterance; they are constructed by speakers and hearers alike by virtue of their knowledge of the language.[5] In similar fashion, the reader of a line of metrical verse constructs a metrical grid which is the

---

[5] It is significant that the index of Liberman (1996), presenting what is arguably the most important body of acoustic phonetic work of the second half of the 20th century, does not include an entry for word.

formal embodiment of the meter of the line. In this regard we conceive the present study as a contribution to the research program initiated by Noam Chomsky into the nature of language and mind.[6] The rules of meter share many properties with the rules of phonology and morphology: they generate abstract elements that are not directly present in the acoustic speech signal, and they account for specific aspects of the signal in terms of these abstract entities and their interactions with other aspects of language.

Poets and their audiences have the ability to judge that lines are metrical, and this ability is part of the human capacity for language. This capacity, which must minimally include the ability to judge certain word sequences as syntactically well formed, includes, in our view, also the ability to judge word sequences as metrically well formed. Though little is known at present about these metrical judgments, their reality is warranted by the existence of poetry.

We assume that a metrical grid can be associated with any sequence of syllables. What distinguishes proper lines of metrical poetry from a random sequence of syllables is that metrical grids of such lines satisfy specific conditions of well-formedness. Since grids are abstract structures, we need to make them visible in some way for purposes of exposition. We do this with the help of such notational devices as asterisks, parentheses and arrays of them, as illustrated in (16) (see also (13) above), but as already noted, we do not mean that such arrays are necessarily constructed by individuals while reading metrical poetry or composing it. They are one specific way of making explicit the computation and its results.

(16)   And bréathed in the fáce of the fóe as he pássed:

```
*      * )     *    * * ) *   * * ) *   *  * )      0
       ) *           * )          *        * )      1
       ) *                                 * )      2
                                           *        3
```

The first step in generating the grid from the line is to project its syllables as asterisks, which means writing an asterisk under each syllable and labeling the sequence of asterisks 'Gridline 0'. The rule in question is stated as (17); it is a rule which, with some variations, is used as the first step in all metrical poetry in all languages.

(17)   Project each syllable as an asterisk on Gridline 0.

---

[6] For discussion of this program, see Adriana Belletti, Noam Chomsky and Luigi Rizzi 'An interview on minimalism' in Chomsky (2002: 92–161).

The result of applying the projection rule (17) to one line from each of our sample texts is shown in (18).

(18)   a.   At a tóuch swéet pléasure mélteth,

            *   *   *   *   *   *   *   *   0

         b.   And bréathed in the fáce of the fóe as he pássed:

      *   *   *   *   *   *   *   *   *   *   *   0

In the second step of grid construction special diacritic marks (represented by ordinary right or left parentheses) are inserted among the asterisks. The parentheses have the effect of splitting the asterisks in the sequence into groups, where the term 'group' is a technical notion defined by convention (19).

(19)   A left parenthesis groups the asterisks on its right; a right parenthesis groups the asterisks on its left. Asterisks that are neither to the right of a left parenthesis, nor to the left of a right parenthesis, are ungrouped.

Parentheses are inserted into asterisk sequences by ordinary rules and also by a class of special rules that play a pivotal role in the characterization of the meters in poetry. The crucial feature of these special rules is that they are *iterative rules*, that is, they start applying at one end of the asterisk sequence and continue to the other end, syllable by syllable, inserting parentheses wherever the conditions for their insertion are met.

The iterative rules were discovered by Idsardi (1992) in a study of stress systems of different languages.[7] The role of iterative rules in the characterization of meters in poetry has been explored in Halle and Keyser (1999), Halle (2008), Fabb (2002a,b, 2006), and Fabb and Halle (2006a,b), and these rules are also the major topic of this book. The iterative rules have a common format, which involves the setting of the five parameters in (20).

(20)   i.   Insertion starts either just at the edge of the Gridline, or one asterisk in, or two asterisks in.

        ii.   Edge of the sequence (Left (L) / Right (R)) at which insertion begins.

      iii.   Nature of parenthesis inserted (L/R).

      iv.   Interval between consecutive insertions (2/3 asterisks).

       v.   Location of head in each group (L/R).

---

[7] Additional studies documenting the role of iterative rules in the assignment of stress are Halle and Idsardi (1995), and Halle (1998). See also section 1.11.

In the following we explore each of these five parameters. In (21a) we have given trochaic tetrameter lines from Keats and in (21b) anapaestic tetrameter lines from Byron. The direction in which parentheses are inserted in each Gridline is indicated by writing $\Rightarrow$ (left to right) or $\Leftarrow$ (right to left) in the margin.

(21) a. Éver let the Fáncy róam,
         (* * (*   * (* * (*   0 $\Rightarrow$

         Pléasure néver is at hóme;
          (* *   (* *(* * (*   0 $\Rightarrow$

         At a tóuch swéet pleasure mélteth,
         (* *(*   *   (* *   (* *(0 $\Rightarrow$

         Líke to búbbles when ráin pélteth;
         (*   * (* *   (*   * (* *(0 $\Rightarrow$

      b. For the Ángel of Déath spréad his wíngs on the blást,
) *   * *) * *   *)   *   * *) *   * *)   0 $\Leftarrow$

         And bréathed in the fáce of the fóe as he pássed:
         *   *)   *   * *) *   * *)* * *)   0 $\Leftarrow$

         And the éyes of the sléepers wáxed déadly and chíll,
)*   * *) * * *)*   *   *) * *   *)   0 $\Leftarrow$

         And their héarts but once héaved, and foréver grew stíll.
)*   * *)   * *   *)   *   * *)* *   *) 0 $\Leftarrow$

As we have seen, in (21a) the lines include between seven and eight syllables, whereas in (21b) line length varies between eleven and twelve. These differences in length can be readily explained on the assumption that the syllables (asterisks) are grouped by parentheses that are inserted into the sequence. In (21a) the parentheses are inserted at *binary* intervals, while in (21b) the parentheses are inserted at *ternary* intervals. Since there are four groups in each line, the expected length of each line would be eight syllables (four binary groups) in (21a) and twelve syllables (four ternary groups) in (21b). The fact that a group can fall short explains why there are only seven syllables in one of the lines of (21a) and only eleven syllables in one of the lines in (21b). Formally these differences in the overall length of the lines are accounted for by different settings of the parameter (20iv), which governs the interval between consecutive parenthesis insertions: in (21a) the parameter (20iv) is set to TWO, in (21b), it is set to THREE.

It was also noted in section 1.1 that in applying an iterative rule, the last group to be formed can be incomplete. In (21a) the incomplete group was at the right edge of the line, in (21b) the incomplete group was at the left edge. This property of the lines is captured by setting the parameter (20ii) to LEFT in (21a), so that grouping begins at the left edge of the line and ends at the right edge of the line (where an incomplete group can arise). The parameter is set to RIGHT in (21b).

Perhaps the most obvious difference between the lines in (21a) and (21b) is their respective rhythms. Somewhat crudely the 'trochaic' rhythm in (21a) might be represented as

DUMdaDUMdaDUMdaDUM(da)

whereas the 'anapaestic' rhythm of (21b) might be represented as

(da)daDUMdadaDUMdadaDUMdadaDUM

In the two cases illustrated above, a stressed *DUM* syllable alternates with one or two unstressed *da* syllables. To capture these rhythms formally we exploit the fact that in every group there is a special syllable, which we have called the head and which projects to the next Gridline. On a particular Gridline in a particular meter, the head is (consistently) either the left- or the rightmost asterisk in each group. This is shown for the two lines in (22).

(22)   a.   Pléasure néver is at hóme;

```
( *   *   ( *  *( *  *   ( *            0 ⇒
    *       *    *       *              1
```

     At a tóuch swéet pléasure mélteth,

```
(*   * ( *       *   ( *  *   ( *  *(   0 ⇒
   *     *           *        *         1
```

   b.   For the Ángel of Déath spréad his wíngs on the blást,

```
) *      * *) *  *    *)       *    *  *)  *     *  *)   0 ⇐
         *            *             *         *          1
```

     And bréathed in the fáce of the fóe as he pássed:

```
*       *)    *    * *) *    * *) *   *  *)          0 ⇐
        *         *         *        *               1
```

In order to obtain the above placement of heads in the groups, parameter (20v) is set to LEFT in the trochaic meter of (22a) and to RIGHT in the anapaestic meter of (22b).

Convention (19) explains how parenthesis insertion into a sequence of asterisks segments the sequence into groups. The theory admits both left '(' and right ')' parentheses, and the choice between them is governed by different settings of parameter (20ii). In (22a) this parameter is set to LEFT and in (22b) the parameter is set to RIGHT. In the so-called strict meters of English, of which the two stanzas discussed here are typical examples, the choice of parenthesis kind is correlated with the edge at which grouping begins. Where grouping begins at the left edge, left parentheses are inserted, but where grouping begins at the right edge, right parentheses are inserted. This restriction does not hold universally. For example, as discussed in Chapter 6, in classical Greek there are both iambic meters where insertion starts at the right edge and iambic meters with insertion starting at the left edge.

Parenthesis insertion need not always start flush at the edge of the line. It may start one asterisk (occasionally even two asterisks) inside the line. We illustrate this in (23a) with lines where the grouping starts at the left edge and can skip one asterisk (at the left), and in (23b) with a stanza where grouping begins at the right edge and can skip one asterisk (at the right). These variations are determined by parameter (20i); in these poems the parameter is set to JUST AT THE EDGE, or ONE ASTERISK IN.

(23)   a. And the enjoying of the spring ...

```
        *     ( * * ( * * ( *    *   ( *              0 ⇒
              *     *     *         *                 1
```

        To banish Even from her sky ...

```
        * ( * * ( * * ( *    *   ( *                  0 ⇒
            *     *     *         *                   1
```

        From dewy sward or thorny spray ...

```
        *   ( * * ( * * ( * * ( *                     0 ⇒
            *     *     *     *                       1
```

        The daisy and the marigold ...

```
        * ( * *( *      * ( * *( *                    0 ⇒
            *   *         *   *                       1
```

        And Jove grew languid. – Break the mesh ...

```
        *    ( *    *  ( *   *     ( *   * ( *         0 ⇒
             *          *          *        *         1
```

John Keats, 'Fancy' selected lines

    b. Though the sound overpowers,

```
         ) *        *  * )  *  * * )                  0 ⇐
                    *         *                       1
```

        Sing again, with your dear voice revealing

```
        ) *  * * )   *    *    * )  *    * * ) *       0 ⇐
             *              *           *             1
```

        A tone

```
        *  * )                                        0 ⇐
           *                                          1
```

        Of some world far from ours,

```
        ) *   *     * )   *   *   * )                  0 ⇐
              *            *                           1
```

Where music and moonlight and feeling

```
     *        *)*  *        * )  *      *       * )*              0 ⇐
              *                 *                  *              1
```

Are one.

```
     *     * )                                                   0 ⇐
           *                                                     1
```

Percy Bysshe Shelley, 'To Jane' final stanza

As already shown in (21a), the lines in Keats's 'Fancy' are composed of left-headed binary groups, where grouping starts at the left edge. In the great majority of lines in 'Fancy', including those quoted in (21a), the groupings start directly ('just') at the left edge of the line. In the lines quoted in (23a), grouping starts not directly at the left edge, but one syllable in. (The groups are still left-headed.)

Like the lines by Byron quoted in (21b), the lines by Shelley in (23b) are composed of anapaests, that is of groups that are right-headed and ternary, and grouping starts at the right edge. In (23b) the number of groups per line varies systematically: there are two groups in the first and fourth line, three groups in the second and fifth line, and a single group in the third and sixth line. This metrical organization is supported by the rhyme scheme: AbCAbC, where the first line rhymes with the fourth, the second with the fifth, and the third with the sixth. The feminine rhyme in the second and fifth lines is made possible by the fact that the grouping of the syllables in these lines does not start at the right edge directly, but one syllable in. The starting point of parenthesis insertion in the lines of both (23a) and (23b) is determined by the setting of parameter (20i).

In (23b) the second and fifth lines end with feminine rhymes, while the other lines in the stanza have masculine rhymes. Occasionally, English verse makes use of rhymes like those in the stanza (24) from Canto I of Byron's *Don Juan*, which includes both the triple rhymes *goddesses – bodices – Odysseys* and *apology – mythology* and the feminine rhymes *puzzle – bustle – tussle*.

(24)   His classic studies made a little puzzle,
       Because of filthy loves of gods and goddesses,
       Who in the earlier ages raised a bustle,
       But never put on pantaloons or bodices;
       His reverend tutors had at times a tussle,
       And for the Aeneids, Iliads, and Odysseys,
       Were forced to make an odd sort of apology,

For Dónna Ínez dréaded the mythólogy.

```
)  *    *  )  * * ) *     *  ) *    *  )  *   *) *  *        0 ⇐
   *       *          *          *         *                 1
```

As shown below the last line in (24) triple rhymes are accounted for by starting syllable groupings not at the right edge of the line, but two syllables in, by setting parameter (20i) to TWO.

In discussing the lines in (22) we noted that in English verse there was a definite tendency for syllables bearing the word stress to appear in positions that project to Gridline 1. We return to this issue here.

In addition to grouping the syllables most metrical systems impose conditions on the groups. For the purpose of stating these conditions, the syllables that compose the lines are always partitioned into two classes. The principles that divide the syllables into the two classes differ from language to language, and also from tradition to tradition. As discussed below, in the quantitative poetry of Greek, Sanskrit, and Arabic, syllables are classified as heavy vs. light, based on the nature of the syllable rhyme; in Chinese and Vietnamese poetry, syllables divide into two classes based on their inherent tone; in Old English poetry, syllables bearing the word stress are classed as alliterating vs. non-alliterating depending on the nature of the syllable onset. A given language may class its syllables differently for different meters. For example, in Latin there is quantitative verse based on the same classification of syllables as in classical Greek. But Latin has also saturnian verse (see section 4.7), which, like English verse, is based on restrictions on the placement of syllables bearing the word stress.

In English the classification depends on stress placement, but, as explained below, in a manner somewhat more complex than is usually understood. In advance of more discussion of this distinction we label the marked class of syllables in English metrical poetry as maxima (sg. *maximum*) and contrast them with the rest of the syllables (which are unmarked, and given no specific label; we never need to refer to 'non-maxima'). This allows us to state the well-formedness condition of English metrical poetry in the simple form in (25) below.

(25)   Maxima must project to Gridline 1.

This is a condition which checks on the results of rule application. In particular, it checks whether after the grid has been constructed, a particular type of syllable has a projection on Gridline 1. As a condition, it is therefore distinct from the two projection rules (17) and (6), which generate the grid.

As a first approximation it might be assumed that in English verse all syllables bearing the word stress are maxima. If this were the case, then once the grid is generated from the line, all syllables bearing word stress would be located such that they project to Gridline 1. But this is clearly incorrect as shown by an examination of the lines in (22), where there are syllables bearing word stress which do not project to Gridline 1, and yet the lines in (22) are metrical. The identification of maximum with stress-bearing syllable is thus untenable.

An indication of how the definition of maximum must be modified is provided by the concocted line in (26), which is obviously not well-formed in the meter of Keats's lines quoted above.

(26)   Pléasure is néver at hóme
    (*   * (*   *(*   *   (*   0 ⇒
     *   *   *   *   1

The metricality of the line is restored when it is changed to (27).

(27)   Pléasure's néver in its hóme
    (* *   (* *(*   *   (*   0 ⇒
     *   *   *   *   1

But the metricality is lost again when (27) is changed to (28).

(28)   Pléasure's alóne in its hóme
    (* *   (* * (*   *   (*   0 ⇒
     *   *   *   *   1

Closer examination reveals that the unmetricality of (26) and (28) is due to the placement of the stress of a polysyllabic word such as *never* or *alone*. In the metrical lines the stresses of polysyllabic words appear in positions that project to Gridline 1; in the unmetrical lines the stresses of polysyllabic words appear in positions that do not project to Gridline 1. Formally, we capture this fact by defining the maximum mentioned in (25) as in (29).

(29)   The syllable bearing the word stress in a polysyllabic word is a maximum.

The definition (29) will be somewhat modified below.

A line is correctly scanned when the grid generated from it by a specific set of rules meets all conditions. We have seen two such conditions so far: condition (11) which is found in all meters requires that there be one asterisk on the final Gridline, and condition (25) which is specific to English requires that all maxima be projected to Gridline 1. Given that there are many possible sets of rules which might in principle generate a grid from a Gridline, how is the right set of rules chosen? The answer is that the right set of rules is chosen by trial and error, such that a line is assigned a grid which satisfies the conditions. We assume that this is as true for the metrical theorist, who must determine which set of rules (and conditions) constitutes a specific meter, as it is for the listener, who unconsciously chooses a set of rules and generates a grid from the line. A rule is determined by a combination of the parameters in (20); we try various combinations of the parameters until we have a set of rules which generate a well-formed grid whose relation to the line satisfies the relevant conditions. In principle, several distinct sets of rules may be satisfactory. For example, we could have assigned grid (30) instead of grid (16).

(30)   And bréathed in the fáce of the fóe as he pássed:

```
*      * )     *     * * ) *    * * ) *   *  * )        0
       ) *                 * )         *       * )      1
                           ) *                 * )      2
                            *                          3
```

No condition is violated by this grid, which is generated by a rule forming a left-headed group on Gridline 2. Similarly, though this grid can be generated by a rule inserting right parentheses from right to left on Gridline 2, it could also be generated by a rule inserting right parentheses from left to right on Gridline 2. It is often the case that a number of alternative grids are equally viable. When poems with a large number of lines are considered, the choice among alternative accounts becomes easier because the larger the set of lines, the clearer the evidence for the choice among the alternatives.

1.5 How verse length is controlled

At the end of section 1.1 we explained how grouping on the Gridlines above Gridline 0 made it possible to restrict the length of the lines. In the meters discussed to this point, incomplete groups are admitted only at the edges, and grouping need not always begin at the edge of the line, but may begin one or two syllables into the line. These options account for some variation in line length. By far the most important control on line length, however, is the number of Gridlines that make up the grid. A grid with groups on two Gridlines admits lines of nine syllables at most (i.e., if ternary groups are formed on both Gridlines), plus possibly one or two extra syllables constituting the (feminine) rhyme.

In order to make use of the grid as the means for restricting line length we propose the condition (31).

(31)   The number of Gridlines in the grid assigned to the lines in a poem (or part of a poem) is the same as that required for its longest line.

In the light of condition (31), *all* the lines in Shelley's stanza quoted as (23b) above have grids with groups on two Gridlines, as shown in (32), even though the shortest lines contain only two syllables.

(32)   Though the sound overpowers,

```
   ) *        * * )    *   * * ) *              0 ⇐
           *            * )                     1 ⇐
                         *                      2
```

Sing again, with your dear voice revealing

```
   ) *    * * )    *     *    * )   *    * * ) *    0 ⇐
          *                  *           * )        1 ⇐
                                          *         2
```

A tone

```
   *   * )                                       0 ⇐
        * )                                      1 ⇐
         *                                       2
```

Of some world far from ours,

```
   ) *    *     * )    *    *    * )              0 ⇐
          *                  * )                  1 ⇐
                              *                   2
```

Where music and moonlight and feeling

```
       *     * ) *  *     * )  *    *    * ) *    0 ⇐
             *           *           * )          1 ⇐
                                      *           2
```

Are one.

```
   *    * )                                       0 ⇐
        * )                                      1 ⇐
         *                                       2
```

It is obvious that the six lines in the stanza (32) are organized into two sub-stanzas of three lines, where the first line consists of two groups, the second of three groups, and the third of one group. This fact is captured formally by the rules in (33b) below that group the asterisks on Gridline 1 into a single ternary group, which is complete in the second line (of the sub-stanza) and incomplete elsewhere. Moreover, in the second line of the sub-stanza the grouping on Gridline 0 begins one syllable in (feminine rhyme), while in two other lines, the grouping begins just at tho right odgo. We state the grouping rules for this poem in (33).

(33)   a.   Gridline 0: starting ⟨ just / one asterisk in ⟩ at the R edge, insert a R parenthesis, form ternary groups, heads R.

      i. Incomplete groups are admitted.

      ii. Ungrouped asterisks are admitted.

  b. Gridline 1: starting just at the R edge, insert a R parenthesis, form ternary groups, heads R.

      i. Incomplete groups are admitted.

It will be noticed that the rules for the two Gridlines in (33) are almost identical. This is not always the case as will become evident below, where meters of greater variety are discussed.

The other poems (Keats's trochaic tetrameter 'Fancy', and Byron's anapaestic tetrameter 'Destruction...') discussed to this point require an additional Gridline in order to accommodate the fact that these poems include longer lines, lines with more than three Gridline 0 groups (i.e., more than three 'feet' in traditional terms). In (34) we give the rules for Keats's poem, and reproduce the grid assigned to one of the lines.

(34) Rules for trochaic tetrameter

  a. Gridline 0: starting just at the L edge, insert a L parenthesis, form binary groups, heads L.

      i. Incomplete groups are admitted.

  b. Gridline 1: starting just at the L edge, insert a L parenthesis, form binary groups, heads L.

  c. Gridline 2: starting just at the L edge, insert a L parenthesis, form binary groups, heads L.

(35) Pléasure néver is at hóme;

```
( *   *    ( * *( *   *   ( *            0 ⇒
( *         *   ( *        * (           1 ⇒
( *              *  (                    2 ⇒
    *                                    3
```

In (36) we give the rules for Byron's poem and reproduce the grid assigned to one of the lines.

(36) Rules for anapaestic tetrameter

  a. Gridline 0: starting just at the R edge, insert a R parenthesis, form ternary groups, heads R.

      i. Incomplete groups are admitted.

  b. Gridline 1: starting just at the R edge, insert a R parenthesis, form binary groups, heads R.

  c. Gridline 2: starting just at the R edge, insert a R parenthesis, form binary groups, heads R.

(37) For the Ángel of Déath spréad his wíngs on the blást,

```
) *     * * )  *   *    * )      *    *   * )  *    *   * )   0 ⇐
    ) *          * )              *            * )   1 ⇐
        ) *                                    * )   2 ⇐
                                               *     3
```

Examination of (34) and (36) shows that the two sets of rules are symmetrical counterparts, except for the stipulation of different group sizes on Gridline 0. The simple relation between different meters which we find in the English tradition is not generally the case; as will be seen below, rule types of greater variety are employed in other languages and poetic traditions. The metrical grids generated above are in addition subject to conditions such as (25), which holds for English metrical verse, but not elsewhere.

1.6 Comparison with the traditional approach

The generative approach to meter illustrated above contrasts with the classificatory, taxonomic account of traditional metrics (exemplified by Fussell 1979, Lennard 2005, and Fry 2005). Like the generative account, the taxonomic account partitions all syllables into two classes and it also groups the syllables. It is at this point that the two approaches diverge fundamentally. As illustrated above, in the generative account the groups on a given Gridline are identical both in the number of syllables per group (except at the edges) and in the location of the head. The traditional account does not observe these constraints. It admits lines with different feet (Gridline 0 groups). It also countenances feet of great variety; in fact, the traditional approach recognizes as legitimate feet, the entire list of twenty-eight syllable sequences, varying in length from two to four syllables, given in (38).

(38) **disyllabic** (4): trochee, iamb, pyrrhic, spondee

trisyllabic (8): dactyl, anapaest, amphibrach, tribrach, bacchius, antibacchius, amphimacer, molosssus

quadrisyllabic (16): proceleusmatic; first, second, third and fourth paeon; ionic a majore, ditrochee, choriamb, antispast, diamb, ionic a minore; first, second, third and fourth epitrite; dispondee.

It is not usually noted that the 28 'feet' listed in (38) include all possible sequences (groups) of syllables of length 2, 3 or 4, where the syllables belong to two classes (such as stressed vs. stressless, heavy vs.

light, etc.) Specifically, there are $2^2 = 4$ such groups of length 2, $2^3 = 8$ groups of length 3, and $2^4 = 16$ such groups of length 4; the total is 28.

The immediate objection to the list in (38) is that the list is arbitrary and unmotivated. It excludes – without reason – groups of one syllable, and it provides no justification for excluding groups of five or more syllables. Moreover, it is well known that the great majority of the feet in (38) rarely comes up in discussions of meters. For example, Fry (2005: 121) quotes from a letter by Edmund Wilson, who writes to Vladimir Nabokov that 'we have simplified our [English – NF&MH] metrics to five kinds of feet ... trochee, iambus, anapest, dactyl and spondee. We do not need any more'. The fact that only a handful of the feet in the list are of use in English metrics brings out a major shortcoming of lists (and of theories relying on lists): they fail to provide an explanation for their content. If for the treatment of English meters the list of feet can be reduced from twenty-eight to five, as Wilson claims, it is not sufficient just to list the latter, we need to be told at a minimum what distinguishes these five from the remaining twenty-three.

The problem is compounded by the fact that the traditional theory allows for foot substitution and hence for lines that are composed of feet of several different kinds. Here again the traditional approach is to list the allowable substitutions, but it is not sufficient to state, for example, that in English iambic verse, trochaic inversion (a trochee replacing an iamb) is admitted line-initially. This fact needs to be explained; i.e., deduced from principles that determine the nature of English metrical verse, or of metrical verse in general. To answer these questions – as well as others that the traditional theory fails to address – is one of the aims of the theory of this book.

The traditional theory differs from our approach also in that in the traditional account, the metrical scansion is matched to the phonetic surface of the line; that is, the feet are chosen and combined so that the heads of feet always match stressed syllables. The sequence of metrical feet thus directly represents the 'rhythm' of the line. In contrast, in our approach the metrical grid has a fully regular and periodic structure because it is generated from the line by iterative rules. The stressed syllables do not necessarily match heads of groups (though the grid assigned must conform to the condition (25) that maxima project to Gridline 1).[8] In our approach, rhythm and meter are quite distinct; in

---

[8] Our metrical grid is thus fundamentally different from the metrical grids proposed for poetry by Hayes (1983), which are not generated by iterative rules.

the traditional approach, rhythm and meter are two sides of the same coin.

We end this section with remarks on the relation between the meter of a poem and the recitation of its lines (its performance). A common practice is to recite classical Greek and Latin verse so as to disregard totally the stress placement of the individual words that make up the line. For example, in reading the first line of Virgil's *Aenead* below, stress is placed as in (39) on the final syllable of *cano:* and *Tro:iae:* in open violation of the rules of Latin word stress.

(39) Árma virúmque canó: Tro:iáe: qui: prí:mus ab óri:s

According to this tradition the metrical grid assigned to a line determines how the line is read. This is not the generally accepted way of reading English poetry, nor of poetry in many other languages. This is readily seen once one considers the performance of well-known iambic pentameter lines such those below.

(40) Painting thy outward walls so costly gay?

William Shakespeare, Sonnet 146

Lawrence, of virtuous father virtuous son,

John Milton, 'Lawrence of Virtuous Father'

Milton! Thou shouldst be living at this hour:
England hath need of thee: she is a fen

William Wordsworth, 'London, 1802'

Silent upon a peak in Darien.

John Keats, 'On First Looking in Chapman's Homer'

Looking as if she were alive. I call

Robert Browning, 'My Last Duchess'

All of these iambic lines begin with a word that bears stress on the initial syllable followed by an unstressed syllable. As explained in Chapter 2, the syllable bearing the word stress in verse-initial position is not a maximum, and the fact that its stressed syllable does not project to Gridline 1 is therefore not a violation of condition (25). In reading these lines, however, the normal, phonetically trochaic stress patterns of these words are produced, in spite of the fact that these stresses occupy positions which contradict the iambic sequence in the grid. The lines in

(40) are thus counterexamples to the proposition that the metrical grid must be reproduced in performing lines of verse.

Additional evidence for the proposition that performance does not mimic the meter comes from the treatment of lines with syllables that are not projected onto Gridline 0 and are therefore omitted in computing the meter of the line (English examples can be seen in sections 2.7 and 3.5.2). When such lines are read, the syllables omitted in the count may nevertheless be pronounced, especially where failure to pronounce them would make the utterance incomprehensible.

The situation is even more striking in the Romance languages, where word-final vowels are not counted if followed by a vowel-initial word (see section 4.2 for examples and discussion). These metrical omissions are very extensive, and so the syllables must be prononuced or the poetry would be unintelligible. Syllables that do not project to Gridline 0 and can play no role in determining the metrical well-formedness can always be pronounced. Intelligibility thus takes precedence over metrical transparency. (For some additional remarks, see section 1.10.)

1.7 The strict meters of English verse

Above we have illustrated lines with Gridline 0 groups that were left-headed and binary as well as lines with Gridline 0 groups that were right-headed and ternary. We begin this section by scanning lines that are the symmetrical counterparts of the meters above, that is lines with Gridline 0 groups that are left-headed and ternary (dactyls) and lines with Gridline 0 groups that are right-headed and binary (iambs).

Dactylic verse, where the Gridline 0 groups are ternary with heads left, is relatively rare in English poetry. We cite an example in (41), and show grids for the last two lines in (42).

(41)   Pibroch of Donuil Dhu,
       Pibroch of Donuil,
       Wake thy wild voice anew,
       Summon Clan-Conuil.
       Come away, come away,
       Hark to the summons!
       Come in your war array,
       Gentles and commons.

Sir Walter Scott, 'Pibroch of Donuil Dhu' first stanza

(42) Come in your war array,

```
( *      *    *    ( *  *   * (        0 ⇒
( *                 * (                1 ⇒
   *                                  2
```

Gentles and commons.

```
( *  *    *    ( *      *              0 ⇒
( *                * (                 1 ⇒
   *                                  2
```

The rules grouping the syllables are stated in (43).

(43) a. Gridline 0: starting just at the L edge, insert a L parenthesis, form ternary groups, heads L.

  i. Incomplete groups are admitted.

  b. Gridline 1: starting just at the L edge, insert a L parenthesis, form binary groups, heads L.

The fourth and last type of elementary meter is iambic meter, illustrated in (44)

(44) Thou sorrow, venom elf:

```
) *     * ) *      * ) *    * )        0 ⇐
        * )         *       * )        1 ⇐
      ) *                    * )        2 ⇐
                              *         3
```

Is this thy play,

```
)*     * )    *     * )                0 ⇐
     ) *            * )                1 ⇐
                    * )                2 ⇐
                     *                 3
```

To spin a web out of thyself

```
) *    * ) *    * )  *   * )   * * )    0 ⇐
     ) *         * )       *      * )   1 ⇐
             ) *                   * )   2 ⇐
                                   *    3
```

To catch a fly?

```
) *  * )    *    * )                   0 ⇐
    ) *            * )                 1 ⇐
                   * )                 2 ⇐
                    *                  3
```

For why?

```
) *        * )                        0 ⇐
           * )                        1 ⇐
           * )                        2 ⇐
            *                         3
```

Edward Taylor, 'Upon a Spider Catching a Fly' stanza

The lines in (44) vary in length from having four groups on Gridline 0 to one group, in the pattern 3–2–4–2–1. The rules for this type of iambic tetrameter in which line length varies radically are given in (45). They differ from the rules for the anapaestic tetrameter in (36) not only in forming binary rather than ternary groups on Gridline 0, but also in admitting incomplete groups on all Gridlines.

(45)   a.   Gridline 0: starting just at the R edge, insert a R parenthesis, form binary groups, heads R.

   i.   Incomplete groups are admitted.

   b.   Gridline 1: starting just at the R edge, insert a R parenthesis, form binary groups, heads R.

   i.   Incomplete groups are admitted.

   c.   Gridline 2: starting just at the R edge, insert a R parenthesis, form binary groups, heads R.

   i.   Incomplete groups are admitted.

1.8 Grid transformations

Condition (11) establishes a fixed number of Gridlines for all lines in a poem (or for a clearly delimited section of a poem). Grids of this kind terminate in a Gridline with a single asterisk. The syllable from which this asterisk projects is called the head of the verse, and this syllable plays a special role in the account of different metrical regularities. An example of this special role of the head of the verse is the following metrical experiment by Tennyson:

(46)   O you chorus of indolent reviewers,
       Irresponsible, indolent reviewers,
       Look, I come to the test, a tiny poem
       All composed in a metre of Catullus,   4
       All in quantity, careful of my motion,
       Like the skater on ice that hardly bears him,
       Lest I fall unawares before the people,
       Waking laughter in indolent reviewers.   8
       Should I flounder awhile without a tumble
       Thro' this metrification of Catullus,
       They should speak to me not without a welcome,
       All that chorus of indolent reviewers.   12
       Hard, hard, hard it is, only not to tumble,

So fantastical is the dainty meter.
Wherefore slight me not wholly, nor believe me
Too presumptuous, indolent reviewers.   16
O blatant Magazines, regard me rather –
Since I blush to belaud myself a moment –
As some rare little rose, a piece of inmost
Horticultural art, or half-coquette-like   20
Maiden, not to be greeted unbenignly.

Alfred, Lord Tennyson, 'Hendecasyllabics'

Examination of (46) reveals that every one of its twenty-one lines is composed of eleven syllables ending with a feminine rhyme, i.e., the 'hendecasyllabic' (eleven-syllable) count after which the meter is named. Iambic lines with feminine rhymes are the province of parameter (20i), which allows parenthesis insertion to begin inside the line rather than at its edge (see rule (47a)). At first sight it may appear that (46) is in iambic pentameter lines, and at least one of the lines, line 17, is a clear instance of this meter, which formally is expressed with the help of the rules in (47).

(47)   a. Gridline 0: starting one asterisk in at the R edge, insert a R parenthesis, form binary groups, heads R.

   b. Gridline 1: starting just at the R edge, insert a R parenthesis, form ternary groups, heads R.

      i. The last (leftmost) group must be incomplete – binary.[9]

   c. Gridline 2: starting just at the L edge, insert a L parenthesis, form binary groups, heads L.

We show in (48) the metrical grid that these rules assign to line 17.

(48)   O blatant Magazines, regard me rather –

```
)*    *) *     *) * * )    * * )    * * ) *        0 ⇐
      *         *) *       *        * )            1 ⇐
                ( *                 * (            2 ⇒
                *                                  3
```

While several other lines in the poem generate grids that may be lawful instances of the iambic pentameter (e.g., lines 13 and 18), the great majority of its twenty-one lines are direct violations of condition (25). We quote three such lines in (49).

---

[9] We have previously seen rules in which a ternary group is *permitted* to be binary. Here we must *require* that the last group constructed on Gridline 1 is binary, to ensure that there are exactly five asterisks on this Gridline.

(49)   a. Irresponsible, indolent reviewers,

```
)*  * ) *  *)*  * ) * *)   * * ) *        0 ⇐
    *      *)    *    *       *)           1 ⇐
         ( *                * (            2 ⇒
            *                              3
```

      b. Thro' this metrification of Catullus,

```
 ) *    * )  * *)* *) *  *) * *)*          0 ⇐
```

      c. Horticultural art, or half-coquette-like

```
 ) *  *)* *)* *)  *   *) *   *)   *        0 ⇐
```

In each of these lines, the third syllable is occupied by a maximum, the stressed syllable of a polysyllabic word. Since in iambic pentameter lines odd-numbered syllables do not project to Gridline 1, this is a blatant violation of condition (25), which requires maxima to project to Gridline 1. We note that there is one violation in each line, and that the violation is located in the Gridline 0 group that contains the head of the verse.[10]

It would be an error to think that this line should be assigned a different grid, as in (50).

(50)   Irrespónsible, índolent revíewers,

```
)*  * ) *  *)* * ) **)   * * ) *          0 ⇐
    * )       *   *         *)            1 ⇐
         ( *              * (             2 ⇒
            *                             3
```

A grid is generated from a line of verse by iterative rules (it is not preconstructed and then attached to the line). Though this grid does conform to condition (25), the grid cannot be generated by the iterative rules, because it has an inconsistent mix of right and left heads on Gridline 0. The iterative rules that group the asterisks are incapable of generating aperiodicities, and so any aperiodicities cannot be explained by the iterative rules alone.

The problem posed by the lines in (49) is how such lines should be accounted for by the theory. A possible solution is to weaken the theory by adding to it a list of exceptions, admitting as metrical, for example, lines where a maximum does not project to Gridline 1 but is in the same Gridline 0 group as the syllable projecting to Gridline 1. Taken

---

[10] In line 3,

        Look, I come to the test, a tiny poem
```
   ) *    * )*    * ) * * )  * *)* *)*
```
the third syllable is not a maximum as defined by (29), and this line is therefore technically not a violation of (25). As discussed in section 1.9, for purposes of some meters, stressed monosyllabic words are maxima where followed by two or more syllables with less stress. On this conception of maximum, the verse above violates condition (25) in exactly the same way as the other lines in (46), but, this is 'corrected' by the application of rule (52), as explained below.

literally, this suggestion would gut condition (25), for it would no longer exclude most sequences of ten or eleven syllables. This alternative must therefore be discarded.

In order not to empty (25) of content, it might be proposed that the weakening of (25) only be allowed for syllables in the same group as the head of the verse. To be specific, we might replace condition (25) with condition (51).

(51)   Maxima must project to Gridline 1 or appear in the same Gridline 0 group with the syllable which projects to Gridline 3 (the head of the verse).

This modification accurately reflects the situation in Tennyson's poem (46), where all maxima that fail to project to Gridline 1 are in the same Gridline 0 group as the (uniquely identifiable) head of the verse. In spite of its empirical accuracy, however, we do not adopt (51) because of its ad hoc character, for there is no intrinsic relation between the requirements that a syllable project to Gridline 1 and that it be adjacent to the syllable that projects to Gridline 3.

Since we regard the metrical grid of a line as the embodiment of its meter, it seemed natural to us to adopt a solution that makes maximal use of the metrical grid and its properties. Rather than modify condition (25), we modify the metrical grid that is subject to condition (25). To this end we posit the rule (52) that transforms the grid of which condition (25) holds.

(52)   Delete the Gridline 0 asterisk which projects to the head of the verse.

Deleting this Gridline 0 asterisk in (49) has the effect of removing also the other asterisks projecting from it. The deletion, however, does not affect the grouping of the remaining asterisks. Instead, deleting the Gridline 0 asterisk changes the second group in (49a) from binary to unary, and as shown in (53), the remaining asterisk in that group is now head of the verse.[11] Note that it is the Gridline 0 projection of the syllable which is deleted by rule (52), not the syllable itself: metrical rules do not alter the way we pronounce the words that make up the line.

---

[11] Here and below we have indicated where an asterisk has been deleted by writing the Greek letter Δ (delta) as a place marker. This is purely for the reader's convenience; the delta does not form part of the grid (i.e., is not like an asterisk or parenthesis), and so cannot be referred to by a rule or condition.

(53)   Irresponsible, indolent reviewers,

```
)*  * )  *   Δ) *   * )  * * )    *  * )  *          0 ⇐
    *   * )       *      *      * )              1 ⇐
      ( *                      * (              2 ⇒
        *                                        3
```

The grid in (53) fully conforms to condition (25): the three stressed syllables in polysyllabic words all project to Gridline 1. Rule (52) applies also to all other lines in the poem, with the sole exception of line 17. In the other lines it 'corrects' the grid by bringing the grid into conformity with condition (25).[12]

Though rule (52) is not in wide use in English poetry – Tennyson's poem is the only example we have encountered – rules deleting a projection of the head of the verse are essential parts of the explanation of Spanish hendecasyllabic poetry (section 4.3), various Greek (sections 6.3.4, 6.4.1, 6.4.2), Arabic (section 7.2), and Sanskrit (sections 8.1.4, 8.3.1, 8.3.2, 8.4.3, 8.5) meters, as well as in Catullus's meter which was imitated by Tennyson. The deletion rule (52) targets a unique projection in the line: the asterisk which projects to the head of the verse. The head of the verse is the only line-internal syllable which can be uniquely identified by a rule or condition. The deletion rule (52) can thus be used as a diagnostic for the head of the verse, and can thus determine the iterative rules that generate the grid such that this syllable will project to the head of the verse. (As we will see, other rules or conditions which target a unique syllable can also be shown to apply to the head of the verse.)

The deletion rule (52) tells us two important things about metrical verse. First, deletion documents the fact that metrical grids may be subject to modification and the computation of a given grid may involve intermediate grids which differ significantly from the grid to which the well-formedness conditions such as (25) and (11) apply. The cognitive status of such intermediate grids is not well understood at this time, but our present ignorance about intermediate representations does not impugn their status. Intermediate representations arose naturally in the attempt to account for the metrical facts, and it is unlikely that the metrical facts can be accounted more insightfully by excluding intermediate representations. It is far more likely that as cognitive science advances, such representations will be fully integrated into the theory.

---

[12]   As pointed out to us by S. J. Keyser, the exceptional character of line 17 is signaled by the word *blatant*, meaning that the meter of the line is given directly and does not require the deletion rule (52).

Second, the deletion rule (52) brings out the special role of the head of the verse, i.e., of the unique syllable that projects to the bottom line of the metrical grid. It is this unique syllable in the grid that is targeted by the deletion rule (52), and, as we will see below, it is also the target of similar operations in other languages and poetic traditions.

1.9 Loose meters

In this section we look at a different kind of meter, exemplified by William Blake's 'The Lilly'.

(54)   The modest Rose puts forth a thorn:
          The humble Sheep, a threatning horn:
          While the Lilly white, shall in Love delight,
          Nor a thorn nor a threat stain her beauty bright.

William Blake, 'The Lilly' complete

The first two lines of this poem, eight syllables long, can be analyzed as regular iambic tetrameter, but the third and fourth lines cannot; these lines have ten and eleven syllables respectively, and the distance between consecutive marked syllables also varies (i.e., stressed syllables are sometimes two, sometimes three syllables apart). Lines of the type shown in (54) were characterized by Robert Frost as being in 'loose' iambics, in contrast with the normal 'strict' iambic lines (see Chapter 3).

The main difference between these two kinds of meter is that in strict meters the grouping of the syllables on Gridline 0 determines the placement of the maxima, whereas in loose meters it is the placement of the maxima that determines the grouping. This difference is formally captured in our account by the addition of the rule (55).

(55)   On Gridline 0, insert a R parenthesis to the right of an asterisk projecting from a maximum.

Rule (55) inserts parentheses into the asterisk sequence, and can be applied several times. However, its form is not determined by choosing from the parameters set in (20), and it is not a rule which iterates from one end of the line to the other. This *non-iterative rule* is applied to the Gridline 0 sequence of asterisks before parentheses are inserted by the iterative rules for this poem, which are given in (58). This ordering differentiates rule (55) from other non-iterative rules such as (52) above, which crucially must be applied after parentheses have been inserted by the iterative rules (47). Like in generative phonology, the ordering of rules is the primary means available in our theory of meter for capturing interactions among rules.[13]

In loose meters the definition of maximum (stated in (56)) is generalized somewhat beyond the definition of maximum (29) in strict meters.

(56)   Syllables bearing the stress of polysyllabic words are maxima, and so are stressed monosyllabic words if those words are followed by two or more syllables with less stress.

In (57) we illustrate the effects of (55) (using the definition of maximum (56)) on all four lines of Blake's poem. The right parentheses inserted by (55) are printed in bold type here and below.[14]

(57)   The modest Rose puts forth a thorn:
           * ***)** *   *   *   *   *

        The humble Sheep, a threatning horn:
           * ***)** *   * * ***)** *   *

        While the Lilly white, shall in Love delight,
        *   * ***)** * ***)** * * * ***)**

        Nor a thorn nor a threat stain her beauty bright.
        * * ***)** * * ***)** * * ***)** * *

The sequence of asterisks and parentheses inserted by (55) is then subject to the iterative rules in (58).

(58)   a. Gridline 0: starting just at the R edge, insert a L parenthesis, form binary groups, heads R.

         i. Ungrouped asterisks are admitted freely.

       b. Gridline 1: starting just at the R edge, insert a R parenthesis, form binary groups, heads R.

       c. Gridline 2: starting just at the R edge, insert a R parenthesis, form binary groups, heads R.

---

[13] It will be recalled from the discussion of Tennyson's poem that the non-iterative rule (52) deletes the Gridline 0 projection of the head of the verse. In order to determine which syllable is head of verse the metrical grid for the verse line must be available, and this requires prior application of the iterative rules (47). For some recent discussion of rule order see Halle and Nevins (2008).

[14] The use of bold type for parentheses inserted by non-iterative rules is for the reader's convenience. The metrical rules and conditions operate just with right and left parentheses, and no rule or condition differentiates parentheses inserted by non-iterative rules from parentheses inserted by iterative rules.

Convention (19), which we repeat here, holds in this meter, just as it holds in all meters.

(19)   A left parenthesis groups the asterisks on its right; a right parenthesis groups the asterisks on its left. Asterisks that are neither to the right of a left parenthesis, nor to the left of a right parenthesis are ungrouped.

In (59) we have illustrated the application of the iterative rules (58) to the four lines in (57).

(59)   The modest Rose puts forth a thorn:

```
( *   *)(*    *   ( *   *   ( *   * (        0 ⇐
        ) *       *) )       *      *)       1 ⇐
        ) *                         *)       2 ⇐
                                    *        3
```

The humble Sheep, a threatning horn:

```
( *   *) ( *    *   ( *   *) ) ( *   * (     0 ⇐
        ) *         *) )        *      *)    1 ⇐
        ) *                            *)    2 ⇐
                                       *     3
```

While the Lilly white, shall in Love delight,

```
*    ( *  *)(*    *)   * ( *    *   ( **) (  0 ⇐
         ) *      *)        *    *      * )  1 ⇐
         ) *                            *)   2 ⇐
                                        *    3
```

Nor a thorn nor a threat stain her beauty bright.

```
* ( *   *)   * ( *    *)   *   ( *   *) ( *   * (    0 ⇐
      ) *          *) )               *     *)      1 ⇐
      ) *                                    *)      2 ⇐
                                             *       3
```

In the last two verses of (59) there are ungrouped asterisks; i.e., asterisks that neither precede a left parenthesis, nor follow a right parenthesis. By admitting ungrouped syllables on Gridline 0 we account for the variability in line lengths in (59), which vary between eight and eleven syllables, yet every line is composed of exactly four feet. The 'loose' meters of English are discussed further in Chapter 3, where we explain how the rules interact.

We observe in conclusion, that lines of both strict and loose metrical verse give rise to grids which satisfy specific conditions of well-formedness. While a metrical grid may be assigned to any sequence of syllables in the ways illustrated above, only some of these grids will both satisfy the stated well-formedness conditions, such as condition (25) or its analog in different languages and metrical traditions, and will also satisfy the universal requirement (11) that (exactly) one asterisk be projected to the bottom of the grid. Syllable sequences that give rise to metrical grids that satisfy these conditions are perceived as instances of metrical verse and as being distinct from ordinary prose.

1.10 Appendix A: The metrical grids in music and in performance

Poetry is not the only art form that has a meter. Music also has meter, and, as shown in this section, musical meters are constructed by iterative rules of parenthesis insertion of the same kind as those employed above in assigning metrical grids to lines of poetry. We reproduce in (60) the five-Gridline metrical grid assigned by Lerdahl and Jackendoff (1983) to the ten notes and one rest forming the opening of Mozart's *Symphony 40* (in their grid, the ninth note is the most prominent; in our grid it is the head of the sequence).

(60)

The grid in (60) is an object of the same kind (minus parentheses) as the grids of the poetic meters encountered above, and, as we show directly, like the metrical grids in poetry, a grid like that of (60) is readily generated by rules of iterative parenthesis insertion with the five parameters in (20).

The segment in (60) consists of eleven units of which the first ten are pitches and the eleventh is a silence. The fact that pauses (silences) are part of the metrical grid distinguishes musical meters fundamentally from those of poetry. In poetry, as we have seen above – and as is also shown by many of the examples in the rest of this book – metrical grids are assigned exclusively to sequences of syllables. Only syllables project to Gridline 0 in poetry, and pauses have no metrical status, though they are a crucial factor in how the lines are performed.

We propose to capture this basic difference between poetry and music formally by positing that in music the entities projecting to Gridline 0 are time intervals, rather than syllables; it is the shortest note in the segment that determines the smallest time interval. In the Mozart melody the shortest time interval is that of an eighth note (quaver), but in (63) below the shortest time interval is a sixteenth note (semiquaver). Different pieces of music differ in the length of their shortest time interval. In (60) pitches and silences are associated with one or more time intervals. As shown in (61), Gridline 0 of the melody consists of sixteen time intervals which are grouped by the parentheses in the fashion that should, by now, be familiar.

(61)

```
( * * ( * * ( *  * ( * *  ( *  * ( * * ( * * ( * * (      0 ⇒
) *     * ) *    * )   *    * ) *   * )             1 ⇐
      ( *         *        ( *       * (           2 ⇒
      ) *                  * )                     3 ⇐
                 *                                 4
```

The rules that generate the grid in (61) are listed in (62) below.

(62)   a.   Gridline 0: starting just at the L edge, insert a L parenthesis, form binary groups, heads L.

      b.   Gridline 1: starting just at the R edge, insert a R parenthesis, form binary groups, heads R.

      c.   Gridline 2: starting just at the L edge, insert a L parenthesis, form binary groups, heads L.

      d.   Gridline 3: starting just at the R edge, insert a R parenthesis, form binary groups, heads R.

When a metrical text is set to music, a distinct musical grid is created which usually shows no particular resemblance to the grid of the text, as the two grids are generated by separate grouping rules. There is thus no necessary connection between the meter of a line of poetry and the way it is set to music. What has been shown above is that the meters of poetry and the meters (or beat structure) of certain kinds of music are constructed by rules of the same kind.[15]

To make clear the difference between the two kinds of grid we compare the metrical grid assigned to the first musical 'line' of the American birthday greeting 'Happy birthday to you' in (63) with the metrical grid that is assigned to the first few words of the greeting shown in (65).

---

[15] For text setting, see J. Halle and Lerdahl (1993), J. Halle (1999, 2008), Dell and J. Halle (2008).

(63)

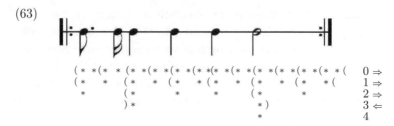

```
( * *( *  * (*  *(* *(*  *(* *(*  *(* *(* *(* *(* *(  0 ⇒
( *    * (*    * (*    * (*    * (*    * (*    * (    1 ⇒
       *       (*       *       *       (*       *    2 ⇒
       ) *                      * )                   3 ⇐
                               *                     4
```

The rules that generate the grid in (63) are given in (64).

(64)   a. Gridline 0: starting just at the L edge, insert a L parenthesis, form binary groups, heads L.

    b. Gridline 1: starting just at the L edge, insert a L parenthesis, form binary groups, heads L.

    c. Gridline 2: starting one asterisk in at the L edge, insert a L parenthesis, form ternary groups, heads L.

       i. The last (rightmost) group must be incomplete – binary.

    d. Gridline 3: starting just at the R edge, insert a R parenthesis, form binary groups, heads R.

The words to which (63) is set have a metrical grid of their own, which, as shown below in (65), differs substantially from the metrical grid in (63).

(65)   Happy birthday to you
```
      *) *  *) (*   *  *(     0 ⇐
      (*      *      (*       1 ⇒
       )*             *)      2 ⇐
                      *       3
```

(65) is a loose anapaestic meter with a grid generated by the non-iterative rule (55) plus the iterative rules in (66).

(55)   Insert a right parenthesis after a Gridline 0 asterisk projecting from a maximum.

(66)   a. Gridline 0: starting just at the R edge, insert a L parenthesis, form ternary groups, heads R.

    b. Gridline 1: starting just at the L edge, insert a L parenthesis, form binary groups, heads R.

       i. The last (rightmost) group must be incomplete.

    c. Gridline 2: starting just at the R edge, insert a R parenthesis, form binary groups, heads R.

The fact that (63) and (65) are different objects is unsurprising since these grids are constructed by the different sets of rules (64) and (55, 66), respectively. In (65) the asterisks on Gridline 0 project from the consecutive syllables of the text; in (63) they project from consecutive time intervals of the melody.

The fundamental difference between the meter of a poem and the meter of the melody to which the poem is sung is that the Gridline 0 asterisks project from different entities in the two cases. In poems the asterisks project from syllables; in melodies, the asterisk project from time intervals. The metrical grid assigned to a melody of a song is therefore distinct from the grid assigned to the words that are sung to this melody. From this perspective, the recitation of a poem is tantamount to the assignment of a melody to a text, and the metrical grid of a poem is distinct from the grid of its recitation, which, as just noted, consists of the assigning of a melody to a text.[16]

1.11 Appendix B: A note on the assignment of stresses to words

In early theories of stress such as those of Chomsky and Halle (1968/1991) and Halle and Keyser (1971), stress was treated as a phonetic feature of vowels and other sonorants on a par with such features as [+/–back], [+/–nasal], [+/–round]. Liberman (1975), however, showed that stress is unlike other phonetic features in that its distribution is directly tied to specific groupings of the syllables that make up the words and the phrases. Originally the syllable groups were regarded as special kinds of constituents, analogous to the nested Immediate Constituents that make up the syntactic structure of words and phrases (cf. e.g., Hayes 1981 and Halle and Vergnaud 1987). It was subsequently shown by Idsardi (1992) that stress phenomena of various kinds can be characterized more effectively by the same formalism as the one used above (and elsewhere in this book) to account for metrical verse. The groupings of elements generated by this formalism differ substantively from the nested constituents encountered in the syntax.

One of the two main innovations of Idsardi's formalism was the in-

---

[16] Here we differ from Attridge (1982), and others, for whom there is just one scansion of a poem, incorporating both metrical and performed elements in a single representation (including, for example, unrealized beats corresponding to silences in the text). In contrast, it is fundamental to our approach that metrical form is not given the same representation as performed (or perceived) rhythm or any other aspect of performance.

troduction of special diacritic marks to delimit the groups. To this end, Idsardi borrowed from syntax ordinary parentheses, and his usage has also been followed in this book. It is, however, essential to note that parentheses function in radically different ways in metrics and stress assignment than in syntax. Simply put, in syntax parentheses are (redundant) marks that, like the blank spaces between words in a line of type, make visible the consecutive units in a sequence; they make visible the edges of the units, but do not generate the units. By contrast, parentheses in metrics, and also in stress assignment, generate the units. It is by virtue of convention (19) that the parentheses break up a sequence of syllables into groups, and that syllables which happen *not* to be to the right of a left parenthesis or to left of a right parenthesis remain ungrouped.

Idsardi's second innovation was the introduction of iterative rules, i.e., rules whose application begins with the element at one edge of a sequence and proceeds to the opposite edge, element by element. Not all rules that insert parentheses and split up a sequence into groups are iterative. However, to our knowledge the only iterative rules are rules that insert parentheses.

The Idsardi formalism has been applied in the treatment of stress phenomena in a variety of languages. (Some examples, in addition to Idsardi 1992, are Halle and Idsardi 1994, 1995, 2000; and Halle 1998.) In this brief note we discuss stress facts from a few languages in the light of the Idsardi formalism in order to make clear that like the tunes in section 1.10 these rather different kinds of data are subject to the same formal treatment as the meters of poetry that are the main subject of this book.

In many languages stresses are assigned to some of the syllables that make up a word. Phonetically, stress is usually realized by changes in the fundamental frequency (F0) of the syllable nucleus, and it is not uncommon for there to be several stresses with distinct degrees of prominence in a single word. We illustrate this in (67) with words from the Australian language Maranungku (Hayes 1981: 51). This language distinguishes vowels with main stress from those with secondary stress, and in addition also from vowels that are stressless. In (67) an acute accent indicates main stress, a grave accent indicates secondary stress, whereas absence of an accent mark indicates stresslessness.

(67)   mérepèt   yángarmàta   lángkaràtetì
        'beard'   'the Pleiades'   'prawn'

It is self-evident in (67) that main stress falls on the first syllable of the word, that secondary stress falls on odd numbered syllables except for the first, and that all other syllables are stressless.

There is also another way of thinking about these facts. The word in Maranungku can be analyzed into binary groups with heads on the left, like the lines of poetry above. This will project all odd-numbered syllables onto Gridline 1. On Gridline 1, a non-iterative rule inserts a left parenthesis before the leftmost syllable (asterisk), and so distinguishes the initial syllable from the rest of the stressed syllables.

We state this formally in (68).

(68)   a. Project each syllable in the word as an asterisk on Gridline 0.

   b. Gridline 0: starting just at the L edge, insert a L parenthesis, form binary groups, heads L.

      i. The last (rightmost) group may be incomplete.

   c. Gridline 1: insert a L parenthesis at left edge.

These rules generate the metrical grids in (69).

(69)   mérepèt   yángarmàta   lángkaràtetì

(* * (*	(* * (* * (	(* *(* *(*	0 ⇒
(* *	(* *	(* * *	1
*	*	*	2

The stress contours of the words are supplied by rules (70) and (71).

(70)   Assign stress (high pitch) to syllables projecting to Gridline 1.

(71)   Assign main stress (extra high pitch) to the syllable projecting to Gridline 2 (i.e., the head of the word).

Although the metrical grids in (69) are formally identical with the grids assigned to lines of metrical verse, there is an important difference between the two kinds of grid. The metrical grid of a word is subject to the rules (70) and (71), and these affect the way the syllable sequence is pronounced. In contrast, the metrical grid of a line of verse embodies its meter, but has no effect on its pronunciation.[17]

In another Australian language, Pintupi (Hayes 1995: 62), words have

---

[17] Rules which affect the pronunciation of a line of verse are rhythmic rules, not metrical ones. It seems that in some cases, rhythmic rules refer to a grid formed by the metrical rules, and in effect 're-use' or 're-purpose' this grid, to guide pronunciation. For an example of this in Sanskrit, see section 8.3.1.

stress patterns which differ minimally from those just seen in Maranungku. In both languages, odd-numbered syllables are stressed, but
in Pintupi word-final syllables are stressless (even if odd-numbered), as
shown in (72).

(72)   tjúTaya   máLawàna   púLiNkàlatju
           'many'   'through from behind'   'we (sat) on the hill'

We suggest that in constructing the grids for words in Pintupi, right
rather than left parentheses are inserted on Gridline 0, as shown in (73).

```
(73)   tjúTaya          máLawàna            púLiNkàlatju
       ) *  * ) *       ) *  * ) * * )      ) * * )  * * ) *   0 ⇒
       ( *              ( *    *            ( *      *         1
         *                *                   *                2
```

The rules for Pintupi are identical to those of Maranungku in (68), (70),
and (71), except that the Gridline 0 rule in (68b) must be modified to
insert right rather than left parentheses. As a result, in Pintupi, unlike
in Maranungku, the final syllable will not be grouped if the word has
an odd number of syllables, and hence will be incapable of projecting
to Gridline 1. As shown in (73), the change in the orientation of the
parentheses on Gridline 0 results in a different stress pattern.

We conclude this discussion of word stress assignment with a brief look
at the remarkable stress pattern of Creek, an American Indian language
spoken in Oklahoma and Southern Florida (Haas 1977). As shown in
(74), in a class of words in Creek only one syllable in the word carries
stress: this is the last even-numbered syllable, counting from left to
right.

(74)   hicíta   ahicitá
           'one to see one'   'one to watch one'

              imahicíta   isimahicitá
           'one to look after'   'one to sight at one'

To capture these stress patterns we posit the rules in (75), which generate
the metrical grids shown in (76).

(75)   a. Gridline 0: starting at the L edge, insert a R parenthesis,
              form binary groups, heads R.

         b. Gridline 1: insert a R parenthesis at the R edge, head R.

```
(76)   hicíta        ahicitá        imahicíta       itiwanayipíta
       ) * * ) *     ) * * ) * * )  ) *  * ) * * ) *  ) * * ) * * ) * * ) *   0 ⇒
          * )            *    * )         *    * )       *     *    * )       1
            *              *                *                        *        2
```

The metrical grids in (76) are quite similar to those of Pintupi. Parenthesis insertion in Creek differs from that in Pintupi only in head location: in Pintupi heads are left, in Creek heads are right. The stress patterns of words in these languages are, however, very different: as shown in (72) there are many stressed syllables in the words of Pintupi, but there is only a single stress in Creek words. Formally this difference is easily accounted for by positing that in Creek, words are subject only to rule (71), whereas in Pintupi, both rule (70) and (71) apply.

In order to locate the rightmost even-numbered syllable in Creek words, the syllables must be put into binary right-headed groups, realized as a pattern of asterisks on Gridline 1, as shown in (76). But unlike in Maranungku and Pintupi, this binary grouping of the syllables in Creek is not realized phonetically as a binary stress pattern: the fact that a syllable projects to Gridline 1 does not affect its pronunciation. The grid is used here as a means of grouping syllables, rather than as an abstract model of the concrete stress patterns of the words. The same is true of the grid in metrical poetry: it is a theory of the organization of the syllables in the line, not a representation of its rhythm.

2

English strict meters

The strict meters of English are often called 'accentual-syllabic', because in addition to strict control over the number of syllables in a line, there is in these meters also some control over the distribution of the accented (stressed) syllables. Thus, in perhaps the best known accentual-syllabic meter, the iambic pentameter, each line is said to consist of ten syllables (plus or minus one) with the stressed syllables in even-numbered positions (a description to be made more precise in what follows).

2.1 The four basic strict meters

As explained in Chapter 1, the grouping of asterisks is always the result of parentheses insertion, and this is implemented primarily by iterative rules that are determined by the setting of the five parameters in (20) of the previous chapter, repeated here as (1).

(1) i. Insertion starts just at the edge of the Gridline, one asterisk in, or two asterisks in.

ii. Edge of the sequence (L/R) at which insertion begins.

iii. Nature of parenthesis inserted (L/R).

iv. Interval between consecutive insertions (2/3).

v. Head location in group (L/R).

The four basic strict meters of Engish are called 'iambic', 'trochaic', 'anapaestic', and 'dactylic'. They are differentiated by the rule inserting parentheses at Gridline 0. In these meters the parameters (1ii), (1iii), and (1v) are set in tandem: all three are set either 'left' or 'right'. The interval between consecutive insertions of parentheses can be two or three asterisks, giving binary or ternary meters. The combination of all-left or all-right and binary or ternary gives rise to four meters, defined by the Gridline 0 rules in (2).

(2)   a. **Iambic:** Gridline 0: starting just at the R edge insert a R parenthesis, form binary groups, heads R.

        b. **Trochaic:** Gridline 0: starting just at the L edge insert a L parenthesis, form binary groups, heads L.

        c. **Anapaestic:** Gridline 0: starting just at the R edge insert a R parenthesis, form ternary groups, heads R.

        d. **Dactylic:** Gridline 0: starting just at the L edge insert a L parenthesis, form ternary groups, heads L.

The four meters above project different syllables to Gridline 1. As explained in the first chapter, in English metrical verse, there are restrictions on the syllables that project to Gridline 1: all syllables bearing the stress in polysyllabic words must project to Gridline 1. We capture this formally with the help of the definition (3) and the requirement that condition (4) checks the line against the constructed grid.

(3)   The syllable bearing the main stress in a polysyllabic word is a maximum.

(4)   Maxima must project to Gridline 1.

2.2 Strict iambic meters

In (5) we apply rule (2a) to four lines by Tennyson.

(5)   He is not here, but far away

```
        ′         ′   ′
He is not here, but far away
)* *) *    *)    *    *)* *)              0
    *        *        *    *              1
```
```
     ′        ′    ′     ′
The noise of life begins again
)*   *)   *   *)   * *)   * *)           0
     *        *        *     *            1
```
```
     ′         ′          ′
And ghastly through the drizzling rain
)*       *) *    *)     * *) *    *)      0
         *        *        *       *      1
```
```
      ′     ′    ′         ′    ′
On the bald street, breaks the blank day.
)*    *) *     *)     *    *) *     *)     0
      *        *           *       *       1
```

Alfred, Lord Tennyson, *In Memoriam* VII

In Chapter 1, we have distinguished the meter of a line from its rhythm. The meter is defined by the metrical grid assigned to the line, and it is completely regular as shown in (5). The rhythm of the line, by contrast, which is the pattern produced by the different stresses of the syllables in the line (shown here by accent marks), is not regular, as can also be seen in (5).   Given the definition in (3), all maxima project to Gridline 1. Note that the last line, which is rhythmically the least regular, also has no maxima; in this line the distribution of stressed syllables is entirely free. In general, in English metrical verse (particularly iambic) monosyllables are not controlled by the metrical rules and this permits a great degree of rhythmic freedom.[1]

The fact that the stresses of polysyllabic words are treated differently in English verse from the stresses of monosyllables has been known at least since Steele (1775); for a more recent discussion see Kiparsky (1977). However, there is reason to think that even some of the syllables carrying main stress in a polysyllablic word are not maxima. This is illustrated by the two lines from *In Memoriam* in (6). In the first line the stressed syllable of polysyllabic *Christmas* is promoted to Gridline 1 (as are all other word stresses), but in the second line the stressed syllable of polysyllabic *Answer* is not promoted to Gridline 1.

(6)   The Christmas bells from hill to hill
)*   *)   *   *)   *   *) * *)   0
               *   *   *   *   1

      Answer each other in the mist.
)*   *) *   *) * *)   *   *)   0
            *   *   *   *   1

In traditional analyses lines such as (6) are said to exhibit 'trochaic inversion' or 'trochaic substitution' implying that the first 'iamb' in the line is replaced by a 'trochee'. (These suggestions depend on the notion

---

[1] Attridge (1982: 42) discusses an earlier formulation of this same idea by Halle and Keyser (1971). He invents a line of ten monosyllables 'John is dead drunk and weeps tears from red eyes', and remarks that Halle and Keyser permit this line to be metrical in iambic pentameter. He asserts that the invented line can only be metrical in anapaestic or dactylic tetrameter, and concludes that the theory is wrong to permit the line to be iambic pentameter. In light of the distribution of word stresses in (5) and in many examples below we do not think that Attridge is correct in excluding an iambic analysis of his invented line. The meter of a line cannot be determined by taking it in isolation from the rest of the poem; hence a ten-syllable line composed only of monosyllables could be in iambic pentameter or some other meter. Attridge's invented line will be judged in light of the other lines in the poem and in light of the plausibility of the further assumption that the poem is composed of lines in a single meter.

of 'foot' as a building block, a notion we reject.) We take it as evidence requiring a redefinition of maximum as in (7).

(7) The syllable bearing the word stress in a polysyllabic word is a maximum, if it is preceded and followed in the same line by a syllable with less stress.

This definition means that a syllable cannot be a maximum if it is the first syllable in a line (or the last syllable), and as a result the first position in the line can be filled by the syllable carrying stress in a polysyllabic word, as in (6).[2]

The redefinition of maximum in (7) also explains why the stressed syllable in a polysyllabic word can fail to project to Gridline 1 if it is adjacent to a strongly stressed syllable inside the line. Examples of this are shown in (8) and (9).

(8) Of the wide world dreaming on things to come

```
)*    *)*    *)   *  *)*   *)   * *)      0
      *      *       *      *     *        1
```

And peace proclaims olives of endless age.

```
)*    *)   * *)  **)  * *)  *  *)         0
      *        *    *     *     *          1
```

William Shakespeare, Sonnet 107

(9) Her audit, though delayed, answered must be,

```
)* *)*    *)   **)   *   *)   *   *)      0
   *      *     *        *         *       1
```

William Shakespeare, Sonnet 126

We next turn to variations in length. Peripheral length variations in iambic lines have traditionally been referred to as extrametrical when there is an additional syllable at the right edge, and as catalectic when there is a missing syllable at the left edge. Both are illustrated in (10).

(10) I left his arm that night myself
      For what's-his-name's, the new prose-poet
      Who wrote the book there, on the shelf –
      How, forsooth, was I to know it   4
      If Waring meant to glide away
      Like a ghost at break of day?

Robert Browning, from 'Waring'

---

[2] This reanalysis of 'trochaic inversion' and related issues are discussed also in Fabb (2001, 2002b, 2003) and Attridge (2003).

Browning's poem is in iambic tetrameter, just like Tennyson's poem in
(5). While Tennyson's poem has eight syllables in each line, Browning's
varies between nine, eight and seven syllables. This involves two distinct
kinds of variation, which must be written into the rule as (11).

(11) Gridline 0: starting ⟨ just / one asterisk in ⟩ at the R edge insert
      a R parenthesis, form binary groups, heads R.

      i. The last (leftmost) group may be incomplete.

The first variation permits parenthesis insertion to start just at the
(right) edge, as in (12), or one asterisk in, as in (13).

(12) I left his arm that night myself
)* *) * *)   *   *)   * *)   0 ⇐
          *   *   *   *   1

(13) For what's-his-name's, the new prose-poet
) *   *)   *   *)   * *)   *   *)*   0 ⇐
          *   *   *   *   1

Parentheses are inserted by rule (11) from right to left, and in (13)
the insertion of the first parenthesis one asterisk in (rather than just
at the right edge) has the crucial consequence that the first syllable of
poet – which is a maximum – projects, as it should, to Gridline 1. In
iambic lines which end on an unstressed syllable (as in so-called 'feminine
rhyme'), there will generally be an initial skip of the rightmost syllable.

The other variation, also an option, is illustrated in the last line.
Because the parentheses are inserted and so groups are formed from
right to left, the last-generated group will be the leftmost, and in the
last line of (10) (as well as in the fourth line) this group is incomplete.

(14) Like a ghost at break of day?
      *) *   *) *   *) *   *)   0 ⇐
        *   *   *   *   1

This line has an incomplete leftmost group, and in isolation this line
would be better scanned as a trochaic tetrameter. However, since the
other lines in Browning's poem are iambic, we assume that this is also
true of (14). Implicit in this scansion is a general assumption which we
call the 'principle of isometricality', stated in (15).

(15) Unless there is specific evidence to the contrary, the lines in a
      poem are composed in the same meter, and the syllables are
      grouped by variants of the same Gridline 0 rule.

2.3 Trochaic meters

The most famous trochaic poem in Engish is probably *Hiawatha*. Lewis Carroll's parody of Longfellow's poem in (16) is in the same meter.

(16)   From his shoulder Hiawatha
Took the camera of rosewood,
Made of sliding, folding rosewood;
Neatly put it all together.

Lewis Carroll, from 'Hiawatha's Photographing'

The simplest formulation in (17) of the trochaic rule will scan these lines, as shown in (18).

(17)   Gridline 0: starting just at the L edge insert a L parenthesis, form binary groups, heads L.

(18)   Made of sliding, folding rosewood;

```
( *    *  ( * *   ( * *   ( *    * (        0 ⇒
  *       *       *       *                 1
```

We know that this is the correct scansion because it is only in this grid that the three maxima (the first syllables in *sliding*, *folding* and *rosewood*) all project to Gridline 1.

We note that in trochaic poetry, there is a much stronger tendency for all stressed syllables to project to Gridline 1 (though not vice versa: Gridline 1 asterisks need not project from a stresed syllable). This suggests that one of the ways in which English meters might show typical rhythmic differences is by varying the definition of maximum, while always requiring maxima to project to Gridline 1.

The most common variation in trochaic meters is for the rightmost group to be incomplete, often in even-numbered lines. This is illustrated in the stanza quoted in (19), which is in the same trochaic tetrameter as (16) but whose odd-numbered lines have eight syllables and whose even-numbered lines have seven.

(19)   See! the smoking bowl before us,
Mark our jovial ragged ring!
Round and round take up the chorus,
And in raptures let us sing.

Robert Burns, 'Love and Liberty. A cantata' stanza 1

For lines where it occurs, we write the variation into the rule by adding a special proviso, as in (20i). We scan two lines in (21).

(20) Gridline 0: starting just at the L edge insert a L parenthesis, form binary groups, heads L.

  i. In even-numbered lines the last (rightmost) group must be incomplete.

(21) See! the smoking bowl before us,

```
( *    *  ( *  *    ( *    * ( *   * (        0 ⇒
  *         *         *       *              1
```

Mark our jovial ragged ring!

```
( *    *  ( *  *  ( *  *  ( *               0 ⇒
  *         *       *       *               1
```

Trochaic meter is relatively rare in English poetry, and it is worth considering the possibility that all 'trochaic' texts are in fact scanned by variants on the iambic rules. This is technically possible; the lines above would then be scanned by rule (22) with results in (23).

(22) Gridline 0: starting ⟨ just / one asterisk in ⟩ at the R edge insert a L parenthesis, form binary groups, heads L.

  i. In odd-numbered lines the 'one asterisk in' option is chosen, and in even-numbered lines the 'just' option is chosen.

  ii. In all lines the last (leftmost) group must be incomplete.

(23) See! the smoking bowl before us,

```
 * )   *    * ) *    * )   * * )   *        0 ⇒
 *          *        *       *              1
```

Mark our jovial ragged ring!

```
 * )   *    * ) *   * )  *   * )             0 ⇒
 *          *       *        *               1
```

We do not adopt this option, of scanning all binary meters as iambic, because the rule (22) is more complex than (20), while producing the same results.

In some poems whose meter groups syllables into pairs, every line has an odd number of syllables, and in this type of poetry both an iambic and a trochaic analysis is possible, with no rule more complex than the other. An example of such poetry is shown in (24); we scan the third line as iambic in (25) and as trochaic in (26).[3] This poem is indeed metrically ambiguous, and there is no reason to prefer one scansion over the other.

---

[3] Schipper (1910: 246) analyzes seven-syllable lines like this as trochaic, though without argument and evidence. See Fabb (2002a: 108–122) for more discussion of metrically ambiguous lines, including seven-syllable lines like these; also Fabb and Halle (2006a).

(24)   Julia, if I chance to die
         Ere I print my poetry,
         I most humbly thee desire
         To commit it to the fire:
         Better 'twere my book were dead,
         Than to live not perfected.

Robert Herrick, 'His request to Julia' complete

(25) I most humbly thee desire
      *) *   *) *   *) **)   0 ⇐
      *   *   *   *   1

(26) I most humbly thee desire
      (* * (* * (* *(*   0 ⇒
      *   *   *   *   1

2.4 Anapaestic meters

An anapaestic meter is a ternary meter, in which the syllables are
grouped into triplets, and the rightmost member of each triplet is the
marked syllable; any maxima must be in this position. Four lines of
anapaestic verse are shown in (27).

(27)   The Assyrian came down like the wolf on the fold,
         And his cohorts were gleaming in purple and gold;
         And the sheen of their spears was like stars on the sea,
         When the blue wave rolls nightly on deep Galilee.

George Gordon, Lord Byron, 'The Destruction of Sennacherib' stanza 1

The lines can be scanned by the basic rule of the anapaestic meter,
stated in (28), as shown in (29).

(28)   Gridline 0: starting just at the R edge insert a R parenthesis,
         form ternary groups, heads R.

(29)   The Assyrian came down like the wolf on the fold,
)* * *)*   *   *)   *   * *) *   * *)   0 ⇐
         *   *   *   *   1

The line has just one maximum (the second syllable in *Assyrian*), which
is projected to Gridline 1 as required.

In a ternary meter, an incomplete group can in principle contain either
one or two asterisks, as illustrated by the anapaestic poem by Charlotte
Brontë in (30).

(30)   Look into thought and say what dost thou see;
Dive, be not fearful how dark the waves flow;
Sink through the surge, and bring pearls up to me;
Deeper, ay, deeper; the fairest lie low.   4

'I have dived, I have sought them, but none have I found;
In the gloom that closed o'er me no form floated by;
As I sunk through the void depths, so black and profound,
How dim died the sun and how far hung the sky!   8

'What had I given to hear the soft sweep
Of a breeze bearing life through that vast realm of death!
Thoughts were untroubled and dreams were asleep:
The spirit lay dreadless and hopeless beneath.'   12

Charlotte Brontë, 'Diving' complete

The Gridline 0 rule must be modified as in (31) for this poem by building in this variation as option (i).

(31)   Gridline 0: starting just at the R edge insert a R parenthesis, form ternary groups, heads R.

        i. The last (leftmost) group may be incomplete – binary or unary.

Lines 5, 6, 7, and 10 have a complete leftmost group, as scanned in (32); lines 8 and 12 have an incomplete leftmost group of two asterisks, as scanned in (33); lines 1, 2, 3, 4, 9, and 11 have an incomplete leftmost group of one asterisk, as scanned in (34). All lines have four Gridline 0 groups, and so all lines are tetrameter.

(32)   'I have dived, I have sought them, but none have I found;

```
)*  *    *)   *  *    *)     *    *   *)   *  *  *)    0 ⇐
     *           *             *            *     1
```

(33)   How dim died the sun and how far hung the sky!

```
 *    *)   *    *  *) *    *   *)  *     *   *)      0 ⇐
      *          *          *            *     1
```

(34)   Look into thought and say what dost thou see;

```
 *)  *   *    *)    *    *     *)  *     *   *)     0 ⇐
 *            *                *          *     1
```

In an anapaestic meter, the first parenthesis can be inserted just at the right edge of Gridline 0 (as in the poems above), or it can be inserted one asterisk in, or two asterisks in, as illustrated by lines in the limericks cited in (35).

(35)　　There was a Young Lady of Parma,
　　　　　Whose conduct grew calmer and calmer;
　　　　　　　When they said, 'Are you dumb?'
　　　　　　　She merely said, 'Hum!'
　　　　　That provoking Young Lady of Parma.

　　　　　There was a Young Lady of Portugal,
　　　　　Whose ideas were excessively nautical:
　　　　　　　She climbed up a tree,
　　　　　　　To examine the sea,
　　　　　But declared she would never leave Portugal.

Edward Lear, two complete limericks

These limericks are scanned by a version of the anapaestic rule which states all the possible variations as options, (36). Note that the limericks have complete leftmost groups in addition to having incomplete (binary) leftmost groups. [4]

(36)　　Gridline 0: starting ⟨ just / one asterisk in / two asterisks in ⟩ at the R edge insert a R parenthesis, form binary groups, heads R.

　　　i. The last (leftmost) group may be incomplete – binary or unary.

Two lines are scanned below, illustrating insertion one asterisk in, and two asterisks in. The fact that maxima are placed correctly in both lines (and particularly that the rightmost maxima are placed correctly) tells us that the rightmost one (or two) asterisks must be skipped in order to scan these lines correctly.

(37)　　That provoking Young Lady of Parma.
　　　　) *　　* *) *　　　*　　　*) * *　　*) *　　*　　　　0 ⇐
　　　　　　　*　　　　　　　　　　*　　　　*　　　　　　　　1

(38)　　But declared she would never leave Portugal.
　　　　) *　　* *)　　　*　　*　　*) *　　*　　　*) * *　　　0 ⇐
　　　　　　　*　　　　　　　　　　*　　　　　*　　　　　　　1

───────────

[4] An example of a line beginning with a unary group is the fourth line of this limerick (from Legman 1969). 'A complacent old don of Divinity / Made boast of his daughter's virginity. / They must have been dawdlin' / Down at old Magdalen – / It could not have happened at Trinity.'

Limericks have a characteristic rhythm in performance, with pauses at
the end of each line. This suggests that there may be a performance
grid, analogous to the musical grids discussed in Chapter 1, in which
time intervals project to Gridline 0, allowing 'rests' at various points
in the line. The performance (declamation) of the lines is not totally
determined by the metrical form of the poem, but may deviate from it
in various ways. (See also remarks in section 1.10 above.)

2.5 Dactylic meters

Dactylic meters are organized on Gridline 0 as left-headed triplets. This
type of meter is rare in English and the best known example is probably
Tennyson's 'Charge of the Light Brigade'. We quote the first two stanzas
in (39), where we have included an indication of how it was performed
by Tennyson himself (as recorded on wax cylinder by Thomas Edison in
1888). Strongly stressed syllables are marked with accents, and pauses
are marked with ‖; Tennyson also pronounces *rode* by extending the
length of the vowel and giving it a falling tone (the remainder of this
line has hardly any stresses at all).

(39)   Hálf a léague hálf a léague,
         Hálf a léague ónwárd, ‖
         Áll in the válley of Déath
         Róde the six hundred: ‖   4

         'Fórward, the Líght Brigáde! ‖
         Chárge for the gúns' he sáid: ‖
         Into the válley of Déath ‖
         Róde the six hundred.

         Alfred, Lord Tennyson, 'Charge of the Light Brigade' stanza 1

In Tennyson's performance the rhythm of the lines is not regular, and
his rhythm cannot be predicted from the text of the poem. Unpredictable aspects of rhythm include: stress on *all* in line 3 but not on the
equivalently-placed first syllable in *into* in line 7; stress on both syllables in *onward* in line 3 and on *said* in line 6; emphasis on *Rode* more
than any other word, and no stress on *six hundred* at all. Pauses are
also unpredictable. It is not at all clear that there are generalizations
about the performed rhythm. The regularity resides not in the rhythm
of Tennyson's performance of the poem, but in the meter of the lines,
which are scanned as dactylic dimeter by the rules in (40).

(40) a. Gridline 0: starting just at the L edge, insert a L parenthesis, form ternary groups, heads L.

  i. The last (rightmost) group may be incomplete – binary.

  b. Gridline 1: starting just at the L edge, insert a L parenthesis, form binary groups, heads L.

There is also no relation between Tennyson's performed rhythm and the metrical grid structure. The metrical rules correctly control the number of syllables in the line (five or six), and the placement of stressed syllables in polysyllabic words (always projecting to Gridline 1). Note in particular that *hundred* is required by the metrical condition (4) to have its first syllable in head position because this is a polysyllable whose first syllable carries greatest stress (even though in performing the line Tennyson does not stress this syllable). The condition requiring certain syllables to project to Gridline 1 is thus based on the inherent stress of words, not on how the words are stressed in performance.

(41) Hálf a léague hálf a léague,

```
( *    *   *     ( *   *   * (          0 ⇒
( *               * (                   1 ⇒
  *                                     2
```

Hálf a léague ónwárd,

```
( *    *   *     ( *    *                0 ⇒
( *             * (                      1 ⇒
  *                                      2
```

Áll in the válley of Déath

```
(*    *    * ( *  Δ   *    * (           0 ⇒
(*             * (                       1 ⇒
  *                                      2
```

Róde the six hundred.

```
( *     * *   ( *    *                   0 ⇒
( *            * (                       1 ⇒
  *                                      2
```

In the third line of (41) the word *valley* has two syllables, but projects just one asterisk on Gridline 0. It is not uncommon in English metrical poetry for syllables to be omitted from the count, especially for syllables whose nuclei are unstressed word-final vowels in hiatus (before word-initial vowels). If the syllable were counted, the line would have three Gridline 0 feet, the third of which would be unary; no other line in the poem has this structure. The possibility of non-projection is extensively used in most types of metrical poetry, including English, and we explore it further below. The fact that the syllable is not projected is indicated here by marking it with a delta, Δ.[5]

---

[5] See section 2.7 for additional examples and discussion.

We note that this poem could be analyzed as anapaestic, with the leftmost Gridline 0 group incomplete (containing one syllable), and beginning by skipping one or two asterisks at the right edge of the Gridline, as shown in (42).

(42)   Hálf a léague hálf a léague,

```
    * ) * *        * ) *  *                    0 ⇐
    ( *            * (                         1 ⇒
      *                                        2
```

Because it requires skipping and incomplete groups, this anapaestic grid is generated with a more complex rule than the dactylic (40a), and so we do not adopt an anapaestic analysis.

There are, however, some poems with lines in a ternary meter. Given that the goal is to minimize skipping and incomplete groups in deciding on a scansion, the consequence is that some lines are more simply analyzed as dactyls and others more simply analyzed as anapaests. The general principle of isometricality, (15), suggests that we should decide either to scan the whole poem as dactyls or the whole poem as anapaests. An example of such a poem is shown in (43).

(43)   The bleak wind of March
           Made her tremble and shiver
           But not the dark arch,
           Or the black flowing river: 4
           Mad from life's history,
           Glad to death's mystery
           Swift to be hurl'd —
           Any where, any where   8
           Out of the world!

                              Thomas Hood, 'The Bridge of Sighs' stanza 12

The fifth line is simpler scanned as dactyls, (44), than as anapaests, (45).

(44)   Mad from life's history,
```
    ( *    *    *    ( * * * (                  0 ⇒
      *              *                          1
```
(45)   Mad from life's history,
```
    * )    *    *    * ) * *                    0 ⇐
      *              *                          1
```

The second is simpler scanned as anapaests, (47), than as dactyls, (46).

(46)   Made her tremble and shiver
```
    *    * ( *    * *    ( * *                  0 ⇒
           *           *                        1
```

(47)   Made her tremble and shiver
```
       ) *     *    * )   * *     * ) *              0 ⇐
                *             *                      1
```

These facts suggest either that the poem can be analyzed as freely in one or the other meter, or that we make a decision as to meter based on the preponderance of one or the other meters in the poem (possibly a shifting decision, as the poem proceeds through primarily anapaestic or primarily dactylic lines).

2.6 Above Gridline 0

The four basic types of English meter are differentiated by the Gridline 0 rules, for which the evidence has been reviewed above. In this section we examine the rules which insert parentheses at Gridlines 1 and 2 in English meters. The best evidence for the groupings on these higher Gridlines comes by looking for meters which can be combined in the same poem; the principle of isometricality (15) suggests that the rule sets for the two lines should be as similar as possible.

Consider, for example, iambic pentameter, which tends to be found in combination with iambic hexameter, as in the 'Spenserian stanza' that is mostly in iambic pentameter, but where the final line is (always) a hexameter, illustrated in (48).

(48)   Then gin I thinke on that which Nature sayd,
           Of that same time when no more *Change* shall be,
           But stedfast rest of all things firmely stayd
           Upon the pillours of Eternity,   4
           That is contrayr to *Mutabilitie*:
           For, all that moueth, doth in *Change* delight:
           But thence-forth all shall rest eternally
           With Him that is the God of Sabbaoth hight: 8
   O thou great Sabbaoth God, graunt me that Sabaoths sight.

Edmund Spenser, Faerie Queene final canto

There is good reason to think that the final iambic hexameter line is scanned by the rules in (49), giving the scansion in (50).

(49)   English iambic hexameter

     a   Gridline 0: starting just at the R edge, insert a R parenthesis, form binary groups, heads R.

     b. Gridline 1: starting just at the R edge, insert a R parenthesis, form ternary groups, heads R.

    c. Gridline 2: starting just at the L edge, insert a L parenthesis, form binary groups, heads L.

(50)   O thou great Sabbaoth God, graunt me that Sabaoths sight.

```
)*      *)    *    *) *        *)      *      *) *   *) *     *)  0 ⇐
        ) *        *        *)              *       *     *)  1 ⇐
                           ( *                             *(  2 ⇒
                            *                                  3
```

Spenser adapted his hexameter from the French hexameter (*alexandrin*, see Chapter 5), where the sixth of the twelve syllables is the head of the verse, and must be word-final. We suggest that a similar condition holds (not altogether consistently) for Spenser's meter, stated in (51). The fact that the sixth syllable must be uniquely identified is evidence for the rules and grid structure proposed here.

(51)   The syllable projecting to the head of the verse must be followed directly by a word boundary (caesura).

Given that iambic hexameter has two ternary groups at Gridline 1, and given its characteristic partnership with iambic pentameter (as opposed to some other length of line), this strongly supports a scansion of the related iambic pentameter lines as having ternary groups at Gridline 1, one of which falls short. This is expressed in (52), and shown in the grid (53).

(52)   English iambic pentameter. Same rules as in (49), but with the rider that on Gridline 1 the leftmost group must be incomplete.

(53)   With Him that is the God of Sabbaoth hight:

```
)*      *)    *  *)   *  *) *  *) *   *)        0 ⇐
        *          *)      *      *      *)      1 ⇐
                  ( *                    * (     2 ⇒
                   *                             3
```

Further support for this grid, and for the left-headed Gridline 2 group, comes from Campion, who says that in the iambic pentameter 'the naturall breathing place of our English Iambick verse is in the last sillable of the second foote' (Campion 1602: 11). Campion's remark attributes special status to the fourth syllable, which we have identified as the head of the verse, suggesting that the performance of the line is sensitive to the metrical form.[6] In both the pentameter (53) and the hexameter (50)

---

[6] As we have noted elsewhere, performance – that is the way a line is recited or read – is often quite unrelated to its meter. In the present instance, however, the meter of the line and its performance proceed hand in hand.

the head of the verse is in the same place: it directly precedes the third binary group counted from the right edge of the line.

We also note that the structural similarity between iambic hexameter and pentameter in English is mirrored (and perhaps influenced) by a similar relation in French meters between 12-syllable *alexandrin*, which we analyze as iambic hexameter, and 10-syllable *décasyllabe*, which we analyze as iambic pentameter (see Chapter 5). The structure assigned to the iambic pentameter here is the same as that assigned to the iambic pentameter in Tennyson's 'Hendecasyllabics' (see section 1.8), where the head of the verse (in fourth position) is deleted.

Another pair of meters which tend to be combined are 8-syllable iambic tetrameter and 6-syllable iambic trimeter, with the longer preceding the shorter line in a couplet, as in (54).

(54)   Sir Drake, whom well the world's end knew,
        Which thou didst compass round,
     And whom both poles of heaven once saw,
        Which north and south do bound,
     The stars above would make thee known,
        If men here silent were;
     The sun himself cannot forget
        His fellow traveller.

Anonymous, from the collection *Wits' Recreations* (1640) complete

We suggest that iambic tetrameter lines are scanned by the rules in (55) and iambic trimeter by the rules in (56). The near-identity of the rule sets explains why the two meters can easily combine in the same poem while still conforming to the principle of isometricality (15).

(55)   English iambic tetrameter

    a. Gridline 0: starting just at the R edge, insert a R parenthesis, form binary groups, heads R.

    b. Gridline 1: starting just at the R edge, insert a R parenthesis, form binary groups, heads R.

    c. Gridline 2: starting just at the R edge, insert a R parenthesis, form binary groups, heads R.

(56)   English iambic trimeter. Same rules as in (55), but with the rider that on Gridline 1 the leftmost group must be incomplete.

In (57) we show a full grid for an iambic tetrameter line followed by a full grid for an iambic trimeter line.

(57)   And whom both poles of heaven once saw,

```
)*        *)    *    *)    *    *)    *      *)      0 ⇐
          ) *          *)         *           *)      1 ⇐
               ) *                             *)      2 ⇐
                                               *       3
```

Which north and south do bound,

```
   )*      *)    *    *)       *    *)      0 ⇐
           *)          *            *)      1 ⇐
           ) *                      *)      2 ⇐
                                    *       3
```

2.7 Non-projection: some syllables are not counted

The iterative rules build a grid from the syllables making up that line.
But syllables are not directly grouped; before they are put into groups,
the syllables must first project asterisks on Gridline 0, thus forming the
initial part of the metrical representation of the line. It is the Gridline 0
asterisks which are grouped, and hence counted. This distancing of the
grouping mechanism from the actual syllables means that syllables can
be present in the line without projecting as asterisks, and because these
syllables are not projected they are not counted for grouping.[7]

This non-projection of specific syllables is always an option in English
verse, particularly in iambic pentameter. Non-projection is generally
applied intermittently; it is used by some poets more than others. John
Donne uses non-projection very extensively, and this is undoubtedly one
reason for the difficulty he presents to readers trying to scan his lines.[8]

(58)   Batter my heart, three-person'd God; for, you
          As yet but knock, breathe, shine, and seek to mend;
          That I may rise, and stand, o'erthrow me, and bend
          Your force, to break, blow, burn, and make me new.
          I, like an usurped town, to another due,
          Labour to admit you, but O, to no end.
          Reason, your viceroy in me, me should defend,
          But is captived, and proves weak or untrue.
          Yet dearly I love you, and would be loved fain,
          But am betrothed unto your enemy,

---

[7] Hanson (1992), and Hanson and Kiparsky (1996) offer a fundamentally different
    approach to theses problems, based on the notion of resolution. Fabb (2002a: 41–
    47) reviews some of the history of ideas about (what we are calling) non-projection.

[8] This difficulty is reflected in Ben Jonson's comment 'that Donne, for not keeping of
    accent, deserved hanging' ('Conversations with William Drummond', Parfitt 1975:
    462), and Coleridge's description of 'Donne, whose muse on dromedary trots' ('On
    Donne's poetry', Keach 1997: 94).

Divorce me, untie, or break that knot again,
Take me to you, imprison me, for I
Except you enthrall me, never shall be free,
Nor ever chaste, except you ravish me.

John Donne, 'Divine Meditations 14' complete

This poem is regular iambic pentameter, but because of its rhythmic irregularity it is not at first easy to see that it is metrically regular. Consider line 13. This line has eleven syllables, and in (59) we attempt to scan it as an eleven-syllable iambic pentameter with a feminine rhyme.

(59) Except you enthrall me, never shall be free,
```
)*   * )   *   * )   *    * ) * * )   *    * )  *        0 ⇐
     *         *           *    *           *            1
```

When we examine the scansion of this line, we find that it violates the condition (4), which requires maxima to project to Gridline 1: the second syllable in *enthrall* and the first syllable in *never* are maxima but do not project to Gridline 1. So this scansion is incorrect. The correct scansion for this line is shown in (60). The third syllable, *you*, does not project as an asterisk. Once scanned in this way, both maxima correctly project to Gridline 1.[9]

(60) Except you enthrall me, never shall be free,
```
)*   * )   Δ   *    * )   *   * )*    * )   *   * )        0 ⇐
     *              *          *     *         *          1
```

We indicate that a syllable does not project by writing a Δ underneath it – a symbol which we have used before to show that a syllable does not have a representative on Gridline 0. A syllable that does not project to Gridline 0 is still pronounced when the line is recited. (This is especially clear in the poetry of the Southern Romance languages discussed in Chapter 4.) And it is this fact which makes Donne's poem difficult to scan. For example, in (61) the non-projected syllable *me* precedes a pause and it would be difficult not to pronounce it in performing the line, even though this disrupts the regular rhythm. In (62) there are two syllables which are not projected, and furthermore the word *loved* must project two asterisks, even though it is normally a monosyllable. (Nor is it necessarily pronounced as two syllables, in spite of the fact that it projects two asterisks.)

---

[9] A similar omission in hiatus has been noted above in the discussion of Tennyson's 'Charge of the Light Brigade'.

(61)   That I may rise, and stand, overthrow me, and bend
) *   *) *   *) *   *)   *   *)   Δ *   *)   0 ⇐
         *   *   *   *   *   1

(62)   Yet dearly I love you, and would be lovèd fain,
) *   *) Δ * *)   Δ   *   *)   * *) *   *)   0 ⇐
           *   *   *   *   *   1

Non-projection of a syllable is a metrical fact, not a phonetic one.
Nevertheless, non-projected syllables tend to be relatively unprominent
and often can be regarded as instances of slurred pronunciation. The
most common type of non-projecting syllable is unstressed, ends on a
vowel, and is followed immediately by another vowel (or is separated
from it by a glide such as [y] or [w]). This is the type of non-projection
which we see in Donne's poem (lines 3, 5, 6, 7, 9, 11, 13): all the
non-projected syllables are vowels (or vowel–glide sequences, as in (61))
preceding vowels. Non-projection of vowels in prevocalic position is central to the meters of the Romance languages, including classical Latin
(see Chapters 4 and 5 for examples). It is likely that at least some of
the English poets who use non-projection may be imitating Romance
models (Dante and Petrarch, as well as Latin poets), though in fact
most metrical traditions permit non-projection, irrespective of whether
the poets were influenced by Romance models.

Another class of syllables which may not project in English is syllables
with consonantal nuclei (i.e., syllables whose nuclei are [l], [r], or a nasal):
this can be seen in the second syllable of *heaven*, which is a word often
treated as a monosyllable for metrical purposes.

Though syllables which are not projected often fall into phonetic
classes of this kind, any syllable can fail to be projected. In (63) (from
Mayor 1901) we illustrate the possibility of targeting a syllable for non-
projection which does not fall into the usual classes.

(63)   Or like stout Cortez when with eagle eyes
       He stared at the Pacific – and all his men
) *   *)   *   *) * *) Δ   *   *)   *   *)   0 ⇐
           *   *   *   *   *   1

       Looked at each other with a wild surmise –
       Silent, upon a peak in Darien.
                         John Keats, 'On first looking into Chapman's Homer' lines 11–14

(64)   Of treasonous malice. And so do I. So all.
) *   *) Δ *   *) Δ   *   *) * *) * *)   0 ⇐
           *   *   *   *   *   1
                         William Shakespeare, *Macbeth* 2.3.138

(65)   In restless ecstasy. Duncan is in his grave

```
)*   *)  *   *)  *  Δ   *)  *  Δ  *)  *    *)        0 ⇐
     *       *           *       *          *          1
```

William Shakespeare, Macbeth 3.2.22

(66)   Was he not born of woman? The sprites that knew

```
)*    *)  *   *)  *   *  Δ)      *      *)     *     *)        0 ⇐
      *       *       *                 *            *          1
```

William Shakespeare, Macbeth 5.3.4

(67)   For in those days might only shall be admired

```
)*  *)   *    *)    *    *  Δ)  *   *)*   *)          0 ⇐
    *         *          *           *    *            1
```

John Milton, Paradise Lost, XI.689

(68)   O tell me, Angela, by the holy loom

```
)*  *)   *   *)  *Δ   *)   *   *)*  *)        0 ⇐
    *        *        *        *    *          1
```

John Keats, 'Eve of St. Agnes' line 115

2.8 On the operation of the iterative rules

In this section we provide a somewhat more formal account of how parentheses are inserted into asterisk sequences. Readers with little interest in these formal niceties may wish to skip this section.

A Gridline is a sequence of entities of several kinds: asterisks, parentheses of two kinds (left or right parentheses), and spaces. It was explained in the preceding chapter (see section 1.4) that each iterative rule inserting parentheses into an asterisk sequence is defined by setting the five parameters in (1) above, repeated here:

(1)   i.   Insertion starts just at the edge of the Gridline, one asterisk in, or two asterisks in.

   ii.   Edge of the sequence (L/R) at which insertion begins.

   iii.   Nature of parenthesis inserted (L/R).

   iv.   Interval between consecutive insertions (2/3).

   v.   Head location in group (L/R).

A good way of visualizing the operation of parenthesis insertion is by thinking of the asterisk sequence as including spaces on both sides of each asterisk, and as being scanned by moving a cursor from one space to the next. The cursor movement is controlled by the operation

SKIP, which, as its name implies, moves the cursor from one space to the next, skipping over an intervening asterisk (or pre-existing parenthesis). We assume that SKIP requires the setting of a binary parameter (1ii), which determines the (L/R) edge at which SKIP begins, and hence the direction in which the cursor moves. If the insertion begins at the L edge, the cursor moves to the right, and vice versa.

The SKIP operation is linked to a second operation, which we call MARK. MARK inserts a space on the left or on the right of the current position of the cursor, inserts either a left or a right parenthesis, and then executes the SKIP operation. The choice of inserted parenthesis is determined by the setting of a separate parameter (1iii). In addition, each MARK operation is subject to contextual conditions. Two separate conditions are involved, depending on whether the cursor is in the middle of an asterisk sequence or whether it is at one of the edges (specifically, at the left edge where SKIP proceeds from left to right, but at the right edge, where SKIP proceeds from right to left).

When the cursor is in the middle of the sequence and SKIP is set to proceed from left to right, MARK applies and inserts its parenthesis only if on the cursor's left there are two (or three) consecutive asterisks; in the absence of such a sub-sequence SKIP applies. The symmetrical procedure applies if parameter (1ii) is set to right and SKIP proceeds from right to left. In either case, the choice between the two lengths of sub-sequence is determined by the setting of parameter (1iv), generating either binary or ternary groups.

When the cursor is at the edge of the asterisk sequence, yet a different decision must be made. Does the MARK operation apply at the edge or is an asterisk sub-sequence skipped before MARK can apply (parameter (1i)). As shown in (69), the setting of this parameter provides three alternatives at each of the two edges of the sequence.[10]

(69)   i.   Insert a parenthesis in the environment: __ #

       ii.   Insert a parenthesis in the environment: __ * #

       iii.   Insert a parenthesis in the environment: __ * * #

       iv.   Insert a parenthesis in the environment: # __

       v.   Insert a parenthesis in the environment: # * __

       vi.   Insert a parenthesis in the environment: # * * __

---

[10] In these rules, # indicates the end of the sequence and __ the location in which the parenthesis is inserted. Thus, if a parenthesis is inserted in the environment __ * #, it is inserted to the left of the rightmost asterisk.

Finally, the setting of parameter (1v) determines whether the leftmost or the rightmost asterisk in each group is promoted to the next Gridline.

We illustrate the preceding by applying the standard iambic rule (2a) to the second line of Tennyson's stanza which was quoted in (5).

(2)   a.   Gridline 0: starting just at the R edge insert a R parenthesis, form binary groups, heads R.

(70)   The noise of life begins again
         *   *   *   *   * *   * *

The first step is determined by (1i, ii, iii). In our example, the three parameters direct us to begin insertion just at (1i) the Right edge (1ii) and to insert a Right parenthesis (1iii). The result of the choices in the case at hand are shown in (71), which shows the position of the cursor after the first insertion.

(71)   The noise of life begins again
         *   *   *   *   * *   * *)   ⇐
                                ↑

The next part of the rule (parameter (1iv)) requires a choice of interval (2 or 3 asterisks) between consecutive insertions, and here a binary interval is chosen. The SKIP rule moves the cursor from right to left, in two skips, until the cursor has two asterisks on its right.

(72)   The noise of life begins again
         *   *   *   *   * *   * *)   ⇐
                         ↑

(73)   The noise of life begins again
         *   *   *   *   * *   * *)   ⇐
                    ↑

Now the MARK rule applies, inserting a R parenthesis to the right of the cursor.

(74)   The noise of life begins again
         *   *   *   *   * *) * *)   ⇐
                    ↑

The SKIP rule now moves the cursor leftwards in two skips, as shown in (75) and (76).

(75)   The noise of life begins again
         *   *   *   *   * *) * *)   ⇐
                  ↑

(76) The noise of life begins again
       *   *   *   *   * *) * *)   ⇐
              ↑

Now the MARK rule applies, inserting a R parenthesis to the right of the cursor:

(77) The noise of life begins again
       *   *   *   *   ) * *) * *)   ⇐
              ↑

In this manner, the SKIP and MARK rules apply repeatedly until the cursor reaches the other end of the line (i.e., the left end, in this case).

3

English loose meters

3.1 Loose iambic meter

Metrical English poetry comes in two varieties, as proposed by Robert Frost (Frost 1939).

All that can be done with words is soon told. So also with meters – particularly in our language where there are virtually but two, strict iambic and loose iambic.

One variety of meter, which following Frost we call 'strict', includes the iambic, trochaic, anapaestic and dactylic meters discussed in the previous chapter; in these meters, syllables are grouped into either ternary or binary groups but never with mixtures of binary and ternary. The other variety of meter is 'loose', and may at first appear to permit the grouping of syllables into mixtures of both binary and ternary groups within a single line (it is sometimes called 'iambic-anapaestic') and admits also one-syllable groups.[1] In this chapter we will show that in loose meters the syllables are grouped into pairs (iambs, trochees) or into triplets (anapaests, dactyls) by parentheses inserted by iterative rules, and that the interactions of this rule with a non-iterative rule of parenthesis insertion generates ungrouped asterisks as part of the sequence, which results in irregular intervals between heads of consecutive Gridline 0 groups.[2]

Loose meters are found in ballads, songs, nursery rhymes and other folk genres, and from Romanticism onwards in art poetry as well. Coleridge claimed to have first introduced loose meter into art poetry in his poem 'Christabel', whose beginning we quote in (1).

---

[1] In addition to Frost's loose iambic meter, we identify also a loose anapaestic meter in English, and discuss this in section 3.4.

[2] For an earlier discussion of the ideas in this chapter, see Halle and Keyser (1999).

(1)   'Tis the middle of night by the castle clock,
      And the owls have awakened the crowing cock;
      Tu – whit! – Tu – whoo!
      And hark, again! the crowing cock,   4
      How drowsily it crew.

      Sir Leoline, the Baron rich,
      Hath a toothless mastiff bitch;
      From her kennel beneath the rock   8
      She maketh answer to the clock,
      Four for the quarters, and twelve for the hour;
      Ever and aye, by shine and shower,
      Sixteen short howls, not over loud;   12
      Some say, she sees my lady's shroud.

Samuel Taylor Coleridge, from 'Christabel' (Keach 1997: 188)

We will show that (with a few exceptions) the lines of this poem are
iambic tetrameter, but that this is a *loose* iambic tetrameter. In strict
iambic tetrameter there are eight (plus or minus one) syllables, while
in this extract we find lines of between seven and eleven syllables. If
we make the usual assumption that maxima are in head positions, we
can also see that the heads are sometimes two and sometimes three
syllables apart: in line 7 the first syllables of *toothless* and *mastiff* are
both maxima and are two syllables apart, but in line 8 the maximum
(first syllable) in *kennel* is separated from the next maximum (second
syllable) in *beneath* by three syllables.

The rules for a strict meter cannot explain the greater variation in
length and the irregular spacing of maxima. To account for these properties we need for loose meters both a new definition of maximum and
a different procedure for grid construction than that in the preceding
chapter. We begin with a new definition of which syllables are maxima
in (2). (We call it 'Definition A' because we will see that some loose
poems operate with a different definition.)

(2)   Definition A of maximum in English loose meters
      The syllable bearing the word stress is a maximum, except when
      it is immediately preceded or followed in the same line by a
      syllable carrying greater stress.

Definition A should be compared with the definition of maximum in
English strict meters established in Chapter 2 and given in (3), where a
narrower range of syllables count as maxima.

(3)   Definition of maximum in English strict meters
      The syllable bearing the word stress in a polysyllabic word is a
      maximum, if it is preceded and followed in the same line by a
      syllable with less stress.

Maxima are thus differently defined in loose and strict English meters.
First, in a loose meter, there is no restriction of maxima to polysyllables:
a monosyllable can be a maximum in a loose meter, and an example is
the monosyllable *night*, which is a maximum in line 1 of the poem in
(1). Second, in a loose meter there is no requirement that a maximum
be preceded or followed by a syllable with lesser stress – only that if
there is a preceding or following syllable, it must not have greater stress.
This means that in a loose meter a maximum can be the first or the last
syllable in the line, and an example is the line-final word *clock*, which
is a maximum in line 1. Third, a pair of adjacent syllables which have
equal stress can both be maxima in a loose meter (but not in a strict
meter).

However, maxima in loose and strict meters share two characteristics.
First, the maximum must be a syllable bearing the word stress (the
syllable with greatest stress in the word). Second, the maximum cannot
be adjacent to a syllable of greater stress; thus *short* (line 12) is stressed
but it is not a maximum because the following syllable, *howls*, carries
greater stress.

Changing the definition of maximum will not by itself explain why
in loose iambic meters maxima are sometimes two and sometimes three
syllables apart and hence why the line can vary so much in length. The
iterative parenthesis insertion rules operate with strict regularity, but
this is disrupted by the previous application of a different rule, which is
found specifically in loose meters. For English loose iambic verse, the
rule is (4). This is a non-iterative rule, and it applies before the iterative
rules apply.

(4)   Insert a R parenthesis on Gridline 0 after an asterisk projecting
      from a maximum.

In strict meters, maxima are relevant only as part of a condition on the
relation between the grid and the line of verse. In loose meters, by virtue
of rule (4), maxima influence the structure of the grid because they force
the insertion of parentheses into the grid before the iterative rules apply,
and so have an effect on how the iterative rules apply. Rule (4) applies
to Gridline 0 and inserts parentheses after the asterisks which project
from maxima, as in (5).

(5)   'Tis the middle of night by the castle clock,
　　　*　　*　***)*　*　*)　　*　*　*)*　*)　　　　　0

Next we apply the iterative rule at Gridline 0 which for this meter is
(6a), inserting left parentheses from right to left (note that this combines
a 'left' decision for parenthesis orientation, and a 'right' decision for the
edge at which the rule begins), and permitting both ungrouped syllables
and incomplete groups within the Gridline.

(6)   Gridline 0: starting just at the R edge, insert a L parenthesis,
　　　form binary groups, heads R.

　　　a. Ungrouped syllables are permitted.

　　　b. Incomplete groups are permitted.

The effect of applying rule (6) to the sequence of asterisks and parentheses in (5) is shown in (7), where the left-pointing arrow indicates that
an iterative rule inserts the left parentheses from right to left.[3]

(7)   'Tis the middle of night by the castle clock,
　　　*　(*　*)*(*　*)　　*　(*　*)(*　*)　(　　　0 ⇐
　　　　*　　　　*　　　　　*　　　*　　　　　1

We now explain how the pre-existing right parentheses influence the
application of the iterative rule, so that some asterisks remain ungrouped
within the Gridline. Because there are two parentheses of different orien-
tations in this Gridline, it is possible to have an asterisk which is on 'the
wrong side' of two differently oriented parentheses, and such asterisks
are ungrouped, as required by convention (19) of Chapter 1 repeated
here as (8).

(8)   A left parenthesis groups the asterisks on its right; a right paren-
　　　thesis groups the asterisks on its left. Asterisks that are neither
　　　to the right of a left parenthesis, nor to the left of a right paren-
　　　thesis are ungrouped.

The iterative rule starts by inserting a left parenthesis at the right
edge of the line, as shown in (9), where an arrow shows the position of
the cursor which will be moving from right to left.

(9)   'Tis the middle of night by the castle clock,
　　　*　　*　*)*　*　*)　　*　*　*)　*　*)　(　　　0 ⇐
　　　　　　　　　　　　　　　　　　　　↑

---

[3] We employ the typographical convention that parentheses inserted non-iteratively
by rule (4) are printed in bold face, parentheses inserted by the iterative rule (6)
are set in ordinary type. Both types of parentheses are subject to convention (8).

The cursor then undergoes the *skip* rule until it has two consecutive asterisks on its right, as in (10), at which point it inserts a left parenthesis as in (11).

(10)   'Tis the middle of night by the castle clock,

          *   *   *) *   *   *)   *   *   *) *   *) (0 ⇐

                                                    ↑

(11)   'Tis the middle of night by the castle clock,

          *   *   *) *   *   *)   *   *   *) (*   *) (0 ⇐

                                                    ↑

The cursor continues to skip, moving from right to left, until it again has two asterisks on its right, at which point it inserts another parenthesis as shown in (12).

(12)   'Tis the middle of night by the castle clock,

          *   *   *) *   *   *)   *   (*   *) (*   *) (0 ⇐

                                              ↑

The cursor continues to move leftwards, but note that when it gets to the position shown in (13), a parenthesis cannot be inserted even though the cursor has skipped over two asterisks since the last insertion.

(13)   'Tis the middle of night by the castle clock,

          *   *   *) *   *   *)   *   (*   *) (*   *) (0 ⇐

                                         ↑

The parenthesis cannot be inserted here because the asterisks are not consecutive * *. Instead the sequence is *) *, which is not the environment in which the MARK rule applies. Instead, the cursor must skip again, until there is a sequence of two consecutive asterisks, at which point the parenthesis is inserted, as in (14).

(14)   'Tis the middle of night by the castle clock,

          *   *   *) * (*   *)   *   (*   *) (*   *) (0 ⇐

                               ↑

Moving further to the left, the cursor encounters yet again the sequence *) * , which requires an additional SKIP before the next (and last) parenthesis can be inserted. The non-iterative parenthesis insertion rule on Gridline 0 thus interacts with the iterative parenthesis insertion rule on Gridline 0, to leave some asterisks unfooted, a possibility explicitly admitted in the iterative rule. The remaining rules for the loose iambic tetrameter of this poem, on Gridlines 1 and 2, are identical to those for strict iambic tetrameter, as shown by the complete set of iterative rules in (15).

(15) a. Gridline 0: starting just at the R edge, insert a L parenthesis, form binary groups, heads R.

      i. Ungrouped syllables are permitted.

      ii. Incomplete groups are permitted.

  b. Gridline 1: starting just at the R edge, insert a R parenthesis, form binary groups, heads R.

  c. Gridline 2: starting just at the R edge, insert a R parenthesis, form binary groups, heads R.

As discussed above, in English loose iambic meters a right parenthesis is inserted by rule (4), but left parentheses are inserted by rule (15a). This has the important consequence that an asterisk may appear in the middle of a Gridline with a right parenthesis on its left and a left parenthesis on its right. By virtue of convention (8), such an asterisk is ungrouped, and in (14) there are two such ungrouped asterisks on the 'wrong' side of the parentheses. Because in a loose meter ungrouped asterisks are possible line-internally, the number of syllables in a loose meter can be greater than in the corresponding strict meter. In an iambic tetrameter line, like that under discussion here, the four binary groups could, in principle, be accompanied by ungrouped asterisks at both ends of the line and between each group (i.e., an extra five ungrouped asterisks in addition to the eight grouped asterisks, giving up to thirteen asterisks in an iambic tetrameter line). Note that only one asterisk can fall between binary groups; if there are two in a row, they will be put into a binary group by the iterative rule. This means that in a loose binary meter two consecutive heads can be separated by at most two non-head asterisks.[4] The full grid for the first two lines is shown in (16).

(16)   'Tis the middle of night by the castle clock,

```
*    ( *   * ) * ( *    * )     *  ( *  * )(*    * ) (      0 ⇐
          ) *             * )               *        * )      1 ⇐
                ) *                                  * )      2 ⇐
                                                     *        3
```

And the owls have awakened the crowing cock

```
*       ( * * )    *  ( *  * ) *    ( *   * )(*    * ) (      0 ⇐
        ) *                 * )           *        * )      1 ⇐
                          ) *                      * )      2 ⇐
                                                   *        3
```

---

[4] This prediction of our theory is confirmed by Tarlinskaja (1993: 57), who, on the basis of her analysis of a large corpus of poetry, concludes that in this type of meter: 'the intervals between adjacent ictuses vary, but not within a wide range: they contain either one or two syllables'. Her ictuses correspond for the most part to our heads.

Some of the lines in the poem could in principle be scanned either as loose iambic tetrameter, or instead as *strict* iambic tetrameter. This shows that as a special case the rules which scan a loose iambic text must accommodate lines which have the same form as strict iambic lines. This is illustrated by line 7 of the poem in (1). We show in (17) what a strict iambic scansion would be for this line (if it were in a strict iambic poem), and then in (18) the actual loose iambic scansion.

(17)   Hath a toothless mastiff bitch
```
    * )    *    * )    *      * ) *    * )          0 ⇐
    ) *          * )           *       * )          1 ⇐
          ) *                          * )          2 ⇐
                                        *           3
```

(18)   Hath a toothless mastiff bitch
```
    * ) ( *    * ) ( *      *)(*    * ) (           0 ⇐
    ) *          * )           *       * )          1 ⇐
          ) *                          * )          2 ⇐
                                        *           3
```

The two scansions above group the asterisks into identical groups at Gridlines 0, 1 and 2 but are produced in different ways. In (17) the four left parentheses on Gridline 0 are inserted by the iterative rule (15a). In (18) the four right parentheses are all inserted by the non-iterative rule (4) after maxima, and left parentheses are inserted by the iterative rule (15b). Note that in both strict and loose English meters, the maxima must project to Gridline 1. The ambiguity in scansion illustrated by (17) and (18) is resolved by the plausible assumption, formalized as the principle of isometricality (Chapter 2, (15)), that in the absence of reasons to the contrary, the lines in a given poem are all in the same meter (assigned by the same parenthesis insertion rule on Gridline 0), and so the correct scansion of this line is as in (18).

3.1.1 Are only stressed syllables counted?

Our approach to loose iambic meter is different from Coleridge's description of his metrical practice in the preface to 'Christabel', where he said that only the accented (stressed) syllables are counted, making this what is sometimes called an 'accentual meter'.[5]

[T]he metre of the Christabel is not, properly speaking, irregular, though it may seem so from its being founded on a new principle: namely, that of *counting in each line the accents, not the syllables*. Though the latter may

---

[5] Though we disagree with this analysis of loose iambic meter, we argue in section 10.4 that it is in fact true of the meter of *Beowulf*.

vary from seven to twelve, yet in each line the accents will be found to be only four.

Samuel Taylor Coleridge, Preface to 'Christabel' (Keach 1997: 187), emphasis supplied

If Coleridge were right, then there would be no need for the iterative parenthesis insertion rule at Gridline 0. Coleridge's 'accents' of (1) would be identified as maxima, and Gridline 0 groupings would be defined entirely by the right parentheses inserted by rule (4). The scansion of the second line would be as in (19) (we omit the arrow on Gridline 0 to indicate that there is no iterative parenthesis insertion here).

(19)   And the owls have awakened the crowing cock

```
 *        * * )     *    *  * ) *      *   * ) *     * )          0
          ) *            * )            *        * )             1 ⇐
                         ) *                     * )             2 ⇐
                                                 *              3
```

This is the wrong result, for two reasons. First, it implies that there could be any number of unstressed syllables between 'accents' (Gridline 0 heads), with no overall limit on the length of the line. We predict otherwise. Because there can be at most one ungrouped asterisk between binary groups, heads of Gridline 0 groups can be separated by at most two syllables, so that while loose meters permit a greater range of variation in length, there are still clear upper limits. Coleridge's claim should incorrectly permit the following invented line to be metrical:

(20)   And the owls have reawakened the crowing cock

```
 *        * * )     *    ** * ) *      *  * ) *      * )          0
          ) *                * )            *        * )         1 ⇐
                             ) *                     * )         2 ⇐
                                                     *          3
```

While Coleridge's account predicts that this line is metrical, we predict that it is not, and it is our iterative rules (15) that exclude this analysis. These rules would scan such a line not as tetrameter but as pentameter, as in (21), thus rejecting it as a line in a generally tetrameter poem.

(21)   And the owls have reawakened the crowing cock

```
 *       ( * * )   ( *    *( * * ) *    ( *   * )( *    * ) (      0 ⇐
          *              * )    *          *        * )           1 ⇐
                         ) *                        * )           2 ⇐
                                                    *            3
```

The fact that no such lines are found in 'Christabel' shows that Coleridge's own practice supports our theory rather than his.

The second reason for rejecting scansions which do not have iterative Gridline 0 rules is that there are lines such as line 9, which have four

Gridline 0 groups but only three maxima. These are lines which in Coleridge's terms have only three 'accents' but are still legitimate metrical lines in his poem. Rule (4) inserts right parentheses, as in (22).

(22) She maketh answer to the clock,

    *   *)*   *) *   *   *   *)   0

If we dispensed with the Gridline 0 iterative rule, the line would incorrectly scan as a trimeter:

(23) She maketh answer to the clock,

    *   *)*   *) *   *   *   *)   0
      *)   *   *)   1 $\Leftarrow$
)*   *)   2 $\Leftarrow$
                              *   3

The rules for loose iambic tetrameter, including the iterative rule at Gridline 0, correctly scan this line as tetrameter in (24).

(24) She maketh answer to the clock,

  (*   *)(*   *) (*   *   (*   *) (0 $\Leftarrow$
)*   *)   *   *)   1 $\Leftarrow$
)*   *)   2 $\Leftarrow$
                          *   3

The word *to* is the head of an iambic group, even though it is not a maximum (it carries no inherent accent). Coleridge might respond that in this line *to* is accented by the performer, perhaps in order to force four groups; but we rejoin that the performer knows that *to* might be accented in this specific line (but not generally) only because the iterative rules tell him that it is in head position of a Gridline 0 group, and that follows only from (24) and not from (23). This iterative rule is required in addition to the non-iterative rule at Gridline 0.

We have found that in all metrical traditions, iterative rules are required for every Gridline. Thus, we would not expect to find a meter such as that explored and rejected here, where parentheses are inserted on Gridline 0 only by a non-iterative rule. The fact that iterative rules are required on every Gridline makes metrical grids different from the grids which assign stress in words. For example, words of Maranungku (section 1.11) are assigned grids where on Gridline 1 a single left parenthesis is inserted by the non-iterative rule (68c), and there is no iterative rule on this Gridline.

3.2 One-syllable groups within the iambic line

We have seen that a loose meter may stretch the line without increasing the number of groups, by permitting a single ungrouped asterisk between two Gridline 0 groups. We now see that a loose meter may also compress the line without decreasing the number of groups, by permitting incomplete groups line-internally.

The rule (15a.ii) permits incomplete groupings at Gridline 0 in a loose iambic meter. In strict meters incomplete groups may be generated only in the last iteration of the insertion rule, and thus only at one end of the line. But where parentheses are inserted by a non-iterative rule, in principle they could be inserted next to each of a pair of adjacent syllables and so generate incomplete groupings *within* the line. We see this in the first and subsequent lines of (25), a nursery rhyme which starts in loose iambic trimeter and finishes in loose iambic tetrameter.

(25)   Ding dong, bell,
```
         * )   * )    * ) (                    0 ⇐
         *     *      *                        1
```
       Pussy's in the well.
```
         * )(*   *    ( *   * ) (              0 ⇐
         *      *       *                      1
```
       Who put her in?
```
          * ) * ) ( *  * ) (                   0 ⇐
          *   *      *                         1
```
       Little Johnny Green.
```
         *)(*   * )  ( *     * ) (             0 ⇐
         *      *     *                        1
```
       Who pulled her out?
```
          * ) * )    ( *  * ) (                0 ⇐
          *   *        *                       1
```
       Little Tommy Stout.
```
         * )(*   * ) ( *    * ) (              0 ⇐
         *      *     *                        1
```
       What a naughty boy was that,
```
          * )(*  * )  ( *   * ) ( *    * ) (   0 ⇐
          *     *      *        *             1
```
       To try to drown poor pussy cat,
```
        ( *    * )(*  * )   ( *   * )(* * ) (  0 ⇐
          *      *     *        *    *        1
```
       Who never did him any harm,
```
        ( *   * )(*  *  ( *   * )(*  * ) (     0 ⇐
          *    *     *      *    *            1
```
       And killed the mice in his father's barn.
```
       (*    * )    ( *  * ) *  ( *  * )(*  * ) (  0 ⇐
          *          *        *        *      1
```

Anonymous, 'Ding, dong, bell' complete (Opie and Opie 1951: 149)

In a loose iambic meter, according to definition (2), a stressed syllable is a maximum unless it is preceded or followed by a syllable with greater stress. For example, in the eighth line of (25), the stressed syllable *poor* cannot be a maximum because the two words on either side have greater stress. In this poem, however, we see stressed syllables whose neighbors have exactly the same stress, for example, in the first line where all three words have the same stress and so are all maxima (defined as in (2)). This means that a right parenthesis is inserted after each syllable by rule (4). This iambic trimeter line thus consists of three Gridline 0 groups generated from just three syllables, and hence all three are maxima. This means that the line does not have an uninterrupted sequence of two asterisks (every asterisk is separated from the preceding one by a parenthesis) and so the iterative rule at Gridline 0 has no effect, other than to insert a parenthesis just at the right edge of the line. In comparison, *strict* iambic trimeter verses must contain at least five syllables; thus the fourth line ('Little Johnny Green') but not the first ('Ding dong, bell') could have alternatively been scanned as strict iambic trimeter.

The very same metrical devices as in the nursery rhyme (25) are found in art poetry, for example, in Tennyson's 'Break, break, break' of which the first stanza is quoted in (26).

(26)　　Break, break, break,
　　　　On thy cold gray stones, O Sea!
　　　　And I would that my tongue could utter
　　　　The thoughts that arise in me.

Alfred, Lord Tennyson 'Break, break, break' stanza 1

Tennyson's poem is in loose iambic trimeter lines, with the third line of the last two stanzas in loose iambic tetrameter. It brings out the great variation in number of syllables which a loose meter can sustain without varying the number of groups. For example, as shown in (27), all lines in the first stanza are composed of three loose iambic groups, but the number of syllables in a line varies radically as 3, 7, 9, and 7.

(27)　Break, break, break,
```
       *)      *)      *)(                        0 ⇐
       *       *       *                          1
```

　　　On thy cold gray stones, O Sea!
```
    *   (*   *   (*    *)  (*   *)(               0 ⇐
            *        *         *                   1
```

　　　And I would that my tongue could utter
```
    *  (*   *)   *   (*  *)    (*   *)*(          0 ⇐
          *          *          *                 1
```

The thoughts that arise in me.
```
(*      *)        * ( * * ) (*      *) (              0 ⇐
      *)             *              *)               1 ⇐
   ) *                               *)               2 ⇐
                                     *                3
```

3.3 Yet another definition of maximum

(28)   The robin and the wren
        Are God's cock and hen.

Anonymous, complete (Munsterberg 1984: 336)

If we apply the definition of maximum (2) to this poem, and then apply the iambic rules, we scan the first line as loose iambic trimeter (29).

(29)   The robin and the wren
```
( * * )(* *      ( *      *) (                0 ⇐
     *)    *          *)                       1 ⇐
   ) *                 *)                       2 ⇐
                        *                       3
```

Note that the conjunction *and* is the head of the second Gridline 0 group in this line, in spite of not bearing stress. This shows again that the rhythm of the line does not fully determine its meter.

The second line, however, can be scanned as in the same meter only if, contrary to condition (2), both syllables of *God's cock* are maxima, even though they are not equal in stress (*cock* has greater stress than *God's*).

(30)   Are God's cock and hen.
```
(*      *)    *) (*      *) (                 0 ⇐
      *)      *          *)                    1 ⇐
   ) *                    *)                    2 ⇐
                          *                     3
```

In order to justify the assumption that both lines are in the same meter – loose iambic trimeter – we must use in this poem a different definition of maximum (31) for loose meters, which expands the number of syllables which can count as maxima.

(31)   Definition B of maximum in English loose meters
        The syllable bearing the word stress is a maximum.

There is thus need for some flexibility in the interpretation of the concept of 'maximum' in different poems, and it is possible to switch between definitions (2) and (31) in the same text, as illustrated in (32).

(32) Three blind mice,

```
  *) *)   *) (                    0 ⇐
  *   *    *                      1
```

See how they run!

```
  *) *)  (*  *) (                 0 ⇐
  *  *        *                   1
```

They all run after the farmer's wife,

```
  (* *) (* *)* (* *) (*    *) (   0 ⇐
     *     *      *     *         1
```

Who cut off their tails with a carving knife,

```
  (* *) *  (*  *)  * (* *)(*   *) ( 0 ⇐
     *       *        *      *      1
```

Did you ever see such a thing in your life,

```
  *  (* *)(*  *) * (* *) * (* *) (  0 ⇐
       *     *       *      *       1
```

As three blind mice?

```
  (*    *) *)   *) (               0 ⇐
      *  *   *                     1
```

Anonymous, 'Three blind mice' complete (Opie and Opie 1951: 306)

The trimeter lines 1,2 and 6 employ one definition of maximum, and the tetrameter lines 3, 4 and 5 employ the other. In particular, stress subordination is taken into account in the longer lines, where the sequence of three stressed words *all run af-* is analyzed as having two maxima, pursuant to (2). In the trimeter lines, stress subordination is not taken into account, pursuant to (31).

3.3.1 'A short, sharp shock': the molossus reinterpreted

In his discussion of ternary feet, Fry (2005: 86) quotes the lines in (33), and proposes that they end with a 'molossus', consisting of three stressed syllables such as *dúll, dárk dóck* (by analogy with the classical foot 'molossus' which was said to consist of three heavy syllables, see (38) in Chapter 1).

(33) To sit in solemn silence in a dull, dark dock,
      In a pestilential prison, with a life-long lock,
      Awaiting the sensation of a short, sharp shock,
      From a cheap and chippy chopper on a big black block!

W. S. Gilbert, *The Mikado*, 1.605–9 (Gilbert and Sullivan 1996)

In (33), all the lines are twelve or thirteen syllables long, and this lack of significant variation in the number of syllables suggests that they are strict iambic hexameters, as in (34).

(34)   Awaiting the sensation of a short, sharp shock,

```
        ′         ′              ′      ′      ′
   s   s s     s  s  s  s  s   s      s      s
   )*  *)*     *) * *) * *) *  *)     *      *)       0 ⇐
        *       *     *     *     *      *      *       1
```

On the scansion in (34), the fact that the line ends with a sequence of three stressed syllables is unconnected to its metrical form, for in a strict meter, stressed monosyllables are freely placed. On this analysis the 'molossus'-effect described by Fry is a rhythmic effect which is unrelated to the metrical form.

However, there is an alternative way of making metrical sense of the rhythmic 'molossus' consisting of the three stressed monosyllables at the end of the line. Nothing in our theory prevents a given sequence of words from having more than one meter. In particular, the verses in (33) can each be analyzed as consisting of two lines of loose iambic trimeter, as shown in (35); this fits with the melody to which the lines are set in the musical score which consists of two distinct segments. Application of rule (4) here assumes the weaker definition of maximum (31), rather than the stricter (2).

(35)   Awaiting the sensation

```
   (*   *)(*    * (*  *) * (          0 ⇐
        *        *      *              1
```

of a short, sharp shock,

```
   * ( *   *)     *)    *) (          0 ⇐
        *       *      *              1
```

We suggest that this poem is in fact metrically ambiguous; either (34) or (35) are possible scansions. The possibility of analyzing (33) as being composed in two meters does not contradict our principle of isometricality ((15) of Chapter 2), which states that normally poems are composed in a single meter. From our present perspective, the syllable sequence (33) represents two distinct poems simultaneously, one composed of lines in strict iambic hexameter, and the other in loose iambic trimeter.

3.4 Loose anapaests in a poem by W. H. Auden

In English, most poetry in loose meters is in iambic meters. In this section we consider a short poem of six lines whose lines are in loose anapaestic tetrameter, and where the number of syllables in the lines varies (12, 16, 12, 13, 14, 14). The poem is by Auden, who wrote much poetry in loose meters.

(36) Perfection, of a kind, was what he was after,
      And the poetry he invented was easy to understand.
      He knew human folly like the back of his hand,
      And was greatly interested in armies and fleets;
      When he laughed, respectable senators burst with laughter,
      And when he cried the little children died in the streets.

W. H. Auden, 'Epitaph on a Tyrant' complete (Auden 1945: 99)

We scan these lines by first applying rule (4) which inserts right parentheses after maxima, defined by the narrower condition (2), to produce the scansion in (37).

(37) Perfection, of a kind, was what he was after,
      *   *) *   * * *)   *   *) * * *) *
      And the poetry he invented was easy to understand.
      *   * *) * * ** *) *   * *) * * *   *   *)
      He knew human folly like the back of his hand,
      *   *) * * *) * *   * *) *   *   *)
      And was greatly interested in armies and fleets;
      *   *   *) * *) * * * * *) * *   *)
      When he laughed, respectable senators burst with laughter,
      *   * *)   * *) * * *) * *   *)   *   *)   *
      And when he cried the little children died in the streets.
      *   * * *) * *) * *) * *) * *)

The first four lines in the poem are tetrameters, and the last two are pentameters. Because these lines have long stretches between the stressed syllables, they must be analyzed as loose ternary rather than binary groups; this involves a new iterative rule at Gridline 0 in place of (15a).

(38) a. Gridline 0: starting just at the R edge, insert a L parenthesis,
         form *ternary* groups, heads R.

      i. Gridline 0 may include incomplete groups.

      ii. Gridline 0 may include ungrouped asterisks.

The effect of applying the iterative rule is shown in (39).

(39) Perfection, of a kind, was what he was after,
      * *) * (* * *)   *   *) (*   * *) * (0 ⇐
         * | *   *   1

      And the poetry he invented was easy to understand.
      (*   * *) * * (** *)(*   * *) * * (*   * *) (0 ⇐
           *   *   *   *   1

A complete anapaestic Gridline 0 group consists of three syllables. In the first line of (39) we see two incomplete groups, one at the left edge (as is always possible in an anapaestic meter), and the other line-internally. The line-internal incomplete group, containing two asterisks, is generated by inserting right parentheses next to maxima which are only two syllables apart.

English loose meters allow ungrouped asterisks (representing syllables) within the line. In the first line in (39), one asterisk is ungrouped, and in the second line there are two places where a sequence of two asterisks is ungrouped. It is because this is a ternary (loose) meter that up to two ungrouped asterisks are permitted. A sequence of three asterisks could not remain ungrouped: they would always be grouped by the iterative rules. While in a loose iambic meter there can be between zero and two syllables between heads of Gridline 0 groups, a loose anapaestic meter permits between zero and four syllables between heads of Gridline 0 groups.

3.5 Hopkins's metrical innovation: Sprung Rhythm

One of the few genuinely new meters in English was invented at the end of the 19th century by Gerard Manley Hopkins. He called it 'Sprung Rhythm' and he saw it as a development of the folk meter which we have analyzed as 'loose iambic meter'. We will show that Hopkins added to the folk tradition of loose iambic meter the option of not projecting certain syllables, which he took from the art meter tradition.

3.5.1 Hopkins's conventional iambic poetry

Almost without exception, all of Hopkins's poetry is in some variant of iambic meter, either strict or loose, or the special variant which Hopkins called 'sprung'.[6] Many of his poems are in strict iambic meters, and from his first poems onwards, Hopkins made enthusiastic use of the possibility of non-projection. Thus, even the words which make up the title of his first poem, 'The Escorial', contain a non-projected syllable (a vowel before a vowel) when used in the strict iambic line (40).

(40)   Unmindful of their Grace, the Escorial
)*   *)   * *)   *   *)   Δ * *)* *)

---

[6] We believe that there are just two non-iambic exceptions, both in anapaestic tetrameter: 'Rosa Mystica' (Hopkins 2002: 100) and 'Consule Jones' (Hopkins 2002: 412).

In addition to non-projection, Hopkins uses every variation allowed in the strict iambic meter. This is well illustrated in the strict iambic pentameter sonnet scanned in (41) (with Hopkins's own markings).

(41) As king fishers catch fire, dragonflies dráw fláme;
```
)*  *)  *  *)  *     *  )   * Δ *)   *    *)
    *       *         *          *        *
```

As tumbled over rim in roundy wells
```
)*   *)   *   *)*  *)  *   *)   *   *)
     *        *    *   *   *    *
```

Stones ring; like each tucked string tells, each hung bell's
```
) *    *)   *   *)   *        *)   *   *)   *    *)
       *        *             *        *         *
```

Bow swung finds tongue to fling out broad its name;   4
```
) *     *)  *    *)    *  *)   *   *)  *   *)
        *        *        *        *       *
```

Each mortal thing does one thing and the same:
```
) *     *) *   *)   *  *)   *  *)   * * *)
        *      *      *       *        *
```

Deals out that being indoors each one dwells;
```
) *    *)   *   *)* *)  *   *)   *      *)
       *        *   *   *    *        *
```

Selves – goes itself; myself it speaks and spells,
```
) *        *) * *)   * *) *   *)   *      *)
       *       *      *      *        *
```

Crying Whát I dó is me: for that I came.   8
```
) *Δ       *) *  *)*   *)  *    *)* *)
       *      *   *       *        *
```

Í say móre: the just man justices;
```
*)*    *)   *  *)   *   *) * *)
*      *        *       *    *
```

Kéeps gráce: thát keeps all his goings graces;
```
*)     *     *)  *   *)  *  *)*     *) *
*             *      *      *       *
```

Acts in God's eye what in God's eye he is –
```
*)  Δ   *   *)    * *)   *   *)  * *)
*           *       *        *     *
```

Chríst. For Christ plays in ten thousand places,   12
```
*)   *    *)  *  *)  *   *)*      *)*
*         *      *      *         *
```

Lovely in limbs, and lovely in eyes not his
```
*) Δ *  *)    *   * Δ)* *)   *    *)
*       *         *    *    *     *
```

To the Father through the features of men's faces.
```
Δ )* *) *    *)   * *)* *)  *    *)*
     *      *      *     *       *
```

Gerard Manley Hopkins, 'As king fishers catch fire' complete (Hopkins 2002: 129)

The strict iambic iterative rules permit two kinds of variation, both of which Hopkins exploits: an incomplete group on the left, and an ungrouped syllable on the right. Lines 10 and 12 combine both variations producing a 'falling rhythm' in a line which is still strict iambic pentameter. In a strict meter, syllables may be present in the line but not projected as Gridline 0 asterisks, and Hopkins uses this possibility in order to disguise the metrical periodicity behind a rhythmic aperiodicity. An example is line 12, which has the expected ten syllables, but arranged with an incomplete leftmost group and an ungrouped rightmost syllable. This presents a problem for the reader in scanning the line, which is compounded by its rhythmic aperiodicity. In performing the line we would probably produce 'Chríst pláys in tén thóusand' with the four stresses shown, but since both *plays* and *ten* are monosyllables and hence not maxima, their appearance in non-head positions is perfectly regular metrically. In fact, since in a strict meter a maximum must be preceded and followed by unstressed syllables (cf. (3)), Hopkins's practice – as throughout this poem – of stacking together the stressed syllables in the line means that there are very few maxima, and it is the number of metrical (i.e., projected) syllables that matters for the meter. Nothing that Hopkins does in this poem differs from previous practice by other poets composing in iambic pentameter, but what makes his poetry distinctive – and recalls the practice of Donne while going far beyond him – is his willingness to use every allowable variation and to combine legitimate variations within the same line, so that the underlying regularities of the meter are disguised.

Hopkins's idiosyncratic use of strict meter is paralleled by his idiosyncratic use of rhyme in the sestet that ends this sonnet. The scheme alternates masculine with feminine rhymes, where the extrametrical syllable of the feminine rhyme is phonetically identical with the masculine rhyme. The same rhyming scheme is found in 'The Windhover', the poem we discuss in the next section.

Hopkins wrote a few additional poems in the kind of loose iambic meter that we have discussed in this chapter. These include the imitation ballad 'The Queen's Crowning' in iambic tetrameter and trimeter (Hopkins 2002: 51), 'A Complaint' in loose iambic hexameter (Hopkins 2002: 76), 'Ad Mariam' in loose iambic tetrameter (Hopkins 2002: 98), 'Moonrise June 19 1876' in loose iambic tetrameter and trimeter (Hopkins 2002: 121), 'The Woodlark' in loose iambic tetrameter (Hopkins 2002: 122), and much later a 'patriotic song for soldiers' (Hopkins 2002: 181). These poems do not differ in their metrical form from the folk poetry which they imitate. However, as we will now see, Hopkins developed from these imitations of folk meters the modified version of loose meter which he called 'Sprung Rhythm'.

3.5.2 Sprung Rhythm: loose iambic plus non-projection

I had long had haunting my ear the echo of a new rhythm which now I realised on paper. To speak shortly, it consists in scanning by accents or stresses alone, without any account of the number of syllables, so that a foot may be one strong syllable or it may be many light and one strong. I do not say the idea is altogether new; there are hints of it in music, in nursery rhymes and popular jingles, in the poets themselves, and, since then I have seen it talked about as a thing possible in critics.

Gerard Manley Hopkins, letter to R. W. Dixon Oct 5 1878 (Hopkins 2002: 334)

Hopkins called his new rhythm 'Sprung Rhythm'. It is famously exemplified by the sonnet in (42).

(42)

> I caught this morning morning's minion, king-
> dom of daylight's dauphin, dapple-dáwn-drawn Falcon in his riding
> Of the rólling level úndernéath him steady áir, and stríding
> High there, how he rung upon the rein of a wimpling wing   4
> In his ecstacy! then off, off forth on swing,
> As a skate's heel sweeps smooth on a bow-bend: the hurl and gliding
> Rebuffed the big wind. My heart in hiding
> Stirred for a bird, — the achieve of, the mastery of the thing!   8
>
> Brute beauty and valour and act, oh, air, pride, plume here
> Buckle! AND the fire that breaks from thee then, a billion
> Times told lovelier, more dangerous, O my chevalier!
>
> No wónder of it; shéer plód makes plóugh down síllion   12
> Shine, and blue-bleak embers, ah my dear,
> Fall, gáll themsélves, and gásh góld-vermílion.

Gerard Manley Hopkins, 'The Windhover' complete (Hopkins 2002: 132)

This poem is in loose iambic pentameter. The scansion for the first line is shown in (43). Maxima are basically defined as in (2), though Hopkins improvises somewhat in what he permits as a maximum. Right

parentheses are inserted after the maxima by rule (4); then the iterative
rule (15a) inserts left parentheses to generate binary groups.[7]

(43)   I caught this morning morning's minion, king-
       (* *   (*   *)(*   *)(*   *)∧(*   *) (⇐
        *   *   *   *   *

However, while the first line is straightforwardly scanned as loose
iambic pentameter, this is not true for line 8, which is tentatively scanned
in (44).

(44)   Stirred for a bird, –   the achieve of, the mastery of the thing!
       *)   *(* *)   *(* *) *   (* *) *(* * (* *)(⇐
        *   *   *   *   *   *

This line has six groups, rather than the expected five groups. Five
of the groups are generated by the non-iterative rule, which finds five
maxima in the line, based on the definition of maximum introduced in
(2).

The sixth group is generated by the iterative rule, which groups the
syllables -*ry of* into a single group. One solution is to analyze the poem
as loose anapaestic meter, as we analyzed Auden's poem in (39) above.

(45)   Stirred for a bird, –   the achieve of, the mastery of the thing!
)   (* *)   (* * *) (*   *)* *(*   *)(⇐
        *   *   *   *   *   *

This solves one problem because the anapaestic scansion (45) gives line
8 five groups, but it creates a different problem: if we scan line 5 by the
same rules, we do not generate five groups, but only four, as shown in
(46).

(46)   In his ecstacy! then off, off forth on swing,
       (*   * *) *(*   * *) * *) *   *) (⇐
        *   *   *   *   *

The solution to this problem is that some of the syllables are not
counted for the meter and are not projected to Gridline 0. As we have
seen, Hopkins, like many other English poets, allows this in poems which
are in strict iambic meter. But this option is otherwise unknown in
loose iambic meter. Hopkins's innovation, which makes loose iambic
meter into the meter which he called 'Sprung Rhythm', is to allow non-
projection in a loose iambic meter. This is shown in (47), where the
delta Δ indicates the non-projected syllables.

---

[7] Hopkins ends the first line of 'The Windhover' with the initial syllable *king-* of
the word *kingdom* and begins the second line with the last syllable of this word.
Hopkins may have known that words can be split across lines in Greek lyric poetry
(see, for example, section 6.4.1, also (14) in Chapter 1).

(47) Stirred for a bird, – the achieve of, the mastery of the thing!

```
 *)     *( *  *)       Δ(* *)  *   (* *)ΔΔ *  (* *)(⇐
 *       *              *          *          *
```

In (47), three monosyllabic prepositions (*for*, *of*, *of*) are projected but not grouped, and a further three syllables are not projected. Two of the syllables which do not project are vowel preceding vowel: *the* before *achieve* and *-y* before *of*. The third syllable which does not project has [r] as its nucleus. These types of syllable are commonly not projected also in strict iambic meters. Non-projected syllables correspond to some extent to the syllables which Hopkins in his own terminology calls 'outrides' ('one or two or three slack syllables added to a foot and not counted in the nominal scanning'). Hopkins in fact permits a wider range of syllables not to project than most English poets.

We scan the whole sonnet in (49), based on the rules in (48). For most verse lines we illustrate only Gridline 0, but for the last line in (49) we give all four lines of the grid. In scanning the lines we assume that Hopkins's stress marks are intended to identify syllables as maxima. We also exceptionally allow both *big* and *wind* in *big wind* to be maxima (i.e., as though Hopkins had marked these with accents; otherwise the line has four rather than five groups on Gridline 0). (We note also that in the rhyme scheme of the octet in (49), like that of the sestet in (41), the ungrouped syllable of the feminine rhyme is identical phonetically with the masculine rhyme of an adjacent line.)

(48) a. Insert a R parenthesis on Gridline 0 after an asterisk projecting from a maximum.

b. Gridline 0: starting just at the R edge, insert L parentheses, form binary groups, heads R.

c. Gridline 1: starting just at the R edge, insert R parentheses, form ternary groups, heads R.

   i. The last (leftmost) group must be incomplete – binary.

d. Gridline 2: starting just at the L edge, insert L parentheses, form binary groups, heads L.

(49)

I caught this morning morning's minion, king-

```
(* *)      (* *)(*   *)(*    *)Δ(* *)(
 *          *     *         *      *
```

dom of daylight's dauphin, dapple-dáwn-drawn Falcon in his riding

```
* (* *)(*    *)  *  (* Δ *)  (* *)Δ * (* *)*(
 *      *        *         *      *
```

Of the rólling level úndernéath him steady áir, and stríding
```
 *  (*  *)*  (* △ *)  *  *)    *   (* △ *)(*      *)*(
    *                 *    *             *           *
```

High there, how he rung upon the rein of a wimpling wing
```
 *)   *    △  (* *)  *(*   △ *) *(*  *) (*    *) (
   *              *             *      *       *
```

In his ecstacy! then off, off forth on swing,
```
 * (*  *)(* *   (*  *)(*   *)  (*    *) (
      *   *       *      *        *
```

As a skate's heel sweeps smooth on a bow-bend: the hurl and gliding
```
 *(*  *)    *   (*     *) * (* *)  *    (* *)(*    *)*(
      *              *        *         *         *
```

Rebuffed the big wind. My heart in hiding
```
(* *)    (* *)  *)   (* *) (*  *)*(
   *       *   *       *      *
```

Stirred for a bird, – the achieve of, the mastery of the thing!
```
 *)   *(* *)      △(* *)  *   (*  *)△△ *  (*  *) (
   *    *         *        *         *           *
```

Brute beauty and valour and act, oh, air, pride, plume here
```
 (*   *) △(*   *)△ (*  *) (* *) (*     *)   *  (
    *     *          *      *      *            *
```

Buckle! AND the fire that breaks from thee then, a billion
```
 *)△  *    (* *)  (*   *)   *   (*  *  (* *) *(
 *            *        *             *      *   *
```

Times told lovelier, more dangerous, O my chevalier!
```
 *)  (*  *) △*  (*   *) △ *  (*  *  (* △*) (
 *     *        *         *     *      *
```

No wónder of it; shéer plód makes plóugh down síllion
```
(*  *) △ *(*    *)  *) (*    *)  (*   *) *(
   *       *    *       *         *
```

Shine, and blue-bleak embers, ah my dear,
```
 *) (*    *) (* *) (*  *  (*  *) (
 *     *      *      *       *
```

Fall, gáll themsélves, and gásh góld-vermílion.
```
(*    *) (*  *)  (*    *)  *) (*  *) *(      0 ⇐
   *      *)        *    *      *)          1 ⇐
        (*                  * (               2 ⇒
        *                                     3
```

Hopkins presented two alternative accounts of what Sprung Rhythm is, one based on counting stressed syllables, and the other based on organization into feet. Hopkins's first explanation is similar to Coleridge's account of 'Christabel meter' (section 3.1): Hopkins says that the verse 'consists in scanning by accents or stresses alone, without any account of the number of syllables'. Under this approach, the lines seem to be in different meters because they have different numbers of stressed syllables; for example, line 9, 'Brute beauty and valour and act, oh, air, pride plume here', has at least seven stressed syllables, while other lines have five. Hopkins's second analysis of Sprung Rhythm is based on the traditional notion of the foot; he says of 'The Windhover' that it is in falling paeonic rhythm ('falling paeonic rhy[th]m, sprung and outriding', Hopkins 2002: 352). A 'falling paeon' is a type of foot in Greek traditional metrics with a structure − ∪ ∪ ∪, whose equivalent in English is a stressed syllable followed by three unstressed syllables.[8] In this version of Hopkins's theory, Sprung Rhythms are 'measured by feet of from one to four syllables, regularly, and for particular effects any number of weak or slack syllables may be used' (Hopkins 2002: 107).

We take a different view of Hopkins's innovations. Hopkins's feet (Gridline 0 groups) are always binary and right-headed (i.e., his verse is always iambic). There are no four-syllable groups (these cannot be generated by the iterative rules, though we will see a special way of deriving a four-syllable group in Spanish, section 4.5.1). He allows syllables not to be projected in a loose meter (a meter with an non-iterative parenthesis insertion rule), and this is the defining features of Sprung Rhythm. He is more liberal than other writers (even Donne) in allowing syllables not to be projected to Gridline 0. Like many other poets, he is inconsistent in his use of the definition of maximum, switching from one definition to another within a text. And he admits more freely than other English poets lines that end in the middle of a word (as in the first line of 'The Windhover').

Hopkins thus introduces a genuine innovation into metrical theory by permitting non-projection of syllables in loose iambic meter. It is worth asking why the innovation of Sprung Rhythm has not given rise to a new metrical tradition, as the basis of new compositions after Hopkins (though we will see a form of Sprung Rhythm in T.S. Eliot's *The Waste Land* in the next section). One answer may be that the odd stressing of words and the optionality in what counts as a maximum mean that it is not always clear how to apply the special parenthesis insertion rule (4). A second possible problem is that in Sprung Rhythm there are two sources of 'ungrouped' syllables: syllables which are projected but not grouped, and syllables which are not projected at all, and so there are also difficulties (similar to those presented by Donne) in establishing which syllables are counted for metrical purposes. Speculations on these lines suggest that there is a gap between the logically possible meters

---

[8] In traditional metrical analysis of Greek the paeon is considered to be a variation of the cretic, see 6.2.6; we treat the cretic as a loose iambic meter, just as we treat Hopkins's 'paeons' as loose iambs.

and those which suit the diverse practical requirements of composition and reception. As we know from psycholinguistic and sociolinguistic studies, actual verbal behavior is limited by performance factors from making free use of some of the possibilities made available by linguistic competence.

3.6 A note on a meter in *The Waste Land*

It is obvious from even a cursory examination of the lines in T.S. Eliot's *The Waste Land* that line length varies radically from one syllable (in lines 121 and 128) to sixteen syllables (in line 161). In spite of this great variability, every line in the poem is in iambic meter, but the poem employs several different kinds of iambic meter. There are lines in strict iambic pentameter: first and foremost, the many lines that are quotations from English poets; e.g., Shakespeare (line 77) or Webster (lines 74–5). There are also many lines in strict iambic meter composed by Eliot himself; e.g., lines 249–251 and 253–256 are in strict iambic pentameter. In addition, there are many lines in loose iambic meter; e.g., lines 8–18, of which we give the Gridline 0 scansion for the first two lines in (50) using the rules (4) and (15a).

(50)　Summer surprised us, coming over the Starnbergersee
```
    *)    *  (*   *) (*    *)(*   *)*   (*   *)  * (*  *(      0 ⇐
    *             *          *    *          *          *      1
```
　　　　With a shower of rain; we stopped in the colonnade,
```
    *  (*    *)*(*   *)  (*   *)    *   (*  *(*  *)(       0 ⇐
         *          *          *           *   *         1
```

Most interesting from the present perspective are the famous seven lines that begin the poem. These are in a loose iambic meter that we have not encountered elsewhere in English poetry. Like in other loose iambic meters, maxima are marked by rule (4), which inserts a right parenthesis to their right. In place of (15a), however, iterative parenthesis insertion on Gridline 0 is governed by rule (51) which inserts right parentheses from left to right.

(51)　　a.　Gridline 0: starting just at the L edge, insert a R parenthesis, form binary groups, heads R.

　　　　　　　i.　Ungrouped syllables are permitted.

　　　　　　　ii.　Incomplete groups are permitted.

We give in (52) the Gridline 0 scansions for the opening lines of the poem. In applying the parenthesis insertion rule (4) we assume that maxima are defined as in (2); i.e., maxima are syllables bearing the word stress except where immediately adjacent to a syllable with greater stress. At major syntactic breaks – such as the one before the word ending the first line below – the stressed syllable on the right has greater stress than the one on the left.

(52)   April is the cruellest month, breeding

)*) * *)   *   *))Δ *   *)   *)*   0 ⇒
*   *   *   *   *   1

      Lilacs out of the dead land, mixing

) *)*   *)) *   *) *   *)   *)*   0 ⇒
*   *   *   *   *   1

      Memory and desire, stirring

) *)Δ * *))   * *)   *)*   0 ⇒
*   *   *   *   1

      Dull roots with spring rain.

) *   *)   Δ   *   *)   0 ⇒
*   *   1

      Winter kept us warm, covering

) *) *   *)) *   *)   *)Δ *   0 ⇒
*   *   *   *   1

      Earth in forgetful snow, feeding

) *)   Δ   *   *)) *   *)   *)*   0 ⇒
*   *   *   *   1

      A little life with dried tubers.

)*   *)) *   *)) *   *)   *)*   0 ⇒
*   *   *   *   1

As in the rest of *The Waste Land*, there is considerable variability in line length: in (52) the lines vary in length from dimeter to pentameter. Like Hopkins's Sprung Rhythm, this is a loose meter with non-projection. As already remarked, the Gridline 0 rule (51) does not have counterparts elsewhere in English poetry.

    Lines in loose meters, where both the rule marking maxima (or designated syllables) and the iterative rule of parenthesis insertion employ parentheses of the same kind are encountered in Arabic (see Chapter 7), in Greek (see Chapter 6) and in German, as we show in (53) with the scansion of three lines from Goethe's *Römische Elegien*.

(53)   Oftmals hab' ich auch schon in ihren Armen gedichtet,

(*   *   (*   ⍄   ⊢ ((*   *(*   * (*   *   *((*   *   0 ⇐
*   *   *   *   *   *   1

      Und des Hexameters Mass, leise mit fingernder Hand,

(*   *   *((* * *   ((*   (* *   *((*   *   *   (*   0 ⇐
*   *   *   *   *   *   1

Ihr auf dem Rücken gezählt. Sie atmet in lieblichen Schlummer
((*   *   * ((*   *   *((*   * (*   * *((*   *   * ((*   *
 *   *   *   *   *   *

'Oft-times I have even composed poems in her arms / And quietly with
fingering hand, counted out the hexameter's measure / On her back. She
breathes in lovely slumber'

These lines are in a loose dactylic hexameter. Left parentheses are inserted non-iteratively to the left of maxima by rule (54a), and iteratively
from left to right forming ternary left-headed groups by rule (54b). Maxima are defined as in (2). Lines in this meter have the characteristic
DUM-da-da DUM-da-da rhythm that used to be widely taught as the
appropriate way of reciting the classical hexameter lines.

(54)   a.   Insert a L parenthesis on Gridline 0 before an asterisk projecting from a maximum.

       b.   Gridline 0: starting just at the L edge, insert L parentheses,
form ternary groups, heads L.

3.7 The characteristics of a loose meter

Many metrical traditions make a distinction between strict and loose
meters. Loose meters share with strict meters the iterative rules which
insert parentheses on every Gridline, and combine asterisks into groups.
But loose meters in addition have a rule which inserts parentheses in specific contexts before the iterative rules apply, thus affecting the grouping
of syllables (represented by asterisks) on Gridline 0, and in principle permitting incomplete groups and ungrouped syllables (asterisks) within the
line. The number of ungrouped syllables (asterisks) in a line is limited
by the iterative rule of parenthesis insertion on Gridline 0. In the absence of this rule, the controlled character of ungrouped syllables in the
line is totally unexplained. It is sometimes claimed that loose meters
have a closer relation to the rhythm of the line, and in a sense this is
true: phonetic characteristics of syllables such as accent or weight help
determine the formation of metrical groups in a loose meter (but not
in a strict meter). However, the metrical form of a loose line does not
necessarily reproduce its rhythmic form: there is still a clear distinction
between rhythm and meter.

3.8 Ordered rules, and conditions

A meter is a set of rules and conditions. Our examination of a number of English meters has demonstrated all the component parts of a meter, which in the rest of this book we will see exploited in different ways in different languages.

We can distinguish three ordered components of a meter: (i) rules which project syllables to Gridline 0, (ii) other rules (of parenthesis insertion, projection to higher Gridlines, and deletion), and (iii) conditions on the grid.

The default rule of projection to Gridline 0 projects every syllable to Gridline 0. As we have seen, in some English lines, some syllables fail to project. In the grid as we have written it out, these syllables are marked with Δ on Gridline 0, to indicate that they have not projected. No subsequent rule or condition can refer to a non-projected syllable; syllables which are marked with Δ are metrically invisible.

Projection to Gridline 0 is followed in principle by the application of three kinds of rule. In English loose meters, non-iterative rules of parenthesis insertion come first. Then the iterative rules apply. Then (only in the hendecasyllabic meter of section 1.8) a deletion rule applies. This order is not the only possible order, and we will see that in other meters, non-iterative rules can apply at a later point (including at Gridlines above Gridline 0), and deletion rules can apply at an earlier stage. When a projection is deleted we indicate this by replacing the projection with Δ, thus indicating that it is invisible to any later rule or condition.

Once the grid is constructed, the combination of line and grid is checked against the conditions of the meter. In English meters, the only condition is that maxima must project to Gridline 1. As we will see, other kinds of condition are found in other meters, and some meters include more than one condition. In English the condition depends on a bifurcation of syllables into maxima and non-maxima; the superficial differences between English and other languages usually depend on other ways of dividing syllables into two metrical classes, some based on stress (Spanish, French, Latvian), others based on weight (Greek, Arabic, Sanskrit), and yet others based on tone (Chinese, Vietnamese) or on whether syllables do or do not alliterate (the Old English poem *Beowulf*). An important general constraint is that a condition cannot 'see' a syllable whose projection cannot be deleted; this will prove important in our explanation of the caesura rule in French, in Chapter 5.

4

Southern Romance

by

Carlos Piera

4.1 Introduction[1]

This chapter is concerned with some of the basic meters of the Spanish tradition, as well as certain key aspects of Italian and Galician-Portuguese metrics. An important feature of the metrical systems studied here is that they make use of both the notion 'stressed syllable' and the more restrictive notion 'maximum'. Failure to make the distinction between the set of stressed syllables and its subset of 'maxima' has often led metrists to cast their otherwise correct intuitions in terms of mere tendencies or preferences, or the equivalent. This in turn paves the way for doubtful conclusions: if, say, the Italian *endecasillabo* is conceived as having only a tendency towards an iambic distribution of stresses, then nothing prevents us from treating it as a syllabic meter, albeit one which properties of the language and universal rhythmic propensities conspire to overlay, somewhat haphazardly, with multiples of two. Why this rhythm should tolerate a maximum in the third position of the line, but not in the fifth, is of course a question that cannot even be posed unless the notion of maximum is available, in spite of the fact that this descriptive generalization has been obvious to scholars for centuries. Every one of the first ten syllables of an *endecasillabo* can bear stress, so the most one can conclude is that the third syllable is much more likely to be tonic than the fifth, or else that a fifth syllable stress is felt to be excessively evocative of a different meter. Why other comparable evocations are not perceived as excessive becomes, then, the unanswered question.

---

[1] This chapter was written by Carlos Piera of Universidad Autónoma de Madrid, in collaboration with the authors of this book.

In these Romance meters, syllables which are maxima are required to fall in certain positions, but in addition other stressed syllables which are not maxima can also be controlled. Thus, in Petrarch and many other poets, a maximum in the third position of an *endecasillabo* will systematically co-occur with a stressed syllable in the sixth position, and this is a stressed syllable which crucially need not be a maximum. In general, we find that in order to account for the distribution of stressed syllables one must previously have a clear idea of which ones can also be maxima. Let us now turn to the specifics.

4.2 Two general properties of Gridline 0 construction in Southern Romance

In the metrics of several Romance languages – Italian, Portuguese, Catalan and Spanish among them – syllables are not counted in certain contexts. Since the metrical grids of the verses and the rules that generate them cannot be properly appreciated without reference to these non-projections (omissions from the count), we turn next to a discussion of these matters. Readers who want to proceed directly to the discussion of the meters in this chapter are advised to take note of rules (3) and (9) before doing so.

A line-internal non-projection rule applies in the following Spanish example:[2]

(1) Descaminado, enfermo, peregrino
     'Gone astray, sick, wandering' Luis de Góngora

In (1) the last vowel of the first word and the first vowel of the second count as a single metrical unit. This line is a Spanish *endecasílabo* (see section 4.3 below), i.e., a line with ten or eleven asterisks at Gridline 0. If every syllable in (1) were projected we would have one asterisk too many. The correct number is obtained by projecting only one of the adjacent vowels, as in (2):

(2) Descaminado, enfermo, peregrino
     * * * * Δ * *   * ** * *

The rule is known traditionally as *synaloepha*; we will refer to it as Vowel

---

[2] We give here more complete references for the examples quoted in this section. (1): Sonnet 'De un caminante enfermo que se enamoró donde fue hospedado', l.1. (4): 'Cantar del alma que se huelga de conoscer a Dios por fe', l.3. (5): Sonnet '¡Oh bien haya Jaén...', l.5. (6): Canción I, l.54. (7): *Os Lusíadas* I.104,1. (8): *Os Lusíadas* X.64,1–2, X.65,1. (14): Égloga II.133. (15): Sonnnet 'A Júpiter' l.3.

Non-Projection. It has precedents in Romance meters going back as far as Classical Latin, but it does not necessarily apply in much medieval poetry; e.g., the rule does not regularly apply in the 13th-century *Libro de Alexandre*.[3] We formulate the rule in (3).

(3) Vowel non-projection

In a sequence of two consecutive vowels separated by a word boundary:

    a. The second vowel is not projected to Gridline 0, if the first is stress-bearing.

    b. Elsewhere, the first vowel is not projected to Gridline 0.

Clause (a) of (3) guarantees the correct application of later rules referring to maxima and/or stressed syllables in the line. Following are three more examples of the application of (3) in Spanish lines.[4] Note that Vowel Non-Projection can apply to more than two adjacent vowels as we see in (6) (and (13)) below.

(4) Aquélla etérna fónte está escondída

    *   * △ * * * * △ * * △ * * *

    'That everlasting fountain is hidden' John of the Cross

(5) Écija se há esmerádo, yó os prométo

    * ** △ * △ ** * * △   * * *

    'Écija did her best, I promise you' Luis de Góngora

(6) conmígo yá que vér en málo o en buéno

    * * * * * * * * △ △ *   * *

    'anything to do with me either bad or good' Garcilaso

In (4) the first vowel in the sequence *a–e* is projected in one case, the second in another, due to the application of the different clauses in (3). In (5) the sequence *e–(h)a–e*, where the *h* is purely graphical, leads to the projection of *a* only, because the auxiliary has some degree of stress. In (6) clause (3b) is applied twice. When lines are read, all the vowels

---

[3] For relevant comparative data and statistics see Duffell (1991).

[4] We mark all stressed vowels with an acute accent, whether this is required by the standard orthography or not. Syllables marked with the nasal sign (tilde) in the Portuguese examples and the grave accent in Italian are stressed. There can be disagreements as to which words are stressed, particularly in the case of monosyllables, but this fact does not affect the arguments we put forward. See footnote 10 below for some of the criteria we have followed in this respect.

are pronounced: it is just that some of them do not count for metrical purposes.

The two sub-parts of rule (3) apply in order, first (3a), then (3b). Each sub-part of the rule scans the entire string for contexts in which it might apply, and the changes are made in all noted contexts in one fell swoop. Observation of rule order is crucial. For instance, in (4) one element of the rightmost *a–e* sequence is non-projected by rule (3a) and only then is the string scanned for other vowel–vowel sequences and their Gridline 0 projections non-projected by rule (3b).

Vowel non-projection is subject to some optionality. It is safe to say that in the unmarked case it applies systematically, from the Renaissance on, in all the languages discussed in this chapter, particularly when both vowels are unstressed. But the non-application of the rule does not lead to unmetricality; witness the sequence *a–e* in the following Portuguese line in which the rule has not applied (and see also the first two syllables in (10) below).

(7) E, séndo a éla o Capitão chegádo
     *   * Δ * * Δ *   * * *   * * *

     'and the Captain having arrived there' Luís de Camões

Starting approximately in the Renaissance, there is another rule which affects the projection of line ends. A traditional interpretation of its consequences is as follows. Lines can indifferently have an ending which is oxytonic (final syllable is stressed), paroxytonic (second syllable from end stressed) or proparoxytonic (third syllable from end stressed). They can in principle be considered instances of the same meter if they all have the same number of *projected* syllables counting rightward up to and including the last stress. Thus, these are all examples of '*decasílabos*' from Camões, in which we underline the syllables following the last stress:[5]

(8) A éste o Réi Cambáico soberbíssi<u>mo</u>
     Fortaléza dará na ríca Dí<u>o</u> [...]
     Destruirá a cidáde Repelím

     'To this man the exceedingly proud King of Cambaia / will give a fortress
     on the rich Dío [...] / He will destroy the city of Repelim' Luís de Camões

---

[5] In Portuguese, Catalan and Provençal, meters are named after the number of their (projected) syllables up to and including the last lexical stress in a standard line. Works on Italian and Spanish add one syllable to this count, thus treating paroxytonic lines as the paradigm case. Hence the Portuguese *decasílabo* is equivalent to the Italian *endecasillabo*, etc.

We attribute these facts to the rule in (9):[6]

(9) Line-end non-projection

    a. If the rightmost word in a line contains a stressed syllable, do not project any syllables to the right of the stressed syllable.

    b. If the rightmost word in a line does not contain a stressed syllable, do not project any syllables to the right of the initial syllable of the rightmost word.

As a consequence of (9a) (together with the other non-projection rule (3)), the first line in (8) will be projected as in (10):

(10) A éste o Réi Cambáico soberbíssimo
　　　 * * Δ *　 *　 *　 * * * * * Δ Δ

It can be shown that the rule for Gridline 0 construction in Italian and Portuguese (hen)decasyllables is often (11), a rule identical to (33a) justified for Spanish in section 4.3.

(11) a. Gridline 0: starting just at the R edge, insert a R parenthesis, form binary groups, heads R.

Assuming this to be the case here, once (10) has been formed in accordance with (9a) above, the asterisks can only be grouped by (11) as in (12):

(12) A éste o Réi Cambáico soberbíssimo
　　　)* *)Δ *　 *)　 *　 *)* *)* *)Δ Δ

(9) entails, correctly, that the notions oxytone, paroxytone, and proparoxytone should not figure in our metrical rules. Italian has a few inflected forms which are pro-proparoxytonic (stress on the fourth syllable from the right) – such as the form *rincantúcciolano* 'take refuge in a corner (3rd pl. present)', in (13). Aside from this all the lexical stresses in these languages occur at most on the third syllable from the end of the word. But combinations of clitics can lengthen the sequence of post-stress syllables, and such longer sequences are also subject to non-projection.　We exemplify this with two facetious Italian hendecasyllables by Arrigo Boito, indicating projected and non-projected syllables for the second line.

(13) Sì crúdo è il vérno che le ríme sdrúcciolanosene
　　　 Tremándo e in fóndo al vérso rincantúcciolanosene
　　　 *　 *　 Δ Δ *　 *　 Δ *　 *　 *　 *　 *　 * Δ Δ Δ Δ Δ

---

[6] As noted in Chapter 11 an analog of part (a) of this rule holds in the very different poetry of the Old Testament.

'So harsh is the winter that rhymes become proparoxytonic, / shivering, and huddle together at the end of the line' Arrigo Boito (Menichetti 1993: 102)

When the last word in a line does not carry lexical stress, clause (9b) applies. Examples are (14) and (15), where the rightmost words are disyllabic and monosyllabic, respectively. There are no three-syllable stressless words in these languages.

(14) y ésto que dígo me contáron cuando
      △)∗ ∗) ∗ ∗)∗ ∗) ∗ ∗) ∗   ∗) △
      'and this that I tell you they told me when' Garcilaso

(15) cuánta plúma ensilláste para el que
) ∗   ∗) ∗ △ ∗) ∗ ∗) ∗ ∗)△ ∗   ∗)
      'how many feathers did you saddle for the one who' Luis de Góngora

Readers should note that the line-end non-projection rule (9) is not yet applicable to Juan de Mena's *arte mayor* (15th century), studied in section 4.5. It is, however, valid for the 16th-century poetry of Garcilaso, from which most of the examples in section 4.3 are taken.[7]

4.3 The Spanish *endecasílabo*

Following several unsuccessful attempts, the Italian *endecasillabo* was adapted for Spanish by the poets Juan Boscán and Garcilaso de la Vega, both of whose works were published in a single volume in 1543. It did not take long for this meter of ten metrical syllables to displace all the other learned meters in the language, and for Garcilaso's metrical practice to become the established metrical standard, in spite of the relatively small size of the corpus of his work. Our study of the Spanish *endecasílabo* is based, in so far as it is possible, on examples from his poetry, as has been done traditionally, and will therefore characterize the Renaissance variants of this meter. Later pre-modern Spanish poetry deviates from the 16th-century system, if at all, in being somewhat more restrictive. In particular, it tends to avoid the 4–7–10 pattern exemplified in (21) below. This sets it apart, although minimally, not just from its Renaissance models, but also from the practice of both earlier and contemporary Spanish poets (see footnote 9 below).

---

[7] We note that, for systems obeying line-end non-projection, rhyme can apply both to syllables that are projected and to syllables that are not. In that sense, rhyme is here indifferent to the distinction between metrical and non-metrical syllables

There is something of a consensus among metrists as to the classification of the different forms of the Spanish *endecasílabo*. The canonical form of the classification is due to T. Navarro Tomás (1972), from whom we draw five main patterns.[8] These patterns are based on the distribution of stresses over the ten metrical syllables of the line. In (16)–(20) we give examples taken from the poetry of Garcilaso; these examples are where possible those cited by Navarro (1972, 1973a). We have indicated which syllables are stressed (by position in the line) in the right margin.

(16) lléna de vencimiéntos y despójos   1–6–10
      'replete with defeats and spoils' Garcilaso, Égloga I line 271

(17) saliéndo de las óndas encendído   2–6–10
      'emerging from the waves alight' Garcilaso, Égloga I line 43

(18) renovár el placér o la tristúra   3–6–10
      'renew the pleasure or the sadness' Garcilaso, Canción III line 11

(19) las cristalínas águas se cubriéron   4–6–10
      'the crystalline waters were covered' Garcilaso, Égloga III line 376

(20) el asperéza de mis máles quiéro   4–8–10
      'the harshness of my ills I wish' Garcilaso, Canción IV line 1

The type in (21) below is also traditionally recognized (Henríquez Ureña 1944). Navarro calls it 'dactylic hendecasyllable' (Navarro 1973a: 107–109). This pattern is often studied separately from the other ones, largely because many Baroque poets avoided it and because 'in the 18th century ... it came to be used as an independent form' (Navarro 1973a: 107). It alternates freely with patterns (16)–(20) in Renaissance and post-Romantic poetry.[9]

(21) y se conviérta ado piénse salvárse   4–7–10
      'and that he turn to where he thinks he will find safety' Garcilaso,
      'Canción I line 19

---

[8] Because Navarro's main criterion is the position of the first stress in the line, he somewhat misleadingly treats patterns 4–6–10 and 4–8–10 as the same type.

[9] Thus, our six types (16)–(21) correspond to what in standard presentations of Navarro's theory are four 'common' types, one of which has two variants, plus the somewhat exceptional 'dactylic' 4–7–10 type. The avoidance of the 4–7–10 *endecasílabo* by Spanish 17th-century poets is often attributed to its perceived similarity with the ternary lines discussed in sections 4.5 and 4.6 below (e.g., Varela *et al.* 2005: 43, 181). This would be consistent with its survival in Italy, where there was no strong tradition of ternary meters. In any case, we will focus here on the richer Renaissance *endecasílabo*.

Though the six patterns shown in (16)–(21) are not the only stress patterns found in *endecasílabo* lines, their identification constitutes an important discovery which we develop further below. We note first that there are other possible patterns of stress, and we now illustrate these.

Among these other patterns are included lines such as (22), which have more than three stresses. Other lines have fewer than three stresses, as in (23), or may have three stressed syllables in positions other than the six canonical types, as in (24).

(22)   tornáron póco a póco en piédra dúra   2, 4, 6, 8, 10
       'turned little by little into hard stone' Garcilaso, Can. V line 92

(23)   enredó sobre nuestros corazónes   3, 10
       '(it) tangled on our hearts' Garcilaso, Epístola line 54

(24)   el frúto que con el sudór sembrámos   2, 8, 10
       'the fruit that with our sweat we sowed' Garcilaso, 'Elegía II line 9

Furthermore, there is no position in the line that cannot be occupied by a stressed syllable. To the ones we have seen (positions 1, 2, 3, 4, 6, 7, and 10) we may add positions 5 and 9:

(25)   con los que venír viéron, nó sabían   5, 6, 8, 10
       'with those they saw coming, they did not know' Garcilaso, Canción
       IV line 28

(26)   en el tendído cuérpo que allí viéron   4, 6, 9, 10
       'on the outstretched body that there they saw' Canción V line 87

The reader can verify in these data that there is also no position in the line which necessarily bears stress. The most regular stress is the one on position 10, but there is an example in Garcilaso of a stressless tenth syllable (e.g. (27)),[10] and lines with stressless tenth syllables are also found in *endecasílabo*s of later canonical poets (e.g., (28)).

---

[10] This is true at least if we follow Navarro's criteria for what counts as a stressed word in Spanish (Navarro 1925; a good summary can be found in Quilis 1999: 390–395). Here we do not deviate from those widely accepted criteria. What potential discrepancies we have been able to consider do not affect the account we put forward. A remark for Hispanists on our application of Navarro's criteria: several editors, including Rivers (1969) and Morros (1995), put a stress mark on *adó* in line (21) above. There is, however, no reason to treat this word differently from all the other *wh*-words introducing a free relative clause, like the final *cuando* in (27). Morros himself, from whose edition we quote, writes *ado* with no stress elsewhere (Égl. II 120). Lines stressed only on 4, 7, and 10, like (21), are certainly less frequent in this period than lines stressed on 1, 4, 7, and 10 – e.g., Égl. II 69 or example (30) below. Hence, perhaps, the editorial stress mark. In any case, due to the special status of first syllable stress (discussed below) all the arguments we base on 4–7–10 could equally well be based on the quite common 1–4–7–10 lines.

(27) y ésto que dígo me contáron cuando   1, 4, 8

'and this that I say to you they told me' Garcilaso, Égl. II line 137

(28) cuánta plúma ensilláste para el que   1, 3, 6

'how many feathers did you saddle for the one who' Luis de Góngora,
'A Júpiter' line 3

Our goal is to provide an account of the *endecasílabo* which accommo-
dates this amount of variation, while at the same time not retreating into
talk of mere rhythmical tendencies. We view all *endecasílabos* as lines
of five iambic Gridline 0 groups, i.e., technically, iambic pentameters (as
has been done by, among others, Bello 1955, Piera 1980, Nespor and
Vogel 1986, Hanson 1996). A line with fully regular iambic stressing
is given above as (22): it has a stressed syllable flanked by unstressed
syllables in each of its even-numbered positions. One of our main tasks
is to show how this line and lines with similarly stressed syllables only
in even-numbered positions can be compatible with metrical lines whose
stressed syllables are in (line-internal) odd positions as in (18), (21),
(25), and (28). At the same time, we must be able to exclude certain
configurations in which a stressed syllable in an odd position triggers
unmetricality. Thus, the fifth syllable can be stressed in a metrical line
if it is adjacent to another stressed syllable (e.g., in (25) the fifth syllable, *-nír*, is stressed and adjacent to a stressed syllable, *vié-*, in sixth
position), but if the fifth syllable is stressed and not adjacent to another
stressed syllable the line is unmetrical (as in the unmetrical construct
(29)).

(29) se me desveló que me hacía mál   5, 8, 10

'it was revealed to me that (it) did me ill' unmetrical

Although a stressed syllable is legitimate in the seventh position ((21)
and (30) below) as well as in the third position ((18) and (23)) it is not
possible to have stressed syllables in both seventh and third positions in
the same line (unmetrical construct (31)).

(30) Cómo pudíste tan présto olvidárte   1, 4, 7, 10

'how could you so soon forget' Garcilaso, 'Égl. II' line 578

(31) cuando lléga de repénte tu olvído   3, 7, 10

'when your forgetfulness suddenly comes' unmetrical

We derive these features of the *endecasílabo* from the fact that the
patterns in (16)–(21), properly interpreted, are indeed the only legitimate instantiations of this meter. We treat them as in an iambic meter

(binary right-headed groups at Gridline 0), grouped into binary groups at Gridline 1. The grouping of Gridline 0 groups into binary groups (two of which are complete and one incomplete) is crucial to our analysis, and differentiates it both from the English iambic pentameter and French *décasyllabe*, and from most traditional and recent treatments of the *endecasílabo*.

In (32) we reproduce the six canonical patterns once again. Their order is not the more standard one as earlier given in (16)–(21), but the one we follow below.

(32) i.   2 – 6 – 10   ii.   4 – 8 – 10
      iii. 4 – 7 – 10   iv.   4 – 6 – 10
      v.   3 – 6 – 10   vi.   1 – 6 – 10

The different possible stress patterns reflect the fact that different grids can be built for the *endecasílabo* line by different variants of the rules on Gridlines 1 and 2.[11]

In (33) we give the rules which generate the grid for the pattern 2–6–10 (that of (17) above), and we show the result in (34).

(33) *Endecasílabo*, pattern 2 – 6 – 10

    a. Gridline 0: starting just at the R edge, insert a R parenthesis, form binary groups, heads R.

    b. Gridline 1: starting just at the L edge, insert a L parenthesis, form binary groups, heads L.

       i. The last (rightmost) group must be incomplete – unary.

    c. Gridline 2: starting just at the L edge, insert a L parenthesis, form binary groups, heads L.

       i. The last (rightmost) group must be incomplete – unary.

    d. Gridline 3: starting just at the L edge, insert a L parenthesis, form binary groups, heads L.

(34) Pattern 2 – 6 – 10

    saliéndo de las óndas encendído

```
  1 2   3   4 5  6   7  8 9  10
) * *)  *   *)* *)  *  *)  *   *)Δ        0 ⇐
  ( *       *  ( *      *   ( *           1 ⇒
  ( *          *        *   ( *           2 ⇒
  ( *                       *  (          3 ⇀
    *                                     4
```

---

[11] The relations between the six canonical Spanish meters in (32) are not unlike those between the sixteen canonical meters of Arabic poetry. For more discussion see Chapter 7.

As we will see, all the variants of the *endecasílabo* share the same rules for Gridlines 0 and 3, but differ in the rules for Gridlines 1 and 2.

For the *endecasílabo*, as for most Renaissance and post-Renaissance Spanish poetry, we define certain stressed syllables as maxima. A maximum in these meters is a syllable bearing the stress of the word, in any word (monosyllable or polysyllable), which is both preceded and followed by a syllable without lexical stress. This excludes unstressed syllables and clitics. It also permits control over the placement of stressed monosyllables, which is a fact of these meters. Thus, the common stressed monosyllable *fin* 'end, goal, purpose' appears in Garcilaso's *endecasílabos*, flanked by stressless syllables, in all the even line-internal positions: respectively, the second, fourth, sixth, and eighth syllables in the four lines quoted in (35).

(35)   a. al fín la fiéra lúcha a despartírse

     b. con quien al fín no báste a derrocálle

     c. témo que ántes del fín anocheciése

     d. d'aquésta bréve vída fín amárgo

     a. 'finally the fierce struggle to conclude' (line 293)
     b. 'with whom in the end will prove unable to topple it' (line 366)
     c. 'I am afraid night would fall before the end' (line 313)
     d. 'bitter end of this brief life' (line 666); all from 'Égl. II'

We also find stressed monosyllables in position 3 in (36) and position in 7 (37):

(36)   débe sér, y sin tiémpo limitádo
     'must be, and without a time limit', El. II line 81

(37)   tus cláros ójos, ¿a quién los volvíste?
     'your light eyes, who did you turn them to?' Égl. I line 128

But we find no such stressed monosyllable configurations in position 5, neither in Garcilaso nor in other poets we have consulted, just as we find no polysyllabic maxima in that position, as shown by unmetrical (29).

This leads us to adopt the definition of maximum in (38):

(38)   The syllable bearing the word stress is a maximum if it is immediately preceded and followed by unstressed syllables in the same line.

In (34) we observe that maxima project to Gridline 2. All our examples in (16)–(21) have this property, as we see directly. We do not commit

ourselves to a condition imposing it on all *endecasílabo* lines – a condition which turns out to be too restrictive. But examples meeting this
condition are helpful, at this stage, in so far as they wear on their sleeve
the crucial property of Navarro's patterns (16)–(21): they represent the
distribution of Gridline 2 asterisks. Thus, in example (34), Gridline
2 asterisks are projected from syllables 2, 6, and 10, embodying in a
transparent way one of the basic patterns.

We now turn to pattern 4–8–10, exemplified by (20). As in most meters of Romance poetry, the Gridline 0 groups are right-headed (iambs).
On Gridlines 1 and 2, this pattern differs from the previous pattern of
2–6–10 only in that its groups are regularly right-headed, as per (39b,c).

(39)   *Endecasílabo*, pattern 4 – 8 – 10

   a. Gridline 0: starting just at the R edge, insert a R parenthesis,
      form binary groups, heads R.

   b. Gridline 1: starting just at the L edge, insert a L parenthesis,
      form binary groups, heads R.

      i. The last (rightmost) group must be incomplete – unary.

   c. Gridline 2: starting just at the L edge, insert a L parenthesis,
      form binary groups, heads R.

      i. The last (rightmost) group must be incomplete – unary.

   d. Gridline 3: starting just at the L edge, insert a L parenthesis,
      form binary groups, heads L.

These rules build a grid for the line cited in (20) as follows:

(40)   Pattern 4 – 8 – 10

   el asperéza de mis máles quiéro

```
   1 2   3 4 5   6   7     8 9     10
   )* *)  * * )*   * ) *     *)*       *)Δ            0 ⇐
       (*     *   (*         *      (*               1 ⇒
             (*           *      (*               2 ⇒
                       (*       * (               3 ⇒
                          *                       4
```

We have generated grids for two of the six canonical patterns of (32),
2–6–10 and 4–8–10. Two further grids can be derived from these by
deleting the head of the verse, by rule (41).

(41)   Delete the Gridline 0 asterisk of the syllable projecting to the
       head of the verse. (Optional)

Deletion of the Gridline 0 projection of the head of the verse reduces a binary group to unary, whose single asterisk – originally not a head at all – now projects to the head of the verse. Since this asterisk also projects to Gridline 2, it can be occupied by a maximum. A line whose grid is generated by the rules in (39) would normally have a 4–8–10 pattern, which after the application of the deletion rule (41) gives the 4–7–10 pattern as in (42).

(42)   Pattern 4 – 7 – 10

   y se conviérta ado piénse salvárse

```
1   2 3    4    5 6    7   8 9 10
)*  * ) *     * ) Δ *  * )   *   Δ ) *   * ) Δ          0 ⇐
    ( *      *    ( *    *      ( *                      1 ⇒
         ( *           *        ( *                      2 ⇒
              ( *              * (                       3 ⇒
                  *                                      4
```

Three syllables here fail to project (and so are marked with the delta symbol Δ, introduced in chapter 1). One of the internal syllables *-ta* in *convierta* is subject to the rule of non-projection of a vowel before a vowel (3). The other internal syllable *-se* fails to project because its Gridline 0 projection has been deleted.

This brings us to the 4–6–10 pattern. This pattern will be derived from 2–6–10, as exemplified by (34). To get the 4–6–10 pattern we delete an asterisk on Gridline 1. The pattern cannot be derived by deleting an asterisk at Gridline 0 because a deletion rule can only shift a projection within its group, and the projection arising from deletion must shift between distinct Gridline 0 groups.

(43)   Delete the Gridline 1 asterisk projecting to the head of the verse. (Optional)

This rule yields the metrical grid illustrated in (44):

(44)   Pattern 4 – 6 – 10

   las cristalínas águas se cubriéron

```
1     2 34 5   6    7    8 9    10
) *     * ) * * ) *   *  ) *    * ) *    * ) Δ           0 ⇐
     ( Δ    *   ( *      *      ( *                      1 ⇒
          ( *     *             ( *                      2 ⇒
          ( *                  * (                       3 ⇒
              *                                          4
```

The next pattern is 3–6–10. We obtain it in two steps: the deletion rule (43) applies to derive the 4–6–10 pattern and then the other deletion rule (41) applies to this derived pattern to produce the further-derived pattern 3–6–10, as shown in (45).

(45) Pattern 3 – 6 – 10

renovár el placér o la tristúra

```
1  2  3   4     5  6  7  8   9  10
)* *)*   Δ)   * *)* *)  *  *)Δ        0 ⇐
  (Δ *        ( *    *    ( *          1 ⇒
  ( *              *      ( *          2 ⇒
  ( *                     * (          3 ⇒
    *                                  4
```

The 3–6–10 pattern must be derived as in (45) above, and cannot be derived from the metrical grid 4–8–10 of (40). In (46) we illustrate the result of deleting an asterisk on Gridline 0 which projects as the head of a 4–8–10 metrical grid. In (47) we delete an asterisk on Gridline 1, which again projects as the head of a 4–8–10 grid. Neither in (46) nor in (47) could a later asterisk deletion yield a Gridline 2 asterisk in the third position, as required by the 3–6–10 pattern.

(46)
```
1  2  3  4  5  6  7  8  9  10
)* *)* *)* *)* *)  Δ)* *)         0 ⇐
  ( *     *  ( *  *     ( *        1 ⇒
       ( *        *     ( *        2 ⇒
                ( *     * (        3 ⇒
                  *                4
```

(47)
```
1  2  3  4  5  6  7  8  9  10
)* *)* *)* *)* *)* *)* *)         0 ⇐
  ( *     *  ( *   Δ    ( *        1 ⇒
       ( *        *     ( *        2 ⇒
                ( *     * (        3 ⇒
                  *                4
```

To conclude our review of the canonical *endecasílabo* patterns, we show how pattern 1–6–10 is derived from 2–6–10 by means of deletion rule (41), giving the grid in (48).

(48) Pattern 1 - 6 - 10

lléna de vencimiéntos y despójos

```
1  2  3   4  5  6   7  8   9  10
)* Δ) *  *) * *)  * *) *  *)Δ       0 ⇐
( *        *   ( *    *    ( *       1 ⇒
( *              *         ( *       2 ⇒
( *                       * (        3 ⇒
  *                                  4
```

The definition (38) of a maximum in Spanish verse requires it to be flanked by stressless syllables. Therefore the leftmost syllable in a line can never be a maximum, and is always entirely free in a meter whose rules only restrict the distribution of maxima. However, a rule to be given below for the *endecasílabo* makes use of the notion 'stressed syllable', which as it is free of contextual constraints can therefore apply to syllable 1. As a consequence, whether we generate pattern 1–6–10 or not will have consequences. We will come back to this issue once the rule in question is introduced.

Let us now turn to the topic of stress and maxima distribution in the *endecasílabo*. We propose that this meter is subject to two rules, one governing the distribution of maxima and one governing the distribution of stressed syllables. We have defined maxima as (38).

(38)   The syllable carrying lexical stress in a word is a maximum if it is immediately preceded and followed by unstressed syllables in the same line.

Consider now the role of maxima in this meter. It is not the case that we can impose on our six patterns the prima facie reasonable condition (49):

(49)   Syllables projecting to Gridline 2 must be maxima and there are no other maxima in the verse.

Condition (49) is violated, for example, by line (22), repeated below, which has maxima in all five positions that project to Gridline 1, and not only in the three positions that project to Gridline 2.

(22)   tornáron póco a póco en piédra dúra   2, 4, 6, 8, 10

The weaker condition (50) cannot be valid either:

(50)   Syllables projecting to Gridline 2 must be maxima.

Recall that line (23) had maxima on syllables 3 and 10 only:

(23)   enredó sobre nuestros corazónes   3, 10

By (50) there should be one more maximum – in position 6, since this line belongs to the 3–6–10 type. Skeptical readers who are tempted to stress the possessive *nuestro* in this line are directed to other examples with fewer than three maxima, such as (51) or John of the Cross's famous (52).

(51)   con la memória de mi desventúra   4, 10
       'with the memory of my misfortune' Garcilaso, 'Elegía II' line 15

(52)   sino la que en el corazón ardía   8, 10
       'but for the one that in the heart was burning' John of the Cross, 'En una noche oscura' line 15

Both of these lines are also counterexamples to (50).

We propose that *endecasílabo* lines are subject to condition (53):

(53)   Maxima must project to Gridline 1.

Rule (53) allows more than one well-formed implementation for each of the six canonical patterns. Condition (54) below imposes restrictions on this diversity. But (53) has interesting consequences by itself. It excludes the possibility of having maxima in just any of the ten positions in the line. It is also not the case, given (53), that maxima may appear only in the five even-numbered positions. The latter generalization is ruled out by virtue of the fact that 4–7–10 and 3–6–10 are among the six canonical patterns of the *endecasílabo*. It does follow from (53), on the other hand, that there can be at most one maximum in an odd-numbered position in any line. This is because a maximum will appear in an odd-numbered position only if it is subject to the deletion rule targeting Gridline 0 asterisks, and this rule can apply only once. In the 4–7–10 pattern the only odd-numbered syllable projecting to Gridline 1 is syllable 7, while in the 3 6 10 pattern the only odd-numbered syllable projecting to Gridline 1 is syllable 3, and there are no other odd-numbered syllables projecting to Gridline 1 anywhere else in the six patterns – except for syllable 1 in the 1–6–10 pattern, which by definition projects from a syllable which cannot be a maximum. This correctly excludes examples like the construct we gave in (31), repeated here, which violates (53):

(31)   cuando lléga de repénte tu olvído   3, 7, 10   unmetrical

The construct in (29) and any other example having a maximum in position 5, is likewise excluded, i.e., cannot be an *endecasílabo*:

(29)   se me desveló que me hacía mal   5, 8, 10   unmetrical

In addition to the condition on stressed syllables which are maxima, we must *also* impose a requirement on the distribution of other syllables in the line which refers to the three syllables projecting to Gridline 2:

(54)   At most one of the three syllables projecting to Gridline 2 may be unstressed.

Two observations are in order concerning our appeal to the notion 'stressed syllable' instead of 'maximum'. We must use 'stressed syllable' instead of 'maximum' in any statement meant to apply to position 10. Even if we admitted that the last unprojected syllable of a line-final paroxytone – as in, e.g., (51) – allows the penultimate to qualify as a maximum, we still would need to deal with oxytonic lines such as (55), whose last syllable cannot possibly be a maximum by our definition:

(55)   Amór, amór, un hábito vestí

> 'Love, love, a garment I donned' Garcilaso, 'Soneto XXVII' line 1

A straightforward consequence of condition (54) is that there are going to be no *endecasílabo*s with a single stressed syllable. There are indeed no such lines in our corpus, nor have they been pointed out in the literature. There is one exception: Dante (*De vulgari eloquentia* II vii) claims that the single adverb *sovramagnificentissimamente* ('very overmagnificently') constitutes an Italian hendecasyllable. No one should pretend to know better than Dante in this area, and his example certainly does sound like a viable line. It can be replicated in Spanish::

(56)   espiritualizadísimamente

> 'in a very spiritualized fashion' Julio Herrera y Reissig 'Idilio espectral'
> standard spelling (Henríquez Ureña 1944: 811)

To accommodate this type of line we might consider replacing (54) with a requirement to the effect that only one of the syllables projecting to Gridline 3 may be unstressed. There is an alternative, however. Both in Spanish and in Italian, adverbs formed with the suffix *-mente* are, together with certain compounds, the only words having lexical secondary stress (here, on the augmentative *-ísim-*). No unwanted consequences follow, so far as we can see, from taking the notion 'stress' in (54), and indeed in our definition of maximum, to include this restricted set of regular, stable and quite perceptible secondary stresses, which in Spanish are even indicated in conventional spelling.[12] The line in (56) would then conform to (54), being stressed on syllables 7 and 10, which both project to Gridline 2 in the 4–7–10 pattern:

(57)   espiritualizadísimaménte   7, 10

To conclude the discussion of (54) and its consequences, we observe that by generating pattern 1–6–10, as in (48), we commit ourselves to the prediction that lines stressed only in 1 and 6, or in 1 and 10, are legitimate lines. We have encountered no such lines in the period we are considering, and this is not particularly surprising. On the one hand,

---

[12] This is confirmed for Italian by Dante's occasional splitting of line-final *-mente* adverbs: *così quélle caróle differénte- / -ménte danzándo, della sua ricchézza* 'thus, those rings, diversely [diverse/ly] dancing, of their richness' (Paradiso XXIV 16–17). A Spanish parallel is found in Fray Luis de León ('Qué descansada vida' 76–77): *y mientras miseráble- / -ménte se están los ótros abrasándo* 'and while the others sadly [sad/ly] burn'. It is far from uncommon for lines of verse to end in the middle of a word; for additional examples, see sections 1.3, 5.5, and 6.4.1.

lines with the strong enjambment effect required for 1–6 are very infrequent in pre-modern times; Góngora's line (28) is an example, however, although it must be analyzed as an instance of the 3–6–10 pattern with an extra stress on 1. On the other hand, a long sequence of unstressed syllables such as is required for the 1–10 alternative is relatively unusual even in prose, and in Southern Romance poetic traditions it would be perceived as exceedingly prosaic – unless, of course, in the hands of a master like John of the Cross: see his example of 8–10 in (52). Even shorter sequences like the ones needed for lines stressed on 2–10 and 3–10 are difficult to come by in Classical poetry. Still, a variant on Góngora's line with no stress on 3, and thus an instance of 1–6 stress, can be fabricated and does not sound unredeemably bad:

(58)   cuénta la que ensilláste para el que   1, 6

'count what you saddled for the one who' (construct)

We tentatively conclude that pattern 1–6–10 must be generated. Thus, we choose to attribute the absence of clear examples of its consequences to properties of the language – or, as the case may be, to literary preferences – and not to specifically metrical restrictions.

4.4 Italian: the Petrarchan paradigm

The Spanish hendecasyllable is an attempt to reproduce the properties of its Italian model and predecessor, the 'most noble verse' of Dante and Petrarch. The task of determining to what extent the Italian model obeys the same set of rules as its Spanish heir and the Portuguese *decasílabo* of Sá de Miranda and Camões[13] is made initially difficult because of certain properties of Italian and, especially, of Italian poetic diction: in the Italian masters, the number of stresses per line is distinctly higher on average than it is in either Spanish or Portuguese.[14]

---

[13] The absence of references to Catalan in these sections is due to the fact that pre-modern Catalan *decasíl·labs* follow the Gallo-Romance pattern discussed in Chapter 5. For Catalan metrics see Oliva (1992) and references cited there.

[14] An example of a line with 80% stressed syllables is given as (61) below. Navarro Tomás (1973b) compares Garcilaso's Canción IV to Petrarch's 'Nel dolce tempo...' (*Rerum Vulgarium Fragmenta* XXIII), which inspired it, and finds that 22.96% of Petrarch's lines have five 'rhythmical' stresses, versus 11.18% in Garcilaso, whereas Garcilaso has 39.13% three-stress lines, versus 19.26% in Petrarch, and 3.87% two-stress lines versus Petrarch's 0.62% (a single example of stress on 6 and 10, also stressed, 'extrarhythmically', on 7). Also, 63.30% of Petrarch's lines contain 'extrarhythmical' stresses, versus Garcilaso's 23.58%. For the proper interpretation of Navarro's figures, see Mas (1962) and Duffell (1991: chapter 7).

This might help explain why the tradition of metrical-theoretical studies on Italian has tended to confine itself to the study of line length and fixed position stresses. Other constants in the distribution of maxima and word stresses are easily masked by the presence of near or adjacent stressed syllables.

Still, more recent studies in the generative tradition (Nespor and Vogel 1986, Hanson 1996) successfully treat the Italian *endecasillabo* as an iambic pentameter,[15] like its Spanish descendant, and sugggest generalizations which would follow from attributing to it a set of rules largely analogous to the one in section 4.3 above. Indeed, the statistical difference between Italian and Spanish verse instances does not seem to follow from a distinction in verse types. We have not found any hendecasyllable in either language in which the distribution of maxima and/or stressed syllables failed to have a parallel in some canonical period of the other language. Furthermore, important regularities pointed out above for Spanish seem to hold in Italian as well. Thus, in Italian, as in Spanish, we find: (a) no maxima in the fifth position, and (b) no more than one maximum in an odd-numbered position. In this section we observe that generalization (b) should be stated in a more restrictive form for the mainstream Italian tradition originating in Petrarch. This restrictive version follows naturally from adopting for Italian the set of rules proposed in section 4.3 and simply replacing one of them with a slightly different one. The same new rule accounts for a much discussed feature of the Petrarchan paradigm, pointed out already by the early commentators. We start by examining this feature.

It is often said that in Petrarch's *Canzoniere* all *endecasillabi* are stressed on either the fourth or the sixth syllable (or both; see e.g., Beltrami 2002: 187). Menichetti (1993: 407ff.) considers potential counterexamples and concludes that they can all be reinterpreted so as to conform to this generalization. These alternative stress options have been traditionally taken to reveal the existence of two different patterns for the hendecasyllable, the *a maiori* (sixth-position stress) and the *a minori* (fourth-position stress). Our set of patterns in section 4.3 above captures this distinction to a certain extent: in two of those patterns the syllable occupying position 4 projects to Gridline 2, whereas the syllable in position 6 does not; in three of them, on the other hand, it is the syllable in position 6 that projects to Gridline 2 whereas syllable 4 does not. But the fact that we recognize as canonical the pattern 4–6–10,

---

[15] Cf. Jakobson and Valesio (1981: 178): 'the hendecasyllable, i.e., the iambic pentameter'. The idea goes back to Gian Giorgio Trissino, in the 16th century.

in which both syllables project to Gridline 2, indicates that we cannot take the distinction between *a maiori* and *a minori* lines to reflect a basic – as opposed to a derived – property of the meter. We thus reject the usual analysis of lines having maxima on both 4 and 6 as being necessarily ambiguous at the pattern level.

Since in all of our patterns at least one of these syllables projects to Gridline 2, we might conclude that Petrarch stresses each of the three syllables projecting to this Gridline. But he has lines like (59), in which only two of those syllables are stressed:

(59) et da la famigliuóla sbigottíta   6, 10
)*   *) * *) *   *)*   *)* *)*

'and (away) from the dear distressed family' *Rerum Vulgarium Fragmenta* XVI:3

What is clear is that Petrarch's *endecasillabi* are constrained beyond the predictions of condition (54) of section 4.3. This condition allows (at most) one of the syllables projecting to Gridline 2 to be unstressed, which does not exclude syllables 4 or 6. Instead Petrarch employs the stricter condition (60):

(60) Syllables projecting to Gridline 2 which do not project to the head of the verse must bear the word stress.

(60) must mention stress, not maxima, since Petrarch has lines where the stressed syllable in position 4 and/or the stressed syllable in position 6 are flanked by other stressed syllables. Example (61) contains both of these configurations:

(61) fiór', fróndi, hérbe, ómbre, ántri, ónde, áure soávi
)*   *) Δ * Δ *) Δ * Δ *) Δ * *) **)*

'flowers, foliage, grasses, shade, grottos, waves, soft breezes' CCCIII 5

In this line there is stress on positions 1 through 7, as well as 10.

Why should some of the syllables projecting to Gridline 2 have properties which exactly one of them does not have? Recall that the syllable projecting to the head of the verse is singled out by deletion rules. The remaining syllables projecting to Gridline 2 are thus the ones that cannot be affected by deletion.

Given the patterns proposed in section 4.3 above, it follows from (60) that every Petrarchan *endecasillabo* will be regularly stressed on one of the set of syllable positions indicated in (62):

(62)   6–10 (for the patterns 1–6–10 & 2–6–10 & 3–6–10 & 4–6–10)
         4–10 (for the patterns 4–7–10 & 4–8–10)

These two sets of obligatorily stressed syllables describe the traditional *a maiori* and *a minori* variants of the *endecasillabo*, respectively.

Condition (60) also sheds interesting light on the generalization that there is no more than one maximum on an odd-numbered syllable. It has been observed that, within the Petrarchan paradigm, lines with maxima on 3 are also stressed on 6, as shown in (63), whereas lines with maxima on 7 are also stressed on 4, as shown in (64):

(63)   nel commúne dolór s'incominciáro   3, 6, 10
         'had their beginning in the common suffering' Petrarch, III.8

(64)   alcún soccórso di tárdi sospíri   2, 4, 7, 10
         'some assistance from belated sighs' Petrarch, XII.1

Previous treatments of this issue have shown that maxima on position 3 revealed an *a maiori* structure, and maxima on 7 an *a minori* structure. But, to our knowledge, there is no account in the literature of the fact that the stress on 6 (or 4) *must* be present. This clearly follows from (60). The maximum in 3 necessarily corresponds to the head of the verse in the 3–6–10 pattern; otherwise the line would violate condition (53) of section 4.3. This condition requires maxima to project to Gridline 1, and it is only in this pattern that position 3 projects to Gridline 1 – see (45). As a consequence, positions 6 and 10 are required to be stressed, by (60). Similarly, the maximum in 7 necessarily corresponds to the head of the verse in the 4–7–10 pattern, given (53); consequently, (60) requires positions 4 and 10 to be stressed in that case. To repeat: in the Spanish Renaissance meter described in section 4.3 only one maximum could be found in an odd-numbered syllable; in Petrarch's system, as a consequence of (60), it is also the case that whenever such a maximum is found, all the remaining syllables projecting to Gridline 2 bear stress. This includes syllable 4, in the case of a maximum in 7, and syllable 6, in the case of a maximum in 3.

We conclude that Petrarch's *endecasillabi* conform to the set of rules we proposed for Spanish in section 4.3, except tht the condition (54) is replaced by (60) above.[16] What we have called the Petrarchan paradigm,

---

[16] A line stressed on 4 and 10 only is not a counterexample: *Né di Lucrétia mi meravigliái* 'I did not even marvel at Lucretia' (CCLXII 9). It can be an instance of the 4–8–0 or the 4–7–0 pattern in which the head syllable is legitimately unstressed. The same would be true, mutatis mutandis, of a line stressed only on 6 and 10.

characterized by (60) and by a restriction on line ends to be discussed below, is of great historical importance. It represents the norm for many Italian poets before the 20th century, and is even exemplified by most of the *endecasillabo* lines written by poets in Italy in the 20th century. It was also adopted by a number of poets outside Italy, including representatives of the Baroque and Neoclassical schools in Portugal and Spain.

Dante, writing earlier, uses a meter whose rules and conditions are less strict, quite possibly equivalent to the ones proposed for Spanish in section 4.3. Although most of his lines are compatible with the 'Petrarchan' (60), he has some in which neither syllable 4 nor syllable 6 are stressed:

(65)   la vípera che Melanési accámpa   2, 8, 10

   'the viper that makes the Milanese set camp' Dante, *Purg.* VIII.80

In his poetry, as later in Garcilaso and Camões, we also find *endecasillabo* lines ending in either proparoxytones, paroxytones, or oxytones:

(66)   nón da piráti, nón da génte argólica

   'not caused by pirates, not caused by Greeks' Dante, *Inf.* XXVIII.84

   Nel mézzo del cammín di nostra víta

   'In the middle of the journey of our life' Dante, *Inf.* I.1

   sí, ch'amendúe hánno un sólo orizzòn

   'in such a way that they both have a single horizon' Dante, *Purg.* IV.70

This conforms to the line-end non-projection rule in (9) of section 4.2. Again, Petrarch's system, and the system adopted by many later Italian poets, is stricter. All of Petrarch's lines are paroxytonic (ending with a stressed followed by an unstressed syllable).[17] Therefore, the non-projection rule (3) is not applicable to Petrarch, and his version of the Gridline 0 rule must be as in (67):

(67)   Gridline 0: starting at the R edge one asterisk in, insert a R parenthesis, form binary groups, heads R.

   a.   The ungrouped asterisk must not project from a monosyllable.

Petrarch generally avoids this type of line, however. Also, recall that we treat adverbs ending in -*mente* as having two metrically relevant stresses. This takes care of apparent counterexamples such as con *sospíri soàveménte rótti* 'with softly broken sighs' (CCXIII 13).

[17] With the exception of two oxytones (CV 16, 19) in the peculiar context of his one *frottola*, a then-popular humorous form.

4.4.1 Dante's eleventh syllable

Dante, on the other hand, admits monosyllables in the eleventh position
of the line, even in cases which are very rare in later poetry.[18]

(68)   Móssimi; e'l dúca mio si mósse per li
       luóghi spedíti ...

   'I started walking, and my guide walked along the / unblocked paths...'
   Dante, *Purg.* XX.4–5

(69)   détto mi fú; e da Beatríce: Di', di'

   'was said to me, and by Beatrice: Speak, speak' Dante, *Par.* V.122

The eleventh-position *li* in (68) is unstressed whereas, more unexpect-
edly, the eleventh-position *dí* in (69) is a stressed monosyllable (a verb).
Both line ends are treated as equivalent to paroxytonic disyllables, and
in fact rhyme accordingly: with *mérli* 'battlements' and *annídi* '(you)
nest', respectively. In fact, for Dante, monosyllables need to be explicitly allowed in such a way that clause (b) of the line-end non-projection
rule (9) can apply in (69). On the other hand, not all line-final monosyllables are treated in this way by Dante; thus, line (70) has a total of
ten syllables:

(70)   Qual è colui che cosa innanzi sè

   'As remains one who, in front of himself' Dante, *Purg.* VII.9

Dante thus replaces rule (9) with the rule (71).

(71)   Dante's rule of line end non-projection

   a. Optionally, if the rightmost word in a line is a monosyllable,
      it may be left unprojected.

   b. If the rightmost word in a line is a polysyllable and contains
      a stressed syllable, do not project any syllables to the right
      of the stressed syllable.

   c. If the rightmost word in a line is a polysyllable and does not
      contain a stressed syllable, do not project any syllables to
      the right of the initial syllable of the rightmost word.

The resulting rule is complex (i.e., longer) in comparison with that of
later poets, which might possibly explain the fact that it was not generally adopted.

---

[18] In this line, as in many others, the possessive *mio* is treated as a monosyllable.

4.5 Spanish *arte mayor* as loose anapaestic meter

The so-called *verso de arte mayor* is the dominant learned meter in the Spanish language between the late 14th century and the middle of the 16th century, after which it was displaced by the Italianate *endecasílabo*. Its most accomplished practitioner is the poet Juan de Mena (1411–1456), whose masterpiece is the poem *El Laberinto de Fortuna* ('Fortune's Labyrinth'), comprising 2376 lines in eight-line stanzas. Like many of our predecessors, we study here the variant of *arte mayor* that is exemplified by this poem (in Kerkhof's 1997 edition).

Arte mayor has puzzled metricians for quite a long time (as discussed by Duffell (1999) and references cited there). In a classic study, Clarke (1964: 51) described it as follows:[19]

It may be roughly defined as a verse whose time measure is 6+6 syllables, and whose basic pattern is: (u) s u u S (u) | (u) s u u S (u). The caesura is movable between stresses, the secondary stresses are not absolutely fixed in required presence or position, and the unstressed syllables in parentheses are not absolutely fixed except that at the caesura at least one of the unstressed syllables is usually present.

That the syllabic measure is only rough can be seen by comparing the nine-syllable line (72) and the thirteen-syllable line (73):

(72)   óras silvándo como dragón
       'now hissing like a dragon' line 1965

(73)   de los que demuéstran y de los demostrádos
       'of those who reveal and of those revealed' line 1028

Lines can have any number of syllables between nine and thirteen. As for Clarke's 'basic stress pattern' of four stresses to the line, it is indeed true for many lines, such as (74):

(74)   los másteles fuértes en cálma temblávan
       'the strong masts quavered on a calm sea' line 1317

Lines, however, can have as few as two lexical stresses, which is close to the minimum that could be expected for a phrase of this length in a language like Spanish:

(75)   a la mendácia de la adulación
       'to the mendacity of adulation' line 750

Furthermore, the notion of a 'movable' caesura is far from clear. Still, a

---

[19]   Clarke's symbols are replaced by u for unstressed syllable, and S and s for syllables bearing primary and secondary stress, respectively; caesura is marked by the | bar.

good many scholars, starting in the modern period with Foulché-Delbosc (1902), have argued that the meter of *arte mayor* depends crucially on the properties of its hemistichs, typically seen as variants on the pattern [(x) stressed unstressed unstressed stressed (y)].

One consequence of this approach, which has been discussed extensively (Lázaro Carreter 1976; see Duffell 1999: 76–78, 83–85), is that it tends to imply that in this meter many words have a specially reassigned (irregular) stress pattern, including a stress on stressless items (Domínguez Caparrós 2001). In this kind of account, the quite common paroxytone *firmézas* in (76) is supposed to be read *fírmezas*, with reassigned initial stress, and the article *la* in (77) would be treated as if it were tonic (i.e., stressed):

(76)   tus grándes discórdias, tus firmézas pócas,
       'your great contradictions, your steadfastness scant' line 11

(77)   tánto que el víso de la crïatúra
       'so much so that the sight of the creature' line 117

Some discrepancy is to be expected between the pronunciation of learned words in Mena's time and circle and the later norm, and it is true that 15th-century writers aimed at a special, elevated style. But the degree of discrepancy thus postulated is very high. *Arte mayor* was in favor for quite a long time, hence not necessarily linked to the general aesthetics of Mena's period, and was also sufficiently popular to have been preserved for centuries in orally transmitted poetry within the Sephardic communities of the Eastern Mediterranean.[20]

We take the opposite tack here from the standard view: it is not the meter of *arte mayor* that determines word stress, but word stress that (partially) determines the metrical analysis – more specifically, the particular shape that the meter takes in each line. A meter in which word stress is taken into account while building the metrical grid is a loose meter, in contrast to the *endecasílabo*, which is a strict meter. As in other loose meters, the non-iterative rule (79a) below inserts a parenthesis next to every maximum in the line. We define maximum as in (38) above, repeated here.

(38)   The syllable bearing the word stress in a word is a maximum if
       it is immediately preceded and followed by unstressed syllables
       in the same line.

---

[20] This has been documented by J. Domínguez Caparrós in recent unpublished work. *Arte mayor* was still used by Miguel de Cervantes (1547–1616), alongside the Italianate meters (Domínguez Caparrós 2002).

By comparison to some other loose meters, the degree of variation in the total number of syllables per line is relatively modest in *arte mayor*. We suggest that this is because in this meter there are no ungrouped syllables within the line, which follows from assuming that the non-iterative rule (79a) inserts a parenthesis with the same (R) orientation as the ones inserted by the non-iterative rule (78). The iterative rules for *arte mayor* are stated in (79), where we interpret *arte mayor* as a loose anapaestic tetrameter.

(78)   Insert a R parenthesis on Gridline 0 after an asterisk projecting from a maximum.

(79)   a. Gridline 0: starting ⟨ just / one syllable in ⟩ at the R edge, insert a R parenthesis, form ternary groups, heads R.

   i. Either of the two options in angled brackets may be chosen. The skipped syllable must not bear the word stress.

   ii. Incomplete groupings are permitted.

   b. Gridline 1: starting just at the R edge, insert a R parenthesis, form binary groups, heads R.

   c. Gridline 2: starting just at the R edge, insert a R parenthesis, form binary groups, heads R.

Observe that, as pointed out in section 4.2 above, the line-end non-projection rule (9) does not apply in *arte mayor*. Evidence for this is the complete absence of proparoxytonic lines in the *Laberinto*. Mena only has paroxytones and oxytones at line end, as in (80) and (81), respectively. His avoidance of proparoxytones in that position is made more significant by the well-known fact that he positively loves using them elsewhere.[21]

A sample scansion is shown in (80). At Gridline 0, four parentheses are inserted by the non-iterative rule, after the four maxima. The iterative rule inserts parentheses, but without creating any other groups (because the parentheses are inserted where there are already parentheses).

---

[21] We have seen elsewhere that non-projection is not usually found in loose meters (though there are occasional examples). In our discussion of Hopkins's English verse in section 3.5.2 we suggested that his 'Sprung Rhythm' has had limited success because it is a loose meter with non-projection; see also our comment on the absence of the Arabic *ramal*-type non-projecting meter from the loose meters of circle 2 (section 7.6). On the other hand, the Latin saturnian meter discussed in this chapter (section 4.7) is a loose meter with non-projection.

(80)   de sábios valiéntes loárte podría

```
 *  * ))*    * * ))  *  * * ))*  *  * ))*   0 ⇐
  ) *         * )           * )        1 ⇐
  ) *                       * )        2 ⇐
                            *          3
```

'I could praise you for brave, wise men' line 997

In lines with four maxima like this one, the iterative rules have a vacuous effect because the non-iterative rule will be able to form all four groups. However, in lines with fewer than four maxima, the iterative rules have an important effect of forming ternary groups within the line. In (81) we give examples in which the Gridline 0 iterative rule is responsible for forming one of the four groups.

(81)   Aristótiles cérca del pádre Platón

```
)* * * *))** * *)) * * *)) * * * )
```

'Aristotle beside Father Plato' line 939

suplíd cobdiciándo mis inconveniéntes

```
 *  * )) *  * * )) *  * * ) *  * * )) *
```

'kindly make up for my shortcomings' line 48

ermáno de aquél buén archéro de Róma

```
 *  * ))*  △ *  * )  *  *  *))* *  * )) *
```

'brother of that fine archer of Rome' line 698

y los qu'en tu ruéda quexósos fallámos

```
 *  * )    *  *  * ))*  * *)) * * * ))*
```

'and those unhappy ones we find on your wheel' line 12

Where maxima are less than three syllables apart, the non-iterative rule will generate an incomplete group within the line as in (82). Where maxima are separated by more than two syllables in something other than a multiple of three, the iterative rule will have the effect of generating an incomplete group as in (83).

(82)   por úso sólo de la su riquéza

```
 *  * )* *))* * * ) * * * ))*
```

'just to make use of their riches' line 1790

(83)   aquésta comiénça de proçedér

```
 *  * ))* * * *) * *) * * * )
```

'this one can be traced back to' line 373

Line-internal unary groups cannot be generated by the non-iterative rule (78) alone, since adjacent stresses are not maxima. But unary Gridline 0 groups can in principle be generated by the application of the iterative rule (79a), as shown in (84). This scansion, however, presents a problem, as it makes the line a pentameter, rather than a tetrameter.

(84)   tan bien en las águas bívas como muértas

    *   *))* * *) * *)*) * *   *))*

'in water with tides and water without' line 403

Not only are there the wrong number of Gridline 0 groups in (84), but this configuration would project Gridline 1 asterisks from two consecutive syllables. This gives rise to a conflict that is avoided in *arte mayor*, and to that end we propose that this meter is subject to readjustment rule (85), which deletes a parenthesis to the right of a single-asterisk group.

(85)   On Gridline 0, delete a parenthesis to the right of an asterisk, if that asterisk has a right parenthesis to its left.

The application of the parenthesis deletion rule to (84) derives (86), which has the requisite four Gridline 0 groups:

(86)   tan bien en las águas bívas como muértas

    *   *))* * *) * *)* * *   *))*

In (86) we have a group consisting of four asterisks. Groups of this size are very rare in any metrical representation (and we have no other examples in this book). This is because iterative rules apply on every Gridline, and iterative rules group asterisks into groups of at most three asterisks. However, there is no reason in principle why a larger group is not possible; we repeat in (87) the definition of group from Chapter 1, and note that this definition sets no upper limit on the size of a group.

(87)   A left parenthesis groups the asterisks on its right; a right parenthesis groups the asterisks on its left. Asterisks that are neither to the right of a left parenthesis, nor to the left of a right parenthesis are ungrouped.

Thus, a rule which undoes the effect of the iterative rules, such as rule (85), would have the effect of permitting groups larger than three. A further example of the application of the deletion rule (85) is given in the thirteen-syllable line (88). We have put a line through the parenthesis that is deleted by rule (85).

(88)   de los que demuestran y de los demostrados

   * *)   * *   *) *+ *   * *) * *   *))*   0 ⇐
) *   *)   *   *)   1 ⇐
) *   *)   2 ⇐
                                          *   3

'of those who reveal and of those revealed' line 1028

Compare (88) with (89), which shows the grid for a nine-syllable line, which is one of the shortest lines in the poem:

(89)   óras silvándo como dragón

```
*)*   *  *)  *  *)  *   * *)              0 ⇐
)*        *)     *        *)              1 ⇐
     )*              *)              2 ⇐
                      *                   3
```

'now hissing like a dragon' line 1965

As it stands, our theory allows for lines ranging between sixteen and seven syllables. Sixteen-syllable lines would be lines of three Gridline 0 groups which contain four asterisks, preceded by a ternary Gridline 0 group, and with a 'feminine' ending. (Leftmost Gridline 0 groups are predicted never to be quaternary.) Seven-syllable lines would be 'masculine' lines composed of three binary groups preceded by a unary group. This range of variation is reduced by the following conditions on the rules applying to Gridline 0:

(90)   a. The parenthesis deletion rule (85) may apply only once in a line of verse.

       b. The iterative rule (79a) must insert at least one non-final parenthesis on Gridline 0.

Parenthesis insertion by (90b) can be vacuous (shown in the lines which have a bold parenthesis inserted by the non-iterative rule immediately followed by a non-bold parenthesis inserted by iterative rules): parentheses are inserted by the iterative rules but have no effect. For the exact import of condition (90a), beyond the fact that it rules out the presence of two or more quaternary Gridline 0 groups per line, see footnote 22.

This restriction limits line lengths to between eight and fourteen syllables. It would be possible to propose restrictions ensuring that the numbers coincide with the thirteen-syllable maximum and nine-syllable minimum actually found in the poem, but we are inclined to think that the absence of these two extremes from the *Laberinto* is not strictly speaking a property of its meter.

Below we modify actual lines to provide examples of the two non-occurring scansions we are allowing. On the basis of (91), which has four ternary Gridline 0 groups followed by a skipped syllable, we construct (92) by creating one quaternary Gridline 0 group. On the basis of (93), which has three binary Gridline 0 groups and one quaternary, we derive (94) which has one unary, two binary, and one ternary:

(91)   do verédes los grándes señóres e réyes

```
) * * *))*   *   *)) *   *  *))* * *))*
```

'where you will see the great lords and kings' line 1779

(92)   do verédes los grándes señóres e los réyes
)＊　＊ ＊))＊　＊　　＊))　＊　＊ ＊)＊+＊　＊　　＊))＊
'where you will see the great lords and the kings' (construct)

(93)   verás el ótro d'éssa condiçión
＊ ＊)＊ ＊)＊　＊) ＊+＊　＊ ＊)
'you will see the other one of this type' line 558

(94)   viéras ótro d'éssa nación
＊)＊　＊) ＊　＊))＊　＊ ＊)
'you will see another one of this nation' (construct)

Pending more extensive research on other *arte mayor* poems, we assume that the constructed lines are metrical.

We note also that nine-syllable lines like (89) above are never 'feminine' in the *Laberinto*. In other words, we do not have the structure in (95), which, like that in (94), can be interpreted as having eight grouped syllables.

(95)   óras silvándo tánto drágo
＊)＊　＊　＊)　＊　＊)＊　＊)＊
'now so many dragons hissing' (constructed line)

The absence of fourteen-syllable lines, as in (92), correlates with a distinct preference for incomplete first Gridline 0 groups – but this preference is far from absolute: see (91) above and line 939, quoted in (81). The absence of shorter lines stressed on the eighth syllable, such as (94) and (95), might be due to the poet's reluctance to blur the lines between *arte mayor* and shorter, more popular meters, collectively called *arte menor*.

We now seek to capture the features of this meter that have led researchers to feel that it was composed of two distinct, clearly marked hemistichs (see Piera 1980: 4.5; Duffell 1999, 2007). We attribute those features to condition (96):

(96)   Syllables projecting to Gridline 2 must bear the word stress.

That these syllables need not be maxima is clear from lines like line 698 (in (81)), or the line in (97), where the syllable projecting to Gridline 2 is *fué-*, in the first instance of *fuégos*, which is adjacent to the stressed monosyllable *dár* and so is not a maximum.

(97)   ca puéde dár fuégos e fuégos robár

```
 *   * )* *   * ) * *   *)* * * )      0 ⇐
 ) *          * )       *       * )      1 ⇐
 ) *          * )       *       * )      2 ⇐
                                *        3
```

'for it can give fire and steal fire' line 360

One consequence of the requirement that syllables projecting to Gridline 2 must bear the word stress is that the final or penultimate syllable must have word stress: thus, as pointed out above, lines can only end in either a paroxytonic or an oxytonic word, including a stressed monosyllable.[22]

Our definition of maximum implies that monosyllables can be maxima in *arte mayor*, just as in English loose meters. Had we restricted maxima to polysyllables, the resulting scansions (i.e., with different applications of the non-iterative rule) would result in a violation of (96). Consider the incorrect scansion in (98), which disregards monosyllabic maxima, and results in unstressed possessive *tu* projecting to Gridline 2.

(98)   menór ví tu fín que nón ví tu médio   incorrect scansion

```
 * ) *   * * ) *   *   * ) * *   * )* *   0 ⇐
 ) *        * )       *       * )         1 ⇐
 ) *        * )               * )         2 ⇐
                             *            3
```

'I saw your end be less than your middle' line 1578

The correct scansion is as in (99), which conforms to (96):

(99)   menór ví tu fín que nón ví tu médio

```
 * * ) * * * *)   * * ) * * * *)*         0 ⇐
 ) *        ) * )       *       * )        1 ⇐
            *                   * )        2 ⇐
                               *           3
```

Below are two more examples of lines in which a monosyllabic maximum correctly prevents the iterative rule from creating a ternary group in the second foot from the right, and thus from shifting leftwards the preceding Gridline 1 head:

---

[22] An example of a line ending in a stressed monosyllable is line 554: *por que las veas entramas a dos* 'in order that you see them both'. Another consequence of this condition is that it rules out one of the cases in which (90a) overgenerates. (90a) permits the structure) *) whenever the parenthesis deletion rule has already applied, hence, potentially, to the left of both internal Gridline 0 groups:

(i) * * *) *) * * *) * [Deleted parenthesis] * * *)

(ii) * * *) *) * * *) * [Deleted parenthesis] * * *) * * *)

But a unary foot to the left of the second foot from the right, as in (i), would be stressless: it can only be created by the iterative rule if it is preceded by a maximum. Therefore (i) would be a violation of (96). Configuration (ii) is of course excluded as having one foot too many.

(100) ví más contra mí venír al encuéntro

      *   *)   *   *   * **)** * *))* *   * **)** *

      'I also saw coming towards me' line 269

(101) Itália, la quál del puéblo románo

      * * **)**)* *   * **)**   *   * **))** * * * **))** *

      'Italy, which by the Roman people' line 367

4.5.1 Unmetrical lines in the Laberinto

The following lines from the *Laberinto* are unmetrical by these rules:

(102) que de lo ganádo súfre méngua tánta

      *   *) * * * **)** * * **)** *   * **)**   * * **))** *

      'which suffers so much want from what it has earned' line 791

(103) de párte del Áustro vímos tóda Grécia

      *   * **))** * *   * **)**   * * **)** *   * **)** *   * **))** *

      'from the southern part we saw all of Greece' line 354

Both lines are structurally identical, which suggests that they might reflect some further rules or conditions. We do not pursue this matter, however, given the scant evidence. The following line is also deemed unmetrical, as a consequence of the inclusion of monosyllables among potential maxima:

(104) rámo ningúno nón avrá menestér

      *) *   *   * **)** * * **)** * * **))** * * *)

      'will have no need for any bough' line 224

Non is almost certainly stressed (see *no* at line end in line 1848). Some inconsistency on the part of the poet is to be expected. There was, to our knowledge, no explicit formulation of the rules, only part of an oral tradition which the poet was expected to acquire, interpret, and improve on from practice. On the other hand, for the text to be metrical by our rules it is not necessary to amend it by introducing a large number of hiatuses, as is done in Kerkhof's edition (e.g., *superïor* in line 350, *Retia, Germania la superior* 'Rhetia, Upper Germania').

4.6 Loose anapaestic meter in Galician-Portuguese *cantigas*

The first large corpus of Romance lyrical poetry from the Iberian Peninsula is written in Galician-Portuguese, a fairly close predecessor to both Portuguese and present-day Galician, or Galego, in Northwestern Spain. Between the late 12th and the 14th century this language played in the Peninsula (outside of Catalonia) a role comparable to that of Provençal elsewhere as the generally accepted medium for the lyric. Galician-Portuguese poetry was collected in *Cancioneiros* (Songbooks) in the late 13th and 14th centuries. The most distinctive are the brief, parallelistic women's love lyrics called *cantigas de amigo* ('male friend songs').

Cancioneiros exhibit considerable metrical diversity (Tavani 1967), reflecting, among other things, various stages of metrical and linguistic regularization. Within the Romance domain, their most peculiar formal characteristic is a frequent use of ternary meters, and this is the only point we touch on here. Consider the *cantiga de amigo* by Nuno Fernandes Torneol of which we reproduce the first stanza in (105):[23]

(105)   Levád', amígo, que dormídes as manhãas frías;
         tódalas áves do múndo d'amór dizían:
         léda m'ánd'éu.

> 'Wake up, friend, you who sleep in the cold mornings / All the birds in the world are speaking of love / *Happy go I.*' Nuno Fernandes Torneol

Scholars have occasionally expressed doubts as to how closely the standard lineation given to *cancioneiro* poetry reflects the actual meters (e.g., Pimpão 1959: 99–102; cf. Clarke 1964). Here we have one more example of a poem whose regularity, we would claim, is masked by its traditional written presentation. We propose that lines should be divided; thus we split 'line 2' of (105) into two verses, each with its own grid, as in (106):[24]

(106)   tódalas áves do múndo
         *) * * *)*   *   *) *
         *   *   *
         d'amór dizían
         *   *) * *)*
         *   *

---

[23] Text in Magán *et al.* (1996), also in *MedDB, Base de datos da lírica profana galego-portuguesa*, http://www.cirp.es/med/meddb.html. We have not eliminated spelling inconsistencies, which are transparent. All the reader needs to note is that the sign ã is meant to represent a stressed [a] followed by the consonant [n], at this stage of the language. We consider only the text of the *cantiga* stanzas. In general, *cantiga* refrains, which can have one or several lines, may differ metrically from the main text, with which they also may or may not rhyme. One-line refrains are by their very nature compatible with several metrical analyses.

[24] In section 5.6 we similarly analyze the French *Chanson de Roland*.

In other words, every one of the lines in (105) is made up of two sub-lines: a trimeter followed by a dimeter. In this example there are ternary groups in the trimeter and binary groups in the dimeter; we observe below that this does not reflect a necessary property of the meter.

The units resulting from the proposed bipartition behave differently within the parallelistic structure of the poem. In (107) we give the first four stanzas:

(107)   (Levád', amígo, que dormídes) 1 (as manhãas frías;) Aa
          (tódalas áves do múndo) 2 (d' amór dizían) Ba

          (Levád', amígo, que dormíde') 1 (-las frías manhãas;) Ab
          (tódalas áves do múndo) 2 (d' amór cantávan) Bb

          (Tóda-las áves do múndo) 2 (d' amór dizíam;) Ba
          (do meu amór e do vóss') 3 (en mént' avían) Ca

          (Tóda-las áves do múndo) 2 (d' amór cantávan;) Bb
          (do meu amór e do vóss') 3 (í enmentávan) Cb

> '[Wake up, friend, you who sleep] [in the cold mornings] / [All the birds in the world] [are speaking of love] // [Wake up, friend, you who sleep] [in the mornings cold] / [All the birds in the world] [are singing of love] // [All the birds in the world] [are speaking of love] / [It's my love and yours] [they have in mind] // [All the birds in the world] [are singing of love] / [It's my love and yours] [they mention (there)]'

Trimeters – the left-hand constituents – are repeated according to the pattern 1-2, 1-2, 2-3, 2-3. The pattern continues as 3-4, 3-4, 4-5 and 4-5. Dimeters, on the other hand, have two variants each, a and b, as in 'are speaking of love' (Ba) and 'are singing of love' (Bb); their pattern is Aa-Ba, Ab-Bb, Ba-Ca, Bb-Cb, which continues as Ca-Da, Cb-Db, Da-Ea and Db-Eb. These contrasting patterns of repetition are clear evidence for the constituents bracketed in (107).

We saw in (106) above that the first line appears to be strict anapestic, whereas the second could be in strict iambs. We will pursue a different analysis; leaving till later the question of how these parentheses are inserted, we offer an alternative analysis as in (106), where Gridline 0 heads project from syllables bearing the word stress. This yields for 'line 1' of (105) a very different configuration, including two binary Gridline 0 groups in the trimeter and a ternary Gridline 0 group in the dimeter:

(108)   Levád', amígo, que dormídes
           * *)   * *)*   * *   *)*
           *   *   *

as manhãas frías
)∗   ∗   ∗)∗   ∗)∗
        ∗   ∗

Note also the four Gridline 0 asterisks in one of the groups in (108). These are all features of a loose meter.

We suggest, indeed, that this *cantiga* is in loose anapaests, more specifically that it obeys the same basic rules and conditions we gave above for *arte mayor*. That is, by (78) a right parenthesis is inserted after a maximum (defined in (38)); ternary right-headed groups are then formed by an iterative rule which inserts right parentheses starting from the right edge; by rule (85), a right parenthesis is deleted when it follows an asterisk which is immediately preceded by another right parenthesis. Finally, groups at higher Gridlines are also right-headed and formed starting from the right, but they are binary. The following scansions are based on these rules, and represent all the possibilities instantiated in this poem:[25]

(109) Levád', amígo, que dormídes

∗ ∗**)**   ∗   ∗)∗+̸   ∗   ∗   ∗))∗
   ∗)   ∗   ∗)
) ∗   ∗   ∗)
                             ∗

as manhãas frías
)∗   ∗   ∗**)**∗   ∗**)**)∗
) ∗   ∗)
            ∗

'line 1' split into two verses

(110) tódalas áves do múndo
∗) ∗ ∗   ∗**))**∗   ∗   ∗ **))** ∗

d'amór dizían
∗   ∗**)** ∗ ∗**)**∗
'line 2' split into two verses

(111) do meu amór e do vóss'
∗)   ∗   ∗   ∗ **))**∗   ∗   ∗)

en mént'avían
∗   ∗**)** ∗ ∗**)**∗
'line 8' split into two verses

(112) do meu amór e do vóss'
∗)   ∗   ∗   **))**∗   ∗   ∗)

[25] In the first quoted line the crossed-out parenthesis is deleted by rule (85). We have considered several alternatives for stress assignment to the words of this poem: they were all compatible with the proposed metrical rules.

í enmentávam
)   *   *))*
'line 11' split into two verses

(113)   vós lhi tolhéstes os rámos
)   * *))* *   *))*

en que pousávan
*)   * * *))*

'you took away the branches / on which they perched' 'line 17' split into
two sub-lines

(114)   e lhis secástes as fóntes
   *) *   * *))* *   *)) *

en que bevían
*)   * * *))*

'and dried up the fountains / from which they drank' 'line 20' split into
two sub-lines

As is typically the case in individual *cantigas*, the brevity of the poem
and the frequency of lines having parallel scansions suggest a cautious
approach to more fine-grained aspects of their rules. In this case we
cannot be sure whether the meter is subject to condition (90), which
restricts the number of four-asterisk and two-asterisk groups per line in
arte mayor. A comparison with some other poems suggests that this may
indeed be a general condition on this type of loose ternary meter, but
we prefer to leave the matter open here. The one remaining condition of
arte mayor is (96), which requires syllables projecting to Gridline 2 to
be stressed; this condition must be replaced for the *cantigas* by (115):

(115)   The syllable projecting to the head of the verse must bear the
   word stress.

This analysis shows that the much-debated issue of the origins of *arte
mayor* is certain to be clarified by more detailed study of the metrical
make-up of both *arte mayor* and *cancioneiro* poetry, as a number of
scholars have suggested.[26] It is clear, at any rate, that the meter of *arte
mayor* is a loose ternary meter of a kind that was already present in
Galician-Portuguese poetry. As we will see next, the same type of meter
can be found already in the saturnian verse of Latin.

---

[26] The reader is referred to Duffell (1993–94, 2007: 136ff.) for a critical review of the
hypotheses that have been put forward. As Duffell (2007: 139) reminds us, the
Marqués de Santillana (1398–1458), a poet and 'the first Spanish literary critic',
believed that *arte mayor* had originated in Galicia.

4.7 A note on the saturnian verse of Latin

In this section we show that the meter of the Latin saturnian verse (3rd–2nd century BCE) is a loose ternary meter, specifically a loose dactylic meter, which differs only minimally from the loose anapaestic meters discussed in sections 4.5 and 4.6. Because more than 1500 years separate the times when these two meters were used, we consider it highly unlikely that the meter of the *cantigas* and the *arte mayor* was in any way influenced by that of the saturnian. We think rather that the two meters are independent original inventions, and that their similarity is due to the fact that they are special cases of the grouping theory that underlies all meters.

The surviving corpus of saturnian verse consists of less than 200 lines. Of these, 140 were studied by Mercado (2005) in an unpublished paper that employed a version of the theory of this book.[27] Our brief discussion is based on Mercado's data, but deviates from his analyses in a number of important details. Mercado's (and hence our) data include Livius Andronicus's metrical translation of the *Odyssey*, Gnaeus Naevius's *Carmen belli Poenici*, various inscriptions including 24 verses from the epitaphs of four Cornelii Scipiones, and lines from a number of miscellaneous sources.

Like in most Latin poetry, word-final vowels and word-final vowel + nasal sequences are not projected onto Gridline 0 if the next word is vowel-initial. We state this condition formally in (116).

(116)   Project an asterisk onto Gridline 0 from each syllable in the verse except for word-final vowels, or vowel + nasal sequences, in position before a word beginning with a vowel.

In the saturnian meter, syllables bearing the word stress in polysyllabic words are maxima. The class of maxima in the saturnian is thus somewhat different from the class of maxima in the *cantigas* and the *arte mayor*. This is formally stated in (117).

(117)   The syllable bearing word stress in a polysyllabic word is a maximum.

Maxima are subject to rule (118), which is ordered before the iterative rules of parenthesis insertion (119) that construct the metrical grid.

(118)   Insert a L parenthesis to the left of a Gridline 0 asterisk which projects from a maximum.

---

[27] See also Mercado (2006). We thank Dr. Mercado for permitting us to use his data for this study; he is not responsible for any shortcomings or errors in this section.

The asterisk sequence with parentheses inserted by (118) is subject to the iterative rules in (119), which complete the generation of the metrical grid of the saturnian line.

(119) a. Gridline 0: starting just at the L edge, insert a R parenthesis, form ternary groups, heads L.

  i. Incomplete groups are admitted.

  b. Gridline 1: starting just at the R edge, insert a R parenthesis, form ternary groups, heads R.

  i. The last (leftmost) group may be incomplete.

  c. Gridline 2: starting just at the R edge, insert a R parenthesis, form binary groups, heads R.

We have illustrated application of these rules with the examples (120)–(126), with partial grids in some cases.

(120) res divas edicit praedicit castus
```
) *  (* *  *)(* *    *)(* * (*  *              0 ⇒
   *        *        *      *                  1
```
'The virtuous man talks and preaches about sacred things' GN 32

(121) immortales mortales si foret fas flere
```
)*    *  (* *    *)(* *   *)(* *   * ) (* *     0 ⇒
      * )        *        *         * )        1 ⇐
      ) *                           *          2 ⇐
                                    *          3
```
'If it were permitted for immortals to shed tears for mortals' GN 1

(122) malum dabunt Metelli Naevio poetae
```
)(* *   (*  *     *)(* * (*  ** ) *(*  *        0 ⇒
   *     *        *    *    *      *            1
```
'The Metelli will punish the poet Naevius', Metelli

(123) sancta puer Saturni filia regina
```
)(*    * ( **   *)(*   *(* ** ) *(*  *          0 ⇒
   *        *      *      *      *              1
```
'Sacred child of Saturn, royal daughter' Andr. 12

(124) honos fama virtusque gloria atque ingenium
```
)(* * (*  *  *)(*    *)(* *∆ *)   ∆* (* ** )    0 ⇒
   *    *      *       *           *            1
```
'Honor, good repute and virtue, glory and genius' Scip 3.3

(125)   obliti sunt Romae loquier lingua Latina

```
)*( * *  *)  ( *   *  ( *   **)( *    *  ( *  * *)          0 ⇒
        *       *)      *      *      *)                   1 ⇐
              ) *                     *)                   2 ⇐
                                       *                   3
```

'They have forgotten to speak the Latin language in Rome' GN 4

(126)   nexebant multa inter se flexu nodorum dubio

```
) *( * *     ( *  Δ *( *   *  ( *  *  *)( *  *   ( * **)    0 ⇒
   ) *        *       *)      *       *      *)            1 ⇐
            ) *                               *)          2 ⇐
                                              *            3
```

'They tied among themselves a confusing winding of knots' Andr. 20

If Gridline 1 has complete groups, then the line will be a hexameter
as in (126); in Mercado's list of of one hundred and forty lines, there
are, according to our scansions, nine hexameter lines (Mercado's sections
3.1 and 4.3). The Gridline 1 rule (119bi) allows the leftmost group to
be incomplete. If the incomplete group has two asterisks, the line will
be a pentameter as in (122), (123), (124) and (125) (seventy-eight lines
in Mercado's list, sections 1 and 4.1). If the incomplete group has one
asterisk, the line will be a tetrameter as in (120) and (121) (fifty in
Mercado's list, sections 1, 2, 3.2, 4.1, 4.2, 4.4). Thus almost all the lines
in Mercado's list are scanned by the rules in (119).[28]

---

[28] Just three surviving lines cannot be scanned by these rules: the heptameter (seven
Gridline 0 groups) line *Mea puera quid verb⟨i⟩ ex tu⟨o⟩ ore supra fugit* 'My child,
what kind of word has escaped your mouth just now?' (Andr. 3), and two
trimeter (three Gridline 0 groups) lines *Amulius divis⟨que⟩ gratulabatur* 'Amulius
was giving thanks to the gods' (Naev. 26.2), and *id quoque paciscunt maenia sint
quae* untranslatable fragment (Naev. 47.1).

5

French

5.1 Introduction[1]

In order to get a proper grasp of the nature of French metrical poetry, it is necessary to be aware of an important result of linguistic research of the last century. It has been established that the phonetic form in which a word or affix is stored in the memory of a speaker of a language is often substantially different from the way the word is pronounced in an actual utterance. One of the earliest discussions of this fact is to be found in Edward Sapir's 'The psychological reality of phonemes', an article first published in French (Sapir 1933). Sapir reported that when speakers of American Indian languages were taught to write in their language, they would often depart radically from the sounds (phonemes) they were actually pronouncing. For example, at the end of words, Sapir's consultants would write vowels and consonants that they did not actually pronounce. On examining these spontaneous additions, Sapir established that they were not random errors of the learner, but reflected rather features of the grammatical structure of the language which were not realized phonetically in the pronunciation of the words, like [b] in the English noun *iamb*, which is pronounced in the related English adjective *iambic*.

Phonological research since 1933 has strongly confirmed the reality of these abstract representations, and it is now standardly assumed in the scientific study of languages that speakers have access to this abstract underlying representation of a word in addition to its actual pro-

[1] We thank François Dell and Benoît de Cornulier for help with this chapter. All errors are the responsibility of the authors NF&MH. In Fabb and Halle (2006b) we compare these French meters with Polish meters modelled on them.

nunciation or surface representation.[2] This important result of modern phonology has not been given its full due in metrical studies. In most cases, this omission has no significant consequences, since the distinction between underlying and surface representation of a word is not crucial for any of the problems that directly affect the metrical form of lines. This, however, is emphatically not the case with regard to the meters of French poetry. Without reference to the underlying representation of the words – in addition to their surface form (pronunciation) – it is difficult to make sense of French metrics.

Of crucial importance for an understanding of French meters is the treatment of word-final syllables whose nucleus is the vowel called in French *e caduc* (i.e., the vowel which linguists call 'schwa', exemplified by the vowel that ends the word *comme*).[3] Although this syllable is often not pronounced, it is nonetheless part of the abstract underlying representation of the word stored in the memory of the speaker (for details see Dell 1973). Syllables with the underlying *e caduc* provide the basis for the partition of the French vocabulary into two classes: on the one hand, the so-called 'feminine' words in (1a) are both polysyllabic and also end with *e caduc*; on the other hand, the 'masculine' words in (1b) are those which do not end with *e caduc*.

(1)   a.   *feminine words*: table, théâtre, Ulysse, lumière, finissent, finisse, berces, parle, veste, visible, théâtre, nombres, ombre, songes

   b.   *masculine words*: fini, liberté, heureux, criminel, charmant, pas, soir, du, doux, reviendra, rossignol, empereur, contemplation

Word stress in French resides on the penultimate syllable in feminine words, and on the last syllable in masculine words. We designate the stress-bearing syllables as maxima (in (4)).

As discussed in Chapter 4, in Italian, Spanish, and Portuguese poetry, word-final vowels are not counted for purposes of the meter where followed by a word beginning with a vowel. Though omitted from the count, these vowels are always pronounced in reading the lines, showing that syllable count for metrical purposes does not depend on pronunciation, in all cases. A similar situation obtains in French, where word-final *e caduc* does not count for purposes of the meter where followed by a

---

[2] For more discussion and examples see Kenstowicz (1994). For a discussion of the parallel evidence from French see Dell (1973).

[3] For a recent discussion of this vowel in French poetry, see Morin (2003).

word beginning with a vowel. The *e caduc* ending a feminine word is not pronounced under a variety of conditions, but the pronunciation or non-pronunciation of this *e caduc* does not determine whether it is counted for purposes of the meter. That is determined solely by what follows next in the line. This difficult issue is not always made clear in studies of French meters, and it is one of the virtues of Gouvard's (1999) monograph on French versification that it explains this matter clearly.

In his chapter on how syllables are counted, Gouvard (1999: 26) quotes the twelve-syllable (*alexandrin*) line by Paul Verlaine reproduced in (2).

(2)   Tu consoles et tu berces, et le chagrin
       'You console and you soothe, and the sorrow'

In a reading (performance) of this line it is normal not to pronounce the final syllables of the verbs *consoles* and *berces*, which in their underlying representations end with an *e caduc* followed by the second person singular suffix /z/. Since this usually unpronounced /z/ separates the *e caduc* from a following word-initial vowel, the syllables ending both words are always counted for purposes of the meter, even though they are rarely pronounced. As Gouvard remarks *le -es de 'consoles' et de 'berces' est bel et bien numéraire* ('the *-es* of *consoles* and of *berces* are both counted for the meter'). In sum, what matters for the purpose of the meter is not a word's pronunciation, but the word's abstract representation in speakers' memories, where verb forms like *berces* and *consoles* end in syllables with *e caduc* followed by the consonant [z], in spite of the fact that this representation is quite remote from the sequence of sounds actually produced by speakers.

It is assumed below that in French poetry (like in that of all languages studied here) syllables which count in determining the meter are projected to Gridline 0; syllables that are omitted from the count are not projected on Gridline 0. We state the French facts formally in (3).

(3)   A word-final syllable with *e caduc* in its nucleus is not projected to Gridline 0 (not counted for the meter)

   i.   verse-finally,

   ii. and verse-medially, where no consonant intervenes between the *e caduc* (of the syllable nucleus) and the following vowel.

We repeat that projection to Gridline 0 does not determine whether or not a given syllable is pronounced in reading the verse.

Omission of syllables from the metrical count is common across metrical traditions. As noted just above, in the meters of Spanish, Italian, and Portuguese, all word-final vowels are not counted in prevocalic position. In English, by contrast, the omission of vowels in the count though not uncommon is sporadic, rather than systematic.[4]

This treatment of line-final extrametrical syllables by non-projection is not adopted in all poetic traditions. As discussed in Chapter 1, in the metrical poetry of modern English as well as in other languages, unstressed syllables at the end of lines are effectively omitted from the count not by means of non-projection, but by having the rule of parenthesis insertion begin one or two syllables inside the verse, rather than just at the edge of the asterisk sequence.

5.2 The simple meters

French meters fall into two major classes: simple and compound. As explained below, the main difference between these two classes is that the lines of the simple meters are shorter and do not obey the caesura condition (see (14) below) requiring a word boundary after a specific syllable.

All metrical verse in French from the *Chanson de Roland* to the poetry of the 20th century is based on iambic groups; i.e., binary right-headed Gridline 0 groupings which are constructed from right to left. Formally this is implemented by an iterative rule (5a) that splits the sequence of Gridline 0 asterisks into groups. This grouping is subject to the condition that the head of the last (rightmost) Gridline 0 group in the line must project from the syllable bearing the word stress, a condition which forces a final unstressed syllable to be skipped (and hence be 'extrametrical').

It will be recalled from Chapter 2 that in English strict meters, syllables bearing the word stress are also subject to special conditions, and that in order to state the conditions economically, we designated such syllables as maxima and imposed the requirement that in English verse, maxima must project to Gridline 1. Following the same procedure here, we define maxima for purposes of French meters in (4).

---

[4] We have encountered one such example in French poetry: line 3 of Verlaine's 'Sur Rimbaud' (Verlaine 1962: 301) quoted below.

    Et dont Noël et Chapsal, chez les pions qui s'indigne

This line has thirteen, rather than twelve, countable syllables. This unusual fact has been rarely noted and when noted, is accompanied by an attempt to explain it away. E.g., the authoritative Bibliothèque de la Pléiade edition (Verlaine 1962: 1143) states: 'One must doubtlessly pronounce *Nouel* [sic, NF&MH] as one syllable in line 3, which without this is faulty'.

(4) The syllable bearing the word stress is a maximum; it is the last syllable in masculine words and the penultimate syllable in feminine words.

The rules that determine the syllable groupings in simple meters are stated in (5).

(5)   a. Gridline 0: starting at the R edge, insert a R parenthesis, form binary groups, heads R.

   b. Gridline 1: starting just at the R edge, insert a R parenthesis, form binary groups, heads R.

   c. Gridline 2: starting just at the R edge, insert a R parenthesis, form binary groups, heads R.

The simple meters are subject to the well-formedness condition (6).[5] They share this condition with all other meters of French poetry.

(6)   The head of the verse must project from a maximum and be directly followed by a word boundary.

Lines with fewer than eight syllables are also scanned by the rules of (5), but for such lines, stipulations are added requiring an incomplete group at the left edge of one or more Gridlines.

In (7) we quote a poem whose metrical grid is generated by these rules. We have shown the entire metrical grid for the last verse of (7), but only Gridline 0, for the other verses.

(7)   O triste, triste était mon âme
)*   *) *   *)Δ* *)   *   *) Δ

      À cause, à cause d'une femme.
)*   *) Δ *   *) *   *)* *)   Δ

      Je ne me suis pas consolé
) *   *) * *)   *   *) * *)

      Bien que mon coeur s'en soit allé,
) *   *) *   *)   *   *) * *)

      ...

      Mon âme dit à mon coeur: Sais-je
)*   *) * *)*   *)   *   *) Δ

      Moi-même, que nous veut ce piège
)*   *) *   *) *   *)   *   *)Δ

---

[5] It will be noticed that the word boundary requirement in (6) is automatically satisfied as a consequence of (3). It may therefore be objected that the requirement is redundant and should not be included in (6). We have not adopted this option here because there are actual lines of French poetry in simple meters that satisfy the maximum condition of (6) but not the requirement that the head of the verse project from a word-final syllable. (For examples and discussion see section 5.5.)

D'être présents bien qu'exilés,
) * *) * *)   *   *) * *)
Encore que loin en allés.
)*   *)*   *) *   *) * *)   0 ⇐
) *   *)   *   *)   1 ⇐
) *   *)   2 ⇐
                         *   3

'O sad, sad was my soul / because, because of a woman. / I did not get
over it / even though my heart left her. / ... / My soul said to my heart:
Do I know / myself, what this trap means to us / of being here though
exiled, / even though far away.' Paul Verlaine, *Romances sans Paroles*
'Ariettes oubliées VII' lines 1–4, 13–14 (Verlaine 1962: 195)

In (7) we use the symbols which we introduced in our discussion of
English (see chapter 2): the asterisks stand for the consecutive syllables
of the verse that are metrically counted, whereas the Greek letter Δ
represents syllables that are not projected by rule (3) and therefore are
omitted from the grouping.

Iterative grouping on Gridline 0 by rule (5a) begins at the right edge
and proceeds leftward. As shown in the last verse of (7), the combined
effect of the rules in (5) is that the rightmost grouped syllable will project
to the head of the verse, and by condition (6) this grouped syllable must
be a maximum. In masculine lines such as the third and fourth lines this
is straightforward because the rightmost syllable is stressed. However, in
feminine lines the rightmost syllable is an unstressed *e caduc*, and so not
a legitimate head of the verse. Such syllables are not projected by virtue
of (3). In this case, the penultimate syllable, which is stressed, projects
to the head of the verse, and is a maximum. It is worth noting in this
connection that the final unstressed syllable can be a monosyllabic word
like *sais-je* in (7), where the two-word sequence ending with a stressless
word (enclitic) rhymes with the disyllabic feminine word *piège*.

Condition (6) states that the head of the verse must be directly followed by a word boundary. This is true in (7) even though the head
of the verse is not the final syllable in its word: the head projects from
â- but the word is *âme*. However, since the final syllable *-me* does not
project as an element in the grid, it is invisible to the condition (6), and
thus as far as this condition is concerned, the line ends in the middle of
the word with the syllable *â-*. Hence the condition is obeyed.

In (7) all lines consisted of eight metrical syllables, which were grouped
into four iambic groups by the rules (5). Since the rules (7) apply to
all French simple verse, shorter lines are grouped in exactly the same
fashion. In the seven-syllable meter of (8), the leftmost Gridline 0 group
is incomplete and so the line has seven grouped asterisks.

(8)   C'est l'extase langoureuse,
       C'est la fatigue amoureuse,
       C'est tous les frissons des bois

```
 * )    *    * )  * * )    *    * )     0 ⇐
 ) *         * )       *         * )     1 ⇐
        ) *             * )     2 ⇐
                          *      3
```

'It's the rapture of languor, / it's the fatigue of love, / it's all the shudders of the trees'. Paul Verlaine, *Romances sans Paroles* 'Ariettes oubliées I' lines 1–3 (Verlaine 1962: 191)

In (9) below, there are incomplete groups at Gridline 0 and at Gridline 1. These feminine lines all have an additional unprojected syllable.

(9)   Dans l'interminable
       Ennui de la plaine,
       La neige incertaine
       Luit comme du sable.

```
 * )    *    * )  *  * ) Δ   0 ⇐
 * )         *       * )     1 ⇐
 ) *                 * )     2 ⇐
                      *      3
```

'In the interminable / boredom of the plain / the uncertain snow / shines like sand.' Paul Verlaine, *Romances sans Paroles*, 'Ariettes oubliées VIII' lines 1–4 (Verlaine 1962: 195)

In (10) below, it is Gridline 2 which ends on an incomplete group, giving masculine lines of four grouped syllables. In the third and sixth (feminine) lines, the Gridline 0 group is also incomplete so that there are three grouped syllables plus an unprojected syllable in each line.

(10)   Les sanglots longs
       Des violons
         De l'automne
       Blessent mon coeur
       D'une langueur

```
 ) *  * ) *    * )
```

         Monotone.

```
 * ) *  * ) Δ      0 ⇐
 ) *      * )       1 ⇐
          * )       2 ⇐
          *         3
```

'The prolonged sobs/ of the violins of autumn/ wound my heart/ with a langor/ (that's) monotonous.' Paul Verlaine, *Poèmes saturniens* 'Chanson d'automne' lines 1–6 (Verlaine 1962: 72)

In the meter of (11), every Gridline ends on an incomplete group, which means that the lines consist of just one grouped syllable, which may or may not be followed by an unprojected syllable.

(11)　Fort
　　　Belle,
　　　Elle

```
 * ) Δ      0 ⇐
 * )        1 ⇐
 * )        2 ⇐
 *          3
```

　　　Dort.

```
  * )       0 ⇐
  * )       1 ⇐
  * )       2 ⇐
  *         3
```

'Most / beautiful / she / sleeps.' Jules Rességuier, 'Sur la mort d'une jeune fille'

5.3 The *alexandrin* and other compound meters

The longer lines of French poetry differ from those reviewed above not only in length but also in a structural feature, the obligatory presence of a word boundary at a specific place in the line (caesura). We refer to French meters with a caesura as compound meters.

The compound meter that has been most popular among French poets since the 16th century is the twelve-syllable *alexandrin*. The rules which build the grid for the *alexandrin* are stated in (12). Other shorter compound meters employ variations of the rules in (12).

(12)　a.　Gridline 0: starting just at the R edge, insert a R parenthesis, form binary groups, heads R.

　　　b.　Gridline 1: starting just at the R edge, insert a R parenthesis, form ternary groups, heads R.

　　　c.　Gridline 2: starting at the L edge, insert a L parenthesis, form binary groups, heads L.

In (13) the full grid generated by these rules is shown for the last of the four verses; for the other three verses, only Gridline 0 is shown. The bar | in (13) indicates the location of the line-medial caesura.

(13)　Seigneur, je viens à vous, pleine d'un juste effroi.
　　　) *　　*)　*　*)　*　*) |　*　*)　*　　*)Δ *　　*)

　　　Votre voix redoubtable a passé jusqu'à moi:
　　　) *　*)　*　　*)　*　　*)Δ|*　*)　*　*)　*　　*)

　　　Je crains qu'un prompt effet n'ait suivi la menace.
　　　) *　　*)　　　*　　　*)　　*　*)|　*　　*)　*　*)　*　*)Δ

S'il en est temps encore, épargnez votre race ...

```
) *  * ) *     * )     *   * ) Δ | *  * )    *    * ) *  * ) Δ        0 ⇐
   ) *         *          * )         *          *    * )             1 ⇐
                        ( *                              * (          2 ⇒
                          *                                           3
```

'Sir, I come to you, full of justified terror, / your dread words have reached
even me, / I am afraid that an immediate execution might have followed
your threat, / if there is still time, preserve your stock (son).' Jean Racine,
Phèdre, IV.4.1167–70 (Racine 1999: 861)

The chief property that distinguishes compound meters from simple
meters is the obligatory caesura, the obligatory word boundary, that
splits lines of compound meters into two parts. In French compound
meters the caesura is usually located before the third Gridline 0 group,
counting from the end of the verse. No such obligatory verse-medial
caesura is found in the simple meters.

Setting aside the special case discussed in section 5.5 below, a word
boundary always appears also at the end of the verse. Given the grid construction rules in (12), these two syllables followed by word boundaries
are also the only ones that project to Gridline 2. Moreover, both of these
syllables also project from maxima, i.e., from syllables bearing the word
stress. We reflect these observations formally in the well-formedness
condition (14), which all compound meters must obey.

(14)   The two syllables projecting to Gridline 2 must be maxima and
       must be followed by a word boundary (caesura).

It will be recalled that in English meters there are also restrictions on
the placement of maxima (section 2.1) but with an important difference.
In English, the restriction holds of any syllable which is a maximum
(it must project to Gridline 1); in French, the restriction holds of any
syllable which projects to Gridline 2 (it must be a maximum). Thus an
English line need not have any maxima, but all maxima in the line are
controlled; in contrast, a French complex line must have two maxima in
specific positions (and any additional maxima are freely distributed).

It is worth special notice that in the second and fourth line of (13) the
head of the verse is followed by an *e caduc*. By virtue of condition (3),
this *e caduc* is not projected onto Gridline 0 and is therefore 'invisible'
for metrical purposes (the Δ symbol is not actually part of the grid, and
is provided only for the reader's convenience). Thus condition (14) is
satisfied.

Below we have reproduced an actual *alexandrin* line (15a) and two invented unmetrical alternatives (15b,c), which have been discussed in some earlier studies (e.g., Quicherat 1850, Cornulier 1995). We indicate the stressed syllable of *temple(s)* with an accent mark.

(15)   a. Oui, je viens dans son témple adorer l'éternel,

```
    ) *    * ) *      * )    *     * )   Δ |*  * )*    * )*    * )       0 ⇐
    ) *            *             * )         *      *     * )       1 ⇐
                            ( *                        * (       2 ⇒
                            *                                    3
```

   b. Oui, je viens dans son témple prier l'éternel,

```
    ) *    * ) *      * )    *    * )    * | *)*    * ) *   * )       0 ⇐
    ) *            *            * )          *     *     * )       1 ⇐
                           ( *                        * (       2 ⇒
                           *                                    3
```

   c. Oui, je viens aux témples adorer l'éternel,

```
    ) *    * ) *      * )    *      * ) |*  * ) *    * )*    * )       0 ⇐
    ) *            *              * )   *     *      * )       1 ⇐
                           ( *                        * (       2 ⇒
                           *                                    3
```

(a) 'Yes, I come to his temple to adore the Eternal'
(b) 'Yes, I come to his temple to pray to the Eternal'
(c) 'Yes, I come to the temples to adore the Eternal'

Example (15a), the opening line of Racine's *Athalie* is, of course, metrically impeccable. By contrast, the two invented lines (15b) and (15c) are both unmetrical. Line (15b) violates condition (14), because the caesura is not directly after the head of the verse (the sixth syllable *tem-*) but after the next (projected) syllable (*-ple*) to its right. Line (15c) is also unmetrical, even though the head of the verse (the sixth syllable *-ples*) is word-final as required by condition (14); the line is unmetrical because the head of the verse is not a maximum, in violation of (14).

As already remarked, the rules in (12) and condition (14) account also for lines in meters other than the *alexandrin*, since incomplete groups may be generated at the end of the grouping procedure of parenthesis insertion. The most common among these is the *décasyllabe* or ten-syllable line illustrated in (16) with four lines from a justly famous sonnet by Joachim du Bellay.

(16)   Nouveau venu, qui cherches Rome en Rome

```
     ) *    * )   *  * ) | *    * )   *    * ) Δ *    * ) Δ
```

Et rien de Rome en Rome n'apperçois,

```
     )*    * )   *   * ) Δ | *    * ) *   * )   * * )
```

Ces vieux palais, ces vieux arcz que tu vois,

```
     ) *    * )     * * ) | *    * )   *       * ) *  * )
```

Et ces vieux murs, c'est ce que Rome on nomme.

```
)*   *)  *      *)|   *   *)  *   *)Δ*    *)   Δ      0 ⇐
     *        *)         *      *          *)          1 ⇐
              (*                            *(          2 ⇒
     *                                       *          3
```

'Newly arrived, you who seek Rome in Rome, / but find of Rome nothing in Rome. / Those old palaces, those old arches that you see, / and these old walls; that is what is called Rome.' Joachim du Bellay, *Les Antiquitez de Rome*, lines 1–4 (Bellay 1971: 28)

The *décasyllabe* lines in (16) are supplied with their metrical grid by the rules in (12), which were used for the *alexandrin*, but with the additional stipulation that the leftmost (i.e., last-constructed) group on Gridline 1 must be incomplete, specifically binary rather than ternary.

Both the twelve-syllable *alexandrin* and the ten-syllable *décasyllabe* have their caesura in the same place: in both meters the caesura falls after the syllable which projects to the head of the verse.

5.3.1 Villon's meter

Before the 16th-century reforms of the Pléiade, the *décasyllabe* was the favourite meter of French poetry. In the earlier poetry, as exemplified by the poetry of Villon, Marot and others, the head of the verse was line-final and subject to condition (6) but the two syllables projecting to Gridline 2 were subject to condition (17), a weaker version of condition (14).

(17) The two syllables projecting to Gridline 2 must be followed by a word boundary (caesura).

We illustrate this in (18) with some well-known lines by Villon.

(18) Dame du ciel, regente terienne,
```
      )*   *)  *   *)|  * *)  *   *)**)Δ
```

Emperiere des infernaulx paluz,
```
      )*    *)* *)|* *) *   *)    * *)
```
Recevez moy, vostre humble crestienne,
```
      )* *)*    *)|  *  Δ  *)   *     *)**)Δ
```

Que comprinse soye entre voz esleuz,
```
      )* *)   *  *)|*  Δ*)  *  *)  * *)      0 ⇐
         *         *)      *      *)          1 ⇐
                   )*                *)       2 ⇐
                                      *       3
```

'Mistress of heaven, earthly ruler, / empress of the infernal marshes, / accept me, your humble Christian woman, / that I may be included among your elect' François Villon, 'Ballade pour prier Nostre Dame' lines 1–4 (Villon 1974: 82)

The grid of (18) differs from the grids of the post-Pléiade poetry discussed above in locating the head of the verse at the right edge of the verse rather verse-medially. Formally this is implemented by replacing the Gridline 2 rule (12c) with (19).

(19) Gridline 2: starting just at the R edge, insert R parentheses, form binary groups, heads R.

The reforms of the Pléiade consisted in replacing (19) and (17) with (12c) and (14). We return to this topic in section 5.6 below.

5.4 Nine-syllable lines and related matters

To this point we have discussed simple meters with lines of up to 8 syllables, and compound meters (with the mid-line caesura) of 10 and 12 syllables. In this section we consider three types of nine-syllable line, two of which are compound (with caesura) and the third of which is simple (lacking caesura).

The compound meter in (20) is a variant of the ten-syllable line, but with an incomplete group on Gridline 0. It is illustrated by the first two lines of (20); the second two lines are standard ten-syllable *décasyllabes*.

(20) Sus debout la merveille des Belles.

```
* )   *   * ) | *   * ) * * ) *   * )Δ        0 ⇐
  *       * )       *     *       * )          1 ⇐
        ( *                     * (            2 ⇒
          *                                    3
```

Allons voir sur les herbes nouvelles
Luire un esmail dont la vive peinture
Deffend à l'art d'imiter la nature.

```
) * * )   *   * ) |  *   * )*  * ) * * )Δ      0 ⇐
  *         * )      *    *     * )            1 ⇐
        ( *                 * (                2 ⇒
          *                                    3
```

'Stand up, marvel of beauties, / let's go look shimmering on the new lawn / an enamel whose lively painting / makes it impossible for art to imitate nature.' François de Malherbe, 'Chanson' (Gouvard 1999: 141)

All four lines of (20) obey the caesura condition (14), which requires the head of the line to be followed by a word boundary. We can say that the caesura in the nine-syllable line is in the same position as in the ten-syllable line only if we construct the Gridline 0 groups from right to left. The first line of (20) thus provides evidence in support of (12a), where grouping starts at the right edge.

A somewhat more complex variant of the compound meter is that in Verlaine's 'Kyrie Eleison', of which the first five lines are quoted in (21). As shown below, the lines are instances of a compound meter and obey the caesura condition (14).

(21)   Ayez pitié de nous, Seigneur!
```
         )*  * ) | *  * ) *  * )    *    * )        0 ⇐
            * )    *    *         * )                1 ⇐
          ( *                   * (                  2 ⇒
            *                                        3
```

Christ, ayez pitié de nous!
```
          * ) | * * )  * * ) *  * )              0 ⇐
          * )    *    *    * )                    1 ⇐
        ( *              * (                      2 ⇒
          *                                       3
```

Donnez-nous la victoire et l'honneur
```
      * )  *   * ) | *  * ) * Δ * )    *    * )    0 ⇐
      *        * )    *    *        * )            1 ⇐
        ( *                   * (                  2 ⇒
          *                                        3
```

Sur l'Ennemi de nous tous.
```
          * ) | *   * ) *  * ) *      * )
```

Ayez pitié de nous, Seigneur.
```
         )*  * ) | *  * ) *  * )    *    * )
```

'Have pity on us, Lord! / Christ, have pity on us! / Give us victory and honor/ over the Enemy of all of us. / Have pity on us, Lord!' Paul Verlaine, *Liturgies intimes* 'Kyrie Eleison' lines 1–5 (Verlaine 1992: 420)

The poem consists of twenty-one lines arranged into eight stanzas with the line lengths below:

87 978 977 978 997 988 977 8

The meter of the poem is a shortened version of the *décasyllabe* with an incomplete group appearing at the left edge of the line not only on Gridline 0, as in (20), but also on Gridline 1. A stipulation to this effect can readily be added to the Gridline 0 and Gridline 1 rules of (12). As in the other examples of compound meters, the head of the verse in (21) is followed by three Gridline 0 groups without regard to what precedes. It thus further supports the rule (12b), specifically the stipulation that Gridline 1 groupings start at the right edge.[6]

---

[6] Verlaine's 'Délicatesse' (1962: 431) is a shortened variant of the *alexandrin*, where each verse has eleven syllables and a caesura after the seventh syllable, counting from the right edge. It is thus a precise counterpart to the nine-syllable lines discussed here, which are shortened version of the *décasyllabe*.

Gouvard (1999: 145) quotes a poem by Ronsard and a stanza by the 18th-century poet Sedaine, which are nine syllables in length but unlike the poems quoted in this section above have no line-internal caesuras. Gouvard refers to such lines as 'the nine-syllable line without meter' (*le 9-syllabe sans mètre*), but they are not without meter; they are instead best analyzed as lines without line-medial caesura. Formally they are instances of the simple meter and are accounted for by the rules (5) and condition (6), with a modification of (5b), so that instead of binary, ternary groups are formed on Gridline 1. Like the other simple meters, the nine-syllable meter admits incomplete groups at the left edge of the verse on both Gridline 0 and 1. We illustrate this with the lines from Sedaine quoted by Gouvard.[7]

(22) Je reconnais le triste bocage

```
    * ) * * ) *   * ) * * ) * *)Δ         0 ⇐
    *   * )       *   *   *)             1 ⇐
      ) *                 * )             2 ⇐
                          *               3
```

Si funeste à ma tranquillité.

```
    * ) * * ) Δ *   * )  *    *)* * )
```

C'est sur ce gazon, sous cet ombrage

```
    * )   *   * ) * * )   *   *)  *   * )Δ
```

Que j'ai perdu ma félicité.

```
    * )  *   * ) *   * ) * *)* * )
```

'I recognized the sad grove / so fateful for my peace of mind. / It was on this lawn, in this shady spot / that I lost my happiness.'

A nine-syllable line of a kind different from those reviewed above is that of Verlaine's famous 'Art poétique' of which the first and the fourth stanzas are reproduced in (23).

(23) De la musique avant toute chose,

```
    * ) *   *)*  Δ * ) *    * ) *   *)Δ
```

Et pour cela préfère l'Impair

```
    * )   *   *)*  *)* * ) *   * )
```

Plus vague et plus soluble dans l'air,

```
    * )  *  Δ * )  *  *)* * ) *    * )
```

Sans rien en lui qui pèse et qui pose.

```
    * )   *  * )  *   * ) * Δ * )  *  *)Δ
```

...

Car nous voulons la Nuance encor,

```
    * )  *   * ) *   * ) * * ) Δ *   * )'
```

---

[7] We have found a fair number of poems in this meter by Verlaine, e.g., 'Bruxelles' (1962: 200), 'La cathédrale est majestueuse' (1962: 701), 'Je revois quasiment triomphal' (1962: 867).

Pas la Couleur, rien que la nuance!
```
*  )  *   *  )  *     *  )    *  *  )  **  )  Δ
```
Oh! la nuance seule fiance
```
*  )    *   *  )*  *  )  *   *  )  *  *  )  Δ
```
Le rêve au rêve et la flûte au cor!
```
*  )  *   Δ  *  )   *  Δ  *  )   *  *  )  Δ   *    *  )
```

'Music, above all things, / and to this end choose the uneven / vaguer
and more soluble in air, / with nothing in it that is heavy and poses. [...]
For we want just the nuance (delicate gradation), / not the color, nothing
but nuance! / Oh! the shade alone joins (marries) / ådream to dream
and flute to horn!' Paul Verlaine, *Jadis et naguère* 'Art poetique' lines
1–4 and 13–16 (Verlaine 1962: 326–7)

Examination of the lines in (23) shows that in this nine-syllable poem,
condition (14) is satisfied by the fourth and the final (ninth) syllable
in each line. Thus, in the first line the maximum of *musique* is also
followed by a word boundary, and so is the maximum of *chose* that ends
the verse.

These facts present a problem. Condition (14) imposes requirements
on the two syllables projecting to Gridline 2. But in (23), the verse-
medial maximum of *musique* is not the head of its Gridline 0 group and
does not project above Gridline 0. Moreover, in the grids for the normal
décasyllabe (see (16), (20), (21)), the head of the verse is, as argued
above, the seventh syllable counting from the right. But in (23), the
syllables in that position grossly violate condition (14). For example, in
the first line in (23) the first syllable of *musique* occupies this position,
and it is neither word-final, nor a maximum.

We propose to repair these problems with the two modifications below.
First, we assume that in the meter of this poem the head of the verse
is two syllables (one Gridline 0 group) to the right of its location in the
other compound meters. We implement this by replacing rule (12b) with
(24), where two of the five parameters of the rule have been changed,
from R to L.

(24)   Gridline 1: starting just at the L edge, insert a L parenthesis,
       form ternary groups, heads R.

We illustrate the effects of this modification in (25) with the grid of
the penultimate line in (23).

(25)   Oh! la nuance seule fiance
```
  *  )    *   *  )*   *  )  *   *  )**  )  Δ          0 ⇐ R
 ( *        *      *      ( *   *                     1 ⇒ R
             ( *          *  (                        2 ⇒ L
                  *                                   3
```

This does not solve the problem completely. As required by (14), the ninth syllable projects to Gridline 2, as it must, but the fourth syllable does not. We recall that the head of the verse must project from a maximum, and we note that in (25) the head of the verse is the last syllable of the word *nuance*, one syllable to the right of a maximum. Our problem would be solved if we had a way of moving the head of the verse one syllable to the left. We achieve this by positing a rule deleting the Gridline 0 projection of the head of the verse; i.e., the same rule that Tennyson used in his 'Hendecasyllabics' (see section 1.8). In (26) we illustrate the effects of applying the deletion rule to (25).

(26)   Oh! la nuance seule fiance

```
     * )    *   *)*  Δ ) *  *)* * )  Δ          0 ⇐ R
     (*          * *       ( *  *                1 ⇒ R
          ( *            * (                2 ⇒ L
                   *                            3
```

This produces the desired result: the fourth syllable now conforms to (14) because it is word-final, a maximum, and projects to Gridline 2. Although this may seem a rather indirect way of getting the required result, we have obtained it by making use of devices that were used and fully motivated elsewhere. The procedure deals correctly with the other thirty-five lines of the poem, as illustrated in (27), where the Δ in bold face is the result of the deletion rule, and the other three Δs represent uncounted (unprojected) syllables.

(27)   Le rêve au rêve et la flûte au cor!

```
     *) *   Δ* )   *  ΔΔ)  *  *)Δ  *    * )      0 ⇐ R
     ( *       *     *       ( *       *          1 ⇒ R
              ( *            * (                2 ⇒ L
                   *                            3
```

5.5 Grids without conditions

Cornulier (1995: 55) has drawn attention to Verlaine's lines reproduced in (28) and (29), which violate the well-formedness condition requiring that a word boundary follow the last syllable in the line. The poem in (28) is in twelve-syllable lines, the poem in (29) in ten-syllable lines. We assume that their metrical grids are assigned by the rules in (12).[8]

(28)   Si je n'avais l'orgueil de vous avoir, à ta-
        Ble d'hôte, vue ainsi que tel ou tel rasta

---

[8] The caesura condition is violated by the last line in the first poem and by the first two lines in the second poem.

...

D'être, grâce à votre talent de femme exquise-
Ment amusante, décoré d'un doigt subtil.

> 'If I had not had the pride of having seen you at the bu- / -ffet as well as some flashy foreigner [...] Being, thanks to your talent of an exquisite- / -ly amusing woman, decorated with a subtle finger.' Paul Verlaine, *Dédicaces LII* 'Á une dame qui partait pour la Colombie' lines 6–7, 13–14 (Verlaine 1962: 590)

(29)   Voyez de Banville, et voyez Lecon-
Te de Lisle, et tôt pratiquons leur con-
Duite et soyons, tels ces deux preux, nature.

> 'See de Banville, and see Lecon- / -te de Lisle [names of French poets], and without delay, let us imitate their be- / -haviour and like these two valiant knights, let us be natural.' Paul Verlaine, *Dédicaces* 'Á Raoul Ponchon' lines 9–11 (Verlaine 1992: 300)

What differentiates these lines from other lines in French poetry is that their grids are subject to neither well-formedness condition (6) nor (14). These conditions require word boundaries and maxima in particular positions in the lines. The condition on line-medial caesura is violated in the bottom line of the first poem in (28), and in the first line of the second poem. Perhaps more striking even is the fact that the condition requiring lines to end with a word boundary is violated in lines 1 and 3 of the first poem, and in line 1 and 2 of the second poem. In terms of our formalism these facts are captured simply by positing that in the poems in (28), the lines need meet no conditions beyond having grids generated by (12).

We have encountered word-internal enjambment also in other poetic traditions. In classical Greek (Chapter 6), as well as in Berber (see Dell and Elmedlaoui 2006), and some other poetic traditions word-internal enjambment is a standard phenomenon with many examples. These examples constitute challenges to the widely held opinion that the end of all lines of verse coincides with a word boundary.

5.6 The meter of the *Chanson de Roland*

The *Chanson de Roland* is an epic poem composed in the late 11th or early 12th centuries,[9] whose lines are often described as consisting of ten syllables with an obligatory caesura after the fourth syllable. In the lines in (30), the vertical bar | indicates the position of the caesura.

---

[9] The text of lines from the *Chanson* quoted here and below is that of the edition of Brault (1978).

(30) Bel sire reis, | fait m'avez un grant dun,
      Eslisez mei | douze de voz baruns,
      Sim cumbatrai | as douze compagnons.

> 'Dear Sire, King, you have bestowed on me a great gift, / choose for me
> twelve of your barons, / and I will fight the twelve companions.' R876–9

As elsewhere in French metrical verse, there can be an extra unstressed
syllable at the end of the line (shown in angled brackets below), which
is not projected to Gridline 0, as required by (3i).

(31) D'altre part est | Turgis de Turtelu⟨se⟩
      Cil est un quens | si est la citét su⟨e⟩.
      De chrestiëns | voelt faire male vo⟨de⟩.

> 'From another part comes Turgis of Turteluse, / he is a count and the
> city is his. / He vows to destroy the Christians.' R916–18

So far, the *Chanson* seems to have the same compound meter as the
décasyllabe lines discussed in section 5.3. This impression is, however,
incorrect, for it overlooks the important fact that in lines of the *Chanson*,
'the same options of variation prevail at the caesura (at the end of the
hemistich) as at the end of the line' (Elwert 1965: 85). This variation is
illustrated in (32), where the fourth syllable is followed by an additional
unstressed syllable, enclosed in angled brackets, as well as by (33) where
both a midline and a final syllable are followed by an unstressed syllable.

(32) Dist a ses ho⟨mes⟩: | Seignors, voz en ireiz,
      Branches d'oli⟨ves⟩ | en voz mains portereiz,

> 'He said to his men: "Lords, you will go, / olive branches you will carry
> in your hands."' R79–80

'Li reis Marsil⟨ie⟩ | de nos ad fait marchet,
Mais as espe⟨es⟩ l'estuvrat esleger.'

> 'King Marsilie has planned our murder, / but he will have to fight for it
> against our swords.' R1150–1

(33) Dis blanches mu⟨les⟩ | fist amener Marsil⟨ies⟩

> 'Ten white mules Marsilie had brought' R89

Jamais en te⟨re⟩ | ne porterat curo⟨ne⟩.

> 'Never on earth will he wear a crown.' R930

Kar vasela⟨ge⟩ | par sens nen est foli⟨e⟩:
Mielz valt mesu⟨re⟩ que ne fait estulti⟨e⟩

> 'For heroic deeds tempered with sense are not folly,/ reason is better than
> recklessness.' R1724–5

In the *Chanson de Roland* both the verse-medial word boundary and the verse-final word boundary are subject to the same conditions (unlike modern French compound meters). Following the lead of Cornulier (1995: 62, n.71), we interpret this as showing that each single (traditional) line of the *Chanson* is in fact a pair of shorter 'sub-lines', each with its own grid. The first sub-line comprises two iambic groups and may have an additional syllable at the end, and the second sub-line comprises three iambic groups and may, like the first sub-line, have an additional syllable at the end.

The meter of the *Chanson* is thus a special case of a simple meter, where the odd-numbered lines are composed of two Gridline 0 groups, and the even-numbered lines of three groups. This is a simple meter because in metrical terms there is no caesura (no condition on the grid requiring a word boundary): the 'caesura' is an artifact, the result of the convention of presenting two actual lines as a single graphic line.

Formally this proposal is expressed by the rules (34), which are all but identical with those in (5), and condition (6), repeated here.

(34)   a. Gridline 0: starting at the R edge, insert a R parenthesis, form binary groups, heads R.

   b. Gridline 1: starting just at the R edge, insert a R parenthesis, form ternary groups, heads R.

      i. Odd-numbered sub-line: Gridline 1 must include an incomplete (binary) group.

(6)   The head of the verse must project from a maximum and be followed by a word boundary.

The application of the rules (34) is illustrated in (35), where the traditional line is split into two sub-lines.[10]

(35)   Carles li reis,

```
   *  * ) *  * )            0 ⇐
      *     * )             1 ⇐
            *               2
```

nostre emperere magnes,

```
   *  Δ * )  * * )*  * ) Δ        0 ⇐
      *      *      * )           1 ⇐
                    *             2
```

[10] Note the non-projection of the second syllable in *nostre* before the vowel-initial word *emperere*; like French verse of all periods the *Chanson* verse was subject to the condition (3) (for details, see Elwert 1965, para. 31–37).

The main difference between the meter of the *Chanson* and that of the simple meters of the modern language is therefore the (obligatory) shortness of the lines in the *Chanson*.

5.7 Conclusion

Looking back on the evolution of meters in French poetry in the light of the theory of this book, we observe that like the meters of other Romance languages, those of French make use of the binary right-headed groupings on Gridline 0 (cf. (5a), (12a), and (34a)). The meter of the *Chanson de Roland* limited line length to a maximum of three binary groups (cf. (34)). We note that such restrictions to very short lines are also found in the Anglo-Saxon *Beowulf* (section 10.4) and in the Latvian *dainas* (Chapter 9). It is conceivable that this reflects a common Indo-European origin, but to substantiate this speculation is beyond the aims of our study.

The meter of the *Chanson* was replaced at a quite early date by a meter which treated the couplet of the earlier meter as a single line of ten or twelve syllables. These lines – exemplified in (18) above – were subject to the caesura condition (36), whose wording is similar to (14), of which it was clearly a forerunner.

(36)   The two syllables projecting to Gridline 2 must be followed by a word boundary.

The next major step were the reforms of Pléiade in the 16th century. These affected the compound meters only and consisted in the replacement of (6) and (35) by condition (14), repeated below.

(14)   The two syllables projecting to Gridline 2 must be maxima and must be followed by a word boundary (caesura).

6

Greek

6.1 Introduction[1]

In his thorough and detailed account of Greek metrical verse, West (1982: 28) describes the range of meters by saying that 'it is doubtful whether a coherent system could be devised, even if the world wanted it. Greek metre itself is too complex and multiform'. In this chapter we respond to this challenge by showing that Greek meters can all be explained using the theoretical machinery developed in the first few chapters of this book. We select some of the most widely used meters and discuss them in three groups. In section 6.2 we look at iambs, trochees, and cretics, and show that they must be analyzed as strict meters. In section 6.3 we show that dactylic hexameter and anapaests are loose variants of trochaic and iambic meters, with a non-iterative parenthesis insertion rule. In section 6.4 we show that a selection of the aeolic meters are strict (iambic) meters.

All kinds of meter involve counting and patterning. In the theory of this book, the counting explains the patterning: for example, by grouping the syllables of an iambic line into right-headed pairs we explain why every second syllable is marked. Greek verse is in quantitative meters, which are based on the distinction between light and heavy syllables.

The Greek meters contrast in this respect with the meters discussed in the preceding chapters, which divide the syllables into two classes on the basis of word stress. Though the phonetic basis of the meters is

[1] Our analysis draws on Dale (1968) and West (1982), and the handbooks of Raven (1998) and Halporn et al. (1994), as well as entries in Hornblower and Spawforth (2003). Other linguistic accounts of Greek meter which we have consulted include Prince (1989) and Golston and Riad (2005). We thank Juan Jose Gonzalez Garcia for his advice. We have greatly benefited from the advice of Tim Barnes of Harvard University, and in some cases have drawn on his unpublished analyses. All errors are the responsibility of the authors NF&MH.

different, the principles of organization – the rules and conditions – are essentially the same.

The unifying feature of all the Greek meters is that they are all subject to the rule stated in (1).

(1) Delete the Gridline 0 asterisk which projects from the first syllable in a sequence of two or more light syllables.

This rule, which is the major innovation of this chapter, is our alternative to what in traditional accounts is the equation for metrical purposes of two light syllables with a single heavy syllable, called 'resolution'. Its interaction with other rules, and above all with the set of iterative rules, is captured here by rule ordering. As shown in section 6.4, in the aeolic meters rule (1) is ordered after the iterative rules, but elsewhere it precedes the iterative rule block.

6.2 Iambs, trochees, and cretics

6.2.1 Iambs

In Greek verse a syllable is classified as light if it ends on a short vowel, and otherwise heavy. A single consonant (and in some cases a pair of consonants) between two vowels attaches to the following syllable; word boundaries are irrelevant in the determination of weight. For this purpose the entire verse line is treated as if it were a single long word. (For extensive discussion of the establishment of syllable weight, see Steriade 1982 and West 1982.) A complication is that the final syllable in certain lines can be actually light where we would expect it to be heavy; in the traditional approach, a light syllable in this position is counted as heavy, called *brevis in longo*.[2] We follow this analysis for some of the meters, where we treat a final syllable as heavy even if phonetically light.[3]

We begin our analysis of Greek meters with iambic verse, illustrated

---

[2] Traditional accounts of Greek verse from the 19th century onwards have identified a higher-level grouping called the 'period', which either coincides with the line (i.e., one period contains one line) or with a group of lines (i.e., one period contains several lines). *Brevis in longo* occurs at the end of the period, and is a diagnostic of a period boundary.

[3] In this chapter, like in much of the literature on Greek meters, the technical terms *dimeter*, *trimeter*, and *tetrameter* refer to the number of metra in a line, where each metron consists of a pair of feet, not syllables. Dimeters thus are composed of two metra or four syllables, trimeters, of three metra or six syllables, etc. An exception to this usage is the term *hexameter*, where the term *meter* designates the feet, rather than the metra.

by the lines in (2), which are in iambic trimeter, and the lines in (3), which are in iambic dimeter. We have written ∪ (breve) beneath each light syllable and − (macron) beneath each heavy syllable. We treat the final syllable as heavy even when it is phonetically light (as in the first line).

(2)   ὦ κοινὸν αὐτάδελφον ᾽Ισμήνης κάρα,
      − − ∪ − ∪ − ∪ − − ∪ −

      ἆρ᾽ οἶσθ᾽ ὅ τι Ζεὺς τῶν ἀπ᾽ Οἰδίπου κακῶν
      − − ∪ − − − ∪ − ∪ − ∪ −

      ὁποῖον οὐχὶ νῷν ἔτι ζώσαιν τελεῖ;
      ∪ −∪ − ∪ − ∪− − − ∪ −

      'Oh, from a common womb, dear Ismene. Do you know what, of the evils ⟨stemming⟩ from Oedipus, Zeus is not bringing to pass for us two who are ⟨alone⟩ still alive?' Sophocles, *Antigone* lines 1–3 (Sophocles 1999: 73)

(3)   ἤκουσας ὡς μαγειρικῶς
      − − ∪ − ∪ − ∪ −

      κομψῶς τε καὶ δειπνητικῶς
      − − ∪ − − −∪ −

      αὐτῶι διακονεῖται;
      − − ∪−∪ − −

      'Did you hear how 'butcherly', how cleverly and 'diningly' he serves (as an attendant) himself?' Aristophanes, *Acharnians* lines 1015–1017 (White 1912: 28)

Any account of iambs must explain why in a particular meter – e.g., iambic trimeter – the line is of a certain length (12 syllables) and has a certain pattern of heavy and light syllables. In this meter, in every sequence of two syllables the second is heavy, and in every sequence of four syllables the third is light. The only exception to this is the final syllable in the line, which the traditional conception is *brevis in longo* (a light syllable which is treated as heavy). Tthus in the traditional approach, every even-numbered syllable including the final syllable in the first line is metrically heavy.

In the traditional analysis, the 12-syllable line is matched to a template consisting of three smaller four-position templates called 'iambic metra' (3 times 4 is 12). The template is × − ∪ −. When used to describe a position in a template, the − symbol designates a 'longum', a position which must be filled by a heavy syllable. The ∪ symbol designates a 'breve', a position which must be filled by a light syllable. The × symbol here designates an 'anceps', a position which can be filled by either a heavy or a light syllable. None of these notions are available in our theory. We do not have templates, and hence no notion of 'metrical position': our theory recognizes a heavy syllable but not a longum, and a light syllable but not a breve.

In our approach the grid is built from the line by applying grouping rules in order, and checking that the required conditions hold of the grid. We note that the syllables in these lines are grouped into right-headed pairs, because even-numbered syllables are always heavy. The line can fall one syllable short at the right edge (be 'catalectic'), as we see in the third line of (3) which has seven syllables, while there are eight syllables in the first two lines. This suggests that asterisks are grouped on Gridline 0 by a rule which inserts left parentheses from left to right, hence permitting the rightmost group to be incomplete. The rule for Gridline 0 is as stated in (4).

(4)   Gridline 0: starting just at the L edge, insert a L parenthesis, form binary groups, heads R.

The rule in (4) assigns the partial grid in (5) to the first line of (2).

(5)   ὦ κοινὸν αὐτάδελφον Ἰσμήνης κάρα,

```
      –   – U   – U –  U   –  –– U  –
     (*  *(*  *(* *(* *  *( *  **( * *(       0 ⇒
      *    *   *   *    *   *    *  *            1
```

Given this partial grid, we can state condition (6), which has the effect that even-numbered syllables are heavy.

(6)   Syllables projecting to Gridline 1 must be heavy.

In (7) we state the full set of rules for the iambic trimeter lines in (2).

(7)   a. Gridline 0: starting just at the L edge, insert a L parenthesis, form binary groups, heads R.

      b. Gridline 1: starting just at the R edge, insert a R parenthesis, form binary groups, heads R.

      c. Gridline 2: starting just at the R edge, insert a R parenthesis, form ternary groups, heads R.

The rules in (7) generate a grid from the first line in (2), as shown in (8).

(8)   ὦ κοινὸν αὐτάδελφον Ἰσμήνης κάρα,

```
      –   – U   – U –  U   –  –– U  –
     (*  *(*  *(* *(* *  *( *  **( * *(       0 ⇒
      )*    *)  *    *    *)  *    *)          1 ⇐
          )*         *         *)              2 ⇐
                                 *             3
```

Groups on Gridline 1 correspond to traditional 'metra'. Iambic dimeter has two metra (rather than the three of iambic trimeter), and so the rules must be altered to generate a binary rather than a ternary group on Gridline 2. This is illustrated in (9), which is moreover a 'catalectic' line in which the rightmost group on Gridline 0 is incomplete.

(9)   αὐτῶι διακονεῖται·
```
        –   –   U–  U  –   –
       ( *   *  ( * *( *   *  ( *              0 ⇒
          ) *     * )   *     * )              1 ⇐
          ) *           * )                    2 ⇐
                        *                      3
```

We have now accounted for the length of the line, and the fact that in every pair of syllables the second is heavy. We have not accounted for the fact that the third out of every four syllables in a four-syllable metron is light. To express this, we state the condition in (10).

(10)   The syllable that projects to Gridline 2 must be preceded by a light syllable, if both belong to the same Gridline 0 group.

Because syllables are organized into right-headed pairs of right-headed pairs, every fourth syllable projects to Gridline 2. The third syllable is in the same Gridline 0 group and so must be light. (In the catalectic line in (9), the second of the two syllables which projects go Gridline 2 does not share a Gridline 0 group with the syllable which precedes it, and so condition (10) does not apply.)

6.2.2 Resolution in iambic meters

A characteristic type of variation in iambic meter, called 'resolution', permits the iambic metron to contain more than four syllables. In traditional terms, one or two of the four positions in the metron can contain a pair of syllables instead of a single syllable, resulting in a metron of five or six syllables instead of the expected four. The position is said to be 'resolved into' two light syllables. Resolution is illustrated by the iambic trimeter lines in (11), which include resolved metra with five rather than the normative four syllables, in the patterns $U\ U - U -$, $- - U\ U -$, $- U\ U\ U -$, and $- - U\ U\ U$, as well as unresolved metra with the normal four-syllable patterns $U - U -$ and $- - U -$.

(11)   ὅτε δὴ κατῆλθ᾽ Εὐριπίδης, ἐπεδείκνυτο
```
       U U   –  U –   – – U –   U U –   U –
```

τοῖς λωποδύταις καὶ τοῖσι βαλλαντιοτόμοις

  –   – ∪ ∪ –   – – ∪ –   – ∪ ∪ ∪ –

καὶ τοῖσι πατραλοίαισι καὶ τοιχωρύχοις

  –   – ∪ ∪ ∪ – – ∪ –   – – ∪ –

'When Euripides first came down here (to the Underworld), he staged a performance for the brigands and the purse snatchers, for the father-beaters and the burglars' Aristophanes, *Frogs* lines 771–773 (Raven 1998: 31)

One of the general principles of metrical poetry is that not all syllables are counted for metrical purposes. We have seen this, for example, in the French *e-muet*, in Spanish synalepha, in English, and elsewhere. We suggest that this is the explanation of 'resolution' in these lines, and have formulated rule (1) above, repeated here, to account for resolution in Greek.[4]

(1) Delete the Gridline 0 asterisk which projects from the first syllable in a sequence of two or more light syllables.

Rule (1) applies in the three lines in (11), sometimes more than once in the same line.

(12) ὅτε δὴ κατῆλθ' Εὐριπίδης, ἐπεδείκνυτο

  ∪ ∪ – ∪ –   – – ∪ – ∪ ∪ – ∪ –
  Δ * * * *   * * * * Δ * *   * *   0

τοῖς λωποδύταις καὶ τοῖσι βαλλαντιοτόμοις

  –   – ∪ ∪ –   – – ∪ –   – ∪ ∪ ∪ –
  *   * Δ * * * * * * * Δ * * *   0

καὶ τοῖσι πατραλοίαισι καὶ τοιχωρύχοις

  – – ∪ ∪ ∪ – – ∪ –   – – ∪ –
  *   * Δ * * * * * *   * * *   0

For each line, rule (1) reduces the number of projected syllables to twelve. The Δ symbols indicate where asterisks have been removed (they are for visual convenience only and are not part of the grid).

---

[4] In the other languages, more than one syllable in a sequence can fail to project to Gridline 0; in Greek only the first of a sequence of light syllables does not project. Though we have formulated the rule for English, French and Southern Romance as a rule of non-projection, it could equally have been a rule which deletes a Gridline 0 projection. In Greek we have no option but to formulate the rule as a deletion rule, for reasons which will be clear when we use it in dactylic hexameter: the asterisk must first project, be subject to a non-iterative parenthesis insertion rule, and then be deleted.

In our theory of meter, rules are applied in a specified sequence. Rule (1) is ordered before the iterative rules that construct the metrical grid, and we next apply the rules for iambic trimeter (7), to generate the grids in (13).

(13) ὅτε δὴ κατῆλθ' Εὐριπίδης, ἐπεδείκνυτο

```
ᴗ ᴗ  –  ᴗ –      – – ᴗ –  ᴗ ᴗ –    ᴗ –
(Δ *   * ( *  *      ( *  * ( *  *  (Δ  *   *  ( *   * (    0 ⇒
    ) *     * )        *   * )       *     * )    1 ⇐
        ) *              *            *     * )    2 ⇐
                                            *      3
```

τοῖς λωποδύταις καὶ τοῖσι βαλλαντιοτόμοις

```
 –   – ᴗ ᴗ  –      – – ᴗ  –    – ᴗ ᴗ ᴗ –
( *    * ( Δ  *   * (    *   * ( *    * (   *  Δ * ( *  * (    0 ⇒
     ) *        * )          *     * )       *     * )    1 ⇐
         ) *                  *                     * )    2 ⇐
                                                    *      3
```

καὶ τοῖσι πατραλοίαισι καὶ τοιχωρύχοις

```
 –   – ᴗ  ᴗ  ᴗ – – ᴗ   –    – – ᴗ  –
( *    * ( Δ   *    * ( *  * ( *    * (    *  * ( *   * (    0 ⇒
     ) *           * )    *     * )        *     * )    1 ⇐
         ) *                 *                     * )    2 ⇐
                                                   *      3
```

The grids so generated conform to condition (10), which requires a light syllable in the position preceding the syllable which projects to Gridline 2. However, they do not conform to condition (6) requiring heavy syllables in certain positions. This is the correct result. Since, in traditional terms, any heavy syllable can be 'resolved' into a pair of light syllables, there can be no requirement that a syllable in any particular position is heavy. Condition (6), which is inviolable in certain other meters, is thus adhered to only in the majority of iambs (i.e., those without resolution). We show below that though generally true, condition (6) can nevertheless be dispensed with because its effects can be derived indirectly from condition (10) in combination with (1).

First, however, we examine some additional examples of resolution, showing the effects of rule (1) in lines which all conform to condition (10). The lines are by Aristophanes, and all are cited by White (1912: 22–23); they are iambic dimeter, except (14), which is iambic trimeter.

(14) ὡς τοὺς κριτάς με φέρετε· ποῦ 'στιν ὁ βασιλεύς;

```
 –   –    ᴗ –  ᴗ ᴗ ᴗ ᴗ   –   ᴗ ᴗ  ᴗ ᴗ –
(*    *   ( * *   Λ( *  * ( *    *    Δ( *   * ( *  * (    0 ⇒
   ) *        * )       *       * )       *     * )    1 ⇐
   ) *                  *                        * )    2 ⇐
                                                 *      3
```

'Bring me to the judges! Where's the "king"?' Aristophanes, *Acharnians* line 1224

(15) ὁ περιπόνηρος Ἀρτέμων

```
U  UU  U – U    –  U  –
Δ ( * *( * *( *    *( *   *(          0 ⇒
    ) *    *)    *       *)           1 ⇐
    ) *            *)                 2 ⇐
                    *                 3
```

'Artemon the really wicked' Aristophanes, *Acharnians* line 850

(16) λαβόντες ὑπὸ φιληδίας

```
U  –  U  U  U  U –U–
( *  *( Δ  *  *( *  *(* *(          0 ⇒
   ) *        *)   *   *)           1 ⇐
   ) *          *)                  2 ⇐
                 *                  3
```

Aristophanes, *Plutus* line 311

(17) βληχώμενοί τε προβατίων

```
–  –  U –  U    U  U  U–
( *  *( *  *( Δ   *  *( * *(          0 ⇒
   ) *    *)          *   *)          1 ⇐
   ) *                *)              2 ⇐
                       *              3
```

Aristophanes, *Plutus* line 293

(18) μέλπουσα καὶ τὴν τοξοφόρον

```
–    –  U  –  –    –  U  U  U
( *    *( *    *( *    *(Δ  *  *(          0 ⇒
   ) *        *)    *        *)            1 ⇐
   ) *                       *)            2 ⇐
                              *            3
```

Aristophanes *Thesmophoriazusae* line 970

(19) στυγερὸς ἐγώ. — μογερὸς ἐγώ

```
U  U  U  U  –       U  U  U  U  –
Δ( *  *( *   *(     Δ  *  *( *  *(          0 ⇒
   ) *     *)           *     *)            1 ⇐
   ) *                        *)            2 ⇐
                              *             3
```

Aristophanes, *Acharnians* line 1208 (Two speakers split this line between them.)

We now return to condition (6), which requires heads of Gridline 0 groups to be heavy, and would appear to be the basic condition on iambs. Since this condition is violated in 'resolved' lines, can it be dispensed with in all lines? Technically, the answer is that it can. In non-resolved lines, a metron (Gridline 1 group) projects from four syllables. If there are four syllables, and the third must be light by (10), then the second and the fourth are necessarily heavy without any special rule directly referring to them.

Consider, for example, the sequence – – ∪ –, which is metrical, as shown in (20).

(20)

```
        –     –    U    –
      ( *     *   ( *    * (            0 ⇒
              *         *                1
```

Given that there is no independent constraint on the second and fourth syllables, could either or both of these also be light, involving a sequence of – U U – or – – U U or – U U U ? The answer is that these four-syllable sequences would all scan as three rather than four Gridline 0 asterisks, because they include sequences of two or more light syllables, one of which does not project, as shown in (21). Thus, these sequences are not possible metra, but are ruled out without recourse to a condition requiring heads to be heavy.

(21)   a.

```
        –     –    U    U
      ( *     *    Δ   ( *            0 ⇒
              *         *              1
```

   b.

```
        –     U    U    –
      ( *     Δ    *   ( *            0 ⇒
              *         *              1
```

   c.

```
        –     U    U    U
      ( *     Δ    *   ( *            0 ⇒
              *         *              1
```

An iambic line without resolution will, therefore, have heavy syllables in even-numbered positions without any special rule requiring it to do so: this is the result instead of a rule (1) and a condition (10) referring only to light syllables.

6.2.3 Resolution in a sequence of five or six light syllables

We have seen that a sequence of four light syllables is projected as three Gridline 0 asterisks, after rule (1) has applied, and that this produces the right result. However, a sequence of five light syllables cannot be correctly scanned, as shown in (22).

(22)   ὧν πόλις ἀνάριθμος ὄλλυται·

```
       –   U U  U U U   U  –   U  –
      ( *   Δ * ( * *( *   * ( *   * ( *        0 ⇒
            * )   *     * )    *    * )          1 ⇐
            * )         *          * )          2 ⇐
            *                     *             3    ill-formed grid
```

Our solution to this problem makes use of the fact that left parentheses are inserted at Gridline 0 from left to right (we know this because the rightmost Gridline 0 group can fall short, and a short group must be the last generated). Rule (7a) requires parenthesis insertion on Gridline

0 to begin flush at the left edge, but, as shown by numerous examples in the preceding chapters, parenthesis insertion may begin one asterisk in. (For some discussion, see section 1.4.) We therefore replace rule (7a) with (23).

(23)   Gridline 0: starting one asterisk in at the L edge, insert a L parenthesis, form binary groups, heads R.

We illustrate the effect of (23) in (24), where the leftmost metron consists of a heavy syllable followed by light syllables, and in (25), where the leftmost metron is composed of six light syllables.

(24)   ὦν πόλις ἀνάριθμος ὄλλυται·

```
     -    U U  U U U    U   -  U   -
 *    Δ(*  *( *  *  ( *   *  ( *  *(      0 ⇒
      ) *    * )        *       * )       1 ⇐
        ) *                     * )       2 ⇐
                               *          3
```

Sophocles, *Oedipus Tyrannus* line 179 (Raven 1998: 37)

(25)   ἐκόμισα παρέδρους καὶ ξυνεμπόρους ἐμοί

```
 U U U U   U U    -     -  U  -  U   -  U   -
 Δ *( *  *  ( *  *  ( *      *( *  *  ( *   *  ( *  *(     0 ⇒
    ) *     * )          *     * )      *      * )        1 ⇐
      ) *                *                     * )        2 ⇐
                                              *           3
```

Euripides, *Bacchae* line 57 (Raven 1998: 28)

6.2.4 Splitting the line

In iambic meters, most examples of resolution involve one resolution per metron, which produces a sequence of three or four light syllables. The resolved metron has five rather than the expected four syllables. We have proposed rule (1) which prevents the first in a sequence of light syllables from being projected to Gridline 0, and this has the effect of permitting five syllables to be represented by four Gridline 0 asterisks. If there are two resolutions, the metron will have six syllables, and in this case rule (1) will reduce this to five, as in (25). If the metron is leftmost in the grid, the initial asterisk can be skipped, which reduces the five asterisks to four grouped asterisks at Gridline 0. This can all be handled well by our rules.

However, there are occasional lines in which a metron that is not at the beginning of the line has two resolutions. One such line is scanned in (26).

(26) σὲ γὰρ ἐκάλεσα, σὲ δὲ κατόμοσα,

```
     U  U  U U U U  U  U  U U U  U
     Δ  * ( * *( *  *  ( *  * ( *  *( *  * (        0 ⇒
              *)     *       *)   *       *)        1 ⇐
              *)              *       *)            2 ⇐
              *                      *              3      ill-formed grid
```

'For it was you I invoked, you I swore by.' Euripides, *Helen* line 348
(Raven 1998: 37)

The lines which precede and follow this line are in iambic dimeter, which normatively has eight syllables, but this line has twelve light syllables. The scansion in (26) fails because there are too many Gridline 0 asterisks.

We solve this problem by splitting the line into two grids, one grid for each metron. Each metron can now be subject to its own skip rule, and as there are two strings of light syllables, rule (1) applies and deletes the first of the two Gridline 0 asterisks in each grid. This successfully scans the line. (The fact that the two halves of this line are parallel in meaning offers some additional support to the analysis of this line into two separate metrical units.)

(27) σὲ γὰρ ἐκάλεσα,

```
     U  U  U U U U
     Δ  * ( * *( *  * (        0 ⇒
            ) *    *)          1 ⇐
                   *)          2 ⇐
                   *           3
```

σὲ δὲ κατόμοσα,

```
     U  U  U U U U
     Δ  * ( *  *( *  * (       0 ⇒
            ) *     *)         1 ⇐
                    *)         2 ⇐
                    *          3
```

6.2.5 Trochees

Trochees are in most respects the 'mirror image' of iambs. In the traditional analysis, the template is a four-position 'trochaic metron' consisting of the positions − ∪ − ×, such that trochaic tetrameter would be a sixteen-syllable line matching four of these metra. Two lines in trochaic tetrameter are given in (28).

(28) Πῶλε Θρηικίη, τί δή με λοξὸν ὄμμασι βλέπουσα

```
      −  ∪   − ∪− ∪ − ∪ − ∪  −  ∪−  ∪ − ∪
```

νηλέως φεύγεις, δοκεῖς δέ μ᾽ οὐδὲν εἰδέναι ὐυψύν,

```
      −  ∪−  − −   ∪ −  −  − ∪ − ∪ −  ∪ −
```

'Thracian pony, why ever do you look askance at me and flee without pity, thinking that I know nothing clever?' Anacreon, Fragment 417 (Campbell 1982: 73)

The iterative rules (29) for trochees differ from (7) for iambs crucially in having left-headed groups both at Gridline 0 and at Gridline 1.

(29) a. Gridline 0: starting just at the L edge, insert a L parenthesis, form binary groups, heads L.

     i. The last (rightmost) group may be incomplete.

    b. Gridline 1: starting just at the L edge, insert a L parenthesis, form binary groups, heads L.

    c. Gridline 2: starting just at the R edge, insert a R parenthesis, form binary groups, heads R.

    d. Gridline 3: starting just at the R edge, insert a R parenthesis, form binary groups, heads R.

The two lines are assigned grids in (30); note that the second line is 'catalectic' (it has fifteen syllables instead of sixteen), because the rightmost group on Gridline 0 is incomplete, as permitted by rule (29ai).

(30)   Πῶλε Θρηικίη, τί δή με λοξὸν ὄμμασι βλέπουσα

```
     –  U     –  U–  U  –  U  –  U   –   U–    U  –  U
    ( *  *   ( * *(  *  ( *  *  ( *  *  ( *   *(  *  * ( *  * (     0 ⇒
    ( *      * ( *     *   ( *  *   ( *         * (     1 ⇒
    ) *          * )            *          * )         2 ⇐
                 ) *                        * )        3 ⇐
                                             *         4
```

νηλέως φεύγεις, δοκεῖς δέ μ' οὐδὲν εἰδέναι σοφόν;

```
     –  U–    –    –      U  –    U    –  U  –U   –   U  –
    ( *  *(   *   ( *     *( *     *  ( *  *  ( * *( *   *( *      0 ⇒
    ( *   *     ( *         *   ( *      *  ( *       * (         1 ⇒
    ) *          * )            *             * )               2 ⇐
                 ) *                           * )               3 ⇐
                                               *                 4
```

Condition (6), which holds for unresolved iambs, also holds for unresolved trochees:

(6) Syllables projecting to Gridline 1 must be heavy.

Condition (31) is the trochaic equivalent of condition (10) in iambs.

(31) The syllable that projects to Gridline 2 must be followed by a light syllable, if both belong to the same Gridline 0 group.

In unresolved trochaic lines, conditions (6) and (31) between them control three of the four syllables in each four-syllable sequence (corresponding to a Gridline 1 group). The first and third syllables must be heavy, and the second must be light. The fourth syllable in each four-syllable sequence is not controlled (in traditional analysis it is called an 'anceps' syllable).

Like iambs, trochees are found with resolution. This arises as a result of the same rule (1) as is found in iambs with resolution: this rule deletes the leftmost of a sequence of asterisks projecting from light syllables. Grids for a pair of lines with resolution are shown in (32).

(32) ταῦτα καὶ καθύβρισ' αὐτόν, ὅτι με δεσμεύειν δοκῶν

```
    –  U   –  U  –  U   –   U   UU  U  –   –  –    U  –
   ( *  *  ( *  * ( *  *  ( *   Δ  *( * * ( *  * ( *   *( *    0 ⇒
   ( *     ( *    *      ( *    *     ( *      *( *    1 ⇒
   ) *        * )             *           * )       2 ⇐
         ) *                             * )       3 ⇐
                                          *        4
```

οὔτ' ἔθιγεν οὔθ' ἥψαθ' ἡμῶν, ἐλπίσιν δ' ἐβόσκετο.

```
    –   U U U   –    –  U  –  –   –   U–    U  –    U  –
   ( *   Δ *( *  *  ( * * ( *  * ( *  *( *   *( *  *( *    0 ⇒
   ( *      *      ( *   * ( *  *    ( *    * (    1 ⇒
   ) *            * )          *        * )       2 ⇐
            ) *                         * )       3 ⇐
                                         *        4
```

Euripides, *Bacchae* lines 616–617 (Raven 1998: 34)

It can be seen that in these trochaic lines with resolution, condition (6) is not obeyed. In fact, this condition need not be stated for any trochaic line (it is derived, as in iambs, as an indirect result of conditions (31) and (1)).

6.2.6 Cretic

In traditional analyses, a 'cretic metron' is the template $[- \cup -]$, matching a heavy–light–heavy sequence of syllables. The lines quoted in (33) consist of five such sequences, followed by a pair of heavy syllables (i.e., it is a cretic hexameter catalectic).

(33) Ἀφροδίτα μὲν οὐκ ἔστι, μάργος δ' Ἔρως οἷα παῖς παίσδει,

```
    –  U – –  U  –   –  U  –   –    U  –   –  U–   –  –
```

ἄκρ' ἐπ' ἄνθη καβαίνων, ἃ μή μοι θίγηις, τῶ κυπαιρίσκω.

```
    –   U   –  U – –  U   –   –  U  –   –  U –    –  –
```

'Now it's not Aphrodite, it's naughty Eros who sports like a child, alighting on the tips of the blooms of the cypress – but don't you (i.e., Eros) touch them!' Alcman, Fragment 58 (West 1982: 54)

It is clear that the heavy–light–heavy sequence forms a group, but though it characteristically has two heavy syllables, it cannot be a double-headed group: a group can never have two heads because only one asterisk can be promoted to the next Gridline from each group by the iterative rules. Instead, we treat this as a ternary group at Gridline 0, which is left-headed.[5] We scan the lines by the rules in (34), which crucially generate ternary groups at Gridline 0.

(34)   a. Gridline 0: starting just at the L edge, insert a L parenthesis, form ternary groups, heads L.

i. The last (rightmost) group must be incomplete (unary or binary).

b. Gridline 1: starting just at the R edge, insert a R parenthesis, form binary groups, heads R.

c. Gridline 2: starting just at the R edge, insert a R parenthesis, form ternary groups, heads R.

The rightmost syllable may be heavy or light. In other meters, we have accounted for this fact by allowing an actually light syllable to be scanned as heavy. However, in this meter we account for it by stipulation (35).[6]

(35) The rightmost syllable of the verse is not projected to Gridline 0.

The rules (35) and (34) assign the grid (36) to the first line of (33).

(36)   Ἀφροδίτα μὲν οὐκ ἔστι, μάργος δ' Ἔρως οἷα παῖς παίσδει,

```
     –    U – –  U   –    –  U   –   –      U  –   –    U –   –   –
    ( *   * *( *  *   *  ( *   *   * ( *      * * ( *    * *  ( *   Δ    0 ⇒
    ) *       * )           * )         * )                      * )       1 ⇐
        ) *            *                                          * )       2 ⇐
                                                                  *         3
```

Cretic is subject to a condition similar to that which we find in trochees and iambs, which requires a light syllable next to a head. It is clear from this grid that the light syllable always follows the head of the Gridline 0 group (not a Gridline 1 group, as for iambs and trochees). Thus, condition (31) for trochees must be altered to (37) for cretic.

(37) The syllable that projects to Gridline 1 must be followed by a light syllable, if both belong to the same Gridline 0 group.

[5] We could alternatively treat it as a right-headed group; however, it must be one or the other.

[6] It is necessary to prevent the rightmost syllable from projecting, or it will violate condition (37). Note that this stipulation can alternatively be formulated as a deletion rule: delete the Gridline 0 projection of the rightmost syllable. This rule would need to precede all other rules. This clarifies the similarity between the non-projection stipulation and the deletion rule (1).

Cretic lines also show resolution. West (1982: 146) quotes seven lines in cretic meter and notes that '[t]he order of frequency of the four possible forms of metron is $- \cup -, - \cup \cup \cup, \cup \cup \cup -, \cup \cup \cup \cup \cup$.' Either or (rarely) both of the heavy syllables can be replaced by two light syllables. We propose that, like iambs and trochees, cretics are subject to rule (1), the rule which deletes the projection of the first of a sequence of light syllables. This can be seen in the first line of (38), which would be traditionally analyzed as a cretic followed by three resolved cretics with the pattern $- \cup \cup \cup$.[7]

(38) ὡς μεμίσηκά σε Κλέωνος ἔτι μᾶλλον, ὃν ἐ-

```
 -     U - - U  U    U - U  UU    -   U  U  U
(*    * *( *  Δ  *   *(*  Δ  **  ( *   Δ   *  Δ        0 ⇒
)*        * )            *            * )             1 ⇐
       ) *                            * )             2 ⇐
                                      *               3
```

γὼ τεμῶ τοῖσιν ἱππεῦσι καττύματα

```
 -   U  -   - U -    -  U  -   - U U
( *  * *  ( * * *   ( *  *  *  ( *  * Δ               0 ⇒
) *           * )       *          * )                1 ⇐
       ) *                         * )                2 ⇐
                                   *                  3
```

'Since I am more full of hatred for you than for even Kleon, whom I shall cut up into soles for horsemen' Aristophanes, *Acharnians* lines 300–301 (Aristophanes 2002)

Note that the second line ends with two light syllables, the second of which is not projected (by rule (35)). The deletion rule (1) does not delete the projection of the first of these two light syllables because the second light syllable is invisible to it, since it is not projected. Finally, we note that, like resolved iambs, the resolved cretics conform to the basic condition (37) on light syllables in cretic lines, but do not always conform to the less strict general condition (6) that heads of Gridline 0 groups must be heavy.

6.3 Dactyls and anapaests

6.3.1 Dactylic hexameter: the traditional approach

In this section we explore the meter used by Homer: dactylic hexameter. Though the name 'dactylic' suggests that this is a ternary meter, we show that it is a binary meter where asterisks on Gridline 0 are

---

[7] This pattern is also called a paeon. Gerard Manley Hopkins claimed to be using paeons as the basis of his Sprung Rhythm, which we instead have analyzed as a loose iambic meter with intermittent non-projection (cf. section 3.5.2 above).

grouped into left-headed pairs, and the extra syllables are deleted by rule (1). Dactyls thus resemble trochees, but with the crucial difference that dactyls in addition have a non-iterative parenthesis insertion rule, which means that in our account, the traditional dactylic hexameter is a loose trochaic meter.

The 'looseness' of the meter is suggested by the fact that Homer's verse has between thirteen and seventeen syllables in the line. This variation in length is illustrated almost in its entirety in the first five lines of the *Odyssey* in (39), which have, respectively, 17, 16, 15, 16, and 14 syllables. The vertical bars indicate caesura positions, where the required presence of a word boundary is determined by a rule which we discuss in section 6.3.4.

(39) ἄνδρα μοι ἔννεπε, μοῦσα, πολύτροπον, ὃς μάλα πολλὰ
    –   ∪   ∪ – ∪ ∪   – ∪| ∪ – ∪ ∪   –   ∪ ∪   – ∪
    πλάγχθη, ἐπεὶ Τροίης ἱερὸν πτολίεθρον ἔπερσε·
    –   ∪ ∪ –   – –|∪∪   ∪ ∪– ∪ ∪ – ∪
    πολλῶν δ' ἀνθρώπων ἴδεν ἄστεα καὶ νόον ἔγνω,
    –   –   –   – –|∪ ∪ – ∪∪ – ∪∪ – –
    πολλὰ δ' ὅ γ' ἐν πόντῳ πάθεν ἄλγεα ὃν κατὰ θυμόν,
    – ∪ ∪   –   – –| ∪ ∪ – ∪∪– ∪ ∪ – ∪
    ἀρνύμενος ἥν τε ψυχὴν καὶ νόστον ἑταίρων.
    – ∪ ∪ – –   –| – –   – – ∪ ∪ – –

    'Sing me the man, O Muse, of many turns, who wandered much indeed,
    once he had sacked the holy citadel of Troy. Many men's cities he saw,
    and he came to know their minds; many the travails he suffered at sea
    in his heart, trying to save his own life and his companions' safe return.'
    Homer, *Odyssey* I lines 1–5

In the traditional approach, the dactylic hexameter is conceptualized as a template such as (40), made up of positions to which syllables of the line are matched (cf. Halporn et al. 1994: 11).

(40)   – $\overline{\cup\cup}$ – $\overline{\cup\cup}$ – $\overline{\cup\cup}$ – $\overline{\cup\cup}$ – ∪∪ – ×

The – symbol is a 'longum' position and must be matched to a single heavy syllable, the ∪ symbol is a 'breve' position and must be matched to a single light syllable. The $\overline{\cup\cup}$ symbol is a 'contractible biceps' position which must be matched either to a single heavy syllable or to two light syllables. The × is an 'anceps' position and may be matched either to a single heavy syllable or a single light syllable. To see how the matching works, consider the third line in (39), where the first and second 'contractible biceps' positions are matched to heavy syllables, but the third and fourth 'contractible biceps' is matched to a pair of light syllables, and the anceps position is matched to a heavy syllable.

(41) $-\ \overset{—}{—}\ -\ \overset{—}{—}\ -\ \cup\cup\ -\ \cup\cup\ -\cup\cup--$

In the traditional analysis, the template (40) is usually interpreted as consisting of six instances of a smaller template with the schema (42a) realized either as a sequence of two heavy syllables, called 'spondee' (see 42b), or as sequence of a heavy followed by two light syllables, called 'dactyl' (see (42c)).

(42)   a. $-\ \overset{—}{\cup\cup}$

      b. $-\ -$ 'spondee'

      c. $-\cup\cup$ 'dactyl'

In such an analysis, the third line has the following structure:

(43)   spondee + spondee + dactyl + dactyl + dactyl + spondee

6.3.2 Dactylic hexameter reanalyzed as a loose trochaic meter

In the traditional treatment, as just noted, the hexameter line is analyzed as being uniformly composed of six pieces, and the variable length of the lines is attributed to the fact that the pieces (groups) composing the line can be either spondees (2 syllables) or dactyls (3 syllables). On this view, every syllable in the line belongs to a group (foot). We retain the notion that the line consists of six pieces (Gridline 0 groups), and we account for the variable length of the lines in (39) not by means of groups of variable length, but rather by excluding one syllable in every pair of light syllables from the metrical grid by the 'resolution rule' (1) which we have already seen in iambs, trochees, and cretics. So-called 'dactylic hexameter' will thus prove to be a binary (not a ternary) meter, similar in some respects to trochees. As shown below, the dactylic hexameter involves non-iterative parenthesis insertion. The dactylic hexameter is therefore in effect a loose trochaic meter.

The first step in generating a grid is to project syllables as asterisks on Gridline 0. The final syllable in the dactylic hexameter line can be either light or heavy. Instead of treating every line-final syllable as heavy even if it is phonetically light, we take a different approach here: we exclude it from any conditions on the grid by rule (35) (a rule previously seen in cretics).

(35)   The rightmost syllable of the verse is not projected to Gridline 0.

Lines 1 and 5 of (39) project to Gridline 0 as shown in (44) and (45).

(44)   ἄνδρα μοι ἔννεπε, μοῦσα, πολύτροπον, ὃς μάλα πολλὰ

```
 −   U   U −   U U   − U   U −   U U   −   U U   −  U
 *   *   * *   * *   * *   * *   * *   *   * *   *  Δ    0
```

(45)   ἀρνύμενος ἥν τε ψυχὴν καὶ νόστον ἑταίρων.

```
 −   U U −   −   −   − −   −   −   U U −   −
 *   * * *   *   *   * *   *   *   * * *   Δ         0
```

Next the non-iterative parenthesis insertion rule (46) applies.

(46)   On Gridline 0 insert a L parenthesis to the right of an asterisk
which projects from a light syllable, if that light syllable is to
the right of a light syllable, i.e., after a sequence of two light
syllables.

Rule (46) inserts a left parenthesis after a sequence of asterisks which
project from two light syllables. This produces the results shown in (47)
and (48).

(47)   ἄνδρα μοι ἔννεπε, μοῦσα, πολύτροπον, ὃς μάλα πολλὰ

```
 −   U   U −   U U   − U   U −   U U   −   U U   −  U
 *   *   *( *   * *   ( * *   *( * *   * (*   * *   (*  Δ    0
```

(48)   ἀρνύμενος ἥν τε ψυχὴν καὶ νόστον ἑταίρων.

```
 −   U U −   −   −   − −   −   −   U U −   −
 *   * *( *   *   *   * *   *   *   * *( *   Δ         0
```

It is at this point – after the non-iterative rule which inserts a left
parenthesis, but before the iterative rules – that the deletion rule (1),
repeated here, applies to the grid.

(1)   Delete the Gridline 0 asterisk which projects from the first syllable in a sequence of two or more light syllables.

This rule has the effect in dactylic hexameter of projecting three-syllable
sequences where two syllables are light as two asterisks on Gridline 0.
Thus, three-syllable dactyls with one heavy and two light syllables become similar to two-syllable spondees where both syllables are heavy,
and this explains why these two types of sequence are apparently inter-
changeable.

We illustrate the effects of rule (1) on the two lines in (47) and (48),
reproduced here as (49) and (50).

(49)   ἄνδρα μοι ἔννεπε, μοῦσα, πολύτροπον, ὃς μάλα πολλὰ

```
 −   U   U −   U U   − U   U −   U U   −   U U   −  U
 *   Δ   *( *   Δ *   (* Δ   *( * Δ   * (*   Δ *   (*  Δ    0
```

(50)   ἀρνύμενος ἥν τε ψυχὴν καὶ νόστον ἑταίρων.

   –   ∪ ∪ – –   –   – – –   –   – ∪ ∪ –   –
   *   * (* *   *   * *   *   *   Δ * (*   Δ   0

The next step in the derivation is application of the iterative rule (51).

(51)   Gridline 0: starting just at the L edge, insert a R parenthesis,
       form binary groups, heads L.

   a. The last (rightmost) group must be incomplete.

   b. Ungrouped asterisks are not permitted.

Application of rule (51) generates the partial grids in (52) and (53).
We have explicitly ruled out the possibility of having an ungrouped
asterisk after a right parenthesis and before a left parenthesis; ungrouped
asterisks are found in loose meters of other languages but not in Greek.

(52)   ἄνδρα μοι ἔννεπε, μοῦσα, πολύτροπον, ὃς μάλα πολλὰ

   –   ∪   ∪ – ∪ ∪   – ∪   ∪ – ∪ ∪   –   ∪ ∪   – ∪
)*   Δ   *)(*   Δ *) (* Δ   *)(* Δ *) (*   Δ *) (* Δ   0 ⇒
   *   *   *   *   *   *   1

(53)   ἀρνύμενος ἥν τε ψυχὴν καὶ νόστον ἑταίρων.

   –   ∪ ∪ – –   –   – – –   –   – ∪ ∪ –   –
)*   Δ *)(*   *) *   *)*   *) *   Δ *)(*   Δ   0 ⇒
   *   *   *   *   *   *   1

Two types of syllable are invisible to the iterative rule (51), because they
are not projected on Gridline 0. This includes the rightmost syllable (not
projected as a result of (35)), and the first of each pair of light syllables
(whose projection is deleted by rule (1), which is ordered before (51)).

   The metrical grids in (52) and (53) must satisfy condition (6), repeated
here, which is also satisfied by many other Greek meters, though not all.

(6)   Syllables projecting to Gridline 1 must be heavy.

Given the rules above, all Gridline 0 groups are binary, and no ungrouped syllables appear on Gridline 0. The binary groups generated on
Gridline 0 by rule (51) are therefore of two kinds only: the two asterisks project either from a heavy–light sequence or from a heavy–heavy
sequence. This is shown graphically in (52) and (53) above. This fact
gives rise to the question as to the manner in which the formalism developed above excludes lines such as those in (54) below, which consist
of six groups, each of which is either heavy–heavy or heavy–light. This
sequence is never found in a line of Homer's verse: we must explain why.

(54)   – ∪ – ∪ – ∪ – ∪ – ∪ ∪ – –

We show in (55) the steps in the generation of the metrical grid that is assigned to this string by the rules (35), (46), and (51).

(55) a.
  − U − U − U − U − U U − −
  * * * * * * * * * * * * *   0   underlying
                                         representation

  b.
  − U − U − U − U − U U − −
  * * * * * * * * * * * * * Δ   0   by (35)

  c.
  − U − U − U − U − U U − −
  * * * * * * * * * * * (* Δ   0   by (46)

  d.
  − U − U − U − U − U U − −
  * * * * * * * * * Δ * (* Δ   0   by (1)

  e.
  − U − U − U − U − U U − −
)* *) * *) * *) * *) * Δ *)(* Δ   0 ⇒   by (51)
   *   *   *   *   *   *   1

Given the conditions stated to this point the derived grid (e) in (55) is perfectly well formed, and yet no lines of this pattern are to be found in dactylic hexameter texts.

To see why lines of this kind are excluded, compare the bottom grid in (55) with the grid assigned to the well-formed line (52), which we reproduce here.

(52)   ἄνδρα μοι ἔννεπε, μοῦσα, πολύτροπον, ὃς μάλα πολλὰ
  −   U U − U U   − U U − U U   −   U U − U
)* Δ *)(* Δ *) (* Δ *)(* Δ *) (* Δ *) (* Δ   0 ⇒
   *   *   *   *   *   *   1

The major difference between the grid in (55e) and the grid in (52) is in the context where we find asterisks projecting from light syllables. In (52) asterisks projecting from light syllables appear exclusively at the end of binary Gridline 0 groups. This is formally reflected in the metrical grid by the fact that on Gridline 0, a light syllable projects an asterisk that is followed by the parenthesis sequence)(where a right parenthesis is followed by a left parenthesis. Significantly such sequences are not found in (55e) and elsewhere. We rule out grids such as (55e) by adding to our account condition (56) as a requirement that Gridline 0 of all well-formed grids must satisfy in dactylic hexameter.

(56)   On Gridline 0 an asterisk projecting from a light syllable must be followed by a right parenthesis which, in turn, is followed by a left parenthesis.

The effect of condition (56) is that every projected light syllable in the dactylic hexameter line is preceded by an unprojected light sylla- ble: thus, in this meter, light syllables always appear in pairs. This is guaranteed by (56) even though one of the two light syllables cannot be directly referred to by any condition or rule once its projection has been deleted by (1). In this way, we differentiate dactylic from trochaic meters.

6.3.3 The cadence

Dactylic hexameter permits some variation in the first two thirds of the line, but it always ends on a fixed pattern or 'cadence' of $-$ ∪ ∪ $-$ ×. This is explained as a secondary result of analyzing the dactylic meter as a loose meter with a non-iterative rule (46), as we now show.

The Gridline 0 rule (51a) specifies that the rightmost group on Gridline 0 must be incomplete. Given binary groups, an incomplete group at the right edge of a Gridline must consist of a single asterisk preceded by a left parenthesis. This asterisk will be the head of its group, and thus by condition (6) must project from a heavy syllable. This is the rightmost projected syllable in the line, and by rule (35) it must be followed by a non-projected syllable. There is no way to impose conditions on syllables that do not figure in the metrical grid. Since the rightmost syllable does not project it does not figure in the grid and it is therefore not controlled by any condition and so can be either a light or a heavy syllable (i.e., 'anceps'). In summary, the combination of (51a) and (35) means that the grid must end with ($-$ ×.

The only source of a left parenthesis is rule (46), which inserts a left parenthesis to the right of a pair of light syllables, which means that the final sequence must now be ∪ ∪ ($-$ ×. In this pair of light syllables, the first will not be projected, leaving one light syllable, which must be combined in a group with the next projected syllable to the left which must be heavy (by (6)), giving a final pattern of $-$ ∪ ∪ ($-$ ×. The cadence is the inevitable consequence of the rules we have posited.

6.3.4 The caesura rule

We now turn to the 'caesura rule', the rule which requires the line to have a word boundary. In traditional analysis, the line has a penthemimeral caesura, that is, it has a word boundary either after the third longum (the head of the third Gridline 0 group) or after the breve following this (i.e., the light syllable following the head of the third Gridline 0 group). Alternatively, the line has a hephthemimeral caesura with a word boundary after the fourth longum (the head of the fourth Gridline 0 group).

In order to locate these positions, we must first generate the full grid for the dactylic hexameter line by the stipulation (35), rules (46) and (1) and the full set of iterative rules (57).

(35) The rightmost syllable of the verse is not projected to Gridline 0.

(46) On Gridline 0, insert a L parenthesis to the right of an asterisk which projects from a light syllable, if that light syllable is to the right of a light syllable, i.e., after a sequence of two light syllables.

(1) Delete the Gridline 0 asterisk which projects from the first syllable in a sequence of two or more light syllables.

(57) a. Gridline 0: starting just at the L edge, insert a R parenthesis, form binary groups, heads L.

 i. The last (rightmost) group must be incomplete.

 ii. Ungrouped asterisks are not permitted.

 b. Gridline 1: starting just at the L edge, insert a L parenthesis, form binary groups, heads L.

 c. Gridline 2: starting just at the R edge, insert a R parenthesis, form binary groups, heads L.

 i. The last (leftmost) group must be incomplete.

 d. Gridline 3: starting just at the R edge, insert a R parenthesis, form binary groups, heads R.

Two lines from the opening passage of the *Odyssey* in (39) are assigned grids: line 2 as (58) and line 1 as (59).

(58) πλάγχθη, ἐπεὶ Τροίης ἱερὸν πτολίεθρον ἔπερσε·

	–	υ υ –	– –|υ υ –	υ υ – υ υ –	υ		
	)*	Δ *)(*	*)* Δ *)(*	Δ *)(* Δ *)(*	Δ	0 ⇒
	(*	*	(* *	(* * (		1 ⇒
	*)		*	*)		2 ⇐
	)*		*)			3 ⇐
			*			4

(59) ἄνδρα μοι ἔννεπε, μοῦσα, πολύτροπον, ὃς μάλα πολλὰ

	–	υ υ–	υ υ	– υ| υ–	υ υ –	υ υ –	υ ‖		
	)*	Δ *)(*	Δ *)	(* Δ *)(*	Δ *)(*	Δ *)(*	Δ	0 ⇒
	(*	*		(* *	(*	* (		1 ⇒
	*)			*	*)			2 ⇐
	)*			*)				3 ⇐
				*				4

The location of the caesura can be determined once we have the full grid, because it is located after the head of the verse:

(60) The head of the verse must be directly followed by a word boundary (caesura).

We begin with the penthemimeral caesura, seen in (58) and (59). Condition (60) is satisfied in both lines. In line (58), the syllable which projects to the head of the verse is in fact word-final. In (59) the syllable which projects to the head of the verse is penultimate in its word, but the final syllable is invisible to the metrical rules because its projection has been deleted by rule (1). Thus the head of the verse projects from the final syllable which is visible to the metrical conditions, thus meeting the condition.[8] Now we turn to the hephthemimeral caesura, where the obligatory word boundary follows the head of the fourth foot (in a word which extends at least from the beginning of the third foot). In the grid as it stands, this is not accounted for by (60), but we suggest that the grid may be adjusted by applying the optional rule (61), which deletes the Gridline 1 asterisk of the head of the verse.

(61) Delete the Gridline 1 asterisk of the head of the verse.

The effect of applying rule (61) is to shift the head of the verse from being the head of the third Gridline 0 group (foot) to that of the fourth Gridline 0 group (foot), and this syllable is followed by the caesura. This is shown in (62).

(62) ἢ Αἴας ἢ Ἰδομενεὺς ἢ δῖος Ὀδυσσεὺς

```
  –   – –    – – U U  –    | – – U   U  –     –
  )*  *) *   *) * Δ *)(*    *) * Δ   *)( *    Δ            0 ⇒
  (*   *    (Δ        *     ( *       * (                  1 ⇒
   * )             *         * )                           2 ⇐
  )*                  * )                                  3 ⇐
                     *                                     4
```

Homer, *Iliad* I line 145

The fact that the caesura rule picks out the heads of adjacent Gridline 0 groups – the third and the fourth – shows that these groups are related. We have captured this by putting them into the same Gridline 1 group, thus permitting the deletion rule (61) to move the head of the verse within this Gridline 1 group.[9]

---

[8] Compare the similar interaction of the caesura condition and non-projection in French, in section 5.3.

[9] For a discussion of a similar treatment of the different variants of the Spanish *endecasílabo*, see section 4.3, and in the meters of circle 4 of classical Arabic, see section 7.2.

6.3.5 Anapaests

In their simplest form anapaestic meters are traditionally conceived of as repeating a small template which is the mirror image of the dactylic template. It takes the form (63a), manifested either as (63b) or as (63c).

(63) a. $\overline{\cup\cup}$ ‾

   b. – –   'spondee'

   c. ∪ ∪ –   'anapaest'

(64) consists of a sequence of lines in 'anapaestic dimeter catalectic'. This is three sequences on the pattern of (63a) followed by a single heavy syllable; for example, the second line in (64) would traditionally be scanned as: [– –][∪ ∪ –][∪ ∪ –][–]. In fact though the final position is thought of as heavy, the final syllable can be light or heavy. (When a light syllable is 'counted as heavy' in this way it is traditionally called *brevis in longo*.)

(64) ἄγετ' ὦ Σπάρτας εὐάνδρου   ∪ ∪ – – – – – –

   κοῦροι πατέρων πολιητᾶν,   – – ∪ ∪ – ∪ ∪ – –

   λαιᾶι μὲν ἴτυν προβάλεσθε,   – – ∪ ∪ – ∪ ∪ – ∪

   δόρυ δ' εὐτόλμως πάλλοντες ...   ∪ ∪ – – – – – –

   μὴ φειδόμενοι τᾶς ζωᾶς·   – – ∪ ∪ – – – –

   οὐ γὰρ πάτριον τᾶι Σπάρται.   – – – – – –

'Come on, sons of the citizen fathers of manly Sparta, throw the shield forth with the left, and courageously shaking the spear ⟨in the right...⟩ not sparing your life. For that's not how we do it in Sparta.' Anon. Spartan march (West 1982: 53)

Like the dactylic meters, we treat anapaestic meters as loose meters, with a non-iterative rule (65) (which is the counterpart of rule (46) for the dactylic hexameter).

(65) On Gridline 0, insert a R parenthesis to the left of an asterisk which projects from a light syllable, if that light syllable is to the left of a light syllable, i.e., before a sequence of two light syllables.

The rightmost syllable is indeterminate in its weight, and, like in the dactylic hexameter, we deal with this by not projecting it, by rule (35).

(35) The rightmost syllable of the verse is not projected to Gridline 0.

Application of this rule also has the consequence of removing from the footing the odd extra syllable at the end; this is now treated as an unprojected and hence ungrouped syllable, and not as an incomplete foot.[10]

Like dactyls (and iambs and trochees), anapaests show 'resolution', where rule (1) makes the first of a pair of light syllables inaccessible to the metrical rules.

(1)　Delete the Gridline 0 asterisk which projects from the first syllable in a sequence of two or more light syllables.

The iterative rules are stated in (66). The Gridline 0 rule is the counterpart of the Gridline 0 rule (51) for dactylic meters (but with no requirement that the final group be incomplete). Note that because the rightmost syllable in these 'catalectic' lines is not projected there are in fact three rather than four Gridline 0 groups in the line.

(66)　a.　Gridline 0: starting just at the R edge, insert a L parenthesis, form binary groups, heads R.

　　　　　i.　Ungrouped asterisks are not permitted.

　　b.　Gridline 1: starting just at the L edge, insert a L parenthesis, form binary groups, heads L.

　　　　　i.　The last (rightmost) group must be incomplete.

　　c.　Gridline 2: starting just at the L edge, insert a L parenthesis, form binary groups, heads L.

The rules (65), (35), (1), and (66) assign the grid in (67) to the second line of (64).

(67)　κοῦροι πατέρων πολιητᾶν,

```
      –    –   U U  –    U U – –
    ( *    * ) Δ(* *  )  Δ(* * Δ(       0 ⇐
    ( *          *       ( *            1 ⇒
    ( *                    * (          2 ⇒
      *                                 3
```

Condition (6), which holds for the dactylic hexameter, also holds for this meter. Anapaests also require condition (68), which is the counterpart (and mirror image) of the dactylic hexameter condition (56).

(6)　Syllables projecting to Gridline 1 must be heavy.

(68)　On Gridline 0 an asterisk projecting from a light syllable must be preceded by a left parenthesis which, in turn, is preceded by a right parenthesis.

---

[10] An anapaestic line which is not catalectic might be dealt with by omitting condition (35).

Our account carries over straightforwardly from our account of dactylic meter. There is no caesura rule in the anapaestic meter, and in this regard the anapaestic meter is simpler.

6.4 Aeolic meters

We have explored two kinds of meter with resolution: strict meters (iambs, trochees, cretics) and loose meters (dactyls, anapaests). In these meters, resolution – where two light syllables project one asterisk to Gridline 0 – is derived by applying rule (1) before the iterative rules. In this final section we consider some of the aeolic meters. These meters do not have resolution, but as we will see, in these meters (1) also plays an important role in dealing with pairs of light syllables. The different effect of (1) arises because in the aeolic meters this rule is ordered after, rather than before, the iterative rules.

A selection of aeolic meters is shown in (69). It is characteristic for adjacent lines to be in different aeolic meters, as here. It is also common, incidentally, for a later section of the text to exactly reproduce the same sequence of meters (the pair of sections is called a 'strophe–antistrophe' pair). The double bars indicate period boundaries, where a light syllable can be counted as heavy (*brevis in longo*, e.g., in the seventh line, where δεινά ends on a short vowel). Following the traditional analysis, we treat any period-final syllable as heavy in this type of meter.

(69)

ἔτλα καὶ Δανάας οὐράνιον φῶς	− − − ∪ ∪ − − ∪ ∪ − − ‖
ἀλλάξαι δέμας ἐν χαλκοδέτοις	− − − ∪ ∪ − − ∪ ∪−
αὐλαῖς· κρυπτομένα δ' ἐν	− − − ∪ ∪ − −
τυμβήρει θαλάμωι κατεζεύχθη·	− − − ∪ ∪ − ∪ − − − ‖
καίτοι καὶ γενέαι τίμιος, ὦ παῖ παῖ,	− − − ∪ ∪ − − ∪ ∪ − − − ‖
καὶ Ζηνὸς ταμιεύεσκε γονὰς χρυσορύτους.	− − − ∪ ∪ − − ∪ ∪ − − ∪ ∪−
ἀλλ' ἁ μοιριδία τις δύνασις δεινά·	− − − ∪ ∪ − − ∪ ∪ − − − ‖
οὔτ' ἄν νιν ὄλβος οὔτ' Ἄρης,	− − ∪ − ∪ − ∪−
οὐ πύργος, οὐχ ἁλίκτυποι	− − ∪ − ∪ − ∪−
κελαιναὶ νᾶες ἐκφύγοιεν.	∪ − − − ∪ − ∪ − − ‖

> 'Even the body of Danae endured to be deprived of the light of heaven in a golden room; and she was bound fast hidden in a tomb-like chamber. And yet she too was of honored stock, O child, child, and tended Zeus's offspring born in a torrent of gold. But Fate has a kind of fearsome ability; neither wealth nor war, not fortifications, not dark sea-drumming ships could escape it.' Sophocles, *Antigone* lines 944–954 (Sophocles 1999: 285)

Aeolic meters are traditionally analyzed 'by colon', a metrical unit which corresponds to all or most of the metrical line. The weight-patterns of the syllables are fixed, except at the beginning of the colon (where ancipitia are permitted). Often the verse is taken up entirely by the colon, or the colon plus a small metrical section. (70) shows the third line of (69) analyzed as a single colon called a 'pherecratean', which is traditionally modelled as a template consisting of a set of seven positions [× × − ∪∪ − −], of which the first two positions can in principle be occupied either by a light or by a heavy syllable.

(70) αὐλαῖς· κρυπτομένα δ' ἐν

$$\begin{array}{ll}
-\quad\quad -\ \cup\ \cup\ -\quad - & \text{a. syllables}\\
\left[\times\quad\times\quad -\ \cup\ \cup\ -\quad -\right] & \text{b. positions}\\
\quad\quad\text{pherecratean colon} & \text{c. types of section}
\end{array}$$

The fourth line is analyzed in (71) into a colon of the glyconic type, a set of positions [× × − ∪∪ − ∪−], followed by a metrical section [− −], which Griffith calls a 'catalectic bacchiac'.

(71) τυμβήρει θαλάμωι κατεζεύχθη·

$$\begin{array}{ll}
-\ -\ -\ \cup\ \cup\ -\ \ \cup\ -\ -\quad - & \text{a. syllables}\\
\left[\times\quad\times\ -\ \cup\ \cup\ -\ \ \cup\ -\right]\!\left[-\quad-\right] & \text{b. positions}\\
\quad\text{glyconic colon}\quad\quad\quad\text{cat.bac} & \text{c. types of section}
\end{array}$$

In the sections which follow, we take lines where the colon and the line coincide, and reanalyze the aeolic cola in our generative framework, in which rules assign grids to lines.

6.4.1 Glyconic and telesillian

The 'glyconic' meter is illustrated by lines 1, 3, and 4 of the song in (72). Line 2 is in the 'telesillian' meter.[11]

(72) ὁ δὲ καρκίνος ὦδ' ἔφα   ∪∪ − ∪∪ − ∪− ‖
      χαλᾶι τὸν ὄφιν λαβών·   − − ∪∪ − ∪− ‖
      εὐθὺν χρὴ τὸν ἑταῖρον ἔμ-   − − − ∪∪ − ∪− ‖
      μεν καὶ μὴ σκολιὰ φρονεῖν.´ − − − ∪∪ − ∪− ‖

'So spoke the crab, seizing the snake in its claw: "A companion must be straight/honest and not harbour crooked/devious thoughts".' Anonymous, Scolia 892 (Campbell 1982: 133)

The glyconic line has eight syllables, of which the first two are ancipitia and the other six syllables follow a fixed pattern depending on weight. It is common in aeolic meters for the leftmost one or two syllables to

---

[11] Note that a word (ἔμμεν) is split between the third and fourth lines. This exemplifies a general possibility in Greek poetry, particularly in aeolic meters, where the line boundary need not coincide with the word boundary (i.e., where words are subject to enjambment).

be uncontrolled in their weight, while all the other syllables are fixed either as heavy or as light. We will formulate conditions to control for the heavy and light syllables. The best way to exclude the first one or two syllables from such conditions is to prevent them from projecting to Gridline 0. They will thus be invisible to further rules and conditions. We do this for the glyconic meter by stipulation (73).[12]

(73)   The leftmost two syllables of a verse are not projected to Gridline 0.

The remaining six syllables form a pattern which contains three light and three heavy syllables, suggesting that the syllables are grouped into pairs. More specifically, we suggest that these are right-headed pairs (i.e., the line is basically iambic), grouped by rule (74a).

(74)   a.   Gridline 0: starting just at the R edge, insert a R parenthesis, form binary groups, heads R.

b.   Gridline 1: starting just at the R edge, insert a R parenthesis, form ternary groups, heads L.

This is the full set of iterative rules for the glyconic colon; in combination with non-projection by (73), the rules assign the grid in (75) to the second line of (72).

(75)   εὐθὺν χρὴ τὸν ἑταῖρον ἔμ-

```
    –   –      –  U  U  –  U  –
    Δ  Δ     ) *  * ) *  * ) *  * )        0 ⇐
             )    *     *     * )          1 ⇐
                  *                        2
```

The grid we see in (75) does not make sense of the pattern of heavy and light syllables. Of the six projected syllables, two of the heavy syllables project to Gridline 1 but the other does not. This problem is simply solved by applying deletion rule (1) now, with the result shown in (76).

(1)   Delete the Gridline 0 asterisk which projects from the first syllable in a sequence of two or more light syllables.

(76)   εὐθὺν χρὴ τὸν ἑταῖρον ἔμ-

```
    –   –      –  U  U  –  U  –
    Δ  Δ     ) *  Δ ) *  * ) *  * )        0 ⇐
             ) *        *     * )          1 ⇐
                  *                        2
```

---

[12] This stipulation might alternatively be formulated as a rule which deletes the Gridline 0 projections of the leftmost two syllables.

Aeolic meters are subject to conditions (6), repeated below, and (77). The grid assigned by the iterative rules to the aeolic line conforms to these conditions, once the deletion rule (1) has applied to this grid.

(6)   Syllables projecting to Gridline 1 must be heavy.

(77)   Syllables which do not project to Gridline 1 must be light.

The heavy–light–light–heavy pattern which we see in this line is traditionally called a 'choriamb', and it is explained in our account by ordering the deletion rule (1) after the iterative rules. In this meter, the rule has the effect of changing the pattern of heavy and light syllables (producing a characteristic aperiodicity), rather than varying the length of the line. Aeolic lines are not variable in their length (they do not have resolution). The reason that rule (1) does not vary the length of the line is that it applies after the iterative rules.

For the glyconic variant called 'telesillian' stipulation (73) must be replaced by stipulation (78). Otherwise the meters are identical.

(78)   The leftmost syllable of a verse is not projected to Gridline 0.

(79)   χαλᾶι τὸν ὄφιν λαβών·

```
        –   –   U   U –   U   –
      Δ ) *   Δ ) * * )   *   * )        0 ⇐
        ) *           *       * )        1 ⇐
          *           *                  2
```

6.4.2 Hipponactean

'Hipponactean' is the name for a type of meter which is similar to the glyconic but with an additional heavy syllable at the end of the line. Thus, the hipponactean colon is thought of as a sequence [× × − UU − U − −]. We suggest that lines in this meter are scanned by the same set of rules as the glyconic, but altering rule (74a) as in (80), so as to require Gridline 0 grouping to begin one asterisk into the line, rather than just at the edge. The effects of the change are shown in (81).

(80)   Gridline 0: starting at the R edge one asterisk in, insert a R parenthesis, form binary groups, heads R.

(81) ὡς ἁμὲς τὸ καλὸν μελίσκον

$$
\begin{array}{ccccccc}
- & - & - & \cup & \cup & - & \cup - - \\
\Delta & \Delta\;)\;* & & \Delta\;)\;*\;*\;) & \;*\;*\;)\;* & & 0 \Leftarrow \\
&)\;* & & * & *\;) & & 1 \Leftarrow \\
& * & & & & & 2
\end{array}
$$

Alcman, Fragment 36 (Campbell 1988: 422

Cola (lines) in aeolic meters are of specific lengths. We have seen in this section that the length of the colon is determined by combining two types of rule. Rule (73), which applies to glyconic and hipponactean, stipulates that the first two syllables are not projected on Gridline 0; rule (78), which applies to telesillian cola, stipulates that only the initial syllable is not projected. Thus, the glyconic colon has 2+6 syllables in total and the hipponactean colon has 2+7 syllables in total, while the telesillian colon has 1+6 syllables in total.

6.4.3 Pherecratean

Like the hipponactean, the 'pherecratean' meter is closely related to the glyconic. Traditionally the pherecratean is regarded as a 'catalectic glyconic' because it is one syllable shorter at the right edge. A typical example is the third line in (82), which differs from the other two (glyconic) lines by ending with a single heavy syllable rather than with the $\cup\;-$ sequence found in lines 1 and 2.

(82) γουνοῦμαί σ' ἐλαφηβόλε $-\;-\;-\cup\cup-\cup-\;\|$
      ξανθὴ παῖ Διὸς ἀγρίων $-\;-\;-\cup\cup-\cup-\;\|$
      δέσποιν' Ἄρτεμι θηρῶν· $-\;-\;-\cup\cup-\;-\;\|$

'I entreat you, Artemis slayer of deer, blonde child of Zeus, mistress of wild animals' Anacreon, Fragment 348 (Campbell 1988: 46)

Our approach to the pherecratean assigns a grid by the same Gridline 0 rule (80) as in the hipponactean, but with an incomplete ternary Group on Gridline 1.

(83) δέσποιν' Ἄρτεμι θηρῶν·

$$
\begin{array}{cccccc}
- & - & - & \cup & \cup & - - \\
\Delta & \Delta\;)\;* & \Delta\;)\;* & \;*\;)\;* & & 0 \Leftarrow \\
& * & & *\;) & & 1 \Leftarrow \\
& * & & & & 2
\end{array}
$$

6.4.4 Choriambic expansion

In traditional accounts of these aeolic meters, the colon is thought of as starting out with a sequence of ancipitia, followed by a 'choriamb' which is a metrical section with the pattern [− ∪ ∪ −] followed by some final syllables. In some of the longer lines, it is said that the 'choriamb' is repeated two or more times (this is called 'choriambic expansion'). It is illustrated in (84), where each of the lines begins with a pair of ancipitia followed by three choriambs, followed by a final pair of syllables.

(84) οἶνον γὰρ Σεμέλας καὶ Διος υἷος λαθικάδεον

     − −   −   ∪ ∪ −   −   ∪∪   − −   ∪ ∪ − ∪−

     ἀνθρώποισιν ἔδωκ'. ἔγχεε κέρναις ἔνα καὶ δύο

     −   − − ∪ ∪ −   − ∪∪ −   − ∪ ∪ − ∪−

'For the son of Semele and Zeus gave men wine as a gift that erases cares; so mix it and mete it out one or two measures of it' Alcaeus, Fragment 346 (Campbell 1982: 60)

Choriambic expansion is straightforwardly accounted for in the approach we have taken. The lines in (84) are first scanned as seven right-headed binary Gridline 0 groups; following the construction of the grid, the deletion rule (1) has applied several times.

(85) οἶνον γὰρ Σεμέλας καὶ Διος υἷος λαθικάδεον

− −	−	∪ ∪ −	−	∪∪	− −	∪ ∪ − ∪−	
△ △	) *	△) * *)	*	△)*	*)*	△)* *) * *)	0 ⇐
	*)		*	*	*)*	* *)	1 ⇐
	) *		*		*)		2 ⇐
	*						3

6.4.5 Anacreontic and ionic: anaclasis as deletion

The text in (86) is in two meters, anacreontic (lines 1–4 and 6) and ionic (line 5), traditionally related by 'anaclasis', the 'redistribution of long and short positions within a colon or metron' (West 1982: 191).

(86) ἄγε δὴ φέρ' ἡμὶν ὦ παῖ   ∪ ∪ − ∪ − ∪ − −

     κελέβην, ὅκως ἄμυστιν   ∪ ∪ − ∪ − ∪ − −

     προπίω, τὰ μὲν δέκ' ἐγχέας   ∪ ∪ − ∪ − ∪ − −

     ὕδατος, τὰ πέντε δ' οἴνου   ∪ ∪ − ∪ − ∪ − −

     κυάθους ὡς ἀνυβρίστως   ∪ ∪ − − ∪∪ − −

     ἀνὰ δηῦτε βασσαρήσω.   ∪ ∪ − ∪ − ∪ − −

'Come on, boy, fetch us a cup, so I may make a toast and drain it in one go; pour in ten parts water and five of wine, so that I may rage like bacchant without doing any harm!' Anacreon, Fragment 356 (Campbell 1988: 54)

We agree with the underlying insight that the meters are related: we generate grids for both meters by the same set of iterative rules, and apply the deletion rule (1) to derive the ionic from the anacreontic.

Neither meter begins with ancipitia (syllables whose weight is uncontrolled), and thus there is no rule of initial non-projection in this meter. For the anacreontic meter we state the iterative rules in (87).

(87)   a. Gridline 0: starting one asterisk in at the L edge, insert a L parenthesis, form binary groups, heads R.

      i. The last (rightmost) group must be incomplete.

    b. Gridline 1: starting just at the R edge, insert a R parenthesis, form binary groups, heads R.

    c. Gridline 2: starting just at the L edge, insert a L parenthesis, form binary groups, heads L.

The rules in (87) assign the grid in (88) to the anacreontic first line of (86), and the grid is then subject to rule (1), which deletes the Gridline 0 projection of the leftmost syllable.

(88)   ἄγε δὴ φέρ' ἡμὶν ὦ παῖ

```
       U  U   –   U    – U  –    –
     Δ( *   * ( *    *( *   *   ( *          0 ⇒
        ) *       * )   *    * )             1 ⇐
                  ( *        * (             2 ⇒
                   *                         3
```

Anacreontic verse is subject to condition (6), which requires syllables projecting to Gridline 1 to be heavy, and (77), which requires all non-heads to be light.

The iterative rules (87) also generate a grid for the fifth line, as shown in (89). After the grid has been constructed, (1) applies twice: it applies to the leftmost syllable, and also to one of the line-internal syllables. Thus, the relation between anacreontic and ionic is clear: both are subject to exactly the same rules.

(89)   κυάθους ὡς ἀνυβρίστως

```
       UU   –    –   U U   –  –
     Δ( *   *  ( *  Δ ( *   * ( *            0 ⇒
        ) *    * )        *   * )            1 ⇐
               ( *            * (            2 ⇒
                *                            3
```

6.5 Conclusion

We began this chapter by quoting West's challenge to any attempt to formulate a coherent system for the Greek meters. We have argued that these superficially very different meters can be accounted for within the theoretical approach of this book, which assigns a grid to a line by applying ordered rules to it, and then checking conditions. This approach accounts for all the Greek meters by the same means as it accounts for all metrical verse in all other traditions. What makes Greek verse distinctive is the use of rule (1), which applies in all meters and deletes the Gridline 0 projection of the first of a series of light syllables. In iambs, trochees, and cretics this is realized as relatively uncontrolled 'resolution', where a heavy syllable (sometimes even a light syllable) is exchanged for two light syllables. Here, the deletion rule (1) applies before the iterative rules. In the dactylic hexameter (and anapaests) there is strictly controlled 'resolution', where a heavy syllable in certain positions can be replaced by two light syllables; here the deletion rule (1) is ordered to apply between non-iterative and iterative rules, and the relative strictness of resolution is explained by condition (56). In the aeolic meters there is no resolution; here the deletion rule (1) is ordered to apply after the iterative rules and explains the characteristic choriambic pattern of heavy–light–light–heavy as a variant of what is essentially an iambic meter. What are traditionally thought of as very different phenomena are thus accounted for by the same rule, ordered differently relative to other rules. This rule distinguishes the Greek meters from other metrical traditions. Though rule (1) is specific to Greek, there is nothing out of the ordinary about it. What we have seen in this chapter is clear evidence that metrical rules must apply in a definite order and that rule order differentiates one meter from another. Rule order in metrics has a parallel in phonology, the theory of the sounds of language, where, like in metrics, several distinct representations are assigned to a given sequence, and the complex relation between the representations is captured by rules applying in a specific order. (For a discussion of rule order in phonology, see Chomsky and Halle 1968/1991.)

7

Classical Arabic

7.1 Circle 3 meters: *rajaz*, *hazaj*, and *ramal*[1]

The fundamental work on which all subsequent analyses of Arabic meters (including this chapter) are based was composed in the 8th century CE by the philologist al-Xalīl Ibn 'Aḥmad (d. 791 CE). Al-Xalīl recognized sixteen canonical meters and their variants, and grouped the meters into five 'circles'. The basic unit of the traditional theory is not the foot (Gridline 0 group), but rather the equivalent of the metron (Gridline 1 group). The Arabic metron is composed of a bisyllabic sequence, called the 'peg' (*watid*) and one or two additional syllables, called 'cords' (*sabab*). The peg normally consists of a light syllable followed by a heavy syllable, and the position of cord is occupied by an anceps, a syllable of either weight, though most often this is a heavy syllable.[2] In circle 3, which, as will be seen, includes the three most basic meters, all three logically possible combinations of peg and two cords are found. These are shown in (1), where P stands for 'peg' and C for 'cord'.

(1) *rajaz*   C C P C C P
     hazaj   P C C P C C
     ramal   C P C C P C

---

[1] Our analysis begins, like all analyses, with the foundational work of Al-Xalīl. We draw on Bohas *et al.* (1990) and Stoetzer (1989). Other linguistic accounts of Classical Arabic meter include Maling (1973), Prince (1989), Golston and Riad (1997). We have benefited especially from the advice of Mohamed Elmedlaoui. Aziz Qutbuddin sourced and translated the Classical Arabic examples for us. All errors are the responsibility of NF&MH.

[2] A syllable is light if it ends with a short vowel and is separated from the following vowel by no more than one consonant; word boundaries are irrelevant here, and the relevant domain – as in most quantitative meters – is the line. Other syllables are heavy. (See Elmedlaoui 1988 for further discussion of syllabification.)

The traditional representations in (1) are readily translated into the framework of our theory, by assuming that, like in other metrical systems, the syllables that make up a line are projected onto Gridline 0. We posit next that the asterisk sequences on Gridline 0 are segmented into binary groups starting at the left edge, and that the groups so generated are right-headed.

What differentiates *rajaz* from *hazaj* is head placement in the Gridline 1 groups: these are right-headed in *rajaz* and left-headed in *hazaj*. We illustrate this in (2).[3]

(2) *rajaz*
$$\begin{array}{ll} \times \;\; \times \;\; \cup \;\; - & \\ (\;*\;\;\;*\;(\;*\;\;\;*\;(& 0 \Rightarrow R \\ \;\;\;\;(\;*\;\;\;\;\;\;\;\;*\;(& 1 \Rightarrow R \\ \;\;\;\;\;\;\;\;\;\;\;\;\;* & 2 \end{array}$$

hazaj
$$\begin{array}{ll} \cup \;\; - \;\; \times \;\; \times & \\ (\;*\;\;\;*\;(\;*\;\;\;*\;(& 0 \Rightarrow R \\ \;\;\;\;(\;*\;\;\;\;\;\;\;*\;(& 1 \Rightarrow L \\ \;\;\;\;\;\;\;* & 2 \end{array}$$

Poems in the *rajaz* meter appear in two variants, where the meter of the longer variant is composed of three metra (12 syllables), and that of the shorter variant, of two metra (8 syllables). We assume that Arabic poetry employs binary groups on all Gridlines exclusively, and as a consequence we must also assume that all meters require grids with four Gridlines. We account for the difference between lines with two metra (8 syllables) and lines with three metra (12 syllables) by positing an incomplete group either on Gridline 1 (shorter variant) or on Gridline 2 (longer variant).

As we show below, all lines of Arabic poetry in the 16 canonical meters satisfy the condition (3).[4]

(3) A syllable projecting to Gridline 2 must be heavy, and if it is part of a branching Gridline 0 group, it must be preceded by a light syllable.

The grid construction rules for both variants of the *rajaz* meter are given in (4).

---

[3] The obvious alternative of treating the long variant of the *rajaz* and the other meters of circles 3 and 4 as forming ternary groups on Gridline 1 must be rejected, because, as discussed in section 7.2, meters of circle 4 differ from those of circle 3 in being subject to a deletion rule. Since deletion rules affect the head of the verse, we have evidence for head-location in these meters, and the deletion evidence clearly requires binary groups on Gridline 1.

[4] The rider 'if it is part of a branching Gridline 0 group' is necessary because, as we will see in circle 4, pegs may be subject to a deletion rule, reducing them to just a heavy syllable followed by a non-projected light syllable.

(4)　*rajaz*

    a. Gridline 0: starting just at the L edge, insert a L parenthesis, form binary groups, heads R.

    b. Gridline 1: starting just at the L edge, insert a L parenthesis, form binary groups, heads R.

    c. Gridline 2: starting just at the L edge, insert a L parenthesis, form binary groups, heads L.

        i. Long variant: The last (rightmost) group must be incomplete.

    d. Gridline 3: starting just at the L edge, insert a L parenthesis, form binary groups, heads L.

        i. Short variant: The last (rightmost) group must be incomplete.

The long (trimeter) version of *rajaz* is illustrated in (5), and the short (dimeter) variant of *rajaz* is illustrated in (6). The grids in both cases conform to condition (3).

(5)　Circle 3 long *rajaz*: $C^2P + C^2P + C^2P$

    mā dustu fī 'arḍi l'udāti ġadwatan

```
   –    –  U  –  –   –  U  – U  –   U  –
      'illā saqā qaṭru ddimā biqā'ahā.
      – –  U  –  –   –   U  –  U  – U  –
waylun lišaybānin 'idā ṣabbaḥtuhā
   –   –  U  –   – –   U  –  –   –  U  –
      wa 'arsalat bīdu ẓẓubā šu'ā'ahā
      U  –   U  –   – –   U  –  U – U  –
      ( *  *  ( * *   ( *  *  ( *  *  ( * *( *  * (         0 ⇒ R
        ( *      *      ( *       *     ( *    * (          1 ⇒ R
          ( *                     *               ( *      2 ⇒ L
          ( *                                   * (        3 ⇒ L
            *                                             4
```

'Never did I set foot in the land of the enemy early in the morning / but the rain of blood sated its lands. / Woe to Shaybān, when I greet them in the morn / when the shining swords send down their rays.' Attrib. 'Antarah bin šaddād al-'absī

(6)　Circle 3 short *rajaz*: $C^2P + C^2P$

    xawdun yafūḥu lmisku min

```
   –    –   U  –  –    –  U  –
( *   *  ( * *( *    * ( *  * (           0 ⇒ R
    ( *       *        ( *    * (         1 ⇒ R
        ( *                    * (        2 ⇒ L
        ( *                  * (          3 ⇒ L
          *                              4
```

'ardānihā wa l'anbarū

– – ∪ – – – ∪ –

yadīqu 'an 'ardāfihā

∪ – ∪ – – – ∪ –

'idā yulātu lmi'zarū

∪ – ∪ – – – ∪ –

'A soft maid whose cuffs exude the smell of musk and amber / and the loin cloth when twisted around her, is too tight for her buttocks!' Attrib. 'Umar bin Abī Rabī'ah

The *hazaj* meter differs from *rajaz* in two ways, as can be seen in the rules in (7). On Gridline 1, groups are left-headed (because the peg is the first rather than the second group in the metron). On Gridline 2, groups are right-headed. We will see evidence for this in section 7.2, where we look at the circle 4 counterpart of this meter, in which the head of the verse is deleted). *Hazaj* exists only as a dimeter (8-syllable).

(7) *hazaj*

    a. Gridline 0: starting just at the L edge, insert a L parenthesis, form binary groups, heads R.

    b. Gridline 1: starting just at the L edge, insert a L parenthesis, form binary groups, heads L.

    c. Gridline 2: starting just at the R edge, insert a R parenthesis, form binary groups, heads R.

    d. Gridline 3: starting just at the L edge, insert a L parenthesis, form binary groups, heads L.

       i. The last (rightmost) group must be incomplete.

In (8) we quote a couplet in *hazaj* and assign a grid to the second line. The grid conforms to condition (3): both syllables which project to Gridline 2 are heavy, and, as both are in branching groups, they are preceded by a light syllable.

(8) Circle 3 *hazaj*: $P\ C^2 + P\ C^2$

    mina lmashūri bi lhubbī

    ∪ – – – ∪ – – –

      'ilā qāsiyati lqalbī

      ∪ – – ∪ ∪ – – –

```
(* * ( * *(* *  (*   *(          0 ⇒ R
( *    * (*      *(          1 ⇒ L
) "         *)               2 ⇐ R
          (*                 3 ⇒ L
          *                 4
```

'From the one famous for love to the cruel hearted maid' Attrib. Baššār bin Burd

There is a third meter in circle 3 called *ramal*. Our analysis of *ramal* differs substantially from the tradition. Traditionally, the four-syllable sequence, which is the basis of *ramal*, is considered to be a cord–peg–cord sequence, where the marked peg is surrounded by unmarked cords. The *ramal* line is generated by doubling or tripling this sequence. Groups with marked elements (i.e., heads) in the middle are not available in our theory; heads can appear only at the edges of a group. We are therefore forced to treat the *ramal* meter as one where the grouping does not begin ('just') at the left edge, but rather one asterisk in. The immediate consequence of this is that *ramal* now is a special case of the *hazaj*, since both are composed of left-headed metra (Gridline 1 groups) of the form $P\ C^2$. It is, however, shown below (see sections 7.2 and 7.3) that the two meters differ in their placement of the heads of Gridline 2 groups; these groups are right-headed in the *hazaj* and left-headed in the *ramal*.

The first step in our formal account is to introduce rule (9), which differentiates *ramal* from *hazaj*.[5]

(9)   Do not project the leftmost syllable.

The iterative rules for *ramal* are given in (10). The Gridline 1 rule is the same as for *hazaj* because the peg is leftmost in the metron; the Gridline 2 rule is the same as for *rajaz* and differs from that of *hazaj*. There is a short (dimeter) and long (trimeter) version of *ramal*

(10)   *ramal*

    a. Gridline 0: starting just at the L edge, insert a L parenthesis, form binary groups, heads R.

    b. Gridline 1: starting just at the L edge, insert a L parenthesis, form binary groups, heads L.

    c. Gridline 2: starting just at the L edge, insert a L parenthesis, form binary groups, heads L.

        i. Long variant: The last (leftmost) group must be incomplete.

    d. Gridline 3: starting just at the L edge, insert a L parenthesis, form binary groups, heads L.

        i. Short variant: The last (leftmost) group must be incomplete.

---

[5] A similar rule is found in the Greek lyric meters (cf. section 6.4.1 above). The Greek rule excludes the leftmost one or two syllables from projecting to Gridline 0.

The long version of *ramal* is scanned in (11) and the short version in (12). In both cases, the grid satisfies condition (3).

(11) Circle 3 *ramal*: $\Delta + P\ C^2 + P\ C^2 + P$

man ra'ānā fa lyuḥaddiṯ nafsahū

```
 –   U – – –   U –  –   – U –
Δ ( * *( *  *  ( *  * ( *   *( *  *(        0 ⇒ R
   ( *     *    ( *      * ( *              1 ⇒ L
   ( *          *          ( *             2 ⇒ L
   ( *          * (                        3 ⇒ L
     *                                     4
```

'annahū mūfin 'alā qarnin zawāl

```
 –  U –  – –  U–  – –   U  –
```

'Whosoever sees us two, should tell himself / that he, in a while, will surely perish.' (two trees in conversation) Attrib. 'Adī bin Zayd

(12) Circle 3 *ramal*: $\Delta + P\ C^2 + P\ C$

mā 'ubālī ba'da yaumī

```
 – U – –  –  U –  –   –
Δ( *  *( *  * ( *  * ( *         0 ⇒ R
  ( *     *   ( *   * (          1 ⇒ L
  ( *          * (               2 ⇒ L
  ( *                            3 ⇒ L
    *                            4
```

ṭāla laylī 'am qaṣur

```
 –U – – –   U –
```

'After this day, I do not care, whether my night is long or short.' Abū Firās al-Hamdānī

The lines in (11) have an incomplete group on Gridline 1, and the lines in (12) an incomplete group on Gridline 0. In strict meters, such as those of circle 3 (and 4), incomplete groups are only admitted at the end of the grouping operation, where the iterative rule runs out of asterisks to group. It is therefore necessary to stipulate that in these meters the last group on either Gridline 0 or 1 must be incomplete. These variants demonstrate that the parentheses which form the Gridline 0 groups are left parentheses inserted from left to right (even though the groups are right-headed at Gridline 0 and may also be right-headed at Gridline 1). Only parentheses inserted in this manner will permit incomplete groups as variations at the right edge.

The templatic patterns of the meters of circle 3 are shown in (13). The patterns we see here are the basic patterns of all the Arabic meters, with the different circles formed by adding rules or conditions to those

of circle 3. A similar abstract relation among different metrical patterns
was noted in the Spanish *endecasílabo* as discussed in section 4.3.

(13)   × × ∪ − × × ∪ − × × ∪ −   *rajaz* (long): $C^2 P + C^2 P + C^2 P$
        × × ∪ − × × ∪ −   *rajaz* (short): $C^2 P + C^2 P$

        ∪ − × × ∪ − × ×   *hazaj*: $P\ C^2 + P\ C^2$

    × ∪ − × × ∪ − × × ∪ − ×   *ramal* (long): $\Delta + P\ C^2 + P\ C^2 + P\ C$
        × ∪ − × × ∪ − ×   *ramal* (short): $\Delta + P\ C^2 + P\ C$

7.2 Circle 4 meters: *munsariḥ, muqtaḍab, muḍāri',* *xafīf,* and *mujtatt*

Each of the circle 3 meters (five in all, counting long and short variants)
has a parallel meter in circle 4, which differs from it in that one of the
obligatory iambic ∪ − sequences is apparently reversed as an obligatory
heavy–light sequence − ∪. In the traditional approach the 'iambic peg'
called *watid majmū'* with the pattern ∪ − is said to be replaced by a
'trochaic peg' called *watid mafrūq* with the pattern − ∪.

We begin our analysis of the circle 4 meters with *muḍāri'*, which we
analyze as a variant of the circle 3 meter *hazaj*. We show templates for
the two meters in (14), where it is clear that the second of the two pegs
is apparently 'inverted' in *muḍāri'*.

(14)   ∪ − × × ∪ − × ×   *hazaj*
                ∪ − × × − ∪ × ×   *muḍāri'*

We propose to scan *muḍāri'* by the rules (7) for *hazaj*, and illustrate
the effect with two lines in (15). We symbolize *muḍāri'* as $P\ C^2 + Q\ C^2$,
where the Q represents a peg which has a variant − ∪ form.

(15)   Circle 4 *muḍāri'*: $P\ C^2 + Q\ C^2$

        wa qad ra'aytu rrijāla
        ∪   −   ∪−   −   ∪−∪

           famā 'arā ġayra Zaydin
           ∪   − ∪−   −   ∪   − −
           (*   * (* * (*   * (*   * (0 ⇒ R
              (*   *   (*   * (1 ⇒ L
) *   *)   2 ⇐ R
                          (*   3 ⇒ L
                           *   4

        'I surveyed the men / I didn't see any but Zayd' Quoted in an early
        12th-century manual on Arabic metrics, *al-qisṭās fī 'ilm al-'arūḍ*

The grid does not conform to (3) (repeated below) because the second
of the two syllables which projects to Gridline 2 is light (rather than
heavy, as required).

(3)   A syllable projecting to Gridline 2 must be heavy, and if it is part of a branching Gridline 0 group, it must be preceded by a light syllable.

Given the formalism of our theory, this violation is easily remedied by adding rule (16) which deletes the Gridline 0 projection of the head of the verse (the syllable that projects to Gridline 4).

(16)   If the syllable projecting to the head of the verse is light, delete the Gridline 0 projection of that syllable.

The effect of applying this rule to the grid in (15) is seen in (17), which conforms to condition (3).

(17)   famā 'arā ġayra Zaydin

```
      U   –  U –   –   U   –  –   –
    ( *   * ( * *  ( *   Δ ( *   * (    0 ⇒ R
      ( *    * ( *         * (    1 ⇒ L
      ) *         * )             2 ⇐ R
              ( *                  3 ⇒ L
               *                   4
```

The deletion rule (16) resembles deletion rules we have seen elsewhere, in that it deletes the Gridline 0 projection of the syllable which projects to the head of the verse. However, this rule is restated for Arabic to make it context-sensitive: it applies only, and always, when the syllable projecting to the head of the verse is light.[6] A special feature of the Arabic deletion rule is that it is context-sensitive: it requires that the asterisk to be deleted project from a light syllable. In this way, deletion is limited to lines where the head of the verse is a light, rather than a heavy, syllable. An additional reason for formulating the rule in this way is that we can now allow the rule to apply to all Arabic meters, but the rule will have an effect only if the grid constructed for a line has a light syllable projecting to the head of the verse. The existence of the circle 4 meters is an inevitable consequence of the existence of circle 3 and the deletion rule (16).

Mujtaṯṯ is a variant of short *ramal*, plus deletion by (16); their templates are compared in (18).

(18)   × U – × × U – ×   *ramal* (short)
              × – U × × U – ×   *mujtaṯṯ*

Mujtaṯṯ is scanned by the rules for short *ramal* plus deletion of the

---

[6] In our discussion of Vedic Sanskrit, we propose another context-sensitive deletion rule, which derives the early caesura pattern, see section 8.1.2.

Gridline 0 projection of the head of the verse, as shown in (19). The rightmost Gridline 0 group falls short (a common variant in *ramal*-type meters), so that the line ends on a single cord (anceps) rather than a pair of cords.

(19)   Circle 4 *mujtaṯṯ* : $\Delta + Q\ C^2 + P\ C$

albaṭnu minhā xamīṣu

– – ∪ – – ∪ – ∪

wa lwajhu miṯlu lhilālī

```
     –   –   ∪   – –   ∪ – –
  Δ ( *   Δ ( *  *  ( * *(*        0 ⇒ R
    ( *          *   ( * * (       1 ⇒ L
    ( *               * (          2 ⇒ L
    ( *                            3 ⇒ L
      *                            4
```

'Her stomach is taut / her face like a crescent moon' Quoted in *al-qisṭās fī 'ilm al-'arūḍ*

Note that the leftmost syllable is not projected, by rule (9), as always in *ramal*-style meters.

Muqtaḍab is a variant of short *rajaz*. We compare templates for the two meters in (20).

(20)   × × ∪ – × × ∪ –   *rajaz* (short)

× × – ∪ × × ∪ –   *muqtaḍab*

Muqtaḍab is scanned by the rules for short *rajaz*, plus deletion, as shown in (21).

(21)   Circle 4 *muqtaḍab*: $C^2 Q + C^2 P$

ḥāmilu lhawā ta'ibū

– ∪– ∪ – ∪∪ –

yastaxiffuhu ṭṭarabū

```
    –   ∪ – ∪ –   ∪ ∪   –
  ( *  *(* Δ( *   *(*  * (        0 ⇒ R
    ( * * (       *    * (        1 ⇒ R
    ( *                * (        2 ⇒ L
    ( *                           3 ⇒ L
      *                           4
```

'The bearer of love, is exhausted, / his load lightened by singing.' Abū Nuwās

We have seen to this point three dimeter circle 4 meters, each of which corresponds straightforwardly to a dimeter circle 3 meter plus deletion. We now turn to the two trimeter circle 4 meters, where an additional deletion rule must also be operating. In this, Arabic resembles Spanish where a projection of the head of the verse is subject to two deletion rules (see section 4.3).

We begin with *munsariḥ*, which is the circle 4 variant of long *rajaz*. The two meters are compared in (22).

(22) × × U − × × U − × × U −   *rajaz* (long)

× × U − × × − U × × U −   *munsariḥ*

An example of *munsariḥ* is shown in (23). We have applied the rules for *rajaz* to the first line.

(23)   Circle 4 *munsariḥ*: $C^2 P + C^2 Q + C^2 P$

man lam yamut 'abṭatan yamut haraman

```
 −    −    U  −   −   U −   U  −  U U  −
(*    *   (*  *  (*  *(*   *  (*  *(*  *(        0 ⇒ R
     (*        *      (*    *      (*   *(        1 ⇒ R
             (*              *           (*       2 ⇒ L
             (*                          *(       3 ⇒ L
              *                                   4
```

almawtu ka'sun wa lmar'u ḏā'iquhā

```
 −    −   U  −  −    −   − U  −U U  −
```

'Whosoever does not die in the prime of his life, will die in old age, / death is a cup, that every man must taste'

If we apply the deletion rule (16) to the Gridline 0 projection of the head of the verse we obtain an incorrect result. Since in the short meters the correct results were obtained with the same placement of head of the verse as in circle 3, we have reason to assume that the head of the verse is identically placed in both circles. To account for the facts of the long meters of circle 4 we assume therefore that these meters are subject to a rule that shifts the position of head of verse. The requisite rule, (24), deletes the Gridline 2 asterisk of the original head of the verse and shifts head position to its neighbor on the right.

(24)   Delete the Gridline 2 projection of the head of the verse if followed by another asterisk on Gridline 3.

The condition on this rule means that this deletion rule only applies in trimeter lines (and not in dimeters, which have just one asterisk on Gridline 3). It must be ordered before the other deletion rule, (16), and applies to the grid in (23) to produce the grid in (25).

(25)   Circle 4 *munsariḥ*: $C^2 P + C^2 Q + C^2 P$

man lam yamut 'abṭatan yamut haraman

```
     –    –    U  –  –    U –    U  –    U U  –
   ( *    *    ( *  *  ( *   *( *    * ( *    *( *    * (        0 ⇒ R
       ( *         *       ( *        ( *        * (            1 ⇒ R
            ( Δ                *                    ( *          2 ⇒ L
                        ( *                    * (              3 ⇒ L
                            *                                    4
```

Next the deletion rule (16) applies to (25) to produce the grid in (26), a grid which conforms to the basic condition (3).

(26)   Circle 4 *munsariḥ*: $C^2 P + C^2 Q + C^2 P$

man lam yamut 'abṭatan yamut haraman

```
     –    –    U  –  –    U –    U  –    U U  –
   ( *    *    ( *  *  ( *   *( *    Δ ( *    *( *    * (        0 ⇒ R
       ( *         *       ( * *        ( *        * (          1 ⇒ R
            ( Δ                *                    ( *          2 ⇒ L
                        ( *                    * (              3 ⇒ L
                            *                                    4
```

Xafīf is a variant of long *ramal*, and is similarly subject to two deletion rules. We compare the two templates in (27). The grid is shown in (28).

(27)   × U – × × U – × × U – ×   *xafīf*

      × U – × × – U × × U – ×   *ramal* (long)

(28)   Circle 4 *xafīf*: $\Delta + P\ C^2 + Q\ C^2 + P\ C$

Yā ṣabāḥa lxamīsi 'ahlan wa sahlā

```
   –  U  – –    U  – U  –  –    U  – – –
```

zādaka lwāḥidu lmuhayminu faḍlā

```
    –  U  –    –  U  –    U  –    U U  –    –
   Δ( *  *    ( *  *( *    Δ( *    *( *   *  ( *       0 ⇒ R
       ( *        *( *           *    ( *   *(          1 ⇒ L
           ( Δ         *              ( *              2 ⇒ L
               ( *                    *                3 ⇒ L
                   *                                   4
```

'Oh Thursday morning welcome, welcome, / may the One, the Absolute master, increase your greatness.' al-Mu'ayyad fī al-dīn al-šīrāzī

7.3 Circle 1 meters: *basīṭ*, *ṭawīl*, and *madīd*

The remaining meters of Arabic are all loose meters, in which there is an additional rule inserting parentheses before the iterative rules apply. We begin with circle 1, and specifically with the *basīṭ* meter, which is best viewed as a variant of *rajaz*, but with longer lines: the two variants of *basīṭ* include one more Gridline 1 group (metron) than their strict meter (circle 3) counterparts in *rajaz*. We compare templates for *basīṭ* and *rajaz* in (29). The comparison shows that in *basīṭ* some of the cords (marked × as they are ancipitia) are missing.

(29)
× × ∪ −	× ∪ − × × ∪ −	× ∪ −	*basīṭ* long
× × ∪ −	× × ∪ − × × ∪ −		*rajaz* long
× × ∪ −	× ∪ − × × ∪ −		*basīṭ* short
	× × ∪ − × × ∪ −		*rajaz* short

The long version of *basīṭ* thus repeats a pattern of $C^2P + CP$ instead of the *rajaz* pattern of $C^2P + C^2P$.

We interpret single cords as incomplete groups, containing just one asterisk at Gridline 0. Incomplete groups internal to a Gridline are found only in loose meters, that is, in meters that have a non-iterative parenthesis insertion rule. The non-iterative rule for Arabic, which is stated in (30), places a left parenthesis before a peg.

(30) On Gridline 0, insert a L parenthesis to the left of an asterisk which projects from a light syllable, if that syllable is followed by a heavy syllable.

Rule (30)[7] applies to every meter in circles 1, 2, and 5. Application of rule (30) is, as noted, what makes these meters loose meters.

It would be possible to apply (30) to *rajaz* with no effects whatsoever (i.e., the rule would be vacuous, reproducing the effect of the iterative rules). The crucial difference between *rajaz* and *basīṭ* is not whether the special rule (30) applies, but the fact that in addition to being subject to rule (30), the loose meter *basīṭ* differs from its strict counterpart *rajaz* in admitting incomplete groups verse-internally. Such groups are not permitted in *rajaz* or the other circle 3 (or circle 4) meters.

Incomplete groups are found in the long version of *basīṭ*, which is a tetrameter line with four Gridline 1 groups, as shown in (31).[8] The grid is generated by the non-iterative rule (30) and the iterative rules for *rajaz* (see (4) above). The generalization that is obvious in (31) and that is readily seen in all other meters of this circle is that metra consisting of C and P alternate with metra consisting of C^2 and P. As

---

[7] Rule (30) shares significant features with rule (46) of Greek, section 6.3.2.

[8] Rule (30) inserts a left parenthesis before every light–heavy sequence. It thus ensures that all pegs are preceded by a left parenthesis, but occasionally also inserts a left parenthesis before a light–heavy sequence which is not a peg, as shown in the first line (first two syllables) of (31).

shown in (31) the alternating pattern is reflected on Gridlines 2 and 3. A Gridline 1 group of the form C^2P projects its head to Gridline 3; a Gridline 1 group of the form CP projects its head to Gridline 2 only. A similar generalization holds for all other meters in circle 1; it further supports the binary grouping of asterisks (heads of cola) on Gridline 2.

(31)   Circle 1 long *basīṭ*: $C^2P + CP + C^2P + CP$

wa jāhilin maddahū fī jahlihī ḍaḥikī

```
    U  −U−    −   U − − − U−   U U −
((* *((* *   (* (* *(* *((* * (* (* *(      0 ⇒ R
   (*  *  (*    *  (*   * (*    *(      1 ⇒ R
       (*       *       (*      * (      2 ⇒ L
       (*               * (      3 ⇒ L
        *                        4
```

ḥattā atathu yadun farrāsatun wa famū

```
   −  −U−  U  U −   − − −U−   U U   −
  (* *((* * (* (* *  (* *((* *  (* (*  * (      0 ⇒ R
   (*  * (*    *    (*   *   (*    * (      1 ⇒ R
       (*       *       (*        * (      2 ⇒ L
       (*               * (      3 ⇒ L
        *                        4
```

'idā ra'ayta nuyūba llayti bārizatan
U − U− U U − − − U −U U −

falā tazunnanna 'anna llayta yabtasimū
U− U − − U − − − U − U U −

'An ignoramus – seeing that I was laughing, sustained his ignorance, until he encountered a predatory hand and mouth. / If you see the fangs of the lion exposed, do not presume that the lion is smiling.' Abū al-Ṭayyib al-Mutanabbī

Incomplete Gridline 0 groups appear in specific places in the long *basīṭ* line: they are obligatory after the two pegs which project to Gridline 3, and are found nowhere else (line-internally). This placement is controlled by a condition, which holds in all the circle 1 meters, and differentiates these meters from the circle 3 meters on which they are based.

(32)   A Gridline 0 group whose head projects only to Gridline 2 must be in the same Gridline 1 group as an incomplete Gridline 0 group.

In (33) we show the grid for short *basīṭ*, which is a trimeter version of the same meter. In this meter, there are three Gridline 1 groups, of which two project to Gridline 3 and the third must contain an incomplete

Gridline 0 group. Thus, unlike the longer version of the meter, this version only has one incomplete Gridline 0 group.

(33)   Circle 1 short *basīṭ*: $C^2P + CP + C^2P$

máḏā wuqūfī 'alā rab'in xalā

$-\ -\ \ \cup\ --\cup-\ -\ -\ \ \cup-$

muxlawliqin dārisin musta'jimī

$-\ -\ \cup-\ \ \ -\ -\cup\ -$		
(* *((* * (*(* * (* *((* (	$0 \Rightarrow$ R	
(* * (* * (* * (	$1 \Rightarrow$ R	
(* * (*	$2 \Rightarrow$ L	
(* * (	$3 \Rightarrow$ L	
*	4	

'Why do I stand at this empty dwelling, / ruined, forgotten, foreign.'
Quoted in *al-qisṭās fī 'ilm al-'arūḍ*

We next consider *ṭawīl*, which is a loose variant of the circle 3 meter *hazaj*. *Ṭawīl* is a tetrameter and hence twice the length of *hazaj* (see (8) above), but this has no consequences for its internal structure.

(34) $\cup\ -\ \ \times\ \cup\ -\times\times\cup\ -\ \ \times\cup-\times\times$ *ṭawīl*
        $\cup\ -\times\times\cup\ -\times\times$ *hazaj*

Like all lines in loose meters, the lines of the *ṭawīl* are subject to parenthesis insertion by rule (30) prior to the application of the iterative grouping rules. A sample scansion of a *ṭawīl* line is shown in (35).

(35)   Circle 1 *ṭawīl*: $PC + PC^2 + PC + PC^2$

'uṭā'inu xaylan min fawārisiha ddahrū

$\cup\ -\cup\ \cup\ \ -\ -\ \ \ -\ \ \cup\ -\cup\cup\ -\ \ \ -\ \ \ -$		
((* *(*(* * (* * ((* *(*(* (* * (	$0 \Rightarrow$ R	
(* * (* * (* * (* * (	$1 \Rightarrow$ L	
) * *) * *)	$2 \Leftarrow$ R	
(* * (	$3 \Rightarrow$ L	
*	4	

waḥīdan wa mā qawlī kaḏā wa ma'i ṣṣabrū

$\cup\ --\ \ \ \cup\ -\ -\ -\cup\ -\ \cup\ \ \cup-\ \ -\ -$

'I battle with horses, among whose riders is Time / all alone I battle –
no! I have fortitude on my side.' Abū al-Ṭayyib al-Mutanabbī

The grid conforms to condition (32): the two metra (Gridline 1 groups) which do not project to Gridline 3 contain incomplete groups.

Like many Arabic meters, *ṭawīl* is found in systematic variants. In one variant of *ṭawīl*, the last two syllables are systematically a light–heavy pair; this is illustrated in (36).

(36)   wa laylin kamawji lbaḥri 'arxā sudūlahū
   U − − U − − − U − − U − U −

   'alayya bi 'anwā'i lhumūmi liyabtalī
   U − U U − −− U − U U − U−

> 'One night, like the wave of the sea lowering its curtains / upon me with deep grief to try me.' Imru' al-Qays

Texts showing this systematic variation are straightforwardly scanned by the rules. A left parenthesis will be inserted before the penultimate light syllable by rule (30), in exactly the position where a left parenthesis would in any case have been inserted by the iterative rules.

Another kind of systematic variation involves a shortening of the line by one syllable; the line then ends with a peg and one cord, rather than a peg and two cords.

(37)   liman ṭalalun 'abṣartuhū fa šajānī
   U − U U − − − U − U U − −

   ka xaṭṭi zabūrin fī 'aṣībi yamānī
   U − U U − − − U− U U − −

> 'Whose ruins have I seen, the sight of which has saddened me, / ruins like writing on a Yemenite palm tree.' Labīd

This is a standard variation permitted in Arabic meters, where the line falls one syllable short at the end. We analyze it as a line where the rightmost group is incomplete. Such lines provide further evidence that Gridline 0 groups are built from left to right. The effect of this variation is to reduce the number of syllables in the line, while preserving intact the number of Gridline 0 groups (feet) and the rest of the metrical grid.

(38)   Circle 1 *ṭawīl*: $PC + PC^2 + PC + PC$

   ka xaṭṭi zabūrin fī 'aṣībi yamānī

```
  U   − U U − −   − U− U U   − −
((*   *(*(* *(*   *((**(*(*   *(*        0 ⇒ R
  (*  *   (*   *  (* *   (* *(          1 ⇒ L
  )*      *)      *       *)            2 ⇐ R
  (*           (*      * (             3 ⇒ L
  *                                    4
```

The third circle 1 meter is *madīd*, which is a variant of *ramal* because on Gridline 0 the first syllable is not counted (it is not projected). We show this in (39), where the syllable sequence constituting the *madīd* is paralleled by that of the long version of the *ramal*.

(39)   × U – × × U –   × U –   *madīd*

         × U – × × U – × × U –   *ramal* long

The grid for *madīd* is generated by first applying the non-iterative rule
(30), followed by the same rules as those for (long) *ramal*. A sample
scansion is shown in (40).

(40)   Circle 1 *madīd*: $\Delta + PC^2 + PC + P$

rubba nārin bittu armuquhā

```
  –  U    – –     – U –    U U  –
Δ (( *   *( *   *(( *  *  ( * ( *  * (        0 ⇒ R
     ( *    *   ( *    *   ( *                 1 ⇒ L
     ( *         *         ( *                 2 ⇒ L
     ( *                   * (                 3 ⇒ L
       *                                       4
```

taqdimu lhindiyya wa lġārā

         –   U – – – U – – – –

'Many a fire – I spent the night watching. / Grinding (with its teeth) the
sword ... and the army.' Quoted in *al-qisṭās fī 'ilm al-'arūḍ*

In the metrical grid above, there is one Gridline 1 group which does
not project to Gridline 3, and this Gridline 1 group contains the only
line-internal incomplete Gridline 0 group, as required by condition (32).

7.4 Circle 5 meters: *mutaqārib* and *mutadārik*

The circle 5 meters are loose meters like those of circle 1 and their metrical grids are also formed by the non-iterative parenthesis insertion rule
(30). However, in the circle 5 meters, *every* peg (i.e., every Gridline 0
group which projects to Gridline 2) is adjacent to an incomplete group:
the meters repeat a peg–cord–peg–cord sequence. We begin with *mutaqārib* which in both of its lengths is a (longer) variant of *hazaj*, as
shown in (41).

(41)   U –   × U –   × U –   × U –   ×   *mutaqārib* long

       U –   × U –   × U –   ×   *mutaqārib* short

       U – × × U – × ×   *hazaj*

The grid for *mutaqārib* is generated by first applying the non-iterative
rule (30), followed by the same rules as those for *hazaj*, but allowing
for longer lines. A sample scansion is shown in (42); note that in this
manifestation of *mutaqārib*, there is no final (single) cord.

(42)   Circle 5 *mutaqārib* : $PC + PC + PC + P$

taqqaddam xuṭan 'aw ta'axxar xuṭan

       U –   –   U –   –   U –   –   U –

fa 'inna ššabāba maša lqahqarā

```
U  –   –   U – U   U –   –   U –
((*  *   (*  (*  *(*  (*  *  (*  (*  *(        0 ⇒ R
 (*  *    (*  *   (*  *    (*             1 ⇒ L
 )*        *)       *      *)           2 ⇐ R
          (*              *(            3 ⇒ L
           *                             4
```

'Take a step forward, or fall back a step / for verily, Youth is taking a walk in retrograde.' Ibn Hānī al-Andalusī

The circle 5 meter *mutaqārib* is generated by exactly the same rules as the circle 1 meter *ṭawīl*: both are loose variants of the circle 3 meter *hazaj*. What differentiates the meters (and the circles) is that in the circle 5 meters, incomplete and complete Gridline 0 groups alternate. Thus, meters of both circle 5 and circle 1 are subject to condition (32) (repeated below), but meters of circle 5 are in addition subject to condition (43).

(32) Circles 1 and 5: A Gridline 1 group which does not project to Gridline 3 must contain an incomplete Gridline 0 group.

(43) Circle 5: Each Gridline 1 group must contain an incomplete Gridline 0 group.

The other circle 5 meter, *mutadārik*, (44), is a variant of *rajaz*.

(44) × U –   × U –   × U –   × U –   *mutadārik* long

      × U –   × U –   × U –   *mutadārik* short

    × × U – × × U – × × U –   *rajaz* long

The grid for *mutadārik* is generated by first applying the non-iterative rule (30), followed by the same rules as those for *rajaz*.

(45) Circle 5 *mutadārik* : $CP + CP + CP + CP$

jā'anā 'āmirun sāliman ṣāliḥan

– U – – U– – U – – U –

ba'damā kāna mā kāna min 'āmiri

```
–   U   –  –  U   –  –  U  –   –  U–
(*  (*   *  (*(*   *  (*(*   *  (*  (* *(        0 ⇒ R
(*       *  (*     *  (*      *  (*     *(        1 ⇒ R
         (*           *       (*       *(        2 ⇒ L
         (*                   *(                3 ⇒ L
          *                                     4
```

'Amir came to us, sound, unscathed, / after what had transpired, from Amir.' Anonymous (often quoted as a rare example of this meter)

The *mutadārik* meter could alternatively be scanned as a variant of *ramal*. Thus, though there are only two meters in circle 5, they correspond as a group to the three basic meters of circle 3.

7.5 The *sarī'* meter

The *sarī'* meter is traditionally grouped with the circle 4 meters (which we analyze by deletion). Maling (1973: 49) and Golston and Riad (1997) have argued that it is actually a variant of the circle 3 meter *rajaz*. We agree. Four lines in *sarī'* are quoted in (46); the lines are one syllable shorter than in *rajaz*.

(46) bi ljiz'i fa lxabtayni 'ašlā'u dār

      – – ∪ –   – – ∪ – – ∪ –

    ḏātu layālin qad tawallat qiṣār

      – ∪ ∪ ––   – ∪ – – ∪ –

  bānū fa bādat 'asafan ba'dahum

    – – ∪ – – ∪ ∪ –   – ∪ –

    wa 'innama nnāsu nufūsu ddiyār

      ∪ – ∪ –   – ∪ ∪ ––   ∪ –

'In [a place called] Jiz' and Xabtayn are the traces of a dwelling, an abode of nights, seemingly short nights, that passed... / They departed, and sadly the abode too faded away, for indeed people are the souls of dwellings.' Ibn Hānī al-Andalusī

A crucial difference between normal *rajaz* lines and the lines of the *sarī'* is that the latter invariably end with an incomplete Gridline 0 group projecting from a heavy syllable. We account for this fact by treating the *sarī'* lines as special instances of a loose meter variant of the *rajaz*, where rule (47) inserts a parenthesis to the left of the last Gridline 0 asterisk.

(47) Insert a L parenthesis before a verse-final asterisk projecting from a heavy syllable.

Rule (47) distinguishes *sarī'* lines from the *rajaz* lines of circle 3; it makes explicit the fact that *sarī'* lines must end with an incomplete group.

(48) *sarī'* : $C^2P + C^2P + C^2P'$

bi ljiz'i fa lxabtayni 'ašlā'u dār

  – – ∪ –   – – ∪ – – ∪ –
```
( *  *( *  *  ( *   *  ( *  *  ( *  *  ( *        0 ⇒ R
   ( *   *      ( *      *   ( *  *  (             1 ⇒ R
      ( *               *      ( *                2 ⇒ L
      ( *                      * (                3 ⇒ L
       *                                          4
```

Rule (47) also accounts for *sarī'* lines that are composed of ten, rather than of eleven syllables; such lines end on two heavy syllables (instead

of the heavy–light–heavy sequence seen in the example quoted above)
and are parenthesized as $(- (- .$ This rule plays an essential role in
the meters of circle 2 discussed in section 7.6.

7.6 Circle 2 meters: *kāmil* and *wāfir*

Circle 2, which completes our review of the Arabic meters, contains
two meters (both with long and short variants). In the circle 3 meters
with which we began, the obligatory ∪ − sequences (pegs) were either
preceded or followed by a pair of ancipitia × × (two cords). In the circle 2
meters, the pegs are either preceded or followed by one of two sequences,
either a two-syllable sequence − ×, or a three syllable sequence ∪ ∪ ×.
We illustrate this for the *kāmil* meter, which is a variant of *rajaz*.

(49) ͜∪∪ × ∪ − ͜∪∪ × ∪ − ͜∪∪ × ∪ −   *kāmil* (long)

× × ∪ − × × ∪ − × × ∪ −   *rajaz* (long)

͜∪∪ × ∪ − ͜∪∪ × ∪ −   *kāmil* (short)

× × ∪ − × × ∪ −   *rajaz* (short)

In (50) we have shown *kāmil*, with the location of the pegs to make it
clear that the peg can be followed either by a heavy syllable plus another
syllable or by two light syllables plus another syllable.

(50) Circle 2 *kāmil*: $C^2 P + C^2 P + C^2 P$, where C^2 is ∪∪ − or − −

wa 'iḍa mru'un madaḥa mra'an linawālihī

∪ ∪ −   ∪ −   ∪ ∪ −   ∪ −   ∪ ∪ − ∪ −
    peg   peg   peg

wa 'aṭāla fīhi faqad 'arāda hijā'ahū

∪ ∪ − ∪ − ∪ ∪ −   ∪ − ∪ ∪ − ∪ −
    peg   peg   peg

law lam yuqaddir fīhi bu'da lmustaqā

− −   ∪ − − − ∪ − − − ∪ −
  peg   peg   peg

'inda lwurūdi lamā aṭāla rišā'ahū

− −   ∪ − ∪ ∪ − ∪ − ∪ ∪ − ∪ −
    peg   peg   peg

'If a man praises another for the sake of his gifts, and lengthens the praise,
then he in reality desires to satirize him. / If he did not gauge the water
to be so distant, upon arriving, he would not have extended such a long
rope.' Ibn al-Rūmī

It can be seen that the lines vary in length: the first two lines are the
longest possible, of 15 syllables, while the third is the shortest possible,
of 12 syllables, and the fourth is 14 syllables long.

kāmil is subject to rule (30), which inserts a left parenthesis before a light–heavy sequence ,as illustrated in (51).

(51) 'inda lwurūdi lamā aṭāla rišā'ahū

```
 −   −   U − U U  − U − U  U − U  −
 *   *   ( * * * ( *   * ( *  * * ( * * ( *   *        0
```

What specifically distinguishes the meters of circle 2 from the other loose meters is that meters of circle 2 permit optional ungrouped asterisks within the line, with the consequence that the line may vary in length. It is thus similar to the English loose meters, in which the iterative rules insert parentheses with a different orientation from the parenthesis pre-inserted by the non-iterative rule. The Gridline 0 rule for circle 2 meters, stated in (52), therefore replaces the Gridline 0 rules (4a) or (7a), which apply in all other Arabic meters.

(52) a. Gridline 0: starting just at the L edge, insert a R parenthesis, form binary groups, heads R.

       i. Ungrouped asterisks are permitted.

Application of this rule to (51) produces (53).

(53) 'inda lwurūdi lamā aṭāla rišā'ahū

```
  −   −   U − U U  − U − U  U − U  −
  ) *  * ) ( * * ) * ( *   * ) ( *  * ) ( *   * ) ( *  * )       0 ⇒
```

The remainder of the iterative rules are the same as those given in (4) for *rajaz*, and generate the grid shown in (54) for the fourth line, or (55) for the first line.

(54) Circle 2 *kāmil*: $C^2 P + C^2 P + C^2 P$, where C^2 is $\cup\cup -$ or $--$

'inda lwurūdi lamā aṭāla rišā'ahū

```
  −   −   U − U U  − U − U  U − U  −
 ) *  * ) ( * * ) * ( *   * ) ( *  * ) ( *   * )       0 ⇒ R
   ( *      *       ( *   *      ( *      * (          1 ⇒ R
      ( *            ( *   *            ( *            2 ⇒ L
      ( *                           * (               3 ⇒ L
         *                                            4
```

(55) Circle 2 *kāmil*: $C^2 P + C^2 P + C^2 P$, where C^2 is $\cup\cup -$ or $--$

wa 'iḏa mru'un madaḥa mra'an linawālihī

```
 U U  −   U −   U U  −   U −  U U  − U −
 * ( *  * ) ( *  * ) * ( *  * ) ( * * ) * ( *  * ( *  * )       0 ⇒ R
   ( *      *       ( *   *      ( *   * (          1 ⇒ R
      ( *            ( *   *            ( *         2 ⇒ L
      ( *                           * (            3 ⇒ L
         *                                         4
```

Application of rule (52) results in ungrouped asterisks in the middle of the line. The line-medial ungrouped syllables occur only in specific places in the line, as stated in (56).

(56) Circle 2: A Gridline 0 group whose head does not project to Gridline 2 may be preceded by an ungrouped light syllable.

A further condition is required, for this meter only. Of the two cords preceding a peg, the rightmost cord is always heavy (i.e., unlike usual cord positions, this is not an anceps position). This requirement, stated in (57), is a stronger form of condition (3).

(57) Circle 2: A syllable which projects to Gridline 1 must be heavy.

The other circle 2 meter is *wāfir*, and is a counterpart of *hazaj*, as shown in (58).

(58)   U – ŪŪ × U – ŪŪ × U – ŪŪ ×   *wāfir* (long)

         U – ŪŪ × U – ŪŪ ×   *wāfir* (short)

         U – × × U – × ×   *hazaj*

The grid for a line in *wāfir* is generated by first applying the non-iterative rule (30), followed by the Gridline 0 rule in (52) with the same rules for the other Gridlines as for *hazaj*. In (59) we scan two couplets, giving a full grid for the second line in each case.

(59) Circle 2 *wāfir*: $P\ C^2 + P\ C^2 + P\ C$, where C^2 is UU – or – –

yaqūlu liya ṭṭabību 'akalta šay'an
U – U U – U – U U – U – –

wa dā'uka fī šarābika wa ṭṭa'āmī
U – U U – U – U U   – U – –
(* *)*(* *)(* *)*(*   *)(* *)(*   0 ⇒ R
  (*   *   (*   *   (* * (1 ⇒ L
    *)   *   *)   2 ⇐ R
  (*   * (3 ⇒ L
    *   4

wa mā fī ṭibbihī 'annī jawādun
U – – – U – – – U – –

'aḍarra bi jismihī ṭūlu ljimāmī
U – U U – U – – – U   – –
(* *) * (* *)(* *) * *)(*   *) (*   0 ⇒ R
  (*   *   (*   *   (* * (1 ⇒ L
    *)   *   *)   2 ⇐ R
  (*   * (3 ⇒ L
    *   4

'The physician says to me you must have eaten something, / your illness is from your food and drink. / But his medicine does not tell him that I am a steed, / whose body has been damaged by an extended period of rest.' Abū al-Ṭayyib al-Mutanabbī

The rightmost Gridline 0 group is incomplete in these lines; since right rather than the usual left parentheses are inserted in this meter, it is not possible to generate an incomplete rightmost group by the iterative rules. We account for this fact by positing that the lines of the *wafir* are subject to rule (47), a rule which was introduced for *sarī'* in section 7.5:

(47)   Insert a L parenthesis before a verse-final asterisk projecting from a heavy syllable.

We note that there is no equivalent to *ramal* in this circle.[9]

7.7 Summary of the main results

Like in the traditional theory of al-Xalīl, the Arabic meters have been organized above into five circles (sets), where the meters in each of the circles share important features.

The meters in circle 3 and 4 are strict meters, in the sense that the rule for grouping the asterisks on Gridline 0 applies directly to the asterisk sequence that projects the syllables of the verse without regard to any prior groupings. The difference between the meters of circle 3 and those of circle 4 is that the latter meters are derived by the deletion rule (16), which deletes the Gridline 0 projection of the head of the verse. As indicated in (60), the meters in circle 3 come in two variants, long and short, and each variant has a counterpart in circle 4.[10]

(60)

	Circle 3	Circle 4
i.	Long *rajaz*	*munsariḥ*
	Short *rajaz*	*muqtaḍab*
ii.	(Short) *hazaj*	*muḍāri'*
iii.	Long *ramal*	*xafīf*
	Short *ramal*	*mujtatt*

The meters of circles 1, 2, and 5 are loose meters in the sense that the earliest application of the iterative grouping rules is preceded by application of rule (30), which inserts a parenthesis into the asterisk sequence to the left of a sequence where a light syllable precedes a heavy

---

[9] This might reflect the tendency to avoid having both non-projection and un-grouped asterisks in the same meter, a combination which may have undermined the longer term success of Hopkins's Sprung Rhythm (cf. section 3.5.2 above).

[10] The circle 3 meter *hazaj* has no long counterpart, and there is no long counterpart of the *hazaj* among the meters of circle 4.

syllable. There are thus three distinct meters in circles 3 and 4, as indicated by the Roman numerals in (60).

Each of the three meters in circle 3 also has counterparts in the meters of the remaining three circles as shown below (we have cited *mutadārik* as a variant of either *rajaz* or *ramal*).

(61)

	Circle 3	Circle 4	Circle 1	Circle 5	Circle 2
i.	*rajaz*	*munsariḥ, muqtaḍab*	*basīṭ*	*mutadārik*	*kāmil*
ii.	*hazaj*	*muḍāriʿ*	*ṭawīl*	*mutaqārib*	*wāfir*
iii.	*ramal*	*xafīf, mujtatt*	*madīd*	*mutadārik*	

The sets (circles) of meters in the three rows of (61) are distinguished by two parameters. The meters in the top row (i) have right-headed groups on Gridline 1; those in rows (ii) and (iii) have left-headed groups on Gridline 1. The meters in rows (i) and (ii) are distinguished from those in the bottom row (iii) by where iterative parenthesis begins on Gridline 0: in the meters of rows (i) and (ii), insertion begins just at the left edge of the asterisk sequence; in the meters of row (iii), insertion begins one asterisk in.

All meters are subject to condition (3). The loose meters in the last three columns are subject to rule (30) and conditions (32) and (56).

Iterative grouping of Gridline 0 asterisks is implemented by the insertion of left parentheses, except for the meters of circle 2, where right parentheses are inserted.

As explained in section 7.5, the *sarīʿ* meter, which traditionally is assigned to circle 4, is in fact a special type of loose meter based on *rajaz*. This is the only case where our classification differs from that of al-Xalīl.

7.8 The Judeo-Spanish poetry of the Middle Ages

The military conquests and the attendant spread of Islam in the early Middle Ages led to the adoption of the Arabic meters in the poetry of many languages. Thiesen (1982) discusses the use of Classical Arabic meters in Persian, Urdu, Kharakhandic, and Ottoman Turkish. West African languages such as Hausa (Hiskett 1975, Schuh 1989) and Fula (Arnott 1985) use meters that are adaptations of the Arabic meters. We conclude this chapter with an examination of the meters of the Hebrew poetry produced in Spain and Provence during the more than 500 years that ended in 1492 CE with the expulsion of both Muslims and Jews from Spain.

It is generally agreed (see Allony 1951: 21) that this type of Hebrew poetry was initiated around 960 CE by Dunash ben Labrat (born in the first third of the 10th century in Fez, Morocco, and died about 990; Allony 1951: 102). Dunash studied with Saadya Gaon (882–942), head of the Jewish academy at Surah in Babylonia (Iraq), and came to Spain, where he was in the service of Hisdai Ibn Shaprut (*c.* 915–970), the Jewish vizier of the caliph of Cordoba. Dunash adopted essentially unchanged the meters of Arabic poetry, but modified the basis for the classification of syllables as 'heavy' vs. 'light'.

In both Arabic and Hebrew traditions, the classification of the syllables for metrical purposes into two classes is based on orthography, except that in Arabic the phonetic aspects of the relationship are a great deal more transparent than in Hebrew. In the Arabic writing system, each consonant is represented by a separate letter. Vowels, by contrast, have two distinct representations: short vowels are represented by diacritic marks, but long vowels are represented by a diacritic mark and a consonant letter, which is taken to close the syllable. Since the diacritics are often omitted in writing, the orthography distinguishes straightforwardly between 'light' syllables, which are written with a single consonant, and the remaining 'heavy' syllables, which are written with two consonants.

This distinction between 'heavy' and 'light' syllables is not reflected as straightforwardly in the writing system of Hebrew as it is in that of Arabic, and this fact made it impossible for Dunash to use the orthographic criteria of Arabic also for Hebrew poetry. He solved this problem by following the orthography rather than the phonetics. He defined 'light' syllables for metrical purposes (such as condition (3)) as the class of syllables that are always written with a single consonant (plus diacritic): these are the syllables whose rhymes consist of the reduced vowel schwa and its congeners (the so-called *ḥăṭāpîm*). He called such syllables Slaves (*ʕăbādîm*); all other syllables Dunash called Kings (*məlākîm*) and identified them with the heavy syllables of Arabic. Thus, condition (3) for the Hebrew verse following Dunash's proposals must be restated as in (62).

(62) A syllable projecting to Gridline 2 must be of the King class, and, if it is part of a branching Gridline 0 group, it must be preceded by a syllable of the Slave class.

An instructive example of these considerations is provided by the treatment of the variants of the Hebrew copula *wə* 'and', which appears as the proclitic [u] both before words beginning with a labial consonant and before words beginning with any consonant followed by schwa. In the first of these two cases, there is no change in syllabification as a result of prefixing the copula. In the second case, on the other hand, the consonant of the word following the copula becomes part of the same syllable with the [u] of the copula, the following schwa is dropped in the pronunciation, and the copula–word sequence now begins with a closed syllable. As shown in the example (63), the copula is treated as a syllable of the Slave class in *û.miʃ́.taʕēr* 'and he is in turmoil' (where the copula precedes the labial consonant [m]), but as a syllable of the King class in *ûl.kâ:* 'and walk!' where the first syllable is closed by the consonant [l]. The lines in (63) are from a poem by Yəhuda Halevi (*c.* 1075–1141), where the first of the two quoted words ends the first line and the second begins the fourth line.[11]

(63)   Hebrew version of *basīṭ*: $C^2 P + CP'$

ya:ʃe:n – wəlibbô: ʕe:r,

  – –   U– – –

bô:ʕe:r, ûmiʃta:ʕe:r

  – – U – – –

cê:ʔ nâʔ wəhinna:ʕe:r

  – – U – – –

ûlkâ:h bəʔô:r pa:nay

  – – U –   – –

```
(*   *   (( *   *   ( *  ( *        0 ⇒ R
   ( *         *   ( *   *  (       1 ⇒ R
           ( *        *  (          2 ⇒ L
           ( *                      3 ⇒ L
             *                      4
```

'He's asleep, yet his heart is awake, burning in turmoil. "Go out! Awake and walk in the light of my countenance!"' Yəhuda Halevi

The poem itself is in a short form of the meter *basīṭ* (see section 7.3). *Basīṭ* is a loose meter, where the first syllable in the sequence U – (i.e., Slave–King) is marked by a L parenthesis (inserted by rule (30)) and the last two long syllables are separated by a L parenthesis inserted by rule (47). The entire line is then subject to the iterative rules (4).

Before scanning additional lines, we note that the definition of a light syllable as a syllable ending in a schwa provides a partial explanation

---

[11] In Shirman (1959: 483), each pair of lines in (63) is printed as a single line. For the transliteration of Hebrew text, see Chapter 11, footnote 3.

for the absence of the meters of circle 2 – *kāmil* and *wāfir* – in the Hebrew poetry (see Allony 1951: 81). These meters require sequences of two Slave syllables, and such sequences are not admitted inside Hebrew words. Although such sequences can arise in Hebrew when a word ending with a schwa like *yeːbkə* 'he will weep' is followed by a word beginning with a syllable ending in schwa like *yəhûːdâh* 'Judah'. It appears, however, that these available options were not utilized by the Hebrew poets writing in these meters.

Three additional meters are illustrated in (64)–(66) below.

(64)   Hebrew version of circle 3 *hazaj*: $P\ C^2 + P\ C^2 + P\ C$

wətappûːaḥ, ʔemet, ʔeːl lô: bəraːʔôː:

```
 U  –    – –    U  –    –  –    U –  –
(* *  (* *   (*   *   (*   * ( * * (*          0 ⇒ R
  (*      *     (*      *    ( *  * (          1 ⇒ L
    *)         *            *)                 2 ⇐ R
  (*                        * (                3 ⇒ L
    *                                          4
```

ləbaːd ʕōneg ləmeːriːaḥ wənôʃeːq
U –   – –   U – – –   U – –

'And the apple indeed, God created it / only for the pleasure of him who smells and kisses it.' Moshe Ibn Ezra (Shirman 1959: 374)

(65)   Hebrew version of circle 3 *rajaz*: $C^2 P + C^2 P + C^2 P'$

zeh rûḥăkaː, cad maʕāraːb, raːqûːaḥ

```
 –   – U –   –    – U –    –  –  –
(*   *(* *  (*    *(* *   (*  *(*            0 ⇒ R
  (*    *     (*    *       (* *(            1 ⇒ R
    (*        *             (  *             2 ⇒ L
    (*                      * (              3 ⇒ L
      *                                      4
```

hanneːrdə biknaːpaːw wəhattappûːaḥ
–   – U –   – –   U – –   – –

'Your spirit, West Wind, is pure perfume, / in its wing is spikenard and apple.' Yəhuda Halevi (Shirman 1959: 504)

(66)   Hebrew version of circle 4 *mujtatt* : $\Delta + Q\ C^2 + P\ C$

hamʕat hḙ̆yôːtî: bətôːk ʕaːm

```
    –   –   U – –   U  –
Δ (*   Δ(* * (* *   (*             0 ⇒ R
  (*      *    (  *   * (          1 ⇒ L
  (*         *      * (            2 ⇒ L
  (*                               3 ⇒ L
    *                              4
```

yaḥʃob ʃəmô:lô: yəma:nî:

— — ∪ — — ∪ — —

'Is it little for me to be among people who think that their left is my right?' Shəlomo ibn Gabirol (Shirman 1959: 208)

We conclude this section with an examination of the meter of the most famous of the poems of Yəhuda Halevi, which for centuries has been included among the prayers said on *tifʕâ bəʔab*, the day commemorating the destruction of the Temple in Jerusalem. Two couplets from this poem are quoted in (67) and (68). The meter of this poem is *basīṭ*, like that of the lines in (63) above. Note that in the second line the special rule (47) inserts a left parenthesis before the rightmost Gridline 0 asterisk.

(67)   Hebrew version of *basīṭ*: $C^2P + CP + C^2P + CP$

ʔeppol ləʔappay ʕăle:y ʔarce:k wəʔerceh ʔăba:-

— — ∪ — — — ∪ — — — ∪ — — ∪ —

```
( *    *(( *  *  ( *   ( * *    ( *   *  (( * * ( *   ( * * (     0 ⇒ R
   ( *     *  ( *      *       ( *       * ( *        * (        1 ⇒ R
      ( *          *              ( *                * (         2 ⇒ L
      ( *                                * (                     3 ⇒ L
         *                                                       4
```

nayik məʔod wă'ăḥô:ne:n ʔet ʕăpa:rayik

— — ∪ — — ∪ — — — ∪ — —

```
( * *  (( * *   ( *(( *  * ( *    * (( *  * ( * ( *          0 ⇒ R
   ( *      *   ( *      *      ( *     * ( * * (            1 ⇒ R
      ( *          *              ( *       * (             2 ⇒ L
      ( *                                 * (               3 ⇒ L
         *                                                  4
```

'I will fall on my face on your soil and I will love your stones greatly, and I will cherish your dust.' (Shirman 1959: 486)

(68)   ʔel mî: yədammû məʃiḥayik wəʔel mî: nəbi-
      ʔayik wəʔel mî: ləwiyyayik wəʃa:rayik

'To whom will be likened your anointed, and to whom your pro- / phets and to whom your priests and princes?' (Shirman 1959: 488)

The fact worth noting especially about these lines is that the first line in (67) ends in the middle of the word *ʔăba:nayik* 'your stones' after the second syllable. This is not an accident; six of the thirty-four couplets that make up the poem share this feature; in each of the six (which include (67) and (68)), the first line of the couplet ends in the middle of a word. Although rarely discussed or even noticed in formal studies of meter, the fact that lines of metrical verse often end in the middle of a word provides strong evidence that the units that compose the lines are not words, phrases, or sentences, but are rather syllables. Just as there is enjambment where a line break occurs in the middle of a syntactic phrase, there is also enjambment in the middle of a word, but there is no enjambment that breaks up a syllable in metrical verse, indicating that the syllable is the ultimate constituent of metrical verse.

8

Sanskrit

8.1 The Vedic meters[1]

The collection of hymns in Vedic Sanskrit called the *Rig-veda* were composed about three and a half thousand years ago, and for a long period were transmitted orally. The hymns are in 3-line, 4-line, or 5-line stanzas, and in quantitative meters (like Greek, based on patterns of heavy and light syllables). The meters can be divided into those with a short line of 8 syllables, and those with a long line of 11 or 12 syllables; there is also a rarer 5-syllable line. In the long-line meters there is a caesura after either the fourth syllable ('early caesura') or the fifth syllable ('late caesura'). We will show that the Vedic meters share iterative rules, and differ by small variations in deletion rules and conditions.

Though they are the oldest metrical texts to have survived, there is nothing 'primitive' about the metrical form of the Vedic hymns: the iterative rules and deletion rules found here are basically the same kinds of rule as we find in all metrical poetry. Like language itself, both the possibility and the nature of metrical poetry arise from our being human, and do not appear to have changed significantly during recorded history. The fact that the oldest metrical texts to have survived are only three and a half thousand years old tells us nothing about how long humans have been composing metrical poetry. Though it is most likely a historical fantasy, a claim made two thousand years ago by the geographer Strabo reminds us of possible lost riches: '[The Turdetanians] are counted the wisest people among the Iberians; they write with an

---

[1] Our analysis draws on Arnold (1905) and Macdonell (1992, 1993) for Vedic Sanskrit, and on Keith (1993), Brough (1978), Coulson (1992) and Deo (2007) for Classical Sanskrit (the latter being the only previous linguistic account of which we are aware). We have benefited from the advice of Ashwini Deo, John Smith, Renate Sohnen and Richard Widdess. All errors are the responsibility of NF&MH.

alphabet and possess prose works and poetry of ancient heritage, and laws composed in meter, six thousand years old, so they say.' (Strabo, *Geography* 3.1.6; cited Woodard 2004: 7).

8.1.1 The 12-syllable line with late caesura

As in the traditional analysis of Greek poetry, the Vedic Sanskrit 12-syllable line with late caesura has been described with reference to a template (1) (Macdonell 1993: 442). The template is made from three types of position: ∪ matches a syllable which in this position must be light, − matches a syllable which in this position must be heavy, and × matches a syllable which is either light or heavy (it is an 'anceps' position). The vertical bar indicates the obligatory word boundary (caesura).

(1) × − × − × | ∪ ∪ − ∪ − ∪ ×

The 12-syllable line is typically found in the four-line *jagatī*, illustrated in (2) by two 12-syllable lines with late caesura.[2]

(2) sá váhniḥ putráḥ pitaróḥ pavítravān
     ∪ − − − − | ∪ ∪ − ∪ − ∪ −

     punáti dhī́ro bhúvanāni māyáyā.
     ∪ − ∪ − − | ∪ ∪ − ∪ − ∪ −

> 'That son of the two parents, the driver, the purifier, wisely purifies beings by his mysterious power.' *Rig-veda* 1.160, 'Hymn to Dyávā-Pṛthiví' stanza 3 lines 1–2 (Macdonell 1992: 39)

Since our approach to meter admits neither templates nor metrical positions, we must explain the regularities with rules which generate the grid from the line, and the conditions holding of that grid. The line has what Macdonell calls a 'prevailingly iambic' pattern with heavy syllables in even-numbered positions. This suggests that syllables are grouped into right-headed pairs. The sixth syllable stands out in two ways – it is light despite being even-numbered and projects as a Gridline 0 head. The syllable moreover is word-initial (i.e., preceded by the caesura), and this suggests that our rules should generate a grid in which this sixth syllable projects to the head of the verse (so that it can be targeted by conditions). The rules in (3) generate the grid in (4).

---

[2] Transcriptions are taken from Macdonell (1992). A heavy syllable ends with either a long vowel or a short vowel followed by two consonants, light syllables end with a short vowel. The two-letter combinations *bh*, *dh*, and *th* stand for single consonants. The vowels *e* and *o* are always long. ṛ heads a syllable and can be pronounced *ri*. The acute accent on a vowel indicates phonemic high pitch (which is not relevant for the meter).

(3) a. Gridline 0: starting just at the L edge, insert a L parenthesis, form binary groups, heads R.

    b. Gridline 1: starting just at the L edge, insert a L parenthesis, form ternary groups, heads R.

    c. Gridline 2: starting just at the L edge, insert a L parenthesis, form binary groups, heads L.

(4) sá váhniḥ putráḥ pitaróḥ pavítravān

```
 U   –   –    –   – | U U  –    U  –  U  –
(*   * (*    * (*    *(* *  (* *(* *(        0 ⇒
 (*        *        *  (*     *    *(        1 ⇒
           (*                *(              2 ⇒
            *                                3
```

The 'generally iambic character' of the meter is captured by the statement of tendency in (5).[3]

(5) Syllables which project to Gridline 1 are heavy.

The unique characteristics of the sixth syllable are captured by the conditions (6) and (7).

(6) The syllable projecting to the head of the verse must be immediately preceded by a word boundary (caesura).

(7) The syllable projecting to the head of the verse must be light.

Condition (7) applies to a syllable which projects both to Gridline 1 and to Gridline 3; it overrides the general tendency (5) requiring syllables projecting to Gridline 1 to be heavy. We will see (in section 8.4) that in Classical Sanskrit, there are also meters which require light syllables to be heads.

8.1.2 The 12-syllable line with early caesura

The 12-syllable line also has a variant with early caesura before the fifth syllable. Its pattern is shown in (8) (Macdonell 1993: 442) and examples are quoted in (9).

(8) × – × – | U U – – U – U ×

(9) té hi Dyávā-Pṛthiví viśváśambhuvā

```
     –  –    – – | Ŭ  U –  – U  –    U  –
```

---

[3] As Macdonell notes, the iambic pattern is a tendency rather than a fixed rule; for example, the second syllable in the line can be light rather than heavy though it tends to be heavy.

ŗtávarī, rájaso dhārayátkavī
U̇– U –| U U –   – U –   U –

'These two, indeed, Heaven and Earth, are beneficial to all, observing order, supporting the sage of the air.' *Rig-veda* 1.160, 'Hymn to Dyávā-Pŗthiví' stanza 1 lines 1–2 (Macdonell 1992: 37)

The iterative rules which we introduced in (3) generate the grid in (10).

(10)   té hi Dyávā-Pŗthiví viśvásaṃbhuvā
       – –   – –| U̇ U – – U –   U –

(* * (* * (* *(* * (* * (* * (	0 ⇒
(* * * (* * * (	1 ⇒
(* * (	2 ⇒
*	3

Though the sixth syllable is here the head of the verse, it is clear that in this line with early caesura, the fifth syllable *should* be head of the verse because while both fifth and sixth syllables are light, it is the fifth syllable which is is immediately preceded by a word boundary as required by condition (6). But the fifth syllable is not in head position. We solve this problem by positing the deletion rule (11) which targets the Gridline 0 projection of the head of the verse. The deletion rule is sensitive to context: it applies only when the head of the verse is followed by a heavy syllable.

(11)   Delete the Gridline 0 asterisk of the light syllable projecting to the head of the verse, when it is to the left of the Gridline 0 asterisk of a heavy syllable.

When applied to the grid in (10), this rule derives the grid in (12).

(12)   té hi Dyávā-Pŗthiví viśvásaṃbhuvā
       – –   – –| U̇ U – – U –   U –

(* * (* * (* Δ(* * (* * (* * (	0 ⇒
(* * * (* * * (	1 ⇒
(* * (	2 ⇒
*	3

Condition (7), requiring the (new) head of the verse to be light, is satisfied by the syllable that assumes head position as the result of deletion.

In the traditional analysis of Vedic Sanskrit, the middle part of the long line (called the 'break') is said to have the pattern | U U –, whether the caesura is early or late. We explain this traditionally-conceived 'break' pattern by making our deletion rule (11) context-sensitive: every 12-syllable line is tested against it, but the rule deletes the sixth asterisk only if the seventh syllable is heavy. If the seventh syllable is heavy, the line is said to have 'early caesura', meaning that the fifth, sixth, and seventh syllables are in the pattern | ∪ ∪ −, forming the traditionally-conceived 'break' sequence. If the seventh syllable is light, the rule does not apply, and so the line has 'late caesura', which means that the sixth and seventh syllables are in the pattern | ∪ ∪. However, since the following, eighth, syllable projects to Gridline 1, it will be heavy and so the 'break' sequence will be | ∪ ∪ −.

The quantity of the syllable preceding the head (and hence preceding the caesura) is metrically irrelevant, and is not controlled by a condition. This is clear in the lines with late caesura in (13), where the syllable preceding the head is heavy in the first line and light in the second line. In other words, while the deletion rule takes into account the context following the head, it disregards the context preceding the head.

(13)	uruvyácasā mahínī asaścátā,
	∪ − ∪ ∪ −| ∪ ∪ − ∪ − ∪ −
	pitá mātá ca, bhúvanāni rakṣataḥ.
	∪ − − − ∪| ∪ ∪ − ∪ − ∪ −

	'As Father and Mother, far extending, great inexhaustible, the two protect
	all beings.' *Rig-veda* 1.160, 'Hymn to Dyā́vā-Pṛthivī́' stanza 2 lines 1–2
	(Macdonell 1992: 38)

8.1.3 11-syllable lines

The 11-syllable line is in its basic pattern identical to the 12-syllable line, but with an incomplete group on Gridline 0 at its right edge. Like the 12-syllable line, it has an early caesura version with caesura after the fourth syllable, which is exemplified by the first line of the couplet in (14), and a late caesura version with caesura before the sixth syllable, which is exemplified by the second line of the couplet.

(14)	śáśvad víśaḥ Savitúr dáiviasya
	− − ∪ −| ∪ ∪ − − ∪− ∪			early caesura
	(* * (* * (* Δ(* *(* * (*			0 ⇒
	    (* * * (* * * (			1 ⇒
	           (* * (			2 ⇒
	           *			3

	upásthe víśvā bhúvanāni tasthuḥ
	∪ − − − −| ∪ ∪ − ∪ − −			late caesura
	(* * (* * (* *(* *(* * (*			0 ⇒
	    (* * (* * * (			1 ⇒
	           (* * (			2 ⇒
	           *			3

	'For ever the settlers and all creatures have rested in the lap of Savitṛ'
	Rig-veda 1.35, 'Hymn to Savitṛ' stanza 5 lines 3–4, Macdonell 1992: 14)

The grid for the 11-syllable line is generated by the same rules as those for the 12-syllable line, but with a condition on Gridline 0, stated in (15).

(15)   The last (rightmost) group must be incomplete.

The fact that the 11-syllable pattern is the same as the 12-syllable pattern except for ending with an incomplete group is evidence for the specific (marked) Gridline 0 rule which we chose (cf. (11) above). An incomplete group must be the last group generated, and this fact shows that even though the groups are clearly iambic (right-headed), they are formed by left parentheses inserted from left to right.

In sum, the four types of long line are closely related. Their metrical grids are built by the same iterative rules (3), with the grids differing only in whether the rightmost group is incomplete (11-syllable) or complete (12-syllable); the application of the deletion rule (11) derives the pattern with early caesura from the pattern with late caesura.

8.1.4   The 8-syllable line

The short Vedic line is 8 syllables long, and is typically found in the 4-line *anuṣṭubh* stanza and 3-line *gāyatrī* stanza. We suggest that the short line is derived by the same iterative rules as those that scan the long line, but with a condition making the second Gridline 1 group unary, thus shortening the line. We focus on two typical quantitative patterns, both involving the last half of the line and traditionally called the 'cadence':[4] the iambic cadence and the trochaic cadence. In the line with iambic cadence, syllables 5, 6, and 7 have the pattern ∪ − ∪. In the line with trochaic cadence, syllable 5 is unrestricted and syllables 6 and 7 have the pattern ∪ −.

We begin with the 8-syllable line with trochaic cadence, illustrated by the second line in the couplet in (16). This is a complete stanza from a hymn in which all the stanzas pair a 12-syllable line with an 8-syllable line.

(16)   trī́ṇi éka urugāyó ví cakrame,
　　　　− ˘∪ − ∪|∪ ∪ − − ∪ − ∪ −

```
( * *(* *(* Δ(* * (*  * (*  * (          0 ⇒
  (*   * *    (*     *    * (            1 ⇒
    (*              *(              ? ⇒
      *                              3
```

---

yátra deváso mádanti.

```
 –  U  – – –   U  –  U
( *   * ( *  *( *    Δ( *   * (          0 ⇒
  ( *     * *         ( *              1 ⇒
    ( *           * (                2 ⇒
          ☥                        3
```

'One, wide-pacing makes three strides to where the gods are exhilarated.'
Rig-veda 8.29, 'Hymn to Víśve deváḥ' stanza 7 (Macdonell 1992: 14)

The pairing of 12- and 8-syllable lines here suggests a relation between them which we have exploited in generating the grids. The 8-syllable and 12-syllable lines are both scanned by the rules in (3), but Gridline 1 of the 8-syllable line is in addition subject to condition (17).

(17)   The last (rightmost) group must be incomplete – unary.

The fact that the incomplete grouping is at the right edge of Gridline 1 shows that the groups on this line are constructed from left to right with left parentheses (even though they are right-headed). Additional evidence that this is indeed the correct structure for the 8-syllable line comes from the fact that the sixth syllable must be the head of the line (because it is targeted by a deletion rule). The sixth asterisk here is deleted by the same rule we earlier used for the long line, (11). We repeat it here.

(11)   Delete the Gridline 0 asterisk of the light syllable projecting to the head of the verse, when it is to the left of the Gridline 0 asterisk of a heavy syllable.

The same deletion rule (11) thus derives both the 'early caesura' pattern in the long line and the 'trochaic cadence' in the short line.

We now consider the 8-syllable line with iambic cadence. This is illustrated in (18) with the first stanza of the first hymn in the *Rig-veda*, the hymn to Agni, the god of fire (whose name is cognate with Latin *ignis* 'fire'). The metrical grid of the first line is shown in (19).

(18)   Agním īḷe puróhitam,
```
        –  U  – –  U – U –
```

yajñásya devám ṛtvíjam,
```
        –  –  U – U  ° U –
```

hotāraṃ ratnadhā́tamam.
```
        – – –   –  U  – U  –
```

'I magnify Agni the domestic priest, the divine ministrant of the sacrifice, the invoker, best bestower of treasure.' *Rig-veda* 1.1, 'Hymn to Agni' stanza 1 (Macdonell 1992: 39)

(19)   Agním īḷe puróhitam,
```
        –   U   – –   U – U –              iambic cadence
      (*    *  ( * *  ( *  *( * * (        0 ⇒
        (*     *     *  ( *               1 ⇒
                   ( *   * (               2 ⇒
                   *                       3
```

Lines with iambic cadence are lines in which the seventh syllable is light.
Thus, the head of the verse is not deleted in these lines. We control the
fifth and sixth syllables by the condition (20), which closely resembles
the basic condition forming pegs in Arabic meters (section 7.1).

(20)   A syllable projecting to the head of the verse must be heavy, and
       if it is part of a branching Gridline 0 group, it must be preceded
       by a light syllable.

   In sum, both the iambic and the trochaic variants of the 8-syllable
line are generated by the same set of iterative rules and conditions. The
iterative rules are the same in both cases, but they differ in whether or
not the deletion rule (11) applies. The deletion rule applies only if the
seventh syllable is heavy. Condition (20) holds of all 8-syllable lines, but
has no effect in lines which have undergone deletion, because in these
lines the syllable projecting to the head of the verse is in a non-branching
Gridline 0 group (since its original partner has been deleted).

8.2 Classical *anuṣṭubh*

All surviving Sanskrit poetry that is later than the Vedas is composed
in Classical Sanskrit, the form of the language described and fixed by
Pāṇini around 500 BCE (Coulson 1992, Jamison 2004: 674). In this section we consider the classical *anuṣṭubh* (sometimes referred to as *śloka*).
The stanza is made up of two couplets with slightly different odd and
even lines, as illustrated by the templates in (21).[5]

(21)   a. × × × × U – – ×   First line of couplet

       b. × × × × U – U ×   Second line of couplet

Lines in this meter are scanned by the same rules as for the 8-syllable
Vedic line (see section 8.1.4), making the sixth syllable the head of the
verse.

---

[5] These are the *pathyā* or regular forms; we do not analyze the less common *vipulā*
forms here. As indicated in (21), in this meter the heavy syllables tend, in addition,
to be stressed.

(22)　apragalbhapadanyāsā
　　　　－　U　－　　U U　－　　－ －

```
(*  * ( *    * ( *   *  ( *  * (          0 ⇒
  ( *        *    *      ( *              1 ⇒
             ( *       * (               2 ⇒
                 *                       3
```

jananīrāgahetavaḥ
　　U U　－ － U　－ U －

```
( *  * ( *  * ( *   * ( *  * (           0 ⇒
  ( *    *    * ( *                      1 ⇒
         ( *   * (                       2 ⇒
             *                           3
```

santy eke bahulālāpāḥ
　　－　　－ －　U U　－ － －

kavayo bālakā iva.
　　U U　－　　－ U　－ U U

'Some poets are like small children: their feet totter, they cause the people
displeasure (they cause their mothers delight), and they are extremely
verbose (they are constantly slavering).' (Brough 1978: 70)

Condition (20) applies in this meter, making the fifth syllable light and
the sixth heavy. In this meter, there is no deletion rule. The difference
between odd and even lines is expressed by the condition (23).

(23)　The syllable which projects to the head of the verse must be
　　　　followed by a heavy syllable in an odd-numbered line, and must
　　　　be followed by a light syllable in an even-numbered line.

The loss of the deletion rule is the fundamental difference between the
Vedic 8-syllable line and the classical *anuṣṭubh* line.

8.3　The fixed syllabic meters of Classical Sanskrit

Classical Sanskrit has a very large number of meters, of which we examine a tiny selection here.[6] It is characteristic of most Classical Sanskrit meters that they control the quantity of *every* syllable in the line,
with the exception of the final (rightmost) syllable. The sequence of
heavy and light syllables is sometimes in a repetetive pattern, sometimes
slightly disrupted in its regularity, and sometimes apparently without
any pattern. As shown below, all these types of meter can be accounted
for straightforwardly by iterative rules that generate a grid, which may
be subject to a deletion rule, and also to the usual conditions on the
relation between the line and the grid.

---

[6] Deo (2007) refers to modern compilations by Velankar (1949) and Patwardhan
(1937) which contain more than 600 meters. Keith (1993: 418–420) lists seventy-
six of these. Deo offers a theoretical analysis of many more meters than we do.

8.3.1 Indravajrā

We begin our account of the fixed Classical Sanskrit meters with *in-dravajrā*, an 11-syllable meter in which every line has the sequence of heavy and light syllables shown in (24), with an obligatory word boundary (caesura) after the fifth syllable. Only the rightmost syllable is free in its weight (i.e., anceps), and so could in principle be either light or heavy, though in fact in all four lines quoted here it is heavy.

(24) $- - \cup - -| \cup \cup - \cup - \times$

(25) nirmānamohā jitasaṃgadoṣā
$- \quad - \quad \cup \quad - \quad -|\cup\cup - \quad \cup - \quad -$

adhyātmanityā vinivṛttakāmāḥ
$- \quad \quad - \quad \cup - \quad -| \cup \cup - \quad \cup - \quad -$

dvandvair vimuktāḥ sukhaduḥkhasamjñair
$- \quad \quad - \quad \cup - \quad - \mid \cup \quad \cup - \quad \cup - \quad \quad -$

gacchanty amūdhāḥ padam avyayam tat.
$- \quad \quad - \quad \cup - \quad - \mid \cup \cup \quad - \quad \cup - \quad \quad -$

> 'Those who are free from pride and delusion, who have conquered the vice (evil) of attachment / who are constant (devoted) to the supreme being and whose desires have been overcome / who are free from the dualities known as happiness and sorrow / those undeluded ones go to (obtain) that eternal (unmoving) state.' *Bhagavad Gītā* 15.5

Like the 11-syllable Vedic line, *indravajrā* is an iambic meter with deletion of the Gridline 0 asterisk which projects to the head of the verse. The grid is built by the same rules as thoseused for the 11-syllable Vedic line, i.e., (3) supplemented by (15). However, unlike in the Vedic line, in this meter the deletion rule (26) is context-free.

(26) Delete the Gridline 0 asterisk of the light syllable projecting to the head of the verse.

(27) nirmānamohā jitasaṃgadoṣā

$- \quad - \quad \cup \quad - \quad -\|\cup\cup- \quad \cup - \quad -$		
(* * (* * (* Δ(* * (* * (*	$0 \Rightarrow$	
(* * * (* * * (	$1 \Rightarrow$	
(* * (	$2 \Rightarrow$	
*	3	

Except for the rightmost syllable (which is always free of conditions on weight in Sanskrit meters), the quantity of every syllable is fixed by (28).

(28) Syllables projecting to Gridline 1 must be heavy; other syllables must be light.

For this meter we need the additional condition (29).

(29)   The leftmost syllable which projects to Gridline 1 must be preceded by a heavy syllable.

Conditions on the grid can incorporate three types of unique position in the line – at the left edge, at the right edge, or projecting to the head of the verse. The condition (29) is an 'edge rule' which exploits the fact that 'leftmost' is a uniquely identifiable location.

In addition to conditions on weight, *indravajrā* requires the fifth syllable to be word-final (i.e., it is subject to a caesura rule). In our account the fifth syllable is the head of the line, and so the caesura condition can be stated as (30).

(30)   The syllable which projects to the head of the verse must be word-final.

It is interesting to compare the (11-syllable) *indravajrā* with the 11-syllable Vedic meter with late caesura, discussed in section 8.1.3. They show similarities in placement of the caesura and some aspects of the pattern of weights (in particular, syllables 6–8 have a ∪ ∪ − pattern in both). However, *indravajrā* is derived by a deletion rule, while the 11-syllable Vedic meter with late caesura is differentiated from the early caesura variant precisely in *not* being subject to deletion. This difference is reflected in the fact that in the Vedic meters, the caesura precedes the syllable projecting to the head of the verse while in *indravajrā* it follows the syllable projecting to the head of the verse.

The Classical Sanskrit meters are characteristically performed according to certain stereotyped rhythms which require certain syllables to be stressed in performance.[7] Deo (2007), in her account of the Classical Sanskrit meters, cites evidence from performance to support her metrical analysis; thus the metrical form of the line is further evidenced by the fact that we can understand a performed rhythm in terms of this metrical form. Though our account is very different from Deo's, we also find that the stereotype rhythm with which *indravajrā* is sometimes performed – stressing the second, fifth, eighth, and eleventh syllables – provides evidence for our hypothesized metrical structure. In this book, we have insisted that there is no necessary relation between the rhythm of a line and its meter. However, in a particular meter, conditions may relate rhythm and meter, and in this case there is indeed a correlation.

---

[7]   Morris Halle recalls being taught at school in Latvia in the 1930s to recite Latin hexameter lines so that every 'longum' is stressed (overriding actual Latin stress). Thus: 'árma virúmque canó : Trōiáe quī prímus ab órīs'. The stressed syllables are those syllables which project to Gridline 1. The hexameters of Latin are subject to the same rules as those of Greek, see section 6.3.2.

(31)   ´   ´   ´   ´   stressed syllables
        labdhodayā candramasīva lekhā
        −   − U − −   U U − U − −
        (*   *(* * (*   Δ (* *(* * (*   0 ⇒
            (*   * *   (*   * * (1 ⇒
              (*   * (2 ⇒
                *   3

'Like the crescent of the risen moon.' (Deo 2007: 65)

The performance of this line is governed by (32).

(32)   a. Syllables projecting to Gridline 2 must be stressed in perfor-
           mance.

        b. Syllables projecting to Gridline 1 must be stressed in perfor-
           mance, unless adjacent to a syllable projecting to Gridline
           2.

The possibility of relating rhythm and meter in this case provides independent evidence for our metrical rules and the grids they generate.

We see another example of rules assigning a rhythm on the basis of
a grid in section 10.1.1. Where rules assign rhythm on the basis of
a metrical grid, the metrical rules are treated – uncharacteristically –
as rules of the phonology, which determine the stress placement in the
words that composed the line (cf. footnote 7 above). Such rules are
distinct from metrical rules, which do not affect the pronunciation of
words at all.

8.3.2 Vasantatilaka

We next look at the *vasantatilaka* meter, with fourteen syllables in the
pattern (33), exemplified in (34).[8]

(33)   − − U − U U U − U U − U − ×

(34)   gacchan vilaṅghya nagaropavanāntarāṇi
        −   −   U −   U U U − U U − U − U

---

[8] This and some other texts we cite are from the sixth canto of the
Rāghavapāṇḍavīya of Kavirāja (12th century CE) a poem which uses a systematic ambiguity called *śleṣa*, such that it tells a story from the *Rāmāyaṇa* at the
same time as telling a story from the *Mahābhārata* (Brough 1978: 154; Keith 1993:
137–139). Thus, (33) also means 'Making his way through the parts which lay between the city and the garden-suburbs, the success of his venture being indicated
by his chariot whose horses were true-running like the straight flight of an arrow,
the hero saw before him as he went the enemy army, proud with its roaring, like
a terrible ocean, whose crocodiles were war-elephants.' We generally give just one
translation for texts of this kind, indicating them with '*śleṣa*' in the gloss.

sampātipattrarathasūcitakāryasiddhiḥ :
```
–   – U –   U U   U – UU –   U–     –
```
vīro dadarśa karinakrakarālam agre
```
– –   U –   U UU –   UU U – U     –   –
```
ghoṣoddhataṃ saḥlarāśim ivārisainyam.
```
– –     U –     UUU – U   U – U –     –
```

'Crossing on his journey mountain chasms and mighty forests, the successful end of his journey having previously been told to him by the bird Sampāti, the hero saw before him the ocean, uplifted in waves and roaring, terrible with whales and sharks, like an enemy army.' Kavirāja, *Rāghavapāṇḍavīya* canto 6 stanza 5 (Brough 1978: 133)

We begin by formulating the iterative rules (35), which build the periodic grid in (36)

(35)   a. Gridline 0: starting just at the R edge, insert a R parenthesis, form ternary groups, heads R.

            i. The last (leftmost) group must be incomplete – binary.

    b. Gridline 1: starting just at the R edge, insert a R parenthesis, form ternary groups, heads R.

            i. The last (leftmost) group must be incomplete – binary.

    c. Gridline 2: starting just at the L edge, insert a L parenthesis, form binary groups, heads L.

(36)   sampātipattrarathasūcitakāryasiddhiḥ
```
        –   – U –   U U   U – UU –   U–     –
    *    *)* *   *)*   * *)* * *)  *   **     *)      0 ⇐
    *         *)          *     *            *)      1 ⇐
            ( *                              * (      2 ⇒
            *                                         3
```

The periodic grid does not directly reflect the aperiodic sequence of heavy and light syllables. The first step in bringing out the rhythm is to apply the rule deleting the head of the verse (26), repeated here. When applied to (36), this rule generates the grid in (37).

(26)   Delete the Gridline 0 projection of the light syllable which projects to the head of the verse.

(37)   sampātipattrarathasūcitakāryasiddhiḥ
```
        –   – U –   U U   U – UU –   U–     –
    *    *)* *   Δ)*   * *)* * *)   * *     *)      0 ⇐
    *     *)          *     *            *)      1 ⇐
            ( *                              * (      2 ⇒
            *                                         3
```

Once the deletion rule has applied, the pattern of syllables projecting to Gridline 1 satisfies conditions similar to those for *indravajrā*, generally requiring that syllables projecting to Gridline 1 are heavy and others are light (cf. (28)). The most significant difference is that condition (29) which required the leftmost head to be preceded by a heavy syllable is used here, supplemented by a similar condition on the rightmost head (38).

(29) The leftmost syllable which projects to Gridline 1 must be preceded by a heavy syllable.

(38) The rightmost syllable which projects to Gridline 1 must be preceded by a heavy syllable.

Thus, *vasantatilaka* is like *indravajrā*; in both cases, periodic grids are generated, and in both cases the grids are readjusted by a deletion rule which gives rise to a surface aperiodicity.

8.4 Classical Sanskrit meters: the division into sub-lines

8.4.1 Mālinī

Many of the Classical Sanskrit meters have one or two caesuras within the line. We have seen this already in *indravajrā*, where a condition located the caesura immediately after the head of the verse. However, in many Classical Sanskrit meters the caesura must be interpreted differently, as an indication that the line must be split into sub-lines with significantly different metrical patterns. One such meter is *mālinī*. The basic pattern of the line is shown in (39), and illustrated in (40).

(39) ∪∪∪∪∪∪ − − | − ∪ − − ∪ − ×

(40) vikalitarathavaṃśaṃ maṅkṣu bhagnākṣabhāvāt
       ∪ ∪∪∪∪ ∪ − − | − ∪ − − ∪ − −
       pramathitabalanāthaṃ ruddhabhīṣmaprabhāvam :
       ∪ ∪ ∪∪∪∪ − − | − ∪ − − ∪ − −
       kṣapitakṛpakṛpāṇaṃ tat tadākarṇakṛṣṭa-
       ∪∪∪∪ ∪∪ − − | − ∪ − − ∪ − −
       sphuritavipulacāpaṃ sa sma sainyaṃ dhunoti.
       ∪∪∪∪ ∪ ∪∪ − − | − ∪ − − ∪ − −

       'Then he swiftly routed that army, so that its chariot poles were broken, and because of the fact that Akṣa was defeated, its leaders were put to flight, and its terrible onset checked; though it had swords which knew no pity, and numerous vibrating bows, stretched to the ear.'(*śleṣa*) Kavirāja, *Rāghavapāṇḍavīya* canto 6 stanza 17 (Brough 1978: 138)

The pattern before the caesura is very different from the pattern after the caesura, and we propose that the two patterns are scanned by different iterative rules. This requires the line to be split into two sub-lines, each with its own metrical grid.[9] Independent evidence in favor of dividing the line into distinct grids is that a sub-part of one meter can sometimes be found as a sub-part of another. Thus, the first half of *mālinī* is also the first half of *śrīpuṭa*, whose pattern is [UUUUUU − −|−U− ×]. The second half of *mālinī* is found as a sub-component in a number of other meters, including *sragdharā* (see section 8.4.2). The calculation of syllable weight depends on the whole line: the final syllable in the whole line is anceps (i.e., not controlled for weight), while the calculation of the weight of a syllable at the end of a sub-line can involve consonants at the beginning of the next sub-line.[10] Thus, we reinterpret the pattern of *mālinī* as two distinct patterns (41), which combine to form this meter.

(41)   a. U U U U U U − −   *mālinī* sub-line 1/2

        b. − U − − U − ×   *mālinī* sub-line 2/2

The first sub-line is scanned by (42). The Gridline 0 rule constructs 'anapaestic' groups (right-headed triplets) and skips the first two asterisks that end the line.

(42)   a. Gridline 0: starting at the R edge two asterisks in, insert a
            R parenthesis, form ternary groups, heads R.

        b. Gridline 1: starting just at the R edge, insert a R parenthesis,
            form binary groups, heads R.

(43)   vikalitarathavaṃśaṃ

```
 U  U U U  U     U −    −            sub-line 1/2
) *  * *)*  *    *) *    *           0 ⇐
    ) *         *  )                 1 ⇐
                *                    2
```

The condition which controls the distribution of heavy and light syllables in this grid is stated in (44).

---

[9] We owe to John Smith (personal communication) both the idea of dividing the line into distinct metrical sections and the observation that sub-parts of the line are recycled in different meters; see Fabb (1997: 93–4). We have found a similar splitting of traditional lines into sub-grids in Latvian (9.1), in the *Chanson de Roland* (5.6), and in Greek (6.2.4).

[10] This can be seen below in (52), where the short vowel at the end of the line heads a heavy syllable because it is followed in the next sub-line by two consonants *k* and *ṣ* and thus places the line break in the middle of a word. A similar treatment of quantity, where the consonants beginning the next line make the final syllable of the preceding line heavy, is found in the Berber meters discussed by Dell and Elmedlaoui (2007, 2008).

(44) Grouped syllables must be light; ungrouped syllables must be heavy.

The second sub-line is scanned by the rules (45), which generate the grid (46).

(45)   a. Gridline 0: starting at the L edge one asterisk in, insert a L parenthesis, form ternary groups, heads L.

     b. Gridline 1: starting just at the R edge, insert a R parenthesis, form binary groups, heads R.

(46)   maṅkṣu bhagnākṣabhāvāt

```
 −   ∪   −   − ∪   − −     sub-line 2/2
*  ( *   *   * ( *   * * (      0 ⇒
   ) *           * )           1 ⇐
                 *             2
```

This grid has two triplets which are 'inverted' dactyls, with a light–heavy–heavy pattern instead of the normal heavy–light–light pattern. Condition (47), which is needed here, recalls condition (7) requiring a light head in Vedic Sanskrit.

(47) Syllables projecting to Gridline 1 must be light; other syllables are heavy.

8.4.2 Sragdharā

Sragdharā is a meter with two caesuras; it is split into three sub-lines, as shown in (48). The meter is illustrated in (49).

(48)   a. − − − − ∪ − −   *sragdharā* sub-line 1/3

     b. ∪ ∪ ∪ ∪ ∪ ∪ −   *sragdharā* sub-line 2/3

     c. − ∪ − − ∪ − −   *sragdharā* sub-line 3/3

(49)   saṃbhrāntadroṇam udyacchakunikalakalaṃ vihvalolūkasārtham
```
−    −  −  − ∪   − −| ∪ ∪ ∪∪∪ ∪− | − ∪−−∪ −   −
```
sadyovikṣiptagulmaṃ kṣapitanṛpataru kṣuṇṇapunnāgapūgam :
```
−  − −− ∪ −   − | ∪∪∪ ∪ ∪∪ −| − ∪− −∪ − −
```
addhā nunnāśvakarṇaṃ pramathitavipulaśrīphalaṃ dhūtadhātrī-
```
−  − − −  ∪ −  − | ∪ ∪ ∪∪∪ ∪−|− ∪ −  −∪ − −
```
cakraṃ cakre saśokāspadam arigahanaṃ prāg aśokābhirāmam.
```
−  −  −   − ∪ − −  ∪∪∪ ∪ − | − ∪− −∪ − −
```

'The garden of the enemy, formerly delightful with its Aśoka trees, he made a place of sorrow, its ravens frightened, with a confused noise of birds flying up, its flocks of owls terrified, in an instant its clumps of trees scattered, its royal trees smashed, its Punnāga trees and betel-nut trees broken, its Aśvakarṇa trees straightway overturned, its thick clumps of Bilva trees crushed, its ring of Myrobalan trees thrown down.' (*śleṣa*)
Kavirāja, *Rāghavapāṇḍavīya* canto 6 stanza 12 (Brough 1978: 136)

The meter requires word boundaries after the seventh and fourteenth syllables in this twentyone-syllable line, and in (49), this is observed in the first three lines[11] but not in the fourth which violates the rule with respect to the first of the two caesura positions. We split each line into three grids, and note that in the fourth line this results in splitting a word across grids.

In the first of the three sub-lines that constitute a traditional line only one syllable is light and all other syllables are heavy. This is best captured by grouping the syllables with the rules (46) and requiring that the head of the line be light, with a condition similar to (47):

(50) Syllables projecting to Gridline 2 must be light; other syllables are heavy.

(51) sadyovikṣiptagulmaṃ

–	– – – ∪ – –			sub-line 1/3
*	(* * * (* * * (			0 ⇒
	) * *)			1 ⇐
	*			2

The second sub-line is scanned in (52). The grid is generated by a variant of the (anapaestic dimeter) iterative rules (42) with the stipulation that the first asterisk be skipped. Condition (44) holds, requiring all syllables in Gridline 0 groups to be light.

(52) kṣapitanṛpataru

∪ ∪ ∪ ∪ ∪ ∪ –		sub-line 2/3
) * * *) * * *) *		0 ⇐
) * *)		1 ⇐
*		2

The third sub-line is identical to the second part of *mālinī*, and is scanned by the same rules and conditions; i.e., (45) and (44).

(53) kṣuṇṇapunnāgapūgam

– ∪ – – ∪ – –		sub-line 3/3
* (* * *(* * * (		0 ⇒
) * *)		1 ⇐
*		2

---

[11] In the first and third lines, the word boundary falls within a larger compound word, which is legitimate. Thus, the compound *udyac-chakuni-kalakalaṃ* has the caesura falling after its first word, and *pramathita-vipula-śrī-phalaṃ* has the caesura falling after its second word.

8.4.3 Sārdūlavikrīḍita

Sārdūlavikrīḍita (the name means 'tigers at play') is a compound meter where the line is broken into the two sub-lines in (54), and is illustrated with the four lines in (55).

(54) a. – – – ∪∪ – ∪ – ∪∪∪–   *sārdūlavikrīḍita* sub-line 1/2

     b. – – ∪ – – ∪ –   *sārdūlavikrīḍita* sub-line 2/2

(55) uḍhā yena mahādhuraḥ suviṣame mārge sadaikākinā
     –   – – ∪   ∪ –   ∪ –˙   ∪ ∪∪   –| –   – ∪ – – – ∪ –
     soḍho yena kadācid eva na nije goṣṭhe 'nyaśauṇḍadhvaniḥ
     –   – – ∪ ∪ – ∪   – ∪ ∪ ∪ –| – ˙   –   ∪ –   –   ∪ –
     āsīd yaś ca gavāṃ gaṇasya tilakas tasyaiva sampraty aho
     – –   –   ∪ ∪ –   ∪ – ∪ ∪∪ – | –   – ∪ –   – ∪ –
     dhik kaṣṭaṃ dhavalasya jātajaraso goḥ paṇyam udghoṣyate.
     –   –˙–   ∪ ∪ – ∪ – ∪ ∪ ∪ –| –   – ∪   –   – ∪ –

     'The white ox which always alone bore the heavy loads on the roughest
     roads, which never tolerated in its own enclosure the slightest suggestion
     of pride from another, which was the chief ornament of the herd – now,
     the minute it show signs of age (ah, wicked shame!) is put up for sale.'
     (Brough 1978: 72)

The first sub-line of *sārdūlavikrīḍita* is an a-rhythmic 12-syllable sequence composed of four triplets. The second and fourth of these are anapaests (∪∪–), and the third an anapaest whose head has been deleted (∪ – ∪), and which before deletion must therefore have projected to the head of the verse. This suggests the rules in (56), supplemented by the deletion rule (26).

(56) a. Gridline 0: starting just at the R edge, insert a R parenthesis,
       form ternary groups, heads R.

     b. Gridline 1: starting just at the L edge, insert a L parenthesis,
       form binary groups, heads L.

     c. Gridline 2: starting just at the R edge, insert a R parenthesis,
       form binary groups, heads R.

(57) ūḍhā yena mahādhuraḥ suviṣame

–	–	– ∪	∪ –	∪ –	∪ ∪∪	–	sub-line 1/2
)*	*	*)*	* *)	* *	Δ)* *	*)	0 ⇐
	(*		*	(*		* (	1 ⇒
	) *			*)			2 ⇐
				*			3

The pattern of heavy and light syllables is controlled in general by condition (28), repeated here, with a special condition (58) overriding condition (28) in the leftmost Gridline 0 group.

(28)   Syllables projecting to Gridline 1 must be heavy; other syllables
       must be light.

(58)   The leftmost syllable which projects to Gridline 1 must be pre-
       ceded by heavy syllables.

The second sub-line of *sārdūlavikrīḍita* is scanned by (59), supplemented by condition (47).

(59)   a. Gridline 0: starting at the R edge one asterisk in, insert a R
           parenthesis, form ternary groups, heads R.
       b. Gridline 1: starting just at the R edge, insert a R parenthesis,
           form binary groups, heads R.

(60)   mārge sadaikākinā

```
 –   – ∪  – – ∪ –          sub-line 2/2
) *   * * )  * * * )*       0 ⇐
      ) *        * )        1 ⇐
                 *          2
```

   This sub-line has the pattern − − ∪ − − ∪ −, which is the mirror-image
of the pattern − ∪ − − ∪ − −, seen in *mālinī* and *sragdharā*. The mirror-
image pattern is produced by a set of rules (59), which resemble those
in (45) but replace 'left' by 'right', and 'right' by 'left'. In this manner,
the various superficially distinct kinds of metrical structure in Classical
Sanskrit meters are generated by very similar types of rule.

8.5 *Āryā* and other 'mora-counting meters'

Traditional Indian metrical theory distinguishes between syllabic meters
(the meters discussed so far) and moraic meters, which we discuss in this
section. We use the term 'mora' to refer to what the Indian theorists call
a *mātrā*. A light syllable counts as one mora, a heavy syllable counts as
two morae, and the line is measured by counting morae (of which there
are a fixed number), rather than by counting syllables (of which there
are a variable number).

   Our theory of meter provides at least three ways of approaching 'mora-
counting meters'. We might reanalyze them as loose meters in which
only syllables project and there is no notion of mora. This approach
is similar to that taken for Greek dactylic hexameter. While such an
approach is possible here, it does not seem the best match for the data.
Alternatively we might project light syllables onto a separate, preliminary Gridline ('Gridline −1') and group these into binary groups which

project a single asterisk on Gridline 0, where they are joined by asterisks
projected from heavy syllables. Apart from the cost of needing an extra
Gridline, and projecting syllables onto distinct Gridlines, this approach
fails to answer the question of why light syllables can be grouped on
Gridline −1 into pairs but not into triplets (given that grouping into
triplets is possible on any other Gridline).

In view of these inadequacies we take the third possible approach here,
which is as stated in (61).

(61)   Project a light syllable as an asterisk on Gridline 0. Project a
       heavy syllable as two asterisks on Gridline 0.

We illustrate our approach with one of the most important Sanskrit
'mora-counting meters', *āryā*, as exemplified by the couplet in (62).

(62)   vyākhyātum eva kecit kuśalāḥ śāstraṃ prayoktum alam anye
       $-$ $-$ $\cup$ $-$ $\cup$ $--$ | $\cup\cup-$ $-$ $-$ $\cup$ $-$ $\cup$ $\cup\cup$ $-$ $-$
       upanāmayati karo 'nnaṃ rasāṃs tu jihvaiva jānāti.
       $\cup$ $\cup$ $-$ $\cup$ $\cup\cup$ $\cup$ $-$ $-$ | $\cup$ $-$ $\cup$ $-$ $-$ $\cup$ $-$ $-$ $-$[b]

       "Some people are clever only at explaining, while others have the ability
       to practice the craft." "True, the hand carries the food to the mouth, but
       only the tongue knows the flavours." 'Poet and critic' (Brough 1978: 70)

The *āryā* couplet consists of a long line followed by a short line; the final
syllable in each is counted as heavy even if light. If, as proposed, we
count a heavy syllable as 2 and a light syllable as 1, the first line adds
up to 30 and the second to 27, and this is always true in an *āryā* couplet. This is what makes it a 'mora-counting meter'. However, syllables
are also controlled. In the traditional formulation, the metrical line is
composed of groups of syllables called *gaṇa*, which have a specific length
measured in morae. In this meter, *gaṇa* must consist of four morae. A
heavy syllable cannot be split between two *gaṇa*, and so in this meter
the possible *gaṇa* have the shapes shown in in (63) (Coulson 1992: 312).

(63)   a. $-$ $-$
       b. $-$ $\cup$ $\cup$
       c. $\cup$ $\cup$ $-$
       d. $\cup$ $\cup$ $\cup$ $\cup$
       e. $\cup$ $-$ $\cup$

The *āryā* line is constructed by combining eight of these *gaṇa* in sequence, giving 32 morae (8 x 4); the fact that some *gaṇa* are incomplete
brings down the overall length. While the line can begin with the se-
quence $\cup$ $\cup$ $-$ $\cup$, a reordering of this sequence as $\cup$ $\cup$ $\cup$ $-$ is not

possible at the beginning of the line, even though it adds up to the same number of morae. The reason for this is that the first four morae cannot be parsed into a group of syllables (since the fourth and fifth morae are part of the same syllable). The meter thus controls both morae and syllables.

The permitted combinations of *gaṇa* are shown for the first line of the couplet in (64); thus only the second and fourth *gaṇa* are completely free in their shape, and the sixth is restricted to just two possible shapes. The third *gaṇa* is followed by a caesura.

(64)

1	2	3 |	4	5	6	7	8
– –	– –	– –	– –	– –		– –	*x*
U U –	U U –	U U –	U U –	U U –		U U –	
– U U	– U U	– U U	– U U	– U U		– U U	
U U U U	U U U U	U U U U	U U U U	U U U U	U U U U	U U U U	
	U – U		U – U		U – U		

The actual pattern in the first line is shown in (65).

(65)

1	2	3 |	4	5	6	7	8
– –	U – U	– –	U U –	– –	U – U	U U –	–

The short lines differ. Using the analysis proposed by Widdess (1995: 180),[12] we show in (66) the schema for the short line, and in (67), the actual pattern of light and heavy syllables in the quoted text.

(66)

1	2	3 |	4	5	6	7	8
– –	– –	– –	– –	– –	U–	–	*x*
U U –	U U –	U U –	U U –	U U –	U U U	U U	
– U U	– U U	– U U	– U U	– U U			
U U U U	U U U U	U U U U	U U U U	U U U U			
	U – U			U – U			

(67)

1	2	3 |	4	5	6	7	8
U U –	U U U U	– –	U – U	– –	U–	–	U

We propose to treat each 'line' of the couplet as consisting of four metrical grids of which each is eight mora in length (sometimes shorter). We note incidentally that the 'line' here resembles the period in Greek verse, as it ends with a syllable whose quantity is indeterminate. This corresponds to the musical/barring analysis discussed by Widdess, to which we return directly. This treatment also makes sense of the differentiation between odd- and even-numbered *gaṇa*. Like in other meters above, ends of grids need not coincide with word ends but, unlike words, (heavy) syllables are never split between consecutive grids. The first three of the four sub-lines in the first part of the couplet and the first

---

[12] In the traditional analysis, the sixth *gaṇa* is a single light syllable, and the seventh a full four-mora unit.

two in the second part are full length, and the grids are generated by rules as stated in (68).

(68)   a.   Gridline 0: starting just at the L edge, insert a L parenthesis, form binary groups, heads L.

       b.   Gridline 1: starting just at the L edge, insert a L parenthesis, form binary groups, heads L.

       c.   Gridline 2: starting just at the R edge, insert a R parenthesis, form binary groups, heads R.

The head of the verse may optionally be deleted by rule (26).

(26)   Delete the Gridline 0 projection of the light syllable projecting to the head of the verse.

The rules generate a grid from an eight-asterisk Gridline 0 (i.e., an eight-mora sequence). Syllable placement is next checked by the condition in (69), which ensures that the fifth mora is syllable-initial.

(69)   A heavy syllable must project its leftmost asterisk to Gridline 1.

(69) predicts that heavy syllables can project their leftmost asterisk as the first, third, fifth or seventh Gridline 0 asterisks. However, it is also possible for a heavy syllable to project its leftmost asterisk as the sixth asterisk; this is made possible by first applying the deletion rule (26). We illustrate this below with two of the sub-lines/grids from (62):

(70)   kecit kuśalāḥ

```
        – –    ∪ ∪ –
      (* *(** ( * *(* * (          0 ⇒
      (*   *  ( *    * (           1 ⇒
      )*         * )               2 ⇐
              *                    3
```

(71)   vyākhyātum eva

```
        –    – ∪   – ∪
      ( * *  ( * *(Δ  *(* * (      0 ⇒
      ( *    *   ( * * (           1 ⇒
      ) *          * )             2 ⇐
              *                    3
```

Three of the eight sub-lines/grids are shorter than eight morae, demostrating the presence of short groups.

Āryā is a meter for texts which can be sung. Widdoes (1995: 180) transcribes an early musical notation for a song in *āryā* in which each mora corresponds to a musical beat; eight beats are grouped into a bar, as shown in (72), where we indicate beats above the line (each dot corresponds to a quarter-note in the score), and heavy and light syllables below the line. Each of our textual lines (corresponding to a metrical grid) matches a musical bar (in this we follow Widdess's analysis).

(72)   •   •   ••   •   ••   •   musical beats
       va- ra- dam va- ram va-
       ∪   ∪   –   ∪   –   ∪   syllables

We suggested in Chapter 1 that music is subject to grouping rules (similar to those found in meter) which generate grids. We also suggested that there is no requirement that the musical grid and the metrical (textual) grid be in the same, or even in similar meters (e.g., a loose-meter text can match a strict musical grid). In (73) we write the first line again with its textual grid below it, and we suggest a possible grid for the musical structure above the line. The grid for the musical structure is based on the assumption that the initial mora (or musical beat) is marked in performance (e.g., by a particular gesture, or a stronger beat), implying that it is the head of the bar.

(73)
```
     *                             3
    ( *              * (           2 ⇒
    ( *        *    ( *      * (    1 ⇒
    ( *    *  ( **  ( *    *(*  * ( 0 ⇒
      •    •   ••    •     ••   •     musical beats
     va- ra- dam   va-   ram  va-
      ∪    ∪   –    ∪     –    ∪      syllables
    ( *    *  ( **  (Δ    *(*  * (   0 ⇒
    ( *        *          ( ** (     1 ⇒
    ) *                   *  )       2 ⇐
                             *       3
```

Though there are similarities between the musical and textual grids, particularly at Gridlines 0 and 1, the two grids differ substantially in the location of the head of the grid, and the fact that the textual grid is subject to a deletion rule. The deletion rule is required in the textual grid to explain the ∪ – ∪ variation found in the second part of the line/grid, but there is no musical reason for positing such a deletion rule: in the musical structure, the sixth beat in the bar does not (optionally) take on characteristics of the fifth beat. As noted in section 1.10, a performance (recitation) of a text need not reproduce the meter of the underlying text. The Sanskrit example under discussion is an instance where the performance must have a different meter than the original text.

The other major difference between musical and textual grids is that there are eight beats in each bar, but there can be fewer than eight morae. Thus, Gridline 0 in the musical grid can have eight asterisks when Gridline 0 in the textual grid has seven or four, as shown in the last two lines of the full sequence in (74). In the third and fourth lines, a heavy syllable can be extended over three or four musical beats. This extension of the length of the syllable is something we find in musical setting or in recitation, but there is no reason to think that a heavy syllable can count as three or four morae in any textual grid.[13]

```
(74)     *                              3
      ( *              * (             2 ⇒
      ( *      *     ( *    * (        1 ⇒
      ( *   *  ( **  ( *    *(*   * (  0 ⇒
       •   •   • •    •    • •    •    musical beats

      va- ra- dam  va- ram  va-
       U   U   –     U   –    U        syllables
      ( *   *  ( **  (Δ    *(*   * (    0 ⇒
      ( *      *     ( ** (            1 ⇒
      ) *            *  )             2 ⇐
                     *                3

         *                            3
      ( *              * (            2 ⇒
      ( *      *     ( *    * (       1 ⇒
      ( **   ( **    ( ** ( ** (      0 ⇒
       • •   • •    • •   • •         musical beats

      re- nyam  go- vin-
       –     –     –    –             syllables
      ( **   ( **   ( ** ( ** (        0 ⇒
      ( *     *     ( *   * (          1 ⇒
      ) *           *  )             2 ⇐
                    *                3

         *                            3
      ( *              * (             2 ⇒
      ( *      *     * ( * (           1 ⇒
      ( *   *  ( **   ( *  *(* * (      0 ⇒
       •   •   • •     •   • • •       musical beats

      da- ka- sam- stu- tam
       U   U   –     U   –            syllables
      ( *   *  ( **   (Δ    *(*        0 ⇒
      ( *      *      ( ** (           1 ⇒
      ) *            *  )             2 ⇐
                     *                3

         *                   3
      ( *      *            2 ⇒
      ( *  *   *  *         1 ⇒
      ( *(* *  ( *(* * (    0 ⇒
       • • •   • • • •      musical beats

      van-    de
       –      –              syllables
      ( **    ( ** (         0 ⇒
      ( ¡      "ʰ           1 ⤵
       * )                 2 ⇐
       *                   3
```

---

[13] This reflects the basic binarity which we find in metrical verse, where, like here, syllables are partitioned into two classes, heavy and light. For musical purposes, syllables are not partitioned in this manner.

9

Latvian

9.1 Trochaic *dainas*[1]

During the 19th century, the Latvian scholar Krišjānis Barons (1835–1923) collected over 30,000 folk songs – called *dainas* – of which the great majority were composed in strict syllable-counting meters. The following account of these meters is based on a detailed examination of the 176 *dainas* (over 1000 lines) reprinted in Endzelīns (1922). We have also examined other *dainas* that came to our attention while reading the papers cited in this chapter.

The great majority of Latvian *dainas* are composed in syllable-counting meters divided into groups which are left-headed pairs (trochaic *dainas*) or left-headed triplets (dactylic *dainas*). A complete example of a typical trochaic *daina* is given in (1).[2]

(1)   Padziedam
        mēs, māsiņas,
       vēl vienā
        vietiņā!
       Dievs to zina,
        citu gadu
       kur mēs kuŗa

---

[1] One of the authors of this book, Morris Halle, a native of Latvia, is a fluent reader, though no longer a fluent speaker of the Latvian language. We thank Kristīne Konrāde for her extensive comments on earlier versions of this chapter and for her generosity in providing us copies of many of the papers referred to in this chapter. Shortcomings and inadequacies remaining in the text are the responsibilities of the authors NF&MH.

[2] All Latvian examples are quoted in the orthography introduced after Latvia became independent in 1918. The different collections of Latvian folk songs are designated here with the following abbrevations: LD/BW = Barons and Wissendorffs' (1894) *Latwju Dainas*; LTD = Endzelīns and Klaustiņš' (1928–36) *Latvju Tautas Dainas*.

dziedāsim:
cita tālu
tautiņās,
cita smilšu
kalniņā.

'Let us sing, sisters, / While still in one place! / God knows, in another year / Who of us will be singing where: / One far away married, / Another in a sandy hill (buried).' LD/BW 269, Endzelīns #9

The variation in length between four and three syllables can be explained by analyzing the lines into two binary groups of which the second maybe incomplete. Formally this is reflected by the rules in (2).

(2)   a. Gridline 0: starting just at the L edge, insert a L parenthesis, form binary groups, heads L.

      i. Incomplete groups are admitted.

    b. Gridline 1: starting just at the R edge, insert a R parenthesis, form binary groups, heads R.

The trochaic *dainas* are traditionally printed as tetrameters (of seven or eight syllables). For example, the *daina* in (1) is usually printed as consisting of six tetrameter lines, although in reality, as argued below, the poem is composed of twelve lines, each consisting of two Gridline 0 groups. The reason for the traditional printing practice seems to be that lines composed of two trochees are very short and thus appear somewhat odd typographically. We owe to Konrāde (personal communication) the information that in Barons's earliest published volume both trochaic and dactylic lines are printed as tetrameters. Beginning with the second volume, however, in dactylic *dainas* dimeters were typographically distinguished from tetrameters, but this distinction was not extended to the trochaic *dainas*, which continued (and continue) to be printed as before as tetrameters. In much of the scholarly literature on the *dainas* all trochaic lines are treated as tetrameters. Our reason for rejecting this analysis is that it makes the statement of the prosodic restrictions needlessly complex. We return to this issue after a review of the main data that are of relevance here.

The grids for the first four lines quoted in (1) are shown in (3).

(3)   Padziedam

```
( *   * ( *          0 ⇒
) *     * )          1 ⇐
        *            2
```

mḗs, mā̃siņas,

```
( *    *( *  * (        0 ⇒
) *       * )          1 ⇐
          *            2
```

vḗl vi̯enā

```
( *   *  ( *           0 ⇒
) *       * )          1 ⇐
          *            2
```

vi̯etiņā!

```
(* *(*                 0 ⇒
) *    * )             1 ⇐
       *               2
```

The trochaic *daina* line of three or four syllables is divided into words of different lengths, as shown in (4); the patterns in (a) and (b) are freely attested in the *dainas*, but not the patterns in (c): a monosyllable cannot be the last word in a four-syllable line, even though it can be the last word in a three-syllable line.

(4) a. Attested 3-syllable lines: 3, 1+2, 2+1, 1+1+1

   b. Attested 4-syllable lines: 4, 1+3, 2+2, 1+1+2

   c. Unattested 4-syllable lines: *3+1, *1+2+1, *2+1+1, *1+1+1+1

In (5) we give examples of the eight attested patterns.

(5) a. 1+3   Ko, brālīši,   What, (my) brothers, were you
     3   domājāt   thinking
     2+2   kalpam mani   giving me to a serf?
     4   vēlēdami?

                              LTD 15327 per Zaube (1960)

   b. 1+3   lai balsīte   let the voice ring out across,
     2+1   pāri skan,
     1+1+1   lai dzird mans   let my ploughman hear,
     3   arājiņš,

                              LD/BW 496, Endzelīns #12

   c. 1+2   Mirt jaunam,   To die young, to die old;
     1+2   mirt vecam;
     3   pusmūžā   only not to die in midlife!
     1+2   vien nemirt!
     4   Pusmūžiņā   For a man at midlife
     3   cilvēkam
     1+1+2   daudz raud žēli many cry grievously.
     3   pakalā.

                              LD/BW 27738, Endzelīns #145

The fact that in a line with four syllables the last word must be poly-syllabic is an important restriction which was already noted by Zanders, who wrote that 'folksongs do not freely admit monosyllabic words in the final position of the dimeter' (Zanders 1893, I: 223), but except for Zeps (1963, 1969) the more recent literature on Latvian *dainas* has failed to emphasize this important restriction. The restriction on trochaic *dainas* is stated as a 'caesura' condition on the grid in (6).[3]

(6)   The Gridline 0 group whose head is the head of the verse must be followed by a word boundary. In trochaic (binary) verses a word boundary may not intervene between the two syllables of this group.

This constraint rules out a possible lineation of a *daina* as shown in (7).

(7)   Padziedam mēs   unmetrical
      (*   * (*   * (0 ⇒
          *   *)   1 ⇐
              *   2

Condition (6) excludes as unmetrical also lines such as those in (8). As indicated in the left margin, these were concocted by adding a mono-syllabic word at the end of well-formed trisyllabic lines.

(8)   a. 3+1   Padziedam tad   cf. (3)
                          mēs, māsiņas
      b. 1+2+1   Mirt jaunam šeit,   cf. (5c)
                          mirt vecam tur,
                          pusmūžā
                          vien nemirt
      c.   Lai balsīte
          2+1+1   pāri skan tur   cf. (5b)
      d. 1+1+1+1   lai to dzird tie   cf. (5b)
                          kurzemnieki

A condition much like (6), requiring that the Gridline 0 group includ-ing the head of the verse be followed by a word boundary, is found also in South Slavic (Serbo-Croatian) epic poetry (for more information, see Lord 1973, and literature cited there). In this poetry the canonical line, called *deseterac,* is traditionally said to be composed of ten syllables

---

[3] The prohibition of a word boundary in a particular position is sometimes charac-terized as requiring a 'bridge' (Greek *zeugma*) in that position.

with an obligatory caesura after the fourth syllable, and with the further condition that no monosyllabic word may occupy the fourth and the tenth position in the verse. A significant simplification in this formulation can be achieved by assuming that the traditional lineation of the South Slavic epic poetry is incorrect and that each traditional verse is composed of a pair of lines, of which the first consists of four syllables, and the second, of six syllables. On this analysis, only a single condition is required, viz. that the head of each verse coincide with the penultimate syllable of a (polysyllabic) word. A similar argument was advanced in Chapter 5 for the meter of the *Chanson de Roland*.

With a handful of exceptions, all words in Latvian are stressed on their first syllable. Though this generally gives the lines 'falling' rhythms (which is why they are traditonally called trochaic or dactylic), stress is metrically irrelevant in the meter of the *daina*. In the lines quoted in (3) we have underlined stressed syllables, and it can readily be seen that they do not fall in any particular position in the line.[4] Here we see an important difference between the rhythm of the line and its meter. The rhythm is a property of the way a sequence of words is read or performed. The meter is represented by the metrical grid and indicates that the line is metrically well-formed. The grid does not determine how the line is read (performed); this depends on factors unconnected to the metrical rules, such as stress, vowel length, syllable structure, and meaning of the words that compose it. The division of a line into Gridline 0 groups is therefore often not directly detectable in the line's performance, though it may have indirect effects.

Syllable quantity (i.e., the differentiation for metrical purposes between light and heavy syllables) is also metrically irrelevant. We make this claim in spite of assertions such as that of Endzelīns (1922: 22) that 'the fourth and the eighth syllables now contain a short vowel ... Apparent exceptions ... are either of late origin, or incorrect deformations of older forms'.

Stronger still is the statement in Bērziņš (1959: 52): 'in the 4-syllable dipody the last syllable is undoubtedly short, in the 3-syllable dipody it is long, or at least potentially long ... Exceptions ... are relatively few; moreover, they can be explained as errors or misunderstandings ... the difference in quantity of the two noted end syllables is not just a rule,

---

[4] In this respect the *dainas* differ most radically from modern Latvian art poetry, which is largely in syllabo-tonic meters, similar to the 19th-century German and Russian poetry that directly influenced it.

it is an unalterable iron law'.[5] The validity of Bērziņš's generalization
has been contested by Rudzītis (1960), Zaube (1960), and Zeps (1963,
1969), who cite numerous counterexamples (including those in (5a,b)).
What remains undeniable nonetheless is that there is a tendency to end
3-syllable trochaic lines with a heavy, rather than with a light syllable,
even though the tendency falls short of being the 'unalterable iron law'
declared by Bērziņš.

9.2 Dactylic dimeters

We quote two dactylic *dainas* in (9) and (10).

(9)   Kāzās iedama,
            bezkauņa biju,
        pametu godiņu
            uz vārtu staba.
        Pāriešu mājā,
            turēšu godu.
        Turēšu godu,
            kā citas meitas.

'Attending weddings, / I was shameless, / I left my honor / on the gate
post. / When I come back home, / I'll keep my honor / I'll keep my
honor/ like other girls.' LD/BW 950, Endzelīns #17

(10)   Apdeju, aplecu
            māmiņas pēdas,
        lai bērni neraud
            staigādami.

'I danced over, jumped over / mother's footprints, / so that children would
not weep / while walking about.' Bērziņš 54

The dactylic iterative rules are similar to those for the trochaic *dainas*
(2a,b), with the single modification that on Gridline 0 the left parentheses are inserted not at binary, but at ternary intervals. The rules are
stated in (11) and the second poem is fully scanned in (12).

(11)   a. Gridline 0: starting just at the L edge, insert a L parenthesis,
            form ternary groups, heads L.

            i. Incomplete groups are admitted.

---

[5] Bērziņš (1959: 50) explains that 'where the syllable count in the dipody is four,
the last syllable consists of a short vowel *a, i, e, u,* or of a short vowel + the
ending *s*; i.e., *as, is, es, us.* However, in all those cases where the dipody has only
three syllables, we never find in the last position any of the eight combinations
just listed'.

b. Gridline 1: starting just at the R edge, insert a R parenthesis, form binary groups, heads R.

(12) Apdeju, aplecu

```
(*   * *(*   * *(        0 ⇒
)*        * )           1 ⇐
          *             2
```

māmiņas pēdas,

```
(*  *  *  (* *           0 ⇒
)*           * )         1 ⇐
             *           2
```

lai bērni neraud

```
(*   *   *(* *           0 ⇒
)*           * )         1 ⇐
             *           2
```

staigādami.

```
(*  *  *  (*             0 ⇒
)*           * )         1 ⇐
             *           2
```

Asterisks on Gridline 0 are grouped into ternary groups, but the final group constructed may be incomplete, either binary or unary, giving five- and four-syllable lines, respectively. Bērziņš's condition on syllable quantity (section 9.1) is occasionally violated in dactylic poetry; for example, in the last line of (12), a line-final dactylic group is headed by a light syllable.

The condition (6) prevents the trochaic line from ending on a monosyllable, and it is generally the case that dactylic lines also do not end on a monosyllable; however, this is not always true in dactylic *dainas*, as is shown in the first verse of (13), and in the third verse of (14).

(13) Zinu gan, zinu gan,
```
(*  *   *   (*  *  *(
```

kur gaļa stāv:
```
(  *   * *  (*
```

'I know indeed, I know indeed, / where the meat is kept' LD/BW 32218 var 3

(14) Nekari šūpuli
```
(*  *  *(*  * *(
```

labā zemē:
```
(*  *   *(*
```

balandes vien aug,
```
(* *   *   (*   *
```

'Don't hang the swing / on good land: / weeds only grow (there)' LD/BW 32289 var 1

9.3 Trochaic and dactylic tetrameters

Though not as common as dimeters, true tetrameters are widely represented in the *dainas*. In true tetrameters only the fourth group can fall short and is subject to condition (6). Examples of trochaic and dactylic tetrameters are given in (15).[6]

(15) Zaķīts kaziņu norēja,
  (* *   (* *(*   * (* * (

nebij vilka rējējiņa,
  (* * (*_ * (* *(* * (
brāļi māsiņu noveda,

  (** (* *(* *(* * (
nebij tautu vedējiņu.

  (* *   (* * (* *(* * (0 ⇒
) *   *)   *   *)   1 ⇐
) *   *)   2 ⇐
                     *   3

'The hare bites the goat to death, / when there is no wolf to do the biting, / the brothers marry their sister, / when there is no unrelated bridegroom.' LTD 66, vii

(16) Visu nakti dziedāju, kā malku cirtu;
  (* * * (*   * *(*   *   * (* * * (

kas mana maksāja par dziedājumu?
  (*   * * (* * * (*   * * (* *

Puisēni maksātu, ne pašiem nava,
  (* * * (* * * (* ** (* *

pašiem puisēniem pliks vēderinis.

  (* *   * (* *   * (* * *(*   0 ⇒
) *   *)   *   *)   1 ⇐
) *   *)   2 ⇐
                        *   3

'I sang all night while chopping wood, / who paid me for singing? / The boys would've paid, but they have nothing, / the boys have (only) a naked belly.' LD/BW 978

In (15) and (16) there are several instances where the second group ends in the middle of a word. For example, this is true of the first and third verse in (15) and of the first verse in (16). These tetrameter lines differ from the dimeters discussed in the earlier sections of this chapter in that here condition (6) is satisfied after every four Gridline 0 groups,

---

[6] In her discussion of trochaic tetrameters such as those in (15), Kursīte (1996: 149) characterized them as 'texts where one or two lines, in contradistinction to the rest, are formed not in accordance with the pattern 4+4, but rather in accordance with the pattern 5+3'. Kursīte's attempt to account for such lines as direct reflexes of Indo-European prototypes is unconvincing since she offers no evidence from actual verses in support of this proposal.

rather than after every pair of such groups. Formally this difference in line length is accounted for by positing an additional Gridline for the verse lines in (15) and (16). The rule is stated in (17); it is identical with the rule for Gridline 1.

(17)　Gridline 2: starting just at the R edge, insert a R parenthesis, form binary groups, heads R.

Addition of rule (17) is the minimal extension necessary to admit tetrameter lines in addition to dimeters. Since longer lines are admitted, additional Gridlines are required. No other changes are required; in particular, there is no need to modify condition (6).

9.4 Alternating trochaic trimeter and tetrameter

As remarked above, among the *dainas* printed in Endzelīns (1922) there are two in meters other than the strict trochaic/dactylic dimeters or tetrameters examined above. One of these is the *daina* in (18) in strict trochees, where we find trimeters as well as tetrameter, in the pattern 3–3–4–3 Gridline 0 groups.

(18)　Apkārt kalnu gāju,
　　　　(*　　*　　(　*　　*　(　*　*　(

　　　　kalniņā uzkāpu,
　　　　(*　　*　(*　*　(　*　*　(

　　　　redzu tautu zeltenīti
　　　　(*　　*　(　*　　*　(　*　*(*　*　(

　　　　gauži raudājam.
　　　　(*　　*　(　*　　*(*　　　　　　0 ⇒
　　　　　*　)　　　*　　　*　)　　　　　1 ⇐
　　　　) *　　　　　　　*　)　　　　　2 ⇐
　　　　　　　　　　　*　　　　　　　　3

'I walked around a mountain, / I climbed the mountain, / I see a young beauty / sorely weeping.' LD/BW 31928, Endzelīns #164

Like the trochaic tetrameter *dainas* of section 9.3, this poem admits an incomplete Gridline 0 group line-finally, and like them, it admits no word-boundaries internal to the line-final Gridline 0 group (see condition (6)). The only metrical difference between (18) and the tetrameters in section 9.3 is that in (18) tetrameter lines alternate with trimeters. We obtain this distribution by permitting Gridline 1 to end on an incomplete group.

9.5 Loose meters in Latvian poetry

9.5.1 A loose trochaic tetrameter

To our knowledge, it has not been noted previously that one well-known *daina* is in a loose trochaic meter, in which the iterative rules are preceded by a non-iterative rule inserting left parentheses. This is the *daina* quoted in (19), where in the column to the right of the text we have shown the number of groups and, in parentheses, the number of syllables in each line of verse.

(19) Viens gans nomira, citi gani raudāja.   5 (12)
　　　) *　　　*)　　(* *)* (* *) (* *) (* *) *

　　　Cūka raka dobīti augstā kalnā;   5 (11)
　　　) (* *) (* *) (* *)* (*　　*) (*　*)

　　　dzeguze zvanīja līkā bērzā;   4 (10)
　　　) (* *) *　　(* *)* (* *) (* *)

　　　dzenis kala krustu sausā eglē;   5 (10)
　　　) (* *) (* *)　(*　*) (* *)(*　*)

　　　sīki mazi putniņi pātarus skaitīja;   5 (13)
　　　)(* *)　(* *) (*　*) * (* *) *　(* *)*

　　　lielais dunduris sprediķi sacīja;   4 (11)
　　　)(*　*)　(*　*) *　(* *)* (* *)*

　　　zīle nesa vēsti tēvam, mātei;   5 (10)
　　　)(* *) (* *) (*　*)(* *)　(*　*)

　　　kaza kāpa debesīs Dievam sūdzēt.   5 (11)
　　　) (*　*) (*　*)(*　*)*　(*　*)　(*　*)　　0 ⇒
　　　　　*　(*　　*　　　(*　　　* (　　　　1 ⇐
　　　　　　) *　　　　　　　　*)　　　　　2 ⇐
　　　　　　　　*　　　　　　　　　　　　　3

'One shepherd died, the other shepherds cried./ The pig dug a grave on a high mountain; / the cuckoo tolled on a crooked birch; / the woodpecker forged a cross on a dry pine; / the tiny little birds said the prayers; / the big wasp pronounced the sermon; / the titmouse carried the news to his father and mother; / the goat climbed to heaven to complain to God.' LD/BW 2692, Endzelīns #26

Several lines in this poem exhibit striking alliterations, but its most remarkable feature is its meter. It is the only *daina* we have encountered that is in a loose meter, specifically in a loose trochaic tetrameter, which is sensitive to the location of maxima, that is, of stressed syllables in polysyllabic words. Maxima are defined as in (20), and a non-iterative parenthesis insertion rule (21) inserts parentheses before maxima.

(20) Definition of maximum in Latvian loose trochaic meter
　　　 The syllable bearing the word stress in a polysyllabic word is a maximum.

(21)   Insert a L parenthesis to the left of the Gridline 0 projection of a maximum.

Following the application of (21), the iterative rules of grid construction in (22) are applied and metrical grids are supplied to each of the lines.

(22)   a.   Gridline 0: starting just at the L edge, insert a R parenthesis, form binary groups, heads L.

      i.   Gridline 0 may include incomplete groups.

     ii.   Gridline 0 may include unfooted syllables.

    b.   Gridline 1: starting ⟨ just / one asterisk in ⟩ at the R edge, insert a L parenthesis, form binary groups, heads R.

    c.   Gridline 2: starting just at the R edge, insert a R parenthesis, form binary groups, heads R.

The complete metrical grid is shown on the bottom of (19). The lengths (in Gridline 0 groups) of the eight lines of the poem, indicated at the right-hand side of (19), exhibit the symmetric (chiastic) structure with numbers of Gridline 0 groups as 5 5 4 5 | 5 4 5 5. This symmetry is further evidence for our hypothesized Gridline 0 grouping.

The loose meter of (19) is very similar to loose meters in both German and Russian poetry. In German such meters are referred to as *Knittelvers*, in Russian they are called *dol'nik*. Whether the meter of this *daina* reflects the influence of German or Russian models is an interesting question that is, however, beyond the scope of this book.

9.5.2 A loose anapaestic dimeter

We conclude this chapter with an examination of *Zemes dēls* ('Son of the Earth') by Fricis Bārda, a poem in loose anapaests, quoted in full in (23). Unlike other poems in this chapter, this is not a folklore poem, but sophisticated art poetry.

(23)   Tu rokās ziedu
      * *)*   *)* (
    pinekļus nesi.
)(*   *)* (
    Tu zemes ziedu
      * *) *   *) * (
    gūsteknis esi...
) (* * *(

Ai, zemes ziediem
*   * **)** *   * **)** * (
maigi var siet:
 ***)**(*   *   * (
Šķiet brīžam – pašas
 *   ***)***   * **)***(
rokas tev zied...
 ***)**(*   *   * (
Šķiet brīžam – šie ziedi
 *   ***)**(*   *   * **)** * (
pēdējs un viss.
 ***)**(*   *   * (
Tik tāla teika
 *   * **)*** * **)** * (
ir debesis.
 *   * **)*** * (
Bet, nakts kad un mūžība
 *   * **)**   (*   *   ***)*** * (
zvaignājā kāp, –
 * **)** (* *   * (
Tu kluss tieci: pinekļos
 (*   *   * **)***   ***)*** * (
rokas tev sāp...
 ***)**(*   *   * (0 ⇐
) *   * **)**   1 ⇐
         *   2

'On your wrists you wear fetters of flowers. / You are the prisoner of Earth's flowers ... / Ah, with Earth's flowers one can gently be tied: / At times it may seem – your very hands are in bloom ... / At times it may seem – these flowers are the end and all, / so distant a tale is heaven's. / But when night and eternity the firmament ascend, / you fall quiet, in your fetters your hands are in pain.' Bārda, 'Zemes dēls'

The poem is in a loose anapaestic dimeter. It requires a different definition of maximum, that in (24), because in this loose meter a stressed monosyllabic word such as *nakts* in the thirteenth line is also a maximum when followed by two or more unstressed syllables.

(24)   Definition of maximum in Latvian loose anapaestic meter

    a. The stressed syllable in a polysyllabic word is a maximum.

    b. A stressed monosyllabic word is a maximum, if followed by two or more unstressed syllables.

A right parenthesis is inserted by rule (25), which applies before the iterative rules in (26). Line 12 differs from the rest in being composed of a single Gridline 0 group (captured by the option for Gridline 1 of having 'incomplete groups admitted').

Like in all loose meters, the maxima in the line are marked on Gridline 0 with the help of rule (25), which inserts a right parenthesis after a maximum. The rest of the metrical grid is generated by the iterative rules in (26), which are ordered after (25).

(25) Insert a R parenthesis to the right of the Gridline 0 projection of a maximum.

(26) a. Gridline 0: starting just at the R edge, insert a L parenthesis, form ternary groups, heads R.

   i. Ungrouped syllables are admitted.

   ii. Incomplete groups are admitted.

   b. Gridline 1: starting just at the R edge, insert a R parenthesis, form binary groups, heads R.

As shown in (23), except for line 12, there are two Gridline 0 groups per line. Line 12 is an exception in having but a single Gridline 0 group.

9.6 Conclusion

The meters of the *dainas* reviewed in this chapter were shown to be composed of left-headed Gridline 0 groups. The meters fall into two classes with respect to the length of the groups: binary (trochaic) vs. ternary (dactylic). The majority of the *dainas* are dimeters; i.e., composed of two Gridline 0 groups. A minority are tetrameters; i.e., composed of four Gridline 0 groups. In addition, we have found a single *daina* with lines that alternate between tetrameter and trimeter (see (18)), as well as one in loose trochaic tetrameter (see (19)). Trochaic *dainas* are subject to condition (6), which limits monosyllabic words in verse-final position. The predominance of short meters is a characteristic that *dainas* share with other well-known types of folk verse, such as the meter of the French *Chanson de Roland* and the South Slavic *deseterac* meter.

10

Meters of the world

Most of the meters considered so far in this book have rules and conditions which presuppose a partitioning of syllables into two types, based either on stress, or on weight. In this chapter, we consider other kinds of binary partition, and argue that in any given metrical tradition only two distinct kinds of syllable are recognized by the metrical rules, though the basis for the partition differs.

10.1 Two vernacular Arabic meters

In Chapter 7 we analyzed the meters of Classical Arabic. In these meters, as in the meters of Sanskrit and Greek, syllables are divided into two classes for metrical purposes: light and heavy. In this section we look at two vernacular Arabic metrical traditions in which syllables are partitioned in a different way. The important claim is that each metrical tradition operates with just one type of binary partition.

10.1.1 A Bedouin accentual meter

We first turn to an accentual meter in a vernacular Arabic poetry. Bailey (2002) has argued that the meters used in Bedouin Arabic songs (from Sinai and the Negev) are based on the counting of stressed syllables. Thus, the bifurcation in this meter is stressed vs. unstressed syllables and not heavy vs. light: one partition is exchanged for another.[1] The stressing of syllables in these songs may override ordinary word stress.

---

[1] Bailey (2002: 397) disagrees with Sowayan (1985), who argues that the Bedouin use classical Arabic meters but with considerable variation. As Bailey points out, Sowayan does not provide extended evidence from any single text that it is consistently in a classical meter; we therefore follow Bailey's treatment here.

The number of stressed syllables in each verse is fixed, but there can be anything between zero and three unstressed syllables between stressed syllables, as illustrated in (1).

(1)   gumt ṭala‘t al-jabal al-yābis ma yaṭā al-xaẓār

    s   s š́   s   š́ s   s   š́ s   š́   s   s š́   s š́

       ḥaṭṭēt in‘ālī fī rijlī māšī lir-ri‘ī dawwār

    s   š́   s   š́ s   s   s š́   š́ s   s   s š́   s   š́

'I rose and climbed a mountain dry, the green'ry there had still not shown; / so putting shoes to both my feet, I sought a spot where pasture'd grown.' Ṭu‘ēmī Mūsā ad-Dagūnī (Bailey 2002: 46, 387)

The fact that in these lines the number of unstressed syllables between consecutive stresses may vary between zero and three shows that the lines are in a loose meter. Since there are at most three unstressed syllables between consecutive stresses, we must assume that the Gridline 0 groups are ternary and the lines therefore are instances of an anapaestic meter, specifically, loose anapaestic hexameter. This assumption implies that there may be as many as five unstressed syllables between stresses, although we have not encountered such examples. The first step in scanning the verse is to insert right parentheses after stressed syllables by rule (2). The next step is to insert left parentheses at ternary intervals by the iterative rules (3)

(2)   On Gridline 0 insert a R parenthesis to the right of an asterisk projecting from a stressed syllable.

(3)   a. Gridline 0: starting just at the R edge, insert a L parenthesis, form ternary groups, heads R.

         i. Gridline 0 may include incomplete groups.

         ii. Up to one ungrouped syllable is permitted between Gridline 0 groups.

     b. Gridline 1: starting just at the R edge, insert a R parenthesis, form ternary groups, heads R.

     c. Gridline 2: starting just at the R edge, insert a R parenthesis, form binary groups, heads R.

A sample grid is shown in (4).

(4)   ḥaṭṭēt inʿālī fī rijlī māšī lir-riʿī dawwār

```
     ́      ́    ́   ́      ́         ́
s    s   s   s  s  s  s   s  s  s    s  s      s
*   *  ) *    *  )*(*  *  *  )   *)*( *   *  * ) *     *  )  (        0 ⇐
  ) *      *       *  )  *           *         * )              1 ⇐
          ) *                                   *  )            2 ⇐
                                                *              3
```

We control for the distribution of stressed and unstressed syllables in this song meter with a special condition.

(5)   Every syllable projecting to Gridline 1 must be stressed, and no other syllable may be stressed.

10.1.2 Superheavy syllables in Ḥassānīya meter

The next non-classical Arabic meter which we review is one in which no distinction is made between light and heavy syllables, but in which superheavy syllables have a special role. Here the heavy–light bifurcation is replaced by a superheavy–other bifurcation, whch is still a quantitative distinction but on a different basis. A superheavy syllable is a syllable ending in two consonants or ending with a long vowel followed by a single consonant. The vernacular in question is Ḥassānīya, the Arabic dialect (and lingua franca) of the Western Sahara, spoken in what is now Mauritania; our source is Norris (1968). Some of the meters involve just syllable-counting, though with the stipulation that superheavy syllables are dispreferred within the verse (as in classical Arabic poetry). Of this type, the 6-syllable meter called *lebtayṯ en-naageṣ* is one of the commonest meters in Ḥassānīya poetry, and the 8-syllable meter *lebtayṯ et-taamm* is also common.

The meters of particular interest here are those in which there is one superheavy syllable within the verse in a designated position. In the common meter *lubbʷayr* illustrated in (6) the hemistich has seven sylla-bles, of which syllables 1–5 can be either light or heavy, syllable 6 must be superheavy, and syllable 7 can be light, heavy, or superheavy, that is, an anceps syllable in the traditional terminology of classical metrics. Superheavy syllables are represented by the = symbol.

(6)   ʿannak baʿd ila kaan ḵuuk
     –   –   –   ∪∪   =   =

     emniḏamb alli ṭaalʿu
     –   ∪ –   – ∪   = ∪

     šakaa-lak wajjah biih buuk
     ∪   –   –   –   –   =   =

fekkuuh emnalli ḵaalʻu

–   –   –   – U   =   U

'If your brother complains to you about a sin which he has committed before God, you should obtain for him the favour of your father, and free him from that which makes him afraid.' (Norris 1968: 46, 161)

We generate a grid for the lines of this meter by the rules in (7), as shown in (8).

(7)   a.   Gridline 0: starting at the R edge one asterisk in, insert a R parenthesis, form ternary groups, heads R.

       b.   Gridline 1: starting just at the R edge, insert a R parenthesis, form binary groups, heads R.

(8)   ʻannak baʻd ila kaan ḵuuk

```
        –    –     –   UU   =      =
   ) *    *    * )  * *    * )     *              0 ⇐
           ) *              * )                   1 ⇐
                            *                     2
```

In this meter, and indeed in all these meters, the final (rightmost) syllable may be of any quantity: light, heavy, or superheavy. But in non-final position a superheavy syllable must also appear in sixth position, and nowhere else. This is required by the condition stated in (9).

(9)   The head of the verse must project from a superheavy syllable.

In some variants of the meter, only the first and third lines in a quatrain have a superheavy syllable in this position.

In other meters, the superheavy syllable can appear in different positions, but there is only ever one (non-final) superheavy syllable in the line. This suggests that different syllables can project to the head of the verse. For example, in the *bu ʻumraan* meter only the second syllable can be superheavy, suggesting that the line has a different grid in which the second syllable projects to the head of the verse.

10.2 Tonal meters

In this section we look at the meters found in two 'tone languages', Chinese and Vietnamese, where the metrical rules distinguish between syllables on the basis of lexical tone. Lexical tone is the fixed pitch or pitch contour which a syllable has in a tone language. It is of particular importance to note that while in both Chinese and Vietnamese there are more than two types of actual lexical tone, nevertheless for metrical purposes the various types of lexical tone are grouped into two classes. Conditions on the meter require that a syllable in a specific position belong to one of the two tonal classes. We see the same phenomenon here as we see in all meters: the language may differentiate a syllable in more than two ways but the meter recognizes only two types of syllable.

10.2.1 Chinese regulated verse

The earliest recorded Chinese verse (*c.*12th–7th centuries BCE) is in 4-syllable lines, that later developed into 5-syllable and 7-syllable lines (Han dynasty, 206 BCE–219 CE). By the time of the T'ang Dynasty (618–907 CE) the 'regulated verse' (*lu shi*) had been invented, in which the tone on certain syllables was controlled. It is the latter type of poetry that is the topic of this section, and which we illustrate with four consecutive lines in 5-syllable verse in (10). Below we explain the difference between actual tone class patterns and idealized tone class patterns.

(10)   kōng shān xīn yǔ hòu

     -   -   - v v   actual tone classes
     -   -   - v v   idealized tone class patterns

   tiān qì wǎn lái qiú

     -   v v - v   actual tone classes
     v v -   - v   idealized tone class patterns

   míng yuè sōng jiān zhāo

     -   v -   -   -   actual tone classes
     v v v -   -   idealized tone class patterns

   qīng quán shí shàng liú

     -   -   - v v   actual tone classes
     -   -   - v v   idealized tone class patterns

'A deserted mountain after new rain / air like an autumn evening / clear moon shining through the pines / pure spring stone over flow' Wang Wei (Yip 1984: 355)

Although there are more than two types of actual tone on syllables, the metrical rules partition the syllables into just two classes. One is called the even-tone class (or 'level', *ping*), and syllables in this class are symbolized with the - symbol in (10). The other is the oblique-tone class (or 'deflected', *zhe*), and this class includes three distinct kinds of phonological tone; syllables in this class are symbolized with the v symbol in (10).[2]

The first goal of the metrical rules is to determine the number of syllables in the line: either five or seven syllables depending on the meter. The second goal of the metrical rules is to characterize the distribution in the line of the syllables belonging to the tonal classes above. Here we must acknowledge a difference between the actual patterns and the idealized patterns which the lines are taken to exemplify. In some cases – such as the first and fourth lines of (10) – the actual and idealized patterns are the same; but in many cases – as in the second and third lines – the actual and idealized patterns are different. For example the second line has the tone pattern even–oblique–oblique–even–oblique, but this is taken to manifest a variation on an idealized pattern of oblique–oblique–even–even–oblique. In the actual tonal pattern only the even-numbered syllables are controlled, requiring just that the fourth syllable is in a different tonal class from the second and the sixth.[3] The actual tonal patterns for the 7- and 5-syllable verse lines are shown in (11) and (12); x represents a syllable of indeterminate quality, analogous to the anceps in Greek poetry and elsewhere.

(11)   7 syllable verse i.   × -   × v   × -   ×
                        ii.   × v   × -   × v   ×

(12)   5 syllable verse i.   × v   × -   ×
                        ii.   × -   × v   ×

It is obvious that the two 5-syllable patterns are contained in the 7-syllable patterns: (12i) in (11i), and (12ii) in (11ii), and that tone is controlled in the even-numbered positions and free in the odd-numbered.

However, traditional accounts of Chinese verse treat these actual tonal patterns as manifestations of the idealized patterns shown in (13) and (14).

---

[2] Duanmu (2004: 71) says that 'the phonetic difference between the tonal categories remains somewhat unclear'. Liu (1962: 22) says that 'these tones differ from each other not only in pitch but in length and movement. The first [ping] tone is relatively long and keeps to the same pitch; the other three are relatively short, and ... move upward or downward in pitch or stop suddenly'. It has also been argued by Duanmu that the meter is organized on the basis of stress rather than tone, with a trochaic stress rhythm; we stay with the traditional analysis in terms of tone classes in this section. See also Chen (1979), Yip (1984), Duanmu (2004); and Fabb (1997: 77–79).

[3] 'Some liberty is allowed to syllables occupying less important positions (usually the 1st and 3rd syllables in a five-syllabic line; the 1st, 3rd and 5th syllables in a seven-syllabic line).' Liu (1962: 26), see also Duanmu (2004: 72).

(13) 7-syllable verse i.   - -   v v   - -   v
                    ii.   v v   - -   vv   -
                    iii.   - -   v v   v -   -
                    iv.   v v   - -   - v   v

(14) 5-syllable verse i.   v v   - -   v
                    ii.   - -   vv   -
                    iii.   v v   v -   -
                    iv.   - -   - v   v

In (10), the first and fourth line has pattern (14iv), the second line (14i) and the third line (14iii). The idealized patterns bring out a further pattern in the lines not visible in the actual patterns, which is that there is a preference for choosing different patterns in adjacent lines.

Although the patterns of distribution of the tones in the lines are not especially complex, our attempt to state them above is not altogether perspicuous. The difficulty is due to lack of a proper theoretical framework for characterizing the facts, and it disappears as soon as the facts are restated in terms of the metrical grid constructed by the rules in (15).

(15)   a. Gridline 0: starting at the R edge one asterisk in, insert a R parenthesis, form binary groups, heads R.
        b. Gridline 1: starting at the L, insert a L parenthesis, form binary groups, heads L.
            i. 7-syllable line: skip the first asterisk encountered at Gridline 1

The rules (15) generate the grid for a 5-syllable line, as shown schematically in (16), and for a 7-syllable line, as shown schematically in (17).[4]

(16)   ) *   *) *   *) *   0 ⇐
                (*   * (1 ⇒
                      *   2
(17)   ) *   *) *   *) *   *) *   0 ⇐
            *   (*   * (1 ⇒
                      *   2

The actual pattern of tonal classes is controlled by the condition (18).

(18)   The syllable projecting to Gridline 2 must be of the opposite tonal class from other syllables projecting to Gridline 1.

---

[4] On Gridline 0 the ungrouped asterisk is obligatory (the line always has five syllables), which is controlled by requiring an initial skip when inserting right parentheses from right to left; similar considerations apply to the obligatory extra asterisk on Gridline 1 of the 7-syllable meter.

Because the Gridline 0 groups are binary and right-headed (i.e., iambic), and because the final odd-numbered syllable is skipped, the even-numbered syllables are the syllables projecting to Gridline 1. In the 5-syllable line the second syllable (head of the verse) is of a different tonal class from the fourth; in the 7-syllable line the fourth syllable (head of the verse) is of a different tonal class from the second and sixth (and the second and sixth are thus of the same tonal class as each other).

The idealized patterns of tonal classes can be derived by adding condition (19) to condition (18).

(19)   The syllable projecting to the head of the verse must be of the same tonal class (i) with the syllable immediately to its right and (ii) with one other syllable to its right.

We illustrate the effects of the conditions by scanning three of the lines of (10) (the fourth has the same pattern as the first and so is not illustrated here).

(20)   kōng shān xīn yǔ hòu

```
   -       -       -     v   v        actual via condition (18)
   -       -       -     v   v        idealized via conditions (18) and (19)
   ) *       * )   *     * ) *              0 ⇐
            ( *          * (                 1 ⇒
                  *                          2
```

tiān qì wǎn lái qiú

```
   -     v   v   -     v        actual via condition (18)
   v     v   -   -     v        idealized via conditions (18) and (19)
   ) *     * ) *   * ) *              0 ⇐
          ( *       * (                1 ⇒
                *                       2
```

míng yuè sōng jiān zhāo

```
   -       v   -     -     -        actual via condition (18)
   v       v   v     -     -        idealized via conditions (18) and (19)
   ) *       * ) *     * )     *            0 ⇐
            ( *         * (                 1 ⇒
                  *                          2
```

The tonal patterns of the lines of Chinese regulated verse are thus straightforwardly related to the metrical grids assigned to the lines by the rules in (15). It is almost as though the poets composing these lines had the grid in their head.

Before Chinese had 5- and 7-syllable lines, it had 4-syllable lines, and the 4-syllable line can be understood as having a clear structural relation to the later 5-syllable line. The 4-syllable line (which has no specific tonal pattern) can have its length measured by the same rules as those for the five-syllable line, but without an initial skip on Gridline 0.

10.2.2 *Vietnamese* ca dao

One of the standard meters of both art and folk verse in Vietnamese is the tonal 'six–eight meter'. A *ca dao* song in this meter is quoted in (21).

(21)   Cái cò là cái cò con.
        Mẹ đi xúc tép để con ở nhà.
        Mẹ đi một quãng đường xa.
        Mẹ xà chân xuống phải mà anh lươn.
        Ông kia có chiếc thuyền nan,
        Chở vào ao rậm xem lươn bắt cò.
        Ông kia chống gậy lò dò.
        Con lươn thụt xuống; con cò bay lên.

> 'Egrets bear egret sons. / Mother's after shrimp. Little one's at home. / Mother Egret has flown far off / to alight... and be roped by Brother Eel! / Nearby, a man poling a bamboo keel / slides through cattails to catch eel and fowl. / Poling clumsily, he rams his prow. / Brother Eel dives. Mother flies off.' (Balaban 2003: 37)

Only the second, fourth, sixth and eighth (i.e., even-numbered) syllables have their tonal class controlled; the odd-numbered syllables are not controlled for tone. The fourth syllable must belong to the Even-tone class (symbolized E in (23) below), and the second, sixth, and eight syllables must belong to the Sharp-tone class (symbolized s).[5] It is clear that the syllables are grouped into right-headed pairs (i.e., iambic groups). Because the fourth syllable is distinctive – it is the only syllable which must carry a Sharp tone – we suggest that it is the head of the verse. The rules in (22) generate the grids in (23).

(22)   a. Gridline 0: starting just at the R edge, insert a R parenthesis, form binary groups, heads R.

        b. Gridline 1: starting just at the L edge, insert a L parenthesis, form binary groups, heads R.

            i. Odd numbered lines: the last (rightmost) group must be incomplete.

        c. Gridline 2: starting just at the L edge, insert a L parenthesis, form binary groups, heads L.

---

[5] The class of Even-tone syllables includes syllables with high-level tone as in *la* (lack of accent indicates high-level tone), and syllables with falling tone as in the word *là*. The class of Sharp-tone syllables includes syllables with falling–rising tone, as in the word *lả*; high–constricted broken tone, as in the word *lã*; high–rising tone, as in the word *á*; or low–constricted tone, as in the word *lạ* (Balaban 2003: 5).

(23)   Cái cò là cái cò con.

```
      s   E  E   s   E  E
   ) *   *) *   *) *   *)                      0 ⇐
       ( *      *      ( *                      1 ⇒
             ( *          * (                   2 ⇒
                   *                            3
```

      Mẹ đi xúc tép để con ở nhà.

```
      s   E  s   s   s   E  E   E
   ) *   *) *   *)   *  *) *   *)               0 ⇐
       ( *      *      ( *      * (             1 ⇒
             ( *              * (               2 ⇒
                   *                            3
```

      Mẹ đi một quãng đường xa.

```
      s   E  E   s   E   E
   ) *   *) *   *)   *   *)                     0 ⇐
       ( *      *       ( *                      1 ⇒
             ( *          * (                    2 ⇒
                   *                             3
```

      Mẹ xà chân xuống phải mà anh lươn.

```
      s   E  s   s   E   E E   E
   ) *   *) *   *)   *  *) *   *)                0 ⇐
       ( *      *      ( *      * (              1 ⇒
             ( *              * (                2 ⇒
                   *                             3
```

Tone is controlled by condition (24).

(24)   The syllable projecting to the head of the verse must have Sharp tone; all other syllables projecting to Gridline 1 must have Even tone.

10.3 Rhyme and meter

In most types of rhyming poetry, rhyme is either line-final or on the final stressed syllable in the line. This by itself does not show that rhyme is determined by the metrical grid because the edge of the line is visible independently of metrical structure, and rhyme is found at the ends of lines also in clearly non-metrical poetry. We have also seen evidence that in Spanish poetry (section 4.2), syllables invisible to the metre (not projected to Gridline 0) can be involved in rhyme. The rhyme in Vietnamese *ca dao* discussed below differs from these in that it is based on a metrical grid, but as we will see, the line is assigned a metrical grid for rhyme which is different from the metrical grid constructed above for the assignment of tone. In (25) we show the number of each rhyming syllable (the rhyme indicated by a letter).

(25)   Cái cò là cái cò con.
                  A
                  6

Mẹ đi xúc tép để con ở nhà.
            A   *B*
            6   8

Mẹ đi một quãng đường xa.
                  B
                  6

Mẹ xà chân xuống phải mà anh lươn.
                  B   *C*
                  6   8

Ông kia có chiếc thuyền nan,
                  C
                  6

Chở vào ao rậm xem lươn bắt cò.
            C   *D*
            6   8

Ông kia chống gậy lò dò.
                  D
                  6

Con lươn thụt xuống; con cò bay lên.
                  D   *E*
                  6   8

As illustrated in (25), in this meter the odd-numbered lines are six syllables long, and the even-numbered lines are eight syllables long. The rhyme scheme is based on the odd-numbered line. Specifically the final syllable of an odd-numbered line rhymes with final syllable of the even-numbered line that precedes it and with the sixth syllable of the even-numbered line that follows it. For example, the third line in (25) ends with *xa*, which rhymes with *nhà* that ends the second line, and with *mà* that is in sixth position in the fourth. Similarly the final syllable of the seventh line is *dò*, which rhymes with *cò* that ends the sixth line and with *cò* that occupies the sixth position in the eighth line.

The rhyme pattern must be formulated as in (26).

(26)   In an even-numbered line, the last syllable rhymes with the last syllable of the following (odd-numbered) line, and the sixth syllable rhymes with the last syllable of the preceding (odd-numbered) line.

To capture these facts most perspicuously we assume that for rhyme-purposes a metrical grid, different from the one in (23), is assigned to each line. The rules for constructing this grid are given in (27).

(27)   a. Gridline 0: starting just at the R edge, insert a R parenthesis, form binary groups, heads R. (same as (22a))

b. Gridline 1: starting just at the L edge, insert a L parenthesis, form binary groups, heads L.

i. Odd numbered lines: the last (rightmost) group must be incomplete.

c. Gridline 2: starting just at the R edge, insert a R parenthesis, form binary groups, heads R.

In (28) we illustrate the metrical grids of lines 3, 4, and 5 in (25).

(28)
$$\begin{array}{c} B \\ 6 \end{array}$$

Mẹ đi một quãng đường xa.

```
) *  * )  *     * )    *     * )              0 ⇐
   ( *          *        ( *                  1 ⇒
) *                     * )                   2 ⇐
                         *                    3
```

$$\begin{array}{cc} B & C \\ 6 & 8 \end{array}$$

Mẹ xà chân xuống phải mà anh lươn.

```
) *  * )  *     * )    *    * )*     * )        0 ⇐
   ( *          *        ( *     * (            1 ⇒
) *                     * )                     2 ⇐
                         *                      3
```

$$\begin{array}{c} C \\ 6 \end{array}$$

Ông kia có chiếc thuyền nan,

```
) *      * )  *     * )     *     * )           0 ⇐
   ( *          *           ( *                 1 ⇒
   ) *                     * )                  2 ⇐
                            *                   3
```

Given the grids in (28), we can state the rhyme rule as in (29).

(29)   In even-numbered lines, the head syllable rhymes with head syllable of the preceding (odd-numbered) line, and the last syllable rhymes with head syllable of the following (odd-numbered) line.

Condition (29), which controls rhyme, refers thus to a different metrical grid than condition (24), which controls tone. The assignment of more than one grid to a given line recalls the assignment of a tune to a text, briefly discussed in sections 1.10 and 8.5 above. Note that rhyme and tone have also different domains of application in this poetry: the condition on rhyme takes adjacent lines as its domain(s), while the conditions

on tone take the single line as their domain. The principle that syllables are partitioned into two exclusive classes holds here too. But the
different domains require different partitions. The classification Sharp
vs. Even tone determines the well-formedness of a single line; rhyme, in
contrast, determines the well-formedness of line sequences.

10.4 The alliterative meter of *Beowulf*

We conclude with an example of the 'alliterative meter' (or 'strong stress
meter') found in Germanic poetry, and exemplified here by the Old
English poem *Beowulf*, from which five lines are quoted in (30)–(34).
Alliterating stressed syllables are marked with *A*, and non-alliterating
stressed syllables with *N*. Our account is based on Halle and Keyser's
analysis (1971: 147–164).[6]

(30) bǽt under béorge.   Béornas géarwe
      s *s*   *s*   *s*   *s*   *s*   *s*   *s*   *s*   all the syllables
      A   *A*   *A*   *N*   only the stressed syllables
     'boat beneath the sea-cliffs. Warriors eagerly' line 221

(31) þæt hē hǽfde mód mícel, þéah þe hē his mǽgum nǽre
      s   *s* *s* *s* *s*   *s s*   *s*   *s* *s* *s*   *s s*   *s s*
           N   *A* *A*   *A*   *N*
     'that he had much courage, though he might not have been with his
     kinsmen' line 1167

(32) þone sélestan sǽcyninga
      s *s* *s s* *s*   *s*   *s s*
            A   *A*
     'the best of sea-kings' line 2382

(33) hréas blǽc; hónd gemúnde
      s   *s*   *s*   *s s*   *s*
      A   *N*   *A*   *N*
     'he fell pale; his hand remembered' line 2488

(34) héard hér cúmen, sóhte hóldne wíne
      s   *s* *s*   *s*   *s* *s*   *s*   *s s*
      A   *A* *N*   *N*   *A*   *N*
     'come boldly here and visited a trusty friend' line 376

One important characteristic of these lines is that they vary greatly in
length. This is true whether we count all syllables or only the stressed

---

[6] In Halle and Keyser (1971), from which the examples are taken, S and W are used
for alliterating and non-alliterating syllables; our change to A and N avoids the
implication of this annotation that the alliterating syllables are relatively 'strong'.
Arnason (2007) on alliteration in Icelandic has been useful in our reanalysis.

syllables. Thus, (33) has six syllables while (31) has fifteen. Similarly, line (32) has two stressed syllables, the lower limit, and line (34) has six stressed syllables, the upper limit. We suggest that the variation in the length of the line arises in part because this is a loose meter, permitting incomplete Gridline 0 groups within the line. The fact that there can be as many as five unstressed syllables between consecutive stresses (e.g., in (31)) means that two complete ternary groups can intervene between two consecutive stresses. And this is not compatible with a number of the analyses above. We assume therefore that for the *Beowulf* meter, unstressed syllables are invisible. By rule (35), only syllables bearing the word stress are projected on Gridline 0 and only these syllables are subject to the iterative rules stated in (37).[7]

(35) Project only syllables bearing the main word stress to Gridline 0.

The second important characteristic of the meter is alliteration; either two or three of the stressed syllables must alliterate, and only certain patterns of alliterating and non-alliterating syllables are permitted. In quoted examples, we write A under syllables which alliterate and N under syllables which do not alliterate. We treat the line as in a loose meter, which begins with the insertion of a parenthesis before each *A* syllable by rule (36), followed by the iterative rules (37).

(36) Insert a L parenthesis to the left of a Gridline 0 asterisk which projects from an alliterating syllable.

(37) a. Gridline 0: starting just at the L edge, insert a R parenthesis, form binary groups, heads L.

  i. Gridline 0 may include incomplete groups.

  b. Gridline 1: starting just at the R edge, insert a L parenthesis, form binary groups, heads L.

  i. An ungrouped asterisk is permitted.

To illustrate how the rules work, we scan (30) in (38). We show all the syllables, but project only the four stressed syllables to Gridline 0, as specified by rule (35). Left parentheses are inserted to the left of the

---

[7] '[O]nly primary-stressed syllables may actualize S's [A] and W's [N]. These syllables are generally to be found only in major lexical items – nouns, verbs, adjectives, non-clitic adverbs, and the first element of compound words. In addition, we assume as a special convention that adjectives always contain primary-stressed vowels, even when they modify nouns. There are occasional lines in which prepositions and personal and demonstrative pronouns actualize S [A] positions.' (Halle and Keyser 1971: 148).

three alliterating syllables by rule (36). There are two incomplete groups at Gridline 0, as permitted by rule (37a.i), and at Gridline 1 one asterisk is ungrouped, as permitted by rule (37b.i)

(38)   bā́t under béorge.   Béornas géarwe

```
    s   s   s   s   s      s   s   s   s
    A       A          A       N
  )( *      ( *        ( *        * )      0 ⇒
     *      ( *         * (                1 ⇐
            *                              2
```

Alliteration is controlled by condition (39).

(39)   A syllable projecting to Gridline 1 must alliterate.

Since each line has either two or three alliterating syllables, these two or three syllables must project to Gridline 1.

The shortest possible line has just two alliterating syllables, with no (stressed) non-alliterating syllables (i.e., no-alliterating syllables which project to Gridline 0), as in (40).

(40)   þone sélestan sǽcyninga

```
       A          A
     ) ( *        ( *            0 ⇒
       ( *        * (            1 ⇐
       *                         2
```

Various patterns of line in which there are also non-alliterating stressed syllables that project to Gridline 0 are shown in (41), (42), and (43).

(41)   héard hḗr cúmen, sṓhte hóldne wíne

```
    A      A   N      N      A   N
  )( *    ( *  * )     *    ( *   * )     0 ⇒
     *    ( *                * (          1 ⇐
          *                               2
```

(42)   þæt hē hǽfde mṓd mícel,   þēah þe hē his mágum nǽre

```
           N      A   A                   A    N
         ) *     ( *  ( *               ( *    * )     0 ⇒
                 *    ( *               * (            1 ⇐
                      *                                2
```

(43)   hrēas blāc; hónd gcmúndc

```
      A    N   A       N
    ) ( *  * ) ( *      * )        0 ⇒
      ( *      * (                 1 ⇐
      *                            2
```

In principle, and given the rules as they stand, each Gridline 0 asterisk projecting from an alliterating syllable could be followed in its group by one asterisk projecting form a non-alliterating syllable, and preceded by one ungrouped asterisk projecting from a non-alliterating syllable, which should give an upper limit as shown in (44).

(44)   N   (A   N)   N   (A   N)   N   (A   N)   N

The actual patterns are more restricted than this as shown in (45), which adapts a table in Halle and Keyser (1971: 154). The number of lines of each type in the entire poem are shown (enclosed in parentheses) on the right.[8]

(45)   N   (A   N)   N   (A   N)   N   (A   N)   N

N	(A	N)	N	(A	N)	N	(A	N)	N	
				(A			(A			(200)
			N	(A			(A			(33)
				(A	N)		(A			(104)
				(A	N)	N	(A			(2)
			N	(A	N)		(A			(3)
				(A			(A	N)		(665)
				(A			(A	N)	N	(21)
			N	(A			(A	N)		(137)
				(A	N)		(A	N)		(430)
				(A	N)		(A	N)	N	(27)
				(A	N)	N	(A	N)		(17)
			N	(A	N)		(A	N)		(19)
	(A			(A			(A			(277)
N	(A			(A			(A			(6)
	(A			(A			(A	N)		(999)
N	(A			(A			(A	N)		(13)
	(A			(A			(A	N)	N	(77)
	(A			(A	N)		(A			(25)
	(A			(A	N)	N	(A			(1)
	(A			(A	N)		(A	N)		(105)
	(A			(A	N)		(A	N)	N	(4)
	(A			(A	N)	N	(A	N)		(3)

[8] We omit the hemistich boundaries shown in the original table: Halle and Keyser (1971: 152) argue against the traditional claim that there is a linguistic basis for the division of the line into two hemistiches (see also Keyser 1969). In our theory, there is no reason for thinking that the line is divided into two hemistiches.

Though in principle our rules permit up to three ungrouped asterisks (projecting from non-alliterating syllables), it is clear that only one such asterisk is actually found, and so we formulate the condition in (46).

(46)   At most one asterisk may be ungrouped at Gridline 0.

The second restriction which is clear from (45) is that if there are three Gridline 0 groups (i.e., three alliterating syllables), the leftmost group must be incomplete. In our grid, this group projects to Gridline 1 as an asterisk which is ungrouped, and hence we can readily identify it by the condition (47).

(47)   An asterisk which is not grouped at Gridline 1 must be projected from a unary Gridline 0 group.

Conditions (46) and (47) permit only the patterns shown in (45).[9]

The *Beowulf* meter differs from other meters reviewed in this book in that it systematically disregards all unstressed syllables and projects to Gridline 0 only syllables that bear word stress. It resembles the other meters in that it partitions the syllables that count for the meter (and are therefore projected to Gridline 0) into two classes. The property underlying the partitioning here is alliteration or its absence, whereas elsewhere the partitioning was based on other properties of syllables, such as stress vs. stressless, heavy vs. light, etc. The comparison between this meter and the Vietnamese meter discussed in the previous section shows us that alliteration and rhyme have fundamentally different relations to meter.[10]

10.5 Conclusion

In this chapter we have seen that superficially very different kinds of metrical system all point in the same general direction – towards the possibilty of metrical universals. In particular we have shown that metrical rules and conditions recognize only a two-way partitioning of syllables within a domain such as the verseline, a partition which can be based on stress (accent), weight (quantity), tone, or, as we have shown in this chapter, based on alliteration.

[9] In *Beowulf*, there are just eight (out of 3176) lines which are ruled unmetrical by our constraints. These are their patterns; the first violates (46) and the second two violate (47).

		N	(A		(A	N)	N	(1)
(A	N)		(A		(A	N)		(6)
(A	N)		(A		(A			(1)

[10] Alliteration is also subject to a locality condition, unlike rhyme; see Fabb (1999).

11

The metrical poetry of the Old Testament

11.1 Introduction[1]

A major portion of the Old Testament (OT) is poetry, and, like all poetry (see Chapter 1), is composed of lines. Most OT poetry is not metrical in that the lines that make up this poetry are not subject to restrictions on length. The topic of this chapter is the small minority of OT poetry that is made up of lines that are subject to restrictions on length, and is therefore metrical. Unlike the other kinds of metrical poetry discussed in this book, the metrical poetry of the OT depends solely on the raw number of syllables that make up its lines. It is unique among the meters in this book in that it has no recourse to the metrical grid and to grouping of syllables inside the line.

The standard text of the OT was established by a group of Jewish scholars, called the Masoretes, at some time between 600 and 800 CE, i.e., a thousand or more years after most of the original writings were composed, and it is well known that the text as it has come down to us fails in various ways to reproduce the original wording. This is shown most clearly with respect to the passages that appear more than once in the Old Testament. For example, Psalms 14 and 53 reproduce the same underlying text, but when compared in detail significant differences between the two versions are readily noted. For example, Psalm 14 refers to the deity both as *yahweh* and *ʔĕlohî:m*, while in Psalm 53 all instances of *yahweh* have been replaced with *ʔĕlohî:m*. In fact, it has been established that in the second of the five sections of the book of Psalms (Psalms 41–72), this replacement is quite systematic, though not total.

[1] We are grateful to John Huehnergard and Elitzur Bar Asher for reading and commenting on an earlier version of this chapter. Remaining inadequacies are the sole responsibility of the authors, NF&MH.

These inaccuracies in the received text present obvious problems to the study of metrical poetry in the OT. Since the metrical structure of the poems depends on the distribution of lines of different lengths (where length is measured in syllables), our results crucially depend on the exact wording of the texts as they were composed, and not as they happen to have come down to us. Each of the OT texts analyzed here has therefore been subject to emendations, all of which are detailed below. Our emendations are, of course, affected by our understanding of the metrical structure of the texts. For instance, it was shown in Halle (1997) that Psalm 54 is composed of two identical stanzas with lines of lengths 8–8–8–7–7–8–8. This statement, however, is true only if in the first stanza three occurrences of trisyllabic *ʔĕlohî:m* are replaced with bisyllabic *yahweh*. This replacement is not implausible in light of the fact noted above, since Psalm 54 is part of the second of the five sections that make up the Psalms.

11.2 Syntactic parallelism and meter

The pervasive role of syntactic parallelism in OT poetry was first documented in 1753 by Robert Lowth, later Archbishop of London. Lowth wrote that 'the poems divide themselves in a manner spontaneously into periods, for the most part equal; so the periods themselves are divided into verses, most commonly couplets, though frequently of greater length ... This is chiefly observable ... when they express the same thing in different words, or different things in a similar form of words; when equals refer to equals, and opposites to opposites' (Lowth 1829: 33).

Lowth believed that in addition to being marked by syntactic parallelism, the poetry of the OT was also metrical; he thought, however, that too much time had elapsed for the metrical system of the OT to be recovered. He writes:

(1) I think we may with safety affirm, that the Hebrew poetry is metrical. One or two of the peculiarities also of their versification ... may at least be reasonably conjectured ... As to the real quantity, the rhythm, or modulation, these from the present state of the language seem to be altogether unknown, and even to admit of no investigation by human art or industry. It is indeed evident, that the true Hebrew pronunciation is totally lost. The rules concerning it, which were devised by the modern Jews many ages after the language of their ancestors had fallen into disuse, have been long since suspected by the learned to be destitute of authority and truth ... it was neither possible for them to recall the true pronunciation of a language long

> since obsolete, and to institute afresh the rules of orthoepy; *nor can*
> *any person in the present age so much as hope to effect any thing to*
> *the purpose by the aid of conjecture, in a matter so remote from our*
> *senses and involved in obscurity.* (Lowth 1829: 33; italics supplied)

It is this last proposition of Lowth's that we challenge in what follows.
We show that there are in the Old Testament a number of metrical texts,
and we establish the principles governing these texts.

The first example illustrating syntactic parallelism in Lowth's book
happens to be subject to restrictions on line length and therefore also
metrical. The text in question, the 'Curse of Lemek' (Genesis 4:23–24),[2]
is quoted in (2), where line lengths are indicated by the numerals printed
between the Hebrew text and its translation into English.[3]

(2)

ʕa:dâ:h wəcillâ:h ʃəmaʕan qô:lî:	10	Adah and Zillah, listen to my voice;
nəʃe:y lemek haʔze:nna:h ʔimra:tî:	10	ye, wives of Lemek, give ear to my speech:
kî: ʔî:ʃ ha:ragtî: ləpicʕî:	8	for I have slain a man over a wound of mine,
wəyeled ləḥabbura:tî:	8	and a boy over a boil,
kî: ʃibʕa:tayî:m yuqqam qa:yin	9	for seven-fold will be avenged Cain,
wəlemek ʃibʕî:m wəʃibʕâ:h	8	and Lemek – seventy-seven-fold.

These lines exhibit syntactic parallelism.[4] These lines, moreover, are
also subject to restrictions on the number of syllables in them, as even
a superficial look at the middle column of (2) shows. The first two lines
of (2) are the preamble; and they are followed by the four lines of the
Curse proper. The two lines of the preamble are each 10 syllables long,
whereas the four lines of the Curse are shorter: three are 8 syllables
long and one is 9 syllables. In fact, as we explain below, when correctly
counted, the '9-syllable' line is also 8 syllables long, like the other three
lines that make up the Curse.

---

[2] Kugel (1981: 203) reports that Immanuel Frances (1618–1710) believed 'that the
first "poem" in the Bible appears to be Lamekh's war boast'.

[3] The Hebrew texts of the poems are transcribed in accordance with a system that
is partly of our own devising. The twenty-two consonants of the Hebrew alphabet
are transcribed as: ʔ b g d h w z ḥ ṭ y k l m n s ʕ p c q r ʃ t. Basic vowels are
a e i o u and ə, which stands for schwa. Vowel length is indicated by a colon.
Reduced vowels (*ḥăte:pî:m*) are indicated by a breve mark above the letter; e.g.,
ă. Circumflex above a vowel letter indicates a long vowel before a non-pronounced
consonant.

[4] Readers without Hebrew can see this by reading the translations on the right, for
the syntax here is preserved in translation.

11.3 Syllable counting in Old Testament metrical poetry

The proposition that there is metrical poetry in the OT is of course not new. As indicated in (1), Lowth entertained the idea. What prevented Lowth from discovering the nature of OT meters was his incorrect belief that all metrical poetry is based on grouping syllables into feet and metrical units of higher order, like the classical poetry of Greek and Latin, or of modern English and French, with which Lowth was familiar. He did not consider the possibility that the metrical poetry of the OT is based on ordinary counting without grouping syllables into pairs/triplets. Such 'foot-less' meters are quite uncommon; in fact as remarked above, the metrical poetry of the OT is the only clear example of purely syllable-counting meter that we have encountered to this time.

Although Lowth never entertained the possibility that OT poetry was based on simple counting, the idea has been explored by a number of scholars during the last century. What differentiates the approaches of this type is how the syllables are counted. In the rest of this section we explain the principles of syllable counting that we make use of and compare them with those utilized by David Noel Freedman, whose metrical studies of some of the same texts as those examined by us here have been collected in his 1980 book *Pottery, Poetry, and Prophecy.*[5]

In counting the syllables of OT poetry, we follow the Masoretic text with the deviations listed in (3).

(3) i.   The count stops with the last stressed syllable in the line.

ii. Secondary *hăte:pî:m* following guttural consonants are omitted from the count; e.g., Masoretic trisyllabic *yaʕăqob* 'Jacob' is read as disyllabic *yaʕqob*.

iii. The *furtive patah* – the vowel /a/ inserted before word-final pharyngeal consonants – is omitted from the count and from the transcription; e.g., the Masoretic disyllabic *koah* 'strength' is represented as a monosyllable.

iv. The schwa is not counted in 'doubly open' syllables of the form $VC_1 \_ C_1V$ where the flanking Cs are different. We read Masoretic *binəʔô:t* 'on pastures' as disyllabic *binʔô:t*, but *cô:rəra:y* 'my enemies' as trisyllabic.

v.   We disregard the effects of degemination of the glide consonants y and w in position before schwa (see Joüon 1947 and Bergsträsser 1962: I,141). Thus, we read *hayyəsô:d* 'the

[5] We thank Professor Freedman for his helpfulness to one of the authors (MH), whose questions and objections he answered in great detail.

foundation' and *ʃeyyəʃallem* 'that will pay' vs. Masoretic *hayəsô:d* and *ʃeyəʃallem*. (This decision affects application of (3iv) above; for some discussion see (13) below.)

vi. The names *yahweh* and *yərû:ʃale:m* are counted everywhere as disyllabic and quadrisyllabic, respectively.[6]

Freedman (1980: 279–280n) explains his way of counting the syllables in (4):

(4)   The vocalization of the Masoretic Text is accepted generally, with certain modifications: secondary vowels (including patah furtive) added in relation to laryngeals in MT are not counted, and segolate formations[7] are treated as monosyllabic ... Vocal schwa, however, is counted since it regularly represents an original full vowel ... We cannot be certain about contractions; e.g., *binʔô:t* (Ps 23: vs. 2; two syllables) for older *bena:ʔô:t* (three syllables).

In both approaches – Freedman's as well as ours – the Masoretic text is taken as basic, but both approaches admit systematic departures from the syllabification. The two approaches agree with regard to the treatment of secondary vowels and furtive *patah* (cf. (3ii, iii)). The approaches differ with respect to the treatment of line-final unstressed syllables: we do not count them (see (3i)), Freedman does. The approaches differ also with respect to the treatment of the segolates. As stated in (4), Freedman treats the disyllabic segolate forms as monosyllables for purposes of the meter, whereas we follow the Masoretic text and count both syllables. We, but not Freedman, deviate from the Masoretic text in not counting the schwa vowel in 'doubly open syllables', (3iv), and in discounting the degemination of glides, (3v).

---

[6] The name of the deity YHWH appears in each of the three psalms analyzed below. Since the meter of these psalms is based on counting the syllables in the lines, the psalms provide information about how the psalmists pronounced this name. The data below indicate that the tetragrammaton YHWH was phonetically a disyllabic word with stress on the last syllable, most likely [yahwé:]. This information is of interest in view of the age-old prohibition against pronouncing this word. The metric data here exclude the trisyllabic pronunciation Jehovah and its variants. Since the Septuagint systematically translates YHWH as κυριος 'lord' we can conclude that the prohibition against pronouncing this name of God was in force already by the time of the Septuagint, parts of which date from the beginning of the 3rd century BCE, while other parts – e.g., the book of Daniel – must be from the middle of the 2nd century BCE or later.

[7] Segolates are disyllabic words, like *yeled* 'boy' with the same vowel in both stem syllables, that have monosyllabic stem alternants, as in *yald-i:* 'my boy' in other contexts.

Because of these differences, the two approaches analyze (scan) a given text in markedly different ways. This gives rise to the question as to which of the two ways of counting is the correct one; i.e., which method of determining line length reflects more accurately the intention of the makers of the poems. A quick preliminary test of the competing approaches is provided by the Curse of Lemek in (2). It was noted above, that in the quatrain that constitutes the Curse the third line differs from the rest in that it has 9 syllables, rather than 8. This irregularity is eliminated by our condition (3i), because the line ends with an unstressed syllable (the second syllable of name *qa:yin* 'Cain'), and condition (3i) stipulates that line-final unstressed syllables are omitted from the count.

Our approach differs from Freedman's also in the treatment of segolates (nouns like the name *Lemek* or like the common noun *yeled* 'boy'). Freedman departs from the Masoretic text of the OT in treating such nouns as monosyllables (see (4)). There are in Lemek's Curse (2) three instances of segolates: the name *Lemek*, which occurs twice, once in the second line and once in the last, and the word *yeled*, in the fourth line.

It is assumed here that all metrical poetry involves restrictions on line length and that the simplest kind of restriction on line length is that sets of lines be of the same length. This simple requirement is satisfied, if the syllables are counted in accordance with (3): the introduction to the Curse consists of a couplet where each of the two lines is of 10 syllables, whereas the Curse itself is composed of four lines, each 8 syllables long. When the same text is counted in accordance with Freedman's conventions (4), these simple regularities disappear. Instead of the syllable count 10–10–8–8–8–8, we get the irregular distribution of line lengths 10–9–8–7–9–7. Since none of the other regularities in the distribution of line lengths that we have studied is improved by following Freedman's conventions in (4), rather than ours in (3), we conclude that (3) rather than (4) is the correct way of counting syllables in OT poetry.

11.4 Psalm 23: meter and gematriya

The text of Psalm 23 is reproduced in (5). The syllable count of the lines indicated by the numbers in the middle of the page is that resulting from following (3). The line-final unstressed syllables, which, pursuant to (3i), are not counted, are enclosed in parentheses. In (5) we have also omitted from the count certain reduced vowels as required by (3ii, iii, iv).

(5)

yahwe:h ro:ʕî: lo:ʔ ʔeḥsa:r	7	Yahweh is my shepherd, I shall not want.
binʔô:t deʃeʔ yarbice:(nî:)	7	He makes me lie down on grassy pastures.
ʕal me:y mənuḥ:ôt yənahle:(nî:)	8	He guides me to still waters.
napʃî: yəʃô:be:b	5	He restores my soul.
yanḥe:nî: bəmaʕgəle:y-cedeq	8	He leads me on paths of righteousness 5
ləmaʕan ʃəmô:	5	for the sake of his name.
gam kî:-ʔe:le:k bəgêʔ calma:(wet)	8	Though I walk in the valley of the shadow
lo:ʔ-ʔî:ra:ʔ raʕâ:h	5	I shall fear no evil, [of death,
kî:-ʔattâ:h ʕimma:dî:	6	for you are with me.
ʃibṭəka: ûmiʃʕante:(ka:)	7	Your rod and your staff 10
he:mmâh yənaḥmû:(nî:)	5	they comfort me.
taʕro:k ləpa:nay ʃulḥa:n	7	You prepare a table for me
neged co:rəra:y	5	in front of my enemies,
diʃʃanta: baʃʃemen ro:ʔʃî:	8	You anoint my head with oil;
kô:sî: rəwa:yâ:h	5	my cup runs over. 15
ʔak ṭô:b wa:ḥesed yirdəpû:(nî:)	8	Only goodness and mercy shall pursue me
kol-yəme:y ḥayya:y	5	all the days of my life.
wəya:ʃabtî: bəbe:yt yahwe:h	8	And I shall dwell in Yahweh's house
ləʔo:rek ya:mî:m	5	to the end of days.

The text in (5) has been emended in two places, and both emendations
are required by the meter. These emendations have only minimal effects
on the semantics of the lines. In line 8 we have replaced *ra:ʕ* 'evil' of the
Masoretic Text (MT) with its synonym *ra:ʕâ:h*. In line 18 MT *wəʃabtî:*
'I shall return' is replaced with *wəya:ʃabtî:* 'I shall dwell', which is both
required by the meter and more appropriate semantically.

All metrical OT texts that we have studied count the name of the
deity YHWH as a bisyllabic word. The prohibition against pronouncing
this name of God was thus not in force at the time that the poems
were composed, and in our transcriptions the name is represented as
yahwe:h.[8]

We owe to Bazak (1987) the important observation that Psalm 23
consists of 55 words, and the suggestion that these 55 words should be
subdivided into two sub-sequences of 26 words separated by a three-word
sequence. It turns out that when this is done, the three-word sequence
occupying the 'numerological' center of the poem, *kî:-ʔattâ:h ʕimma:dî:*
('for you are with me'), is the only six-syllable line in the psalm and, more
important, also epitomizes the point of the poem. Bazak motivates the
segmentation of the 55 words of the poem into 26+3+26 with reference
to the fact that the letters of the Hebrew alphabet have numerical values:

---

[8] Kugel (2007: 38n) expresses a widely held view: 'Since, even in biblical times, this
name came to be considered too sacred to be uttered, its exact pronunciation has
been lost'. The evidence in this chapter allows us to conclude instead that the
name was disyllabic and oxytone. See also footnote 6 above.

ʔalef = 1, beyt = 2, etc. Bazak notes that the numerical values of the Hebrew letters composing the name of the deity *yhwh*, add up to 26.[9] This type of numerology, known as 'gematriya', is widely used as an exegetic principle in the rabbinical literature. (For some discussion see Dornseiff (1925) and the entry *gematriya* in the *Encyclopedia Judaica*). In other words, Bazak proposes that there is a hidden message in the psalm, roughly that shown in (6).

(6)   YHWH, for you are with me, YHWH

We think that an additional hidden message can be decoded in Psalm 23. Given the syllable count of the lines shown in (5), Psalm 23 is composed of 9 couplets plus a single line. As noted, the odd single line, *kî:-ʔatta:h ʕimma:dî:* ('that you are with me'), is the only line in the text that is 6 syllables long; the other lines in the poem are 8 or 7 or 5 syllables long. The nine couplets that make up the rest of the poem share further important metrical regularities: aside from the first couplet, the second line in each couplet has 5 syllables, whereas the first line is either 7 or 8 syllables long. The lines, moreover, can be arranged into three stanzas with the syllable counts shown as the top line of (7). In this arrangement, the first and the last stanza are both composed of four couplets, whereas the middle stanza contains the odd 6-syllable line plus a single couplet.

(7) | 77 85 85 85 | 6 75 | 75 85 85 85 | syllables in each line |
|---|---|---|---|
| 53 | 18 | 51 | syllables in each stanza |
| 26+26(+1) | 18 | 26+26(−1) | see (8) |

In (7) there are two stanzas of 52 syllables (plus or minus one), hence four times 26 (YHWH), and a middle stanza of 18 syllables. To people familiar with Jewish traditions (and superstitions), the number 18 also represents the Hebrew word *ḥay* 'life, vivat', and is widely taken to be a lucky number. On this reading the psalm includes the hidden message in (8), quite similar to the one in (6).

(8)   YHWH YHWH ḤY (*vivat!*) YHWH YHWH

The two hidden messages in (6) and (8) provide an explanation for the lengths of the different lines that make up Psalm 23. The fact that the poem is 55 words long is surely not an accident; rather it is an essential

---

[9] $y = 10$, $h = 5$, $w = 6$, so $yhwh = 10+5+6+5 = 26$

part of the intention of the poet in composing this text, and so are the lengths of each of the nineteen lines that make up the psalm. The particular numbers were chosen for the purpose of conveying the above two hidden messages.

In order to decode the two hidden messages it is necessary to analyze the text so as to establish its midpoint. Once this is done it is not hard to discover that the three-word phrase occupying the center of the poem is 'for you are with me', and also that the stanza in the middle of the poem consists of the lines 8–10 (cf. (5)), whose syllable count adds up to 18.

Examination of the two sequences that flank the center reveals the rest of the messages. In the case of the first hidden message (6), each of the two flanking texts is 26 words long. In the hidden message, (8), the two flanking texts are, respectively, $53 = (26 \times 2) + 1$ and $51 = (26 \times 2) - 1$ syllables long. As noted, the number 26 is the sum total of the letters in *yhwh*, while 18 represents the word *ḥy* meaning 'life'.

The crucial step for discovering the hidden message is the idea of looking for the midpoint of the text. There is evidence that the midpoint of a text was a property of importance in the Jewish tradition. We recall that in the Masoretic text, information about the midpoint is given in the colophons at the end of each of the books of the Old Testament. For example, the colophon at the end of Genesis states that the verses in the book total 1534 and that the verse at the midpoint is Genesis 27:40. In including hidden messages in his text, the author of Psalm 23 must have hoped that they would be decoded in the future by a reader familiar with this tradition.

The claim of 'secret messages' in the text will no doubt remind some readers of the recent claim that particular arrays of the consecutive letters in the book of Genesis encode the names of famous rabbis of recent centuries. (That claim was compellingly controverted by McKay *et al.* 1999.) Unlike the latter claim, our proposition does not require belief in clairvoyance on the part of the author. To encode the messages above the author only had to know that Hebrew letter sequences represent both words and numbers and to make use of this information in ways that are attested elsewhere.

11.5 The meter of Psalm 24

We argued above that in Psalm 23 the rationale for the particular arrangement of line lengths was the intention to code hidden messages. In the two psalms discussed in this and the following section, the rationale is a great deal more concrete: these psalms are pattern or picture poems where the graphic shape generated by the line lengths pictures an object that is related to the subject matter of the psalm. The patterns that are generated in this way are of course crucially dependent on the way syllables are counted, and, as above, we assume that the counting principles are those in (3). Alexandrian Greek pattern poetry is known from this period, and is referred to as *technopaignia* ('games of skill'). Surviving and relevant examples include two poems which constitute pictures of altars, one by Dosiadas, possibly 3rd century BCE, and one by 'Besantinus', of the 2nd century CE. For some additional discussion of pattern poems, see Halle (1987, 1997).

The first of our two examples is Psalm 24, reproduced in (9).

(9)

ləyahwe:h ʔerec umlô:ʔâ:h	8	Yahweh's is earth and its fulness,
te:be:l wəyo:ʃbe:y bâ:h	6	dry land and those who dwell in it.
kî: hûʔ ʕal yammîm yəsa:dâ:h	8	For he has founded it on seas
wəʕal nəha:rô:t kô:nănâ:h	8	and has established it on rivers.
mî: yaʕleh bəhar yahwe:h	7	Who will ascend Yahweh's mountain? 5
û:mî: ya:qû:m bimqôm qo:dʃô:	8	And who will stand up in his holy place?
nəqî:-kappa:yi:m ûbar-le:ba:b	9	Clean of hand and pure of heart,
ʔăʃer lo:ʔ na:ʃâ:ʔ laʃʃa:wʔ ne(peʃ)	8	who does not deceive
wəlo:ʔ niʃbaʕ ləmirmâ:h	7	and has not sworn falsely.
yiʃʃâ:ʔ bəra:kâ:h me:yahwe:h	8	He will receive a blessing from Yahweh 10
û:cda:qa:h me:ʔlo:he:y yiʃʕô:	8	and justice from the god of his salvation.
zeh dô:r do:rʃe:y yahwe:h	6	This is the generation of Yahweh's followers,
məbaqʃe:y pa:neyka: yaʔqob	8	of seekers of your countenance, o Jacob.
selâ:h		Selah
ʃəʔû ʃəʕa:rîm ro:ʔʃe:ykem	8	Lift up your heads, oh gates! 15
wehinna:ʃʔû: pithe:y ʕô:la:m	8	And let the doors of the world open!
wəya:bô:ʔ melek hakka:bô:d	8	And the king of glory shall come.
mî: zeh melek hakka:bô:d	7	Who is the king of glory?
yahwe:h ʕizû:z wəgibbô:r	7	Yahweh is strong and mighty;
yahwe:h gibbô:r milḥa:mâ:h	7	Yahweh is mighty in war! 20

The text in (9) has been emended in the ways listed in (10). Although the primary reason for our emendations is the needs of the meter, the emendations are also independently justified.

(10)   i. Line 1. *ʔerec* 'earth' instead *ha:ʔa:rec* 'the earth'. According to Even-Shoshan (1990), the collocation *ha:ʔa:rec / ʔerec umlô:ʔa:h* '(the) earth and its fullness' occurs seven times in

the OT, not counting its appearance in Psalm 24. Of these seven, all but one are without definite article. Our emendation is thus on the side of the majority. In addition, the absence of the article brings out more clearly the syntactic parallelism with the following line, *te:be:l wəyo:ʃbe:y bâ:h,* 'dry land and those who dwell in it' where *te:be:l* 'dry land', the counter part of *ʔerec* 'earth', appears without definite article. Our attention has been drawn by E. Bar Asher to the fact that in collocations with *te:be:l,* the noun *ʔerec* is usually supplied with a definite article. There are nonetheless cases such as Psalms 90:2 *wattəholle:l ʔerec wəte:be:l* 'earth and dry land became hollow', where *ʔerec* appears without definite article in this collocation.

ii. Line 4. *ko:nănâ:h* instead of MT *yəkonəneha:.* Here we follow the suggestion in the *Biblia Hebraica Stuttgartensia.*

iii. Line 8. *nepeʃ* 'a soul' instead of *napʃi:.* The collocation of the verb *na:ʃa:ʔ* 'carry/bear' with the noun *nepeʃ* 'soul' occurs several times in the OT, but in all but one of these the noun is supplied with a possessor, e.g., Jeremiah 37:9 *ʔal tiʃʃʔû: napʃo:te:ykem,* and is translated 'do not deceive yourselves'. The single occurrence without possessor is in 2 Samuel 14:14, *wəlo:ʔ yiʃʃa:ʔ ʔêlohîm nepeʃ* and is (mis)translated in the King James version as 'neither doth God respect any person'. A more correct translation is, we suggest, 'and God does not deceive (anyone)', which fits with the text that follows this clause – i.e., 'yet doth he devise means that his banished be not expelled from him'. Our proposed emendation therefore leads us to read line 8 in (9) 'who does not deceive', taking the adverb *laʃʃa:wʔ* 'in vain' as serving to emphasize the verb.

iv. Line 10. *me:yahwe:h* instead of *me:ʔet yahwe:h* Here the deletion of the accusative marker *ʔet* is justified by the absence of *ʔet* in the next line, with which line 10 is paired syntactically. A parallel argument was given for the deletion of the definite article in line 1.

v. Line 12. The MT *dô:r dô:rʃa:w* 'the generation of his followers/seekers' has been replaced with *dô:r dô:rʃe:y yahwe:h* 'the generation of Yahweh's followers/seekers'. The replacement makes better sense than the MT *dô:rʃa:w* 'of his followers/seekers', where there is no antecedent for the pronoun 'his'.[10]

vi. The last six lines of the poem are repeated in the MT in a slightly modified form. The repetition is omitted here.

The syllable counts of the lines of (9) are repeated in (11).

(11)   8868 78987 8688 *selâh* 888777

As shown in (11), the poem is composed of four stanzas, of which the first three are separated from the fourth by the word *selâ:h*, which is a word of disputed meaning that appears to 'indicate a break in the singing' (Pfeiffer 1948: 643). Here *selâ:h* separates the first thirteen lines of the poem from the last six. Thus the first part of the poem – lines 1 to 13 – consists of three stanzas: a middle stanza of five lines flanked by two stanzas of four lines each. The line lengths of the middle stanza are symmetrical: 7–8–9–8–7. This stanza is framed by two stanzas with symmetrical line lengths: 8–8–6–8 vs. 8–6–8–8. The shape generated by the lines of the middle stanza can be viewed as representing a hill or mountain; and the two symmetrical stanzas that precede and follow the hill/mountain stanza might be interpreted as parts of a fence or rampart surrounding the hill. This interpretation gains additional support from the content of the stanza, which asks about a person who will ascend Yahweh's mountain, presumably Mount Zion with its temple.

The fourth stanza – lines 14 to 19 – is composed of six lines, of which the first three contain 8 syllables and the last three 7 syllables. We leave the interpretation of this part of the poem as an open question.

11.6 The structure of Psalm 137

Psalm 137 was the subject of Halle's first publication on biblical metrics, his 1981 paper written jointly with John McCarthy, where most of the syllable counting principles given in (3) were first stated. Psalm 137 was discussed again in Halle (1987), where the proposition was first advanced that the psalm is a pattern (picture) poem. The syllable counts of the

---

[10] Several Greek and Syriac translations have replaced *pa:neyka:* 'your countenance' with *ʔǝlǝhǝry* 'god of' (see note in *Biblia Hebraica Stuttgartensia*). This emendation results in a text that seems to us both more transparent in meaning and syntactically parallel with the reading of the preceding verse: 'seekers of Jacob's god' is the proper counterpart of 'Yahweh's followers'. We have not introduced this change into the text of the psalm in (9) because our focus here is on the meter of the poem, and metrically both readings do equally well.

lines of the psalm in (12) are essentially identical with those in Halle and McCarthy (1981).

(12)

ʕal nəha:rô:t bəba:bel	7	On rivers in Babylon
ʃa:m ya:ʃabnû: gam ba:kî:(nû:)	7	there we sat and also wept
bəzo:kre:nû: ʔet ciyyô:n	7	as we recalled Zion.
ʕal-ʕăra:bî:m bətô:kâ:h	7	On laurels in its midst
ta:lî:nû: kinno:rô:te:y(nû:)	7	we hung our harps. 5
kî: ʃa:m ʃəʔe:lû:(nû:)	5	For there we were asked
ʃô:be:ynû: dibre:y-ʃî:r	6	by our captors for words of song,
wətô:la:le:ynû: ʃimḥâ:h	7	and by those who mocked us, for rejoicing
ʃî:rû: la:nû miʃʃîr ciyyôn	8	'Sing for us of Zion's song!'
ʔe:yk na:ʃî:r ʔet-ʃî:re:y-yahwe:h	8	How can we sing Yahweh's songs 10
ʕal ʔadmat ne:ka:r	5	on alien soil?
ʔim ʔeʃkaḥe:k yərûʃa:le:m	8	If I forget you, Jerusalem,
tikḥaʃ yəmî:nî:	5	may my right arm wither!
tidbaq ləʃô:nî: ləḥikkî:	8	May my tongue cleave to my palate
ʔim-lo:ʔ ʔezkəre:(kî:)	5	if I remember you not, 15
ʔim-lo:ʔ ʔaʕleh yərûʃa:le:m	8	if I should not come to Jerusalem
ʕal-ro:ʔʃ ʃimḥa:tî:	5	at my chief joy!
zəko:r yahwe:h libne:y ʔêdô:m	8	Recall, Yahweh, to Edom's sons
ʔet yəme:y yərû:ʃa:le:m	7	the days of Jerusalem,
ha:ʔo:mrî:m ʕa:rû: ʕa:(rû:)	6	who say: 'Strip bare, strip bare 20
ʕad hayyəsô:d ba:h	5	to its very foundation!'
bat-ba:bel haʃʃədû:dâ:h	7	Daughter of Babylon, the doomed!
ʔaʃre:y ʃeyyəʃallem la:k	7	Happy he who renders you
gəmû:le:k ʃegga:malt la:nû:	7	the payment you paid us!
ʔaʃre:y ʃeyyoʔḥe:z wənippe:c	8	Happy he who grasps and smashes 25
ʕo:la:layi:k ʔel-hassa:(laʕ)	7	your babes on the rock!

The text in (12) has been emended as follows:

(13)   i.   In line 1 *nəharô:t bəba:bel* 'rivers in Babylon' replaces MT *nahrô:t ba:bel* 'rivers of Babylon'. The former appears in the partial text of the psalm preserved in the Qumran caves, and it is also required by the meter.

   ii.   In line 10 we read *ʔet ʃire:y yahwe:h* 'Yahweh's songs' (pl) vs. MT *ʔet-ʃîr yahwe:h* 'Yahweh's song' (sg). This emendation is motivated by metrical requirements. Freedman (1980) has suggested the same emendation.

   iii.   In line 13, following Alter (2007: 474) and others, we read *tikḥaʃ* 'wither' for Masoretic *tiʃkaḥ* 'forget'. The change corrects a plausible error of letter transposition in the consonantal text, reading *tʃkḥ* for *tkḥʃ*.

iv. In line 19 the singular in MT *ʔeːt yôːm yərûːʃaːleːm* 'Jerusalem's day' has been replaced with the plural *ʔet yəmeːy yərûːʃaːleːm* 'Jerusalem's days', which is required by the meter of the line. This emendation, like that in line 10, restores one of two consecutive yods that is often omitted in the MT (see (3v) above).

v. In lines 16, 23, and 26 the preposition *ʔet*, which introduces direct object noun phrases in Hebrew has been omitted. This has only minor semantic or other consequences but is required by the meter.

vi. In lines 21 and 23 a geminate yod replaces the single yod of the MT in *hayyəsôːd* and in *ʃeyyəʃalem*. As above, the main reason for this emendation is the needs of the meter. Metrically, the geminate is required to ensure that the immediately following schwa is counted; without the geminates, the rule in (3iv) would have required us to omit this schwa from the count, and would have resulted in a violation of the meter.[11]

vii. Line 25 contains eight syllables, rather than the expected seven. John Hollander has suggested to us that the deviance was introduced into the meter by the poet as a deliberate flaw to convey the message that the poem, like all human deeds, is imperfect, for only God's creations are perfect. The metrical deviance, we submit, also serves to bring out the barbarous content of the last two lines, which so shockingly contrasts with the elegaic mood of the first half of the psalm.

Psalm 137 is composed of 26 lines, a number that is hardly accidental in view of the fact noted above that 26 is the numerical value of the Hebrew letters in the tetragrammaton *yhwh*. The 26 lines of the psalm break up into five stanzas:

---

[11] A well-known rule of biblical Hebrew geminates consonants after both the definite article *ha* and the complementizer *ʃe* 'that' (*daːgeːʃ haːzaːq*). We are grateful to John Huehnergard for drawing our attention to the fact that this gemination is often not reflected in the Masoretic text for consonants other than /bgdptk/. (Bergsträsser (1962: 141) states that 'before schwa, gemination is commonly eliminated, especially of (the glide) /y/ ... but almost never of the (consonants /b d g p k t/)'; see also Joüon (1947). In fact, the MT – inconsistently – retains the geminate in *ʃeyyoʔheːz* in line 25.) We suggest that the degemination reflects a phonetic development that took place after the poems were composed, but before the Masoretic text was established. Since the meter depends on the pronunciation of the poet, and not of the later editor of the text, we disregard the degemination in counting the syllables in the line.

(14)　77777　5678　85 85 85 85　8765　77787

Examination of the line lengths in (12) shows that stanzas 1 and 2 are the symmetrical counterparts of stanzas 4 and 5 respectively, but stanza 3 is composed of four couplets (i.e., pairs of lines) of lengths 8–5. We recall that both the number 26 and couplets with line of lengths 8–5 figured also in Psalm 23. However, these numbers play a different role here than they did in Psalm 23.

The question to be raised at this point concerns the rationale for this distribution of line lengths. Why would a poet write a poem with lines of the lengths in (14)? The answer becomes almost self-evident once the line lengths of the poem are represented as in (15). (Since Hebrew is written from right to left, the lines have been justified on the right.)

(15)

Looking at the pattern in (15) it becomes evident that when rotated ninety degrees to the left as shown in (16), the pattern of asterisks represents a building composed of two wings (stanzas 1 and 5), a roof (stanzas 2 and 4) and a porch with four columns (stanza 3). Framed in these terms it is only a small step to the conclusion that Psalm 137 is a pattern or picture poem representing the temple.

(16)

It has been argued, e.g., by Freedman (1980: 303), that Psalm 137 'was composed in Babylon during the first half of the 6th century BCE'. This seems unlikely to us in the light of the following considerations. The first temple, the one destroyed by the Babylonians in 586 BCE, is known to have had two, not four columns (see the model in the Harvard Semitic Museum). The structure in (16) is therefore more likely to reflect that of the second temple, destroyed by the Romans in 70 CE. We know that the second temple had four columns because it is so depicted in a number of places, including the silver tetradrachm coins minted during the Bar-Koḥba uprising 132–135 CE, the fresco in the synagogue of Dura Europos (in Iraq) dating from 242–243 CE, and in drinking cup from the 4th century CE, found in the catacomb of SS Pietro and Marcellino in Rome (now in the Vatican). All three of these depict the facade of the Jerusalem temple with four columns, and the same feature is reflected in Psalm 137. Moreover, Greek pattern poems are found in Alexandrian and later poetry, posterior to the construction of the second temple, but no Greek pattern poetry is known from the 6th century BCE.

11.7 Summary and conclusion

The meters of the four poems analyzed above involve syllable counting of the most rudimentary kind, without groupings into feet, metra, etc. The lines of all four poems are organized either into stanzas or into couplets. It was shown that in three of the four poems additional structure can be discerned. In Psalm 23 the additional structure is in the nature of a hidden message, while in Psalms 24 and 137 the lengths of the lines form graphic shapes that, we argued, represented Mt. Zion (Psalm 24) and the Jerusalem temple (Psalm 137).

In addition to the four OT texts that were discussed above, metrical analyses of Amos 3:3–8 ('Can two walk together'), Psalm 54 ('Save me oh God by thy name'), and Psalm 114 ('When Israel went out of Egypt') have been published in Halle (1989b, 1997). We know of a number of other syllable-counting texts in the OT. Five texts, on which interested readers might try out their understanding of what has been presented here are Judges 15:16, Zephaniah 1:14–16, Song of Songs 4:8, and Psalms 15 and 93. There are doubtless additional metrical texts to be discovered in the OT. We conclude with R. Shammai that much work remains to be done.

Bibliography

Allony, N. 1951. *Tô:ra:t hamiʃqa:lî:m šel Dûnaʃ, Yəhûdâh ha-Lle:wî:, wəʔabra:ham ʔibn ʕezrâ:h* [The theory of quantities of Dunaš, Yehuda Halevi, and Ibn Ezra]. Jerusalem: Môsa:d ha-Rab Qûq.

Alter, Robert. 2007. *The Book of Psalms: A Translation with Commentary.* New York: Norton.

Aristophanes. 2002. *Acharnians,* ed. S. Douglas Olson. Oxford University Press.

Arnason, Kristján. 2007. On the Principles of Nordic Rhyme and Alliteration. *Arkiv för nordisk filologi* 122: 79–116.

Arnold, E. V. 1905. *Vedic Metre in its Historical Development.* Cambridge University Press.

Arnott, D. W. 1985. Literature in Fula. In *Literatures in African Languages,* ed. B. W. Andrzejewski, S. Piłaszewicz, and W. Tyloch, 72–96. Warsaw: Wiedza Powszechna.

Attridge, Derek. 1982. *The Rhythms of English Poetry.* Harlow: Longman.

Attridge, Derek. 2003. The Rules of English Metre: A Response to Nigel Fabb. *Language and Literature* 12: 71–72.

Auden, W. H. 1945. *The Collected Poetry of W. H. Auden.* New York: Random House.

Bailey, Clinton. 2002. *Bedouin Poetry from Sinai and the Negev.* London: Saqi Books.

Balaban, John. 2003. *Ca Dao Việt Nam: Vietnamese Folk Poetry.* Port Townsend, WA: Copper Canyon Press.

Barons, K. and H. Wissendorffs. 1894. *Latwju Dainas.* Jelgava: H. I. Drawin-Drawneeks.

Bazak, J. 1987. Numerical Devices in Biblical Poetry. *Vetus Testamentum* 38: 333–337.

Bellay, Joachim de. 1971. *Les Antiquitez de Rome. Les Regrets,* ed. F. Joukovsky. Paris: Garnier-Flammarion.

Bello, Andrés. 1955. Principios de la ortología y métrica de la lengua castellana. In *Obras completas,* vol. VI: *Estudios filológicos,* 5–329. Caracas: Ministerio de Educación. (First published 1835.)

Beltrami, Pietro G. 2002. *La metrica italiana,* 4th edn. Bologna: Il Mulino.

Bergsträsser, G. 1962. *Hebräische Grammatik,* vol I. Hildesheim: Georg Olms Verlagsbuchhandlung.

Bērziņš, Ludis. 1959. *Ievads latviešu tautas dzejā* [Introduction to Latvian folk poetry]. Chicago: Čikāgas baltu filologu kopa.

Biblia Hebraica Stuttgartensia. 1984. Stuttgart: Deutsche Bibelgesellschaft.

Bohas, G., J.-P. Guillaume, and D. E. Kouloughi. 1990. *The Arabic Linguistic Tradition.* London: Routledge.

Brault, Gerard J. 1978. *The Song of Roland: An Analytical Edition,* vol. II: *Oxford Text and English Translation.* University Park, PA: Pennsylvania State University Press.

Brough, John. 1978. *Selections from Classical Sanskrit Literature, with English Translation and Notes.* London: School of Oriental and African Studies.

Campbell, David A. (ed.). 1982. *Greek Lyric Poetry.* London: Bristol Classical Press.

Campbell, David A. (ed.). 1988. *Greek Lyric,* vol. II: *Anacreon, Anacreontea, Choral Lyric from Olympus to Alcman* (Loeb Classical Library 143). Cambridge, MA: Harvard University Press.

Campion, Thomas. 1602. *Observations in the Art of English Poesie.* London: Richard Field. (Reprinted 1925, as *Bodley Head Quartos XIV.*)

Chen, Matthew. 1979. Metrical Structure: Evidence from Chinese Poetry. *Linguistic Inquiry* 10(3): 371–420.

Chomsky, Noam. 2002. *On Nature and Language.* Cambridge University Press.

Chomsky, Noam and Morris Halle. 1968/1991. *The Sound Pattern of English.* New York: Harper and Row. (Re-issue 1991, MIT Press.)

Clarke, Dorothy Clotelle. 1964. *Morphology of Fifteenth-Century Castilian Verse* (Duquesne Studies, Philological Series 4). Pittsburgh, PA: Duquesne University Press and Louvain: Nauwelaerts.

Cornulier, Benoît de. 1995. *Art Poëtique: Notions et problèmes de métrique.* Presses de l'Université de Lyon.

Coulson, Michael. 1992. *Sanskrit: An Introduction to the Classical Language,* 2nd edn. London: Hodder and Stoughton.

Dale, A. M. 1968. *The Lyric Metres of Greek Drama,* 2nd edn. Cambridge University Press.

Dell, François. 1973. *Les règles et les sons.* Paris: Hermann.

Dell, François and Mohamed Elmedlaoui. 2007. Mot, vers et domaine de syllabation dans la chanson chleuhe. In *Des sons et des sens: Données et modèles en phonologie et en morphologie,* ed. Élisabeth Delais-Roussarie and Laurence Labrune, 269–286. Paris: Hermès.

Dell, François and Mohamed Elmedlaoui. 2008. *Poetic Meter and Musical Form in the Songs of the Tashlhiyt Berber* (Berber Studies Series). Cologne: Rüdiger Köppe Verlag.

Dell, François and John Halle. 2008. Comparing Musical Textsetting in French and in English Songs. In *Towards a Typology of Poetic Forms,* ed. Jean-Louis Aroui and Andy Arleo. Amsterdam: Elsevier.

Deo, Ashwini. 2007. The Metrical Organization of Classical Sanskrit Verse. *Journal of Linguistics* 43(1): 63–114.

Domínguez Caparrós, José. 2001. *Diccionario de métrica española,* 2nd edn. Madrid: Alianza.

Domínguez Caparrós, José. 2002. *Métrica de Cervantes.* Alcalá de Henares: Centro de Estudios Cervantinos.

Dornseiff, F. 1925. *Das Alphabet in Mystik und Magie.* Leipzig: Teubner.

Duanmu, San. 2004. A Corpus Study of Chinese Regulated Verse: Phrasal Stress and the Analysis of Variability. *Phonology* 21(1): 43–89.

Duffell, Martin J. 1991. The Romance Hendecasyllable: An Exercise in Comparative Metrics. PhD dissertation, Queen Mary and Westfield College University of London.

Duffell, Martin J. 1993–94. Alfonso's *Cantigas* and the Origins of Arte Mayor. *Journal of Hispanic Research* 2(2): 183–204.

Duffell, Martin J. 1999. *Modern Metrical Theory and the 'verso de arte mayor'*. (Papers of the Medieval Hispanic Research Seminar 10). Queen Mary and Westfield College University of London.

Duffell, Martin J. 2007. *Syllable and Accent: Studies on Medieval Hispanic Metrics*. Department of Hispanic Studies, Queen Mary and Westfield College University of London.

Elmedlaoui, Mohamed. 1988. De la gémination. *Langues orientales anciennes: Philologie et linguistique* 1: 117–156.

Elwert, W. Theodor. 1965. *Traité de versification française*. Paris: Edition Klincksieck. (French translation of *Französische Metrik*. Munich: Max Huber Verlag, 1961.)

Encyclopedia Judaica. 1971. Jerusalem: Keter Publishing House.

Endzelīns, Jānis. 1922. *Lettisches Lesebuch*. Heidelberg: Carl Winter Universitätsverlag.

Endzelīns, Janis and K. Klaustiņš (ed.). 1928–36. *Latvju Tautas Dainas*. Riga: Avots.

Even-Shoshan, Avraham. 1990. *A New Concordance of the Bible*. Jerusalem: Kiryat Sefer Publishing House.

Fabb, Nigel. 1997. *Linguistics and Literature: Language in the Verbal Arts of the World*. Oxford: Blackwell.

Fabb, Nigel. 1999. Verse Constituency and the Locality of Alliteration. *Lingua* 108: 223–245.

Fabb, Nigel. 2001. Weak Monosyllables in Iambic Verse and the Communication of Metrical Form. *Lingua* 110: 771–790.

Fabb, Nigel. 2002a. *Language and Literary Structure: The Linguistic Analysis of Form in Verse and Narrative*. Cambridge University Press.

Fabb, Nigel. 2002b. The Metres of Dover Beach. *Language and Literature* 11: 99–117.

Fabb, Nigel. 2003. Metrical Rules and the Notion of 'Maximum': A Reply to Derek Attridge. *Language and Literature* 12: 73–80.

Fabb, Nigel. 2006. Generated Metrical Form and Implied Metrical Form. In *Formal Approaches to Poetry*, ed. Elan Dresher and Nila Friedberg, 77–91. Berlin: Mouton

Fabb, Nigel and Morris Halle. 2006a. Metrical Complexity in Christina Rossetti's Verse. *College Literature* 33(2): 91–114.

Fabb, Nigel and Morris Halle. 2006b. Telling the Numbers: A Unified Account of Syllabo-tonic English and Syllabic French and Polish Verse. *Research in Language* 4: 5–30.

Foulché-Delbosc, Raymond. 1902. Étude sur le *Laberinto* de Juan de Mena. *Revue Hispanique* 9: 75–138.

Freedman, David Noel. 1980. *Pottery, Poetry, and Prophecy: Studies in Early Hebrew Poetry*. Winona Lake, IN: Eisenbrauns.

Frost, Robert. 1939. The Figure a Poem Makes. In *Selected Prose of Robert Frost*, ed. H. Cox and E. C. Lathens, 33–46. New York: Colliers Books, MacMillan Publishing Co.

Fry, Stephen. 2005. *The Ode Less Travelled: Unlocking the Poet Within*. London: Hutchinson.

Fussell, Paul. 1979. *Poetic Meter and Poetic Form*. New York: McGraw Hill.

Gilbert, W. S. and A. Sullivan. 1996. *The Complete Annotated Gilbert and Sullivan*, ed. Ian Bradley. Oxford University Press.

Golston, Chris and Tomas Riad. 1997. The Phonology of Classical Arabic Meter. *Linguistics* 35: 111–132.

Golston, Chris and Tomas Riad. 2005. The Phonology of Greek Lyric Meter *Journal of Linguistics* 41(1): 77–115.

Gouvard, Jean-Michel. 1999. *La versification*. Paris: Presses Universitaires de France.

Haas, Mary R. 1977. Tonal Accent in Creek. In *Studies in Stress and Accent* (Southern California Occasional Papers in Linguistics 4), ed. Larry Hyman, 195–208. Los Angeles: University of Southern California.

Halle, John. 1999. A Grammar of Improvised Textsetting. PhD dissertation, Columbia University.

Halle, John. 2008. Music and Language. In *The Cambridge Encyclopedia of the Language Sciences*, ed. Patrick Hogan. Cambridge University Press.

Halle, John and Fred Lerdahl. 1993. A Generative Textsetting Model. *Current Musicology* 55: 3–23.

Halle, Morris. 1985. Speculations about the Representation of Words in Memory. In *Phonetic Linguistics Essays in Honor of Peter Ladefoged*, ed. Victoria A. Fromkin, 101–114. Orlando, FL: Academic Press.

Halle, Morris. 1987. A Biblical Pattern Poem. In *The Linguistics of Writing*, ed. Nigel Fabb, Derek Attridge, Alan Durant, and Colin MacCabe, 67–75. Manchester University Press.

Halle, Morris. 1989a. Addendum to Prince's 'Metrical Forms'. In *Phonetics and Phonology*, vol. 1: *Rhythm and Meter*, ed. Paul Kiparsky and Gilbert Youmans, 81–86. San Diego, CA: Academic Press.

Halle, Morris. 1989b. Syllable-counting Meters and Pattern Poetry in the Old Testament. In *Studia Linguistica et Orientalia Memoriae Haim Blanc Dedicata*, ed. A. Borg *et al.*, 110–120. Wiesbaden: Otto Harrassowitz.

Halle, Morris. 1997. Metrical Verse in the Psalms. In *India and Beyond*, ed. D. van der Meij, 207–225. London and New York: Kegan Paul International, and Leiden and Amsterdam: International Institute for Asian Studies.

Halle, Morris. 1998. The Stress of English Words. *Linguistic Inquiry* 29: 539–568.

Halle, Morris. 2008. On Stress and Meter and on English Iambics in Particular. In *The Nature of the Word: Studies in Honor of Paul Kiparsky*, ed. Kristin Hanson and Sharon Inkelas. Cambridge MA: MIT Press.

Halle, Morris and William Idsardi. 1994. A Reanalysis of Indonesian Stress. *MIT Working Papers in Linguistics* 21: 1–9.

Halle, Morris and William Idsardi. 1995. General Properties of Stress and Metrical Structure. In *The Handbook of Phonological Theory*, ed. John A. Goldsmith, 403–443. Oxford: Blackwell.

Halle, Morris and William Idsardi. 2000. Stress and Length in Hixkaryana. *The Linguistic Review* 17: 199–218.

Halle, Morris and Samuel Jay Keyser. 1971. *English Stress: Its Form, its Growth, and its Role in Verse*. New York: Harper and Row.

Halle, Morris and Samuel Jay Keyser. 1999. On Meter in General and on Robert Frost's Loose Iambics in Particular. In *Linguistics: In Search of the Human Mind. A Festschrift for Kazuko Inoue*, ed. M. Muraki and

E. Iwamoto, 130–153. Tokyo: Kaitakusha.

Halle, Morris and John J. McCarthy. 1981. The Metrical Structure of Psalm 137. *Journal of Biblical Literature* 100(2): 161–167.

Halle, Morris and Andrew Nevins. 2008. Rule Application in Phonology. In *Contemporary Views on Architecture and Representations in Phonology*, ed. Charles Cairns and Eric Raimy. Cambridge MA: MIT Press.

Halle, Morris and Jean-Roger Vergnaud. 1987. *An Essay on Stress*. Cambridge, MA: MIT Press.

Halporn, James, Martin Ostwald, and Thomas G. Rosenmeyer. 1994. *The Meters of Greek and Latin Poetry*. Indianapolis, IN: Hackett Publishing Company, Inc.

Hanson, Kristin. 1992. Resolution in Modern Meters. PhD dissertation, Stanford University.

Hanson, Kristin. 1996. From Dante to Pinsky: A Theoretical Perspective on the History of the Modern English Iambic Pentameter. *Rivista di Linguistica* 9(1): 53–97.

Hanson, Kristin and Paul Kiparsky. 1996. A Parametric Theory of Poetic Meter. *Language* 72: 287–335.

Hayes, Bruce. 1981. A Metrical Theory of Stress Rules. PhD dissertation, MIT.

Hayes, Bruce. 1983. A Grid-based Theory of English Meter. *Linguistic Inquiry* 14: 357–393.

Hayes, Bruce. 1995. *Metrical Stress Theory*. The University of Chicago Press.

Henríquez Ureña, Pedro. 1944. El endecasílabo castellano. *Boletín de la Academia Argentina de Letras* 13: 725–824.

Hiskett, Mervyn. 1975. *A History of Hausa Islamic Verse*. London: School of Oriental and African Studies.

Hopkins, Gerard Manley. 2002. *The Major Works*, ed. Catherine Phillips. Oxford University Press.

Hornblower, Simon and Antony Spawforth. 2003. *The Oxford Classical Dictionary*, 3rd edn. Oxford University Press.

Idsardi, William J. 1992. The Computation of Prosody. PhD dissertation, MIT.

Jakobson, Roman and Paolo Valesio. 1981. *Vocabulorum constructio* in Dante's Sonnet *Se vedi li occhi miei*. In *Roman Jakobson: Selected Writings*, vol. III: *Poetry of Grammar and Grammar of Poetry*, 176–192. The Hague: Mouton.

Jamison, Stephanie W. 2004. Sanskrit. In *The Cambridge Encyclopedia of the World's Ancient Languages*, ed. Roger D. Woodard, 673–699. Cambridge University Press.

Joüon, Paul. 1947. *Grammaire de l'hébreu biblique*. Rome: Institut biblique pontifical.

Keach, William (ed.). 1997. *Coleridge: The Complete Poems*. London: Penguin.

Keith, A. B. 1993. *A History of Sanskrit Literature*. Delhi: Motilal Banarsidass. (First published 1922.)

Kenstowicz, Michael. 1994. *Phonology in Generative Grammar*. Oxford: Blackwell.

Kerkhof, Maxim P. A. M. (ed.). 1997. *Juan de Mena:* Laberinto de Fortuna. Madrid: Castalia.

Keyser, Samuel Jay. 1969. Old English Prosody. *College English* 30: 331–356.

Kiparsky, Paul. 1977. The Rhythmic Structure of English Verse. *Linguistic Inquiry* 8: 189–247.

Kugel, James L. 1981. *The Idea of Biblical Poetry: Parallelism and its History*. New Haven, CT: Yale University Press.

Kugel, James L. 2007. *How to Read the Bible*. New York: Free Press.

Kursīte, Janīna. 1996. Metrika. In *Latviešu folklora mītu spogulī* [Latvian folklore as reflected in myths], ed. J. Kursīte, 140–156. Rīga: Zinātne.

Lázaro Carreter, Fernando. 1976. La poética del arte mayor castellano. In *Estudios de poética* 75–111. Madrid: Taurus.

Legman, Gershon (ed.). 1969. *The Limerick: 1700 examples, with notes variants and index*. New York: Bell Publishing Company.

Lennard, John. 2005. *The Poetry Handbook*, 2nd edn. Oxford University Press.

Lerdahl, Fred and Ray Jackendoff. 1983. *A Generative Theory of Tonal Music*. Cambridge MA: MIT Press.

Liberman, Alvin M. 1996. *Speech: A Special Code*. Cambridge, MA: MIT Press.

Liberman, Mark. 1975. The Intonational System of English. PhD dissertation, MIT.

Liu, James J. Y. 1962. *The Art of Chinese Poetry*. The University of Chicago Press.

Lord, Albert B. 1973. *The Singer of Tales*. New York: Atheneum.

Lowth, Robert. 1829. *Lectures on the Sacred Poetry of the Hebrews ... translated from the original Latin by A. Gregory, F.A.S.* A new edition with notes by Calvin E. Stowe, A.M. Andover, MA: Codman Press. (Latin original published in 1753.)

Macdonell, Arthur Anthony. 1992. *A Vedic Reader for Students*. Delhi: Motatil Banarsidass Publishers. (First published 1917.)

Macdonell, Arthur Anthony. 1993. *A Vedic Grammar for Students*. Delhi: Motatil Banarsidass Publishers. (First published 1916.)

Magán Abelleira, Fernando *et al.* 1996. *Lírica profana Galego-Portuguesa. Corpus completo das cantigas medievais, con estudio biográfico, análise retórica e bibliografía específica*. Xunta de Galicia – Consellería de Educación e Ordenación Universitaria – Centro de Investigacións Lingüísticas e Literarias Ramón Piñeiro, Santiago de Compostela, 2 vols. (First revised printing 1999.) Texts available on *MedDB. Base de datos da lírica profana galego-portuguesa*. http://www.cirp.es/med/meddb.html.

Maling, Joan. 1973. The Theory of Classical Arabic Metrics. PhD dissertation: MIT.

Mas, Amédée. 1962. Le mouvement ternaire dans l'hendécasyllabe de la troisième églogue de Garcilaso. *Bulletin Hispanique* 64bis: 538–550.

Mayor, Joseph B. 1901. *Chapters on English Metre*. Cambridge University Press.

McKay, Brendan, Dror Bar-Natan, Maya Bar Hillel, and Gil Kalai. 1999. Solving the Bible-code Puzzle. *Statistical Science* 14: 150–173.

Menichetti, Aldo. 1993. *Metrica italiana: Fondamenti metrici, prosodia, rima*. Padova: Editrice Antenore.

Mercado, Angelo. 2005. The Latin Saturnian Meter: Towards a Traditional Description and Generative Analysis. Unpublished paper, LSA Summer Institute of Linguistics.

Mercado, Angelo. 2006. The Latin Saturnian and Latin Verse. PhD dissertation, University of California Los Angeles.

Morin, Yves-Charles. 2003. Le status linguistique du chva ornemental dans la poésie et la chanson françaises. In *Le sens et la mésure: De la pragmatique à la métrique. Hommages á Benoît de Cornulier*, ed. Jean-Louis Aroui, 459–499. Paris: Champion.

Morros, Bienvenido (ed.). 1995. *Garcilaso de la Vega: Obra poética y textos en prosa*. Barcelona: Crítica.

Munsterberg, Peggy. 1984. *The Penguin Book of Bird Poetry*. New York: Penguin.

Navarro Tomás, Tomás. 1925. Palabras sin acento. *Revista de Filología Española* 12: 335–375.

Navarro Tomás, Tomás. 1972. *Métrica española: Reseña histórica y descriptiva*, 3rd revised edn. Madrid: Guadarrama.

Navarro Tomás, Tomás. 1973a. Correspondencia prosódico-rítmica del endecasílabo. In *Los poetas en sus versos*, 87–115. Barcelona: Ariel.

Navarro Tomás, Tomás. 1973b. La musicalidad de Garcilaso. In *Los poetas en sus versos*, 117–136. Barcelona: Ariel.

Nespor, Marina and Irene Vogel. 1986. *Prosodic Phonology*. Dordrecht: Foris.

Norris, H. T. 1968. *Shinqīṭī Folk Literature and Song*. Oxford: Clarendon Press.

Oliva, Salvador. 1992. *La mètrica i el ritme de la prosa* Barcelona: Quaderns Crema.

Opie, Iona and Peter Opie. 1951. *The Oxford Book of Nursery Rhymes*. Oxford University Press.

Parfitt, George. 1975. *Ben Jonson: The Complete Poems*. Harmondsworth: Penguin.

Patwardhan, Madhav. 1937. *Chandoracanā*. Bombay: Karnataka Publishing House.

Pfeiffer, Robert H. 1948. *Introduction to the Old Testament*. New York: Harper and Brothers.

Piera, Carlos. 1980. Spanish Verse and the Theory of Meter. PhD dissertation, University of California Los Angeles.

Pimpão, Álvaro J. da Costa. 1959. *História da literatura portuguesa. Idade Média*, 2nd edn. Coimbra: Atlântida.

Prince, Alan. 1989. Metrical Forms. In *Phonetics and Phonology*, vol. 1: *Rhythm and Meter*, ed. Paul Kiparsky and Gilbert Youmans, 45–80. San Diego, CA: Academic Press.

Quicherat, Louis. 1850. *Traité de versification française*, 2nd edn. Paris: Imprimerie de Crapelet.

Quilis, Antonio. 1999. *Tratado de fonología y fonética españolas*, 2nd edn. Madrid: Gredos.

Racine, Jean. 1999. *Oeuvres complètes I*, ed. Georges Forestier. Paris: Gallimard.

Raven, D. S. 1998. *Greek Metre*. London: Bristol Classical Press.

Rivers, Elias L. (ed.). 1969. *Garcilaso de la Vega: Poesías castellanas completas*. Madrid: Castalia.

Rudzītis, Jānis. 1960. Asimmetriskās strofas latviešu trochaju dziesmās [The asymmetrical stanzas in Latvian trochaic songs]. In *In honorem Endzelini*, ed. E. Hauzenberga-Šturma, 122–131. Chicago: Čikāgas Baltu Filologu Kopa.

Sapir, Edward. 1933. La réalité psychologique des phonèmes. *Journal de psychologie normale et pathologique* 30: 247–265. (English original in *Selected*

Writings of Edward Sapir, ed. D. Mandelbaum, 46–60. Berkeley and Los Angeles: University of California Press, 1949.)

Schipper, Jakob. 1910. *A History of English Versification.* Oxford: Clarendon Press.

Schuh, Russell G. 1989. Towards a Metrical Analysis of Hausa Verse Prosody: Mutadaarik. In *Current Approaches to African Linguistics 6*, ed. I. Haik and L. Tuller, 161–175. Dordrecht: Foris.

Shirman, H. 1959. *Haššîrâh haʕibrît bisparad ûbəprôwans* [Hebrew poetry in Spain and Provence]. Jerusalem and Tel Aviv: Bialik Institute and Dvir.

Sophocles. 1999. *Antigone*, ed. Mark Griffith. Cambridge University Press.

Sowayan, Saad Abdullah. 1985. *Nabaṭi Poetry: The Oral Poetry of Arabia.* Berkeley: University of California Press.

Steele, Joshua. 1775. *An Essay Towards Establishing the Melody and Measure of Speech to be Expressed and Perpetuated by Peculiar Symbols.* London: J. Almon.

Steele, Timothy. 1990. *Missing Measures: Modern Poetry and the Revolt Against Meter.* Fayetteville, AR: University of Arkansas Press.

Steriade, Donca. 1982. Greek Prosodics and the Nature of Syllabification. PhD Dissertation, MIT.

Stoetzer, W. F. G. J. 1989. *Theory and Practice in Arabic Metrics.* Leiden: Het Oosters Instituut.

Tarlinskaja, Marina. 1993. *Strict Stress-meters in English Poetry Compared with German and Russian.* Calgary: University of Calgary Press.

Tavani, Giuseppe. 1967. *Repertorio metrico della lirica galego-portoghese* (Officina Romanica 7). Rome: Ateneo.

Thiesen, Finn. 1982. *A Manual of Classical Persian Prosody with Chapters on Urdu, Karakhandic and Ottoman Prosody.* Wiesbaden: Otto Harrassowitz.

Tomaševskij, Boris V. 1959. *Stix i jazyk* [Verse and language]. Moscow and Leningrad: Gosudarstvennoe izdatel'stvo xudožestvennoj literatury.

Varela, Elena, Pablo Moíño, and Pablo Jauralde. 2005. *Manual de métrica española.* Madrid: Castalia.

Velankar, H. D. 1949. *Jayadāman: A Collection of Ancient Texts on Sanskrit Prosody and a Classified List of Sanskrit Meters with an Alphabetical Index.* Bombay: Haritoṣamālā.

Verlaine, Paul. 1962. *Oeuvres poétiques complètes* (Bibliothèque de la Pléiade). Paris: Editions Gallimard.

Verlaine, Paul. 1992. *Oeuvres poétiques complètes*, ed. Yves-Alain Faure. Paris: Éditions Robert Laffont.

Villon, François. 1974. *Oeuvres d'après le manuscrit Coislin I*, ed. Rika van Deyck. Saint-Aquilin de Pacy: Éditions Maillier.

West, M. L. 1982. *Greek Metre.* Oxford University Press.

White, John Williams. 1912. *The Verse of Greek Comedy.* London: Macmillan.

Widdess, Richard. 1995. *The Ragas of Early Indian Music.* Oxford: Clarendon Press.

Woodard, Roger D. (ed.). 2004. *The Cambridge Encyclopedia of the World's Ancient Languages.* Cambridge University Press.

Yip, Moira. 1984. The Development of Chinese Verse: A Metrical Analysis. In *Language Sound Structure: Studies in Phonology Presented to Morris Halle by his Teacher and Students*, ed. Mark Aronoff and R. T. Oehrle, 346–368. Cambridge MA: MIT Press.

Zanders, J. 1893. Par tautas dzeesmu pantmehru [On the meter of folk songs]. *Austrums* I.1 (1893): 21–27; II.3 (1893): 218–226; III.1 (1894): 119–127.

Zaube, Jānis. 1960. Par kvantitātes nozīmi latviešu tautasdziesmu ritmā [On the role of quantity in the rhythm of Latvian folksongs]. In *In honorem Endzelini*, ed. E. Hauzenberga-Šturma, 132–137. Chicago: Čikāgas Baltu Filologu Kopa.

Zeps, Valdis. 1963. The Meter of the So-called Trochaic Latvian Folksongs. *International Journal of Slavic Linguistics and Poetics* 7: 123–128.

Zeps, Valdis. 1969. The Meter of the Latvian Folk Dactyl. *Ceļi: Rakstu Krājums* (Lund: Ramave) 14: 45–47.

Index